Peter Norton's
Advanced DOS 5 Guide

Peter Norton

Judi N. Fernandez

Ruth Ashley

Brady Publishing

New York   London   Toronto   Sydney   Tokyo   Singapore

Brady Publishing

Published by Brady Publishing
a Division of Prentice Hall
Computer Publishing
15 Columbus Circle
New York, New York 10023

Manufactured in the United States of America

2   3   4   5   6   7   8   9   10

Library of Congress Cataloging-in-Publication Data

Norton, Peter, 1943-

    Peter Norton's Advanced DOS 5 Guide / Peter Norton

      p.   cm.

    Includes index.

    ISBN 0-13-529645-5

    1. Operating systems (Computers) 2. MS-DOS (Computer file)
3. PC DOS (Computer file) 4. Norton utilities (Computer programs)
I. Title. II. Title: Advanced DOS 5 Guide
QA76.76.063N677   1992
005.4'46--dc20   92-10484
                                       CIP

Trademarks

All brand and product names mentioned herein are trademarks or registered trademarks of their respective holders.

Limits of Liability and Disclaimer

The authors and the publisher of this book have used their best efforts in preparing this book and the programs contained in it. These efforts include the development, research, and testing of the theories and programs to determine their effectiveness. The authors and publisher make no warranty of any kind, expressed or implied, with regard to these programs or the documentation contained in this book. The authors and publisher shall not be liable in any event for incidental or consequential damages in connection with or rising out of the furnishing, performance, or use of these programs.

Table of Contents

1   What's New in DOS 5? 1

    Overview of New Features 2

        Installation and Uninstallation 2

        DOS Shell 3

        On-Screen Help 3

        Full-Screen Editor 3

        DOSKEY 3

        Improved Memory Management 4

        Recovery Facilities 4

        QBasic 4

        Other Features 4

        Enhanced Commands 5

        New Commands 7

        Eliminated Features 8

    Working with HELP 9

    Points to Ponder about EDIT 10

    The New DIR Options 12

        Displaying Branches 13

        Selecting Files by Attributes 14

        Sorting the File List 15

        DIR Defaults 17

    Using SETVER 17

        Setting Up SETVER 18

        Setting a Version 18

        SETVER Options 19

2 A Closer Look at DOS Shell 21

Starting DOS Shell 22
Controlling the Shell 24
    Working with Menus 24
    Working with the Drive List 25
    Working with the Directory Tree 26
        Branch Levels 26
    Locating a Subdirectory 27
    Working with the File List 27
        Dragging Files 29
        Display Options 30
        Handling Files from Multiple Directories 30
        Locating Lost Files 32
Running Programs from the Shell 32
    Opening a Program File 33
    Opening an Associated File 33
    Using the File Run Command 34
    Using a Secondary Command Prompt 35
    Opening a Program List Item 35
    Associating File Extensions with Programs...................35
Task Swapping 37
    Setting Up Task Swapping 37
        Swapping and the TEMP Variable 38
    Switching Tasks 39
        Task Hotkeys 40
        Task List Order 40
        Names on the Active Task List 40
        Command Prompt Tasks 41
        Duplicate Tasks 41
        Closing Tasks 41

3 Setting Up DOS Shell 43

Program List Views 44
Structuring the Program List 44
    The Disk Utilities Group 45
Defining New Program Groups 46
    Weak Password Protection 46
Defining Program Items 47
    Required Fields 47
        Calling Batch Programs 47
    Optional Fields 48
        Startup Directories 48
        Application Shortcut Keys 48
        Pause after Exit 49
    Advanced Options 49
        Memory Requirements 50
        Task Switching Limitations 51
    Replaceable Parameter Dialog Box 51
    Modifying Program Group and
    Program Item Definitions 52
    Copying Program Items 52
    Transferring a Setup to Another Computer 52
A Trip through DOSSHELL.INI 53
    Savestate Section 53
    Programstarter Section: Program List Definitions 55
        Program Passwords in DOSSHELL.INI 55
        Color Schemes 56
    File Associations 56

4 DOS at Your Command 59

Redirecting Input and Output 60
Standard Input and Output 60
Standard Error Output 61

Redirecting Output to a File 62
  Overwriting vs. Appending 63
Redirecting I/O to Devices 63
  Some Printer Incompatibilities 64
  NUL: The Road to Nowhere 65
Redirecting Input 65
Piping 67
  Using ECHO to Automate Commands 68
  The Temporary Pipe Files 68
The DOS Filters 68
What's My Line? 69
MORE in a Minute 69
It's Not My SORT 70
  Redirecting SORT I/O 72
SORT Collating Sequence 72
  SORT Limitations 73
  Why You Can't Do a Two-Key Sort 73
  Using Other Sort Programs 74
What a FIND 74
  Locating Lines 75
  Searching All Files for a Text String 76
  Locating Lines in Command Output 76
  Locating Files in a Directory Listing 77

5 At Long Last...DOSKEY 79

Getting DOSKEY Started 80
  DOSKEY's Buffer 80
  But How Can You Uninstall DOSKEY? 81
A History Lesson (DOSKEY Style) 81
Command Line Editing: Now It's Easy 83
  Insert vs. Overstrike Mode 84
Two (or More) Commands for the Price of One 85

Macros 85
   Macros vs. Batch Files 85
   Macro Definition 86
      Special Characters 86
      Sample Macro Definitions 87
   Replaceable Parameters 88
      Accessing All Parameters in a Macro 89
   Generalized Macro Examples 89
      Executing a Macro 89
   Managing Your Macros 90
   Replacing DOS Commands with Macros 91

6   Basically Better Batches 93

A Quick Review of Batch Basics 94
   Batch File Contents 95
   What's in a Name? 95
   Bypassing COM and EXE Files 96
   Floppy Batches 97
      Clobbering the Batch File 97
Message Control 98
   Command-Line Echoing 98
      Echo Messages 101
      Using ECHO in Batch Programs 102
Pausing 103
   Offering Choices via Supplementary Batch Files 105
Replaceable Parameters 108
   A Simple Application of Replaceable Parameters 109
   How Replaceable Parameters Work 109
   Null Parameters 110
   SHIFT 111
   Dumb Replacement 113
      Escaping Replacement 114

7 Batch Logic 115

Linking Batch Files 116
  Chaining vs. Calling 116
  Calling 117
  Chaining 118
  Passing Replaceable Parameters 118
  Multiple Links 119
  Recursion 119
  Killing a Batch Job with Links 119
Branching 120
  Types of Branches 120
    Bypass Branch 120
    Alternative Branches 121
  The IF Command 121
  Exit Codes 122
  The ERRORLEVEL Condition 122
    The Short Life of the Exit Code 123
    IF and Bypass Branches 124
    Telling DOS where to Go 124
  Testing for Files 127
    Testing for a Directory 128
  Comparing Text Strings 128
    Testing for Null Values 128
  Nested IFs 129
Loops 130
  Sample Loop 130
  Loops Involving SHIFT and String Conditions 131
  Using FOR to Create Loops 131
    Global Filespecs in the Item Set 133
    FOR and FIND 133
    Using FOR with CALL 134
    Using FOR with IF 134

8 Directory Management 135

Review of Directory Basics 136
  Subdirectories 136
  Managing Directories 136
  Paths 136
    Special Directory Names 137
    Including Drive Names 137
    Default Directories 137
    Paths with Filespecs 138
    Paths with Command Names 138
  The PATH Command 139
    PATH Recommendations 140
    Invalid Directory Message 140
    Managing the Search Path 140
  Recommendations for Directory Structure 141
TREE 142
  Printing the Tree 143
Restructuring a Directory Tree 144
  ASSIGN 144
  SUBST 145
    Choosing a Drive Name for SUBST 147
    Switching Diskette Drives with SUBST 148
  TRUENAME 149
  APPEND for Your Thoughts 150

9 Copying Files 151

Comparing DOS's Copying Commands 152
  XCOPY vs. DISKCOPY 155
The XCOPY Command 155
  Copying Branches 156
  Copying a File to the Same Directory 157
  Creating New Directories with XCOPY 157

Avoiding Disk Full Termination 158
Pruning and Grafting 159
Renaming Directories 160
Verification 161
Clobbering Files with XCOPY and COPY 161
    Recovering a Clobbered File 161
    Difficulties in Avoiding Clobbering 162
Moving Files 162
The COPY Command 163
Concatenating Files 164
Appending Files 165
The Effect of Concatenation on Certain File Types 166
    Application Data Files 166
    Binary Files 167
Updating Time/Date Stamps 167
Matched Concatenations 168
Copying to and from Devices 168
The ABCs of /A and /B 169
    Clusters and Slack 169
    Avoiding Slack when Accessing Files 169
    COPY Methods 170
    Date Stamping Non-ASCII Files 171
    Copying Files to a Device 171
BACKUP and RESTORE as Copying Tools 171
The REPLACE Command 172
Replacing Missing Files 172
Replacing Existing Files 173
Using REPLACE with /P to Avoid
Clobbering Existing Files 174

10 DOS and the Environment 175

Environment Variables 176
    Displaying Environment Variables 176

DOS's Environment Variables 177
    PATH 177
    PROMPT 177
    TEMP 177
    DIRCMD 178
    COMSPEC 178
Creating an Environment Variable 178
Modifying and Deleting Environment Variables 179
Accessing Environmental Variables 179
    Adding to the Path 179
    Preserving and Restoring Environment Variables 180
    Environment Variables vs. Replaceable
    Parameters 180
Controlling the Command Interpreter
and the Environment 181
    Environment Size 182
    Command Interpreter in Another Location 182
    Using a Third-Party Command Interpreter 183
Loading a Secondary Command Interpreter 183
    Specifying COMSPEC 184
    Omitting COMSPEC 184
    Dynamic Environment Allocation 185
    Starting COMMAND.COM when
    Another Command Interpreter is Primary 186
Loading a New Primary Command Interpreter 186
Executing a Command with COMMAND.COM 187

11 Circumventing DOS's Memory Limitations 189

Memory Layout 190
    Conventional Memory 192
    Upper Memory 193
    Expanded Memory (EMS) 193
    Extended Memory 195
DOS 5's Memory Facilities 197

MEM 198

HIMEM.SYS 200

   Problems in Using HIMEM.SYS 201

Loading DOS into Extended Memory 202

Loading Programs in Conventional Memory
   with LOADFIX 203

Using EMM386 203

   Emulating Expanded Memory 204

   Turning Expanded Memory On and Off 206

   Using Upper Memory Blocks (UMBs) 207

      Controlling the Page Frame Address 209

      Loading Programs into UMBs 210

   Problems with UMBs 210

      MEM and Upper Memory 211

Handling TSRs 212

Typical Startup Files 213

12 Speeding Up Your System 215

Why So Slow? 216

   How DOS Accesses a File 216

   Arm Movement Factors 217

Getting Your Disk Ready 218

   Setting the Interleave Factor 218

   Optimize the Directory Structure 219

   Delete Unnecessary Files 220

   Recovering Lost Allocation Units 222

   Defragment and Relocate Existing Files
      and Subdirectories 222

Disk Caching 223

   SMARTDRV.SYS Features 223

   Installing SMARTDRV.SYS 224

      Extended vs. Expanded Memory Caches 225

      Allowing Windows to Borrow Cache Space 225

      CONFIG.SYS Order 226

      Assessing the Effectiveness of SMARTDRV.SYS 226

IBMCACHE.SYS 226
Disk Buffers 227
FASTOPEN 228
    Installing FASTOPEN 229
    How Many Entries Should You Cache? 230
RAM Drives 230
    Creating a RAM Drive 231
        Locating the RAM Drive 231
        Determining RAM Drive Size 231
        Number of Directory Entries 232
        Determining Sector Size 232
    Using the RAM Drive 232

13 Backing Up and Restoring Files 235

Backup Systems 236
    What to Back Up 236
    Backup Strategies 237
        Daily Full Backups 237
        Daily Supplemental Backups 238
    Storing Backup Diskettes 238
    Working with Archive Attributes 238
Commands for Making Backup Files......................239
    Comparing BACKUP and XCOPY 239
    Using the BACKUP Command 240
        Daily Full Backup 242
        Daily Supplemental Backup 243
    Using the XCOPY Command 244
        Daily Full Backup 244
        Daily Supplemental Backup 245
        Leaving Archive Attributes On 246
Restoring Files..246
    Restoring XCOPYed Backups..........................247
    Using REPLACE to Recover Missing Files 247

Restoring BACKUP Files 247
    Restoring Selected Files 249
    Restoring from Supplemental Backups 250
    Restoring Multiple Files 250
    Restoring the Entire Set 250
    Exit Codes 251

14 An Ounce of Protection 253

Format Protection 254
    The FORMAT Command 254
    Saving Unformatting Information 255
    Unconditional FORMAT Guidelines 256
    Recoverable Formats 257
Protecting the Disk Structure 257
    Hard Disk Architecture (A Very Brief Overview) 258
    Saving Partition Information 259
    Saving Directory Structure Information 260
    Delete-Tracking 260
        Combining Operations 262
        Removing the TSR 262
Verifying Files 262
    CRCs 263
    DOS's Verification 263
        General Verification 263
        Specific Verification 263
Comparing Files 264
    The COMP Command 264
    The FC Command 266
    The DISKCOMP Command 269
Write Protection 269
Additional Data-Protection Needs 270
    Viruses (or Viri) 270
    Parking Your Disk Heads 271

15   A Ton of Cure 273

Checking and Fixing Disks (CHKDSK) 274

The File Allocation Table 275

Examining the FAT 276

Sample FAT Data 277

Detecting and Fixing Errors 278

Lost Allocation Units 278

How Clusters Get Lost 278

Handling Lost Clusters 279

Overfilling the Root Directory 279

Cross-Linked Allocation Units 280

How Files Get Cross-Linked 281

Dealing with Cross-Linked Allocation Units 281

A Single Cross-Linkage 281

Multiple Cross-Linkage 282

Invalid Allocation Units 283

How CHKDSK Fixes Invalid Allocation Units 284

Allocation Errors 284

How CHKDSK Fixes an Allocation Error 284

Dealing with Allocation Errors 285

Invalid Subdirectory Entry 285

What CHKDSK Does 286

Dealing with Invalid Subdirectory Entries 286

Bad FAT Sectors 287

Fragmentation 287

How Fragmentation Occurs 288

Defragmenting Files with DOS Commands 288

Undeleting Files 288

Using UNDELETE 289

How DOS Undeletes a File 289

Problems in Undeleting Files 290

Suggestions for Facilitating Undeletions 291

Using UNDELETE 291

Undeleting All Files 294

Listing the Available Files................................... 294

Rescuing Accidentally Formatted Disks 294

The UNFORMAT Command 295

Restoring Partition Information 296

Viewing Partition Information 296

How Unformatting Works 298

UNFORMAT Using Image Information 299

Missing Image Information 301

UNFORMAT without Image Information 301

Handling Image Files 303

Simulating an UNFORMAT 304

RECOVER 305

Fixing Individual Files................................... 306

Fixing Several Files 306

Mushing an Entire Drive 307

Recovering from RECOVER 308

Sector Not Found Errors 308

16 Console Control 311

DOS and Your Video Monitor 312

The CON Driver 312

The Video Buffer.. 312

What ANSI.SYS Offers................................... 313

The ANSI.SYS Device Driver 314

Sending Commands to ANSI.SYS 314

Typing the Escape Character 315

Using PROMPT 315

Using a Text File 317

Using a Batch File 317

Setting Screen Colors 318

Screen and Cursor Control 320

    Creating a Banner 320

    Displaying a Message Box 322

    Character Wrap 324

    Screen Mode (Graphics) 324

ANSI Keyboard Control 325

    Remapping Individual Keys 327

    Assigning Strings to Keys 328

Controlling the CON (Console) Mode 329

    Identifying the Display Adapter 329

    Specifying Lines and Columns 329

    Controlling Keyboard Response 330

17 Another Country Heard From 333

Overview 334

    Using Special Characters 335

    International Keyboards 336

    The KEYB Command 337

        Code Pages with Keyboards 338

    International Formats 339

    The COUNTRY Configuration Command 340

Using Code Pages 341

    Monitor Code Pages 342

    Printer Code Pages 343

    Preparing Code Pages 344

    Switching Code Pages 346

        Complete Code Page Example 347

    National Language Support 348

        Another Code Page Example 349

    Manipulating Code Pages 350

    Displaying Code Page Information 350

18 Printing through DOS **353**

Printer Types 354
DOS Print Features 354
    Printer Control Commands....................................355
    Echo Printing 356
    Text Screen Printing 356
Configuring a Printer 357
Using Serial Printers 358
    Configuring the Serial Port 358
        Resident Portion of Mode 359
    Redirecting a Serial Printer 360
        Viewing Redirection Status 360
The PRINT Command 361
    Identifying the PRINT Device 362
    Configuring PRINT 362
    Controlling the Print Queue 364
Printing GRAPHICS Screens 365
    How GRAPHICS Works 365
    The GRAPHICS Command 365
    GRAPHICS Switches 367
    Aspect Ratio 368

19 Configuring Disks and Networks **369**

Configuring Physical Disks 370
    DRIVPARM 370
    Change-Line Support 372
Configuring Logical Floppy Disks 372
    Creating an Alternate Drive Name 373
    Setting Up Two Alternate Drive Names..................374
    Adding an External Floppy Disk Drive 375
        DRIVER.SYS or DRIVPARM 375
    Adding an Unsupported Drive 376

Running DOS on a Network 376

    DOS Command Limitations 377

    Logical Drives 378

    Sharing and Locking Files 378

    Special Considerations 378

20   Upgrading to QBASIC 381

QBASIC's Interface 382

    The QBASIC Editor 382

    Smart Editor Effects 383

Converting a GW-BASIC or BASICA Program 384

    Running Programs 384

    Line Numbers 385

        Removing Line Numbers 386

New Constant and Variable Types 386

    Constants 387

    Numeric Variables 387

    String Variables 387

        Additional String Functions 388

    Array Variables 388

    Record Data Type 389

        Records in Arrays 390

        Records in Files 390

New Flow of Control Facilities 391

    Expanded IF Statement 391

    Using a Case Structure 393

    Loop Structures 394

        Contents of Loop 395

Modular Programming 396

    Examining a Structured Program 397

    Creating a New Procedure 397

    Global Variables 399

    Subprograms 399

Passing Values 401
Functions 402
    Creating a New Function 402
Debugging Innovations 403
    The Immediate Window 403
    Tracing a Program 403
    Breakpoints 404

A Exit Codes 405

B IBM Extended Character Set 409

    Index 411

Preface

If you're like most DOS users, you have already learned enough about the operating system to survive. You can boot and reboot, name and rename files, copy and delete files, format diskettes, make and remove subdirectories, list directories, and change drives and directories. Maybe you've gone beyond these basic survival skills and learned to set the system date and time, view or print ASCII files, create a simple batch program, and so on.

TIP	If you have not yet learned these basic skills, you would be better off for now with *Peter Norton's DOS 5 Guide* (also published by Brady). Come back to this book when you feel at home with the basics.

You might suspect there's more you can do with DOS, and you're probably right. Our intention in this book is to help you make better use of your system through DOS. By *better*, we mean faster, safer, easier, more efficient, and more effective. What more could you ask for? And if you're responsible for other people's systems, you'll be able to set them up for better use, too. In particular, you'll be able to simplify tasks that confuse DOS beginners as well as automate their data protection systems to minimize the chance of data loss.

Even if you have a lot of DOS experience, including programming experience, you'll find a wealth of handy information in here, including undocumented commands and features, advanced techniques, warnings about pitfalls and how to circumvent them, and tips for making life easier for your end-users.

Specifically, this book shows you how to:

- Set up a DOS system to simplify and speed everyday tasks through:

    - Better use of DOS Shell features such as the program list and task switching

    - More flexible and powerful batch programs

    - Macros (via DOSKEY and ANSI.SYS)

    - More powerful commands using features such as redirection and DOSKEY command editing

- Make all software run faster via better utilization of resources through:
  - Better memory structuring
  - Optimized hard disk access via better hard disk structuring and caches
  - RAM drives
- Save time, money, and stress by protecting your system's most valuable resource—your data—from all the nasties that go bump in the night (such as viruses and your own memory lapses) through:
  - A well designed and rigorously implemented backup system
  - Preservation of vital system data, especially for deleted files and reformatted diskettes
  - A wide range of data recovery techniques (from locating misplaced files to recovering data from a partially trashed drive)
- Make it all more fun for yourself (and others) through:
  - More colorful displays (including some elementary graphics)
  - More interesting command prompts
  - More interesting messages

And that's not all. This book is jam-packed with handy techniques for using the DOS filters (MORE, SORT, and FIND), capitalizing on the DOS environment, choosing the best copy command (DOS has *four* of them), configuring nonstandard I/O devices, setting up a system for foreign languages, and much more. (For BASIC programmers, the last chapter shows you how to upgrade to DOS 5's QBasic system.) We even explain what DOS doesn't do well and where you would be wise to seek a third-party program (to park disk heads or defragment a hard disk, for example).

But what good are techniques if you don't understand the underlying concepts? You'll find clear-cut, comprehensive explanations of such system features as memory (including the difference between extended and expanded memory), the DOS environment, the File Allocation Table, how files get fragmented, those mysterious and frightening CHKDSK messages, and a lot more.

The DOS 5 Upgrade

This book assumes that you have successfully upgraded to DOS 5; we do not deal with earlier versions for the very good reason that the improvements in DOS 5 are important enough to be well worth the low price of the upgrade package. If you haven't yet made the upgrade, our first few chapters will probably convince you to do so soon. This book is appropriate for readers who have just upgraded to DOS 5 (but know the basics of an earlier DOS version) as well as those who have been using DOS 5 for a while.

Conventions

We have used the following typographical conventions:

italics   Expressions in italics indicate variables to be replaced by specific values. For example, when we say that RECOVER creates generic filenames in the form FILE*xxxx*.REC, the *xxxx* indicates four characters that change from filename to filename. The actual filenames generated by RECOVER are FILE0000.REC, FILE0001.REC, FILE0002.REC, and so on. (Italics are also used for emphasis in some sentences.)

ALL CAPS   In regular text, commands, filenames, directory paths, drive names, and program names are shown in all caps simply to make them stand out from the context. For example, the expression "the copy program" refers to any program that makes a copy, while "the COPY program" refers specifically to the DOS program named COPY.

Commands are shown in all caps even though DOS usually ignores case. You can enter commands in any mixture of cases, and many users prefer to work with all lowercase characters. The few places where DOS is case-sensitive are pointed out in the appropriate chapters.

Command Formats

Many figures in this book provide complete reference information for DOS commands. (Figure 1.3 on page 12 is a typical example.) These figures always include a format statement, such as the following:

```
FASTOPEN d:[[=]n] ... [/X]
```

A legitimate FASTOPEN command might be:

```
FASTOPEN C:=100 D: E:15
```

The conventions used in a command format are described below.

[Square brackets]   In command formats, items enclosed in square brackets are optional. All other items are required. In the above example, the word FASTOPEN and the drive name (represented by *d:*) are required but the expression following the drive name and the /X are optional.

In addition, the expression that follows the drive name includes a nested option, which may be used only within the enclosing option. If you include the *n*, you can precede it with an equal sign, but you can't use the equal sign without the *n*.

ALL CAPS   All caps indicate words or expressions that must be included exactly as shown. (They need not be typed in all caps when you enter commands.) In the FASTOPEN command, the word FASTOPEN must be included as is; it cannot be abbreviated. The /X switch is optional, but if used, it must be used as shown.

italics   Italics indicates items that must be replaced by a value when the command is entered. In the FASTOPEN command, the *d* must be replaced by a drive name. In addition, the *n* must be replaced by a number if you choose to use that option. (The meaning of the expression is discussed in the figure that explains the command.)

Ellipsis...   Three dots indicate that the preceding expression can
                                    be repeated. In the FASTOPEN command, you can
                                    repeat d:[[=] n] for each of your hard drives.

Filespecs

We use the expression *filespec* both in command formats and in regular text
to indicate the conglomeration of elements that identifies a file or set of
files. It can include a drive name, a path, and/or a filename (with or without wildcard characters). In many cases, a drive name alone is sufficient; all
files in the current directory of that drive are implied. In other cases, you
might find it necessary to include a path and/or a filename to identify the
file(s) you want.

CHAPTER 1

WHAT'S NEW IN DOS 5?

Introduction

DOS 5 offers a wealth of new features—some major, some minor—to please both new and experienced users. Some features are especially satisfying to anyone who has struggled with earlier DOS versions and has wished for (perhaps even begged for) some means to undelete files and unformat disks, an easy-to-use ASCII editor, friendly command-line editing, a means to take advantage of memory above the 640K line, and much more. This chapter overviews the new DOS features and examines in detail a few that aren't covered in later chapters, such as the new on-line help system.

Overview of New Features

Because DOS 4 didn't exactly attract a large following, more people are upgrading to DOS 5 from DOS 3 than from DOS 4. This chapter reviews all features added or changed after DOS 3.3 as new features, even if they first appeared with DOS 4, on the assumption that they might be new to you.

Installation and Uninstallation

Installation has become so easy with DOS 5's SETUP program that for many users it is virtually automatic. (Network users and people with incompatible disk managers and/or partitions will have to put some extra effort into installation, however.) Not only that, but DOS 5 sets itself up for simple removal by creating Uninstall diskette(s).

If you install DOS 5 and find that it's incompatible with some of your existing applications, you might want to uninstall it until you resolve the problem. When you start your computer from drive A with an Uninstall diskette, you can opt to remove DOS 5 from your hard disk and restore the former DOS version. (It's saved in the directory named OLD_DOS.n.)

If you decide to keep DOS 5, you can free up some hard disk space by entering the following command, which deletes the OLD_DOS.n directory (or directories, if you've installed DOS 5 more than once) and files from your hard disk:

    DELOLDOS

WARNING

 After you enter this command, you won't be able to use the Uninstall diskettes to uninstall DOS 5.

TIP	If your hard disk won't boot for some reason, the Uninstall diskette will boot DOS 5 from drive A, even if you've removed the old DOS version from your hard disk.

This book does not cover installation or uninstallation any further on the assumption that you've already installed DOS 5 and have decided to keep it.

DOS Shell

DOS Shell provides a modern, graphics interface for managing your PC
using windows, menus, and point-and-shoot mouse operation. The Shell is
a particular boon for inexperienced users, who no longer have to struggle
with awkward command syntax to accomplish such basic functions as
copying and deleting files. Even experienced users will find many likable
features in the Shell. We'll show you what the Shell has to offer and how to
set it up for end-users (as well as yourself) in Chapters 2 and 3.

On-Screen Help

Users can now call up brief documentation about the DOS commands at
the command prompt. The help information shows the format of the command and describes each parameter. You can even modify some of the
help text to provide your own instructions for other users, as you'll see
under *Working with Help* later in this chapter.

Full-Screen Editor

DOS 5 includes an easy-to-use, full-screen, ASCII editor named EDIT,
which features a familiar graphic interface. Most experienced PC users can
start right in using EDIT without any training at all.

DOSKEY

The new DOSKEY program gives you several important command-line facilities. With DOSKEY, you can:

- Edit the current command line easily.
- Recall former commands from a history buffer to the command line.
- Combine two or more commands on one command line.
- Create and use macros, which let you recall a complex command by
  entering a simple one.

Chapter 5 shows you how to set up and use DOSKEY.

Improved Memory Management

DOS 5 includes new features to load drivers, TSRs, and even DOS itself in the upper areas of memory, leaving conventional memory (memory below the 640K line) available for applications. Microsoft's extended memory manager, HIMEM.SYS, has been included in the DOS 5 package. There is also a new memory manager (EMM386) that will convert part of your extended memory into expanded memory. Chapter 11 explores DOS's memory features.

Recovery Facilities

DOS at last incorporates utilities to recover data that was accidentally deleted or reformatted. Chapters 14 and 15 discuss DOS's many data-protection and recovery facilities.

QBasic

DOS 5 now includes QBasic instead of the former GW-BASIC interpreter. While it can run most GW-BASIC or BASICA programs, QBasic is designed to be a structured programming language and runs faster than the earlier forms of BASIC. The major differences between QBasic and GW-BASIC, as well as modular programming techniques, are discussed in Chapter 20.

Other Features

DOS 5 has so many major new features, it's easy to overlook some of the smaller improvements that are listed below:

➲ You can have more than two hard drives, up to 2 gigabytes in size (and you don't have to use SHARE with drives larger than 32M as you did in version 4).

➲ 2.88M diskettes are supported.

➲ More country formats and code pages are available.

➲ More types of monitors and printers are recognized.

⊃ You can specify the location of temporary pipe files.

⊃ HIMEM.SYS (an extended memory manager) and SMARTDRV.SYS (a disk caching system), which were originally developed for Windows, have been improved and included in DOS 5.

⊃ ANSI.SYS has been improved with many new features.

⊃ DISPLAY.SYS can choose the most appropriate type of active display.

⊃ PRINTER.SYS includes enhanced support for the IBM ProPrinter.

⊃ RAMDRIVE.SYS has improved functionality.

⊃ Diskettes are now formatted with unique serial numbers so that DOS can more easily identify when a diskette has been replaced in a drive.

Enhanced Commands

As you can see from the following list, quite a few of the DOS commands have been improved in some way. Most are easily learned and are not covered in this book; see your DOS documentation for more information on them.

ATTRIB	You can manipulate a file's hidden and system attributes with the ATTRIB command.
BACKUP	Automatically formats an unformatted target diskette; you don't need to use /F unless you want to specify the size.
CHKDSK	Displays the volume serial number and number of allocation units.
COMMAND	The COMMAND command includes a /MSG switch to force DOS to store error messages in memory for faster access. COMMAND is covered in detail in Chapter 10.
COMP	COMP includes several new switches to control the results of the file comparison.
COUNTRY	The COUNTRY command references more country codes and code pages. Chapter 17 shows you how to use different country formats on your PC.
DATE	You can set dates up through 2099, but you must use all four digits for years after 1999.
DEL	DEL includes a /P switch to prompt for confirmation.

DIR	DIR has switches to select files by attribute, to list files from subdirectories, and to sort the listing. You can also specify your own default DIR options. The volume serial number is displayed in DIR output. These new features are discussed under *The New DIR Options* later in this chapter.
DISKCOPY	DISKCOPY has added a /V switch to verify the copy.
FASTOPEN	Can be installed from CONFIG.SYS and includes an /X switch to load buffers in expanded memory.
FDISK	Has been substantially improved, both in its user interface and in functionality.
FORMAT	FORMAT can do a nondestructive format of a diskette. It will also format a 2.88M diskette. New switches let you specify the volume label in the command and specify a nondefault size more easily. Chapter 14 discusses the new FORMAT features in detail.
GRAFTABL	Makes more code pages available.
GRAPHICS	More adapters and printers are available.
KEYB	The KEYB command has an /E switch to identify enhanced keyboards and an /ID switch to select a specific keyboard for country codes with more than one possibility. Also, more code pages are available.
MODE	The MODE command offers more monitor and printer options and lets you specify the number of monitor lines and the keyboard repeat rate. Chapter 16 discusses MODE.
MORE	MORE will use the full display on monitors with more than 25 lines.
REM	Can appear in CONFIG.SYS.
REPLACE	Includes a /U switch to update files.
RESTORE	A new RESTORE switch called /D shows you what would be restored but doesn't actually restore anything. RESTORE can restore files from any BACKUP version. Chapter 13 explores the RESTORE utility in detail.
SYS	SYS copies COMMAND.COM along with the system files; the system files no longer need to be contiguous; you can specify the location of the source system files.
TIME	You can specify the time in 12-hour or 24-hour format.
TREE	Uses graphics to depict directory structure.
XCOPY	Does not copy hidden or system files.

New Commands

As you might imagine, all the new DOS 5 features have resulted in several new commands:

DELOLDOS — Deletes older DOS version(s) from your hard disk.

DEVICEHIGH — If you set up your system for it, you can use DEVICEHIGH to load device drivers into upper DOS memory (the area between 640K and 1M) instead of conventional memory. DEVICEHIGH is explained in Chapter 11.

DOS — The DOS command in CONFIG.SYS loads the DOS software in extended memory. It also helps to load software into upper DOS memory. DOS is also explained in Chapter 11.

DOSKEY — The new DOSKEY command starts up and controls the DOSKEY program, which is fully discussed in Chapter 5.

EDIT — The EDIT command starts up the new full-screen editor.

EMM386 — The EMM386 command is used to turn on and off the features of the new memory manager. Chapter 11 discusses EMM386.

EXPAND — The program files supplied on the DOS 5 upgrade diskettes are stored in compressed format. The SETUP program decompresses the files automatically, but if you decide to copy a file from the diskettes to your hard disk after installation, you will have to use EXPAND to decompress it.

HELP — The HELP program displays on-screen documentation for the DOS commands.

INSTALL — Loads programs while CONFIG.SYS is being processed.

LOADFIX — Loads programs higher than the 64K mark.

LOADHIGH — LOADHIGH is used somewhat like DEVICEHIGH to start up a program in upper DOS memory (the area between 640K and 1M) instead of conventional memory. Chapter 11 discusses LOADHIGH.

MEM — The MEM program appeared with version 4 to display current memory usage and availability. With DOS 5, a new switch called /CLASSIFY summarizes the programs currently in conventional and upper memory in a way that is useful even to nonprogrammers. Chapter 11 discusses MEM along with other memory facilities.

MIRROR	The MIRROR program captures vital system information to facilitate the new UNDELETE and UNFORMAT programs. Chapter 14 discusses MIRROR along with other data-protection facilities.
QBASIC	Starts up the QBasic editor.
SETVER	The SETVER command controls the DOS version number that is reported to a program to make DOS 5 compatible with older applications. It's explained under *Using SETVER* later in this chapter.
SWITCHES	The SWITCHES command in CONFIG.SYS forces an enhanced keyboard to behave like a conventional one.
TRUENAME	The TRUENAME command displays the real location of a directory or file when the directory structure has been masked with ASSIGN or SUBST.
UNDELETE	The UNDELETE command can recover files that are marked as deleted but still exist on a disk. Chapter 15 discusses UNDELETE along with other data recovery facilities.
UNFORMAT	The UNFORMAT command can recover much of the former data from a disk that was reformatted. It's also explained in Chapter 15.

Eliminated Features

If you're used to earlier versions of DOS, you might notice that a couple of facilities have been removed. Of these, the most remarkable is SELECT, which was the name of the installation program. This has been replaced in version 5 by SETUP, an entirely new program.

Two extended/expanded memory handlers named XMA2EMS.SYS and XMAEM.SYS appeared with DOS 4, did not work very well, and were replaced in DOS 5 by EMM386.EXE.

Two minor CONFIG.SYS features have also disappeared. The FCBS command used to permit a second parameter to limit the number of files that DOS could close automatically. DOS 5 doesn't close files automatically, so the second parameter is no longer available. The BUFFERS command developed an /X parameter in DOS 4 to place the buffers in expanded memory, but it didn't work well and wasn't used much, and the new memory facilities make it obsolete, so it has been removed from version 5.

Working with HELP

If you're teaching someone to use DOS 5, show them the on-line help system early. They can see individual command documentation (see Figure 1.1. for an example) by entering a command in either of the formats shown below. Both commands produce the same results except that the second format is faster because the HELP program doesn't have to process it.

    HELP [*command*]

or

    command /?

Figure 1.1.

Sample Help
Message.

```
C:\HSG>del /?
Deletes one or more files.

DEL [drive:][path]filename [/P]
ERASE [drive:][path]filename [/P]

 [drive:][path]filename  Specifies the file(s) to delete.  Specify multiple
                         files by using wildcards.
 /P                      Prompts for confirmation before deleting each file.

C:\HSG>
```

HELP with no parameters displays a complete list of DOS commands with a brief explanation of each. The list is automatically paged on a monitor, but it is printed without paging when redirected to a printer like this:

    HELP > PRN

If you are responsible for helping a group of inexperienced people to use DOS, you might want to adapt the help list to include your own notes, comments, and warnings; to document batch commands and macros that you have created; and most particularly, to modify the explanations of commands you have replaced with DOSKEY macros (a technique that is explained in Chapter 5). You can modify the command list by editing the file named DOSHELP.HLP. The beginning of the file (see Figure 1.2) explains the proper way to edit the list.

Figure 1.2.

Beginning of DOSHELP.HLP as Viewed with EDIT.

```
 File  Edit  Search  Options                                          Help
                           ┌──────────── DOSHELP.HLP ────────────┐
@ Copyright (C) 1990-1991 Microsoft Corp.  All rights reserved.          ↑
@ This is the DOS general help file.  It contains a brief
@ description of each command supported by the DOS help command.
@ Type HELP with no arguments to display the text in this file.
@ Lines beginning with @ are comments, and are ignored by HELP.
@ This file may be modified to add new commands.  If the HELP command-name
@ form is to be used, any new commands should support the /? parameter.
@ New commands should start in the first column.  Any extra lines needed
@ for a command description should be preceded by white space.  Commands
@ must be added in alphabetical order.
APPEND   Allows programs to open data files in specified directories as if
         they were in the current directory.
ASSIGN   Redirects requests for disk operations on one drive to a different
         drive.
ATTRIB   Displays or changes file attributes.
BACKUP   Backs up one or more files from one disk to another.
BREAK    Sets or clears extended CTRL+C checking.
CALL     Calls one batch program from another.
CD       Displays the name of or changes the current directory.
CHCP     Displays or sets the active code page number.
CHDIR    Displays the name of or changes the current directory.            ↓
 MS-DOS Editor   <F1=Help> Press ALT to activate menus           |  N 00001:001
```

Individual command documentation, such as that shown in Figure 1.1, is built into the executable program files. You can edit it using DEBUG if you know how to edit a COM or EXE file. Otherwise, it's best to leave it alone.

TIP   If you program additional utilities for your users, include processing of the /? switch to provide on-line documentation similar to what DOS provides.

Points to Ponder about EDIT

DOS has always included an ASCII editor named EDLIN, but it's hard to work with and most inexperienced users ignore it. DOS 5 now makes available an easy editor named EDIT that new users will love. Here are some points to keep in mind about EDIT:

⊃ Don't expect too much from EDIT—it's an editor, not a word processor. That means it doesn't offer font choices, word-wrapping, paragraph or page formatting, or the other bells and whistles everyone has grown accustomed to. Most significantly for people who are used to word processing, they have to press Enter to end each line, and if they want pages numbered, they have to do it manually. EDIT is ideally suited for unformatted ASCII files such as batch files, CONFIG.SYS files, BASIC files (and other program source code), short README files, and the like, but a word processor is a better choice for formatted text documents.

⊃ You can save about 12K of disk space by deleting EDLIN.EXE if you won't use it.

⊃ EDIT is actually QBasic's editor in document mode. It can be used to edit any ASCII file, but it won't work if you remove the file named QBASIC.EXE from the DOS directory. Many QuickBASIC programmers don't plan to keep the smaller QBasic on their hard disks, but if they remove it, they won't be able to use EDIT.

⊃ No matter what word processor you're comfortable with, you'll be right at home with EDIT's keyboard control. EDIT responds to the cursor and delete keys (Left, Home, Del, and so on), but it also recognizes WordStar control combinations such as Ctrl+S to move left one character and Ctrl+Y to delete a line.

⊃ Be sure to set up EDIT's help system, especially for new users. The file named EDIT.HLP must be in a directory that EDIT can locate. If it is not in a directory on the DOS search path, choose **Options Help Path** and enter the correct path for the directory containing EDIT.HLP.

⊃ You can keep EDIT's help window on the screen while working in the text window by dragging the text window's top border up to give it more space. You can toggle from one window to the other by clicking on the appropriate window or pressing F6.

⊃ You can print help text just like any other text. Place the cursor in the help window, select a block of text if desired, and choose **File Print**.

The New DIR Options

The DIR command has finally joined the Nineties. While it's still not perfect, its new functions make it much more useful than before. With DOS 5's DIR, you can:

⊃ select files by their attributes

⊃ list files from an entire branch

⊃ sort the file list

⊃ set up your own default format

Figure 1.3 shows the complete DIR format, which incorporates both old and new options.

Figure 1.3.

DIR Command Format.

DIR

Displays directory listing.

Format:

DIR [*filespec*] [*switches*]

Parameters and Switches:

filespec Identifies the directory and filenames to be listed.

/A[*x*] Specifies the attributes of files to be selected for listing; use a minus sign before an attribute code to exclude files with that attribute. Attribute codes:

A	Archive files (modified files)
D	Directories
H	Hidden files
R	Read-only files
S	System files
none	All files and directories are selected

/B Lists names only with no header or summary lines.

/L Uses lowercase.

/O[*x*] Specifies the order of the list; use a minus sign before a sort key for reverse order. Sort keys:

D	Chronologically by date and time
E	Alphabetically by extension
G	Directories grouped before files
N	Alphabetically by filename
S	By size
none	Equivalent to GNE

/P Pauses after each page.

/S Selects files from an entire branch.

/W Displays names only, five across (wide display).

Displaying Branches

The /S switch lists files from an entire branch—the current or specified directory and all its subdirectories. For example, suppose you want to list all the BAK files in the branch headed by the current directory. The command and DIR's response might look like this:

```
C:\NUFIGS>DIR /S *.BAK

 Volume in drive C is DRIVE C
 Volume Serial Number is 1678-5CCA


Directory of C:\NUFIGS

FIG16-2  BAK    116172 12-11-90  11:10a
TAB5-1   BAK     11536 11-16-90   7:28p
        2 file(s)      127708 bytes

Directory of C:\NUFIGS\NEWSET

FIG11-6  BAK    213016 05-30-91   1:54p
        1 file(s)      213016 bytes

Directory of C:\NUFIGS\NEWSET2

FIG15-2  BAK    217291 05-31-91  12:06p
        1 file(s)      217291 bytes


Total files listed:
        4 file(s)      558015 bytes
                    12759808 bytes free
```

DIR clearly identifies each subdirectory and its contents and summarizes the results at the end. Notice that the new and improved display identifies not only the total number of bytes free on the disk, but also the number of bytes in the listed files, a nice bonus. But it doesn't show the number of bytes actually allocated to the files, and it doesn't edit the figures with commas so that the larger numbers are easily readable. There's still room for improvement in version 6.0.

The /S switch can also help locate missing files when you forget what directory they're in. Suppose you've misplaced RESPROP.SKI. The following command searches every directory on the current drive for it. Each directory is listed, with either the file listing or the message "File not found":

```
DIR \RESPROP.SKI /S
```

It's important to start the search in the root directory when you're looking for a lost file. That's why we included the backslash (\) in the filespec. Add the /B switch to list filespec (including full paths) in a more compact format.

| TIP | If you omit the filename from the preceding command, but include the backslash, the result lists *every file* on the current drive by directory. |

Selecting Files by Attributes

DIR normally lists all files except hidden and system ones, but the /A switch selects files with specified attributes, including the directory attribute. /A limits the listing to files that match the specified attribute(s). For example, /AH lists *only* hidden files. Without /AH, a complete interaction might look like this:

```
C:\>DIR *.SYS

  Volume in drive C is HARD DISK 1
  Volume Serial Number is 1678-5CCA
  Directory of C:\

CONFIG   SYS         209 07-23-91  12:49p
HIMEM    SYS       11304 05-01-90   3:00a
        2 file(s)       11513 bytes
                      4382720 bytes free


C:\>
```

The two files listed are the ones that don't have hidden or system attributes. With /AH added to the command, the output changes to this:

```
C:\>DIR *.SYS /AH

  Volume in drive C is HARD DISK 1
```

```
        Volume Serial Number is 1678-5CCA
        Directory of C:\

IO        SYS      33044 12-13-90    4:09a
MSDOS     SYS      37506 12-13-90    4:09a
        2 file(s)         70550 bytes
                        4382720 bytes free


C:\>
```

Now *only* the hidden files are listed; the nonhidden files (CONFIG.SYS and HIMEM.SYS) do not appear in the display.

If two or more attributes are included with /A, selected files have all specified attributes. /ADH selects only hidden directories, while /ARA selects only modified read-only files.

A minus sign before an attribute code lists files that *don't* have that attribute. /AD–H lists directories that are not hidden, and /A–A lists all files that do not have the archive attribute. /A without any attribute code selects all files and directories, including hidden and system ones.

Sorting the File List

The /O option sorts the list of files. For example, the following command sorts the list in ascending order by size:

```
C:\>DIR *.COM /OS

 Volume in drive C is HARD DISK 1
 Volume Serial Number is 1678-5CCA
 Directory of C:\

EGATEST   COM       6563 07-24-87    7:16p
BAKDOS    COM       6563 02-02-90    5:23p
NDOS      COM      10603 04-29-91    6:00a
COMMAND   COM      46246 12-13-90    4:09a
        4 file(s)         69975 bytes
                        4382720 bytes free


C:\>
```

When no sort keys are specified with /O, DIR lists directories first, then files, in ascending order by name and extension. When more than one sort key is specified, DIR uses the second sort key only when two or more files have the same first sort key. For example, adding an N to the above command changes the outcome only slightly:

```
C:\>DIR *.COM /OSN

 Volume in drive C is HARD DISK 1
 Volume Serial Number is 1678-5CCA
 Directory of C:\

BAKDOS    COM     6563 02-02-90    5:23p
EGATEST   COM     6563 07-24-87    7:16p
NDOS      COM    10603 04-29-91    6:00a
COMMAND   COM    46246 12-13-90    4:09a
        4 file(s)     69975 bytes
                    4382720 bytes free

C:\>
```

The first two files have the same size. In the first example, their order was arbitrary. In the second example, they were placed in alphabetical order by name.

A minus sign before a sort key reverses the order. The following command sorts the listing from large to small; however, files with duplicate sizes are sorted in ascending alphabetical order because there is no minus sign before the N:

```
C:\>DIR *.COM /O-SN

 Volume in drive C is HARD DISK 1
 Volume Serial Number is 1678-5CCA
 Directory of C:\

COMMAND   COM    46246 12-13-90    4:09a
NDOS      COM    10603 04-29-91    6:00a
BAKDOS    COM     6563 02-02-90    5:23p
```

```
EGATEST  COM      6563 07-24-87   7:16p
          4 file(s)        69975 bytes
                         4382720 bytes free

C:\>
```

DIR Defaults

DIR now recognizes an environment variable named DIRCMD, which establishes default DIR options. (Environment variables are explained in Chapter 10.) Suppose you enter this command to define the DIRCMD environment variable:

```
SET DIRCMD=/A /O
```

All subsequent DIR commands would select files with any attributes (because of the /A switch) and sort the listing in ascending order by name and extension with directories listed first (because of the /O switch). To override the default settings for an individual DIR command, you would add the appropriate /A and /O switches to the command.

TIP	Include a SET DIRCMD command in AUTOEXEC.BAT so your favorite DIR options are set up as the default every time you boot.

Using SETVER

Now that you've installed DOS 5, you might find that some older applications won't start up because they check the DOS version number and are designed to work with a specific DOS version earlier than 5. In some cases, the application truly can't work with DOS 5 and you'll need to talk to the manufacturer about getting an updated version. (You might want to uninstall DOS 5 until you resolve the difficulty.) But in most cases, all you have to do is fool the application into thinking that the correct DOS version is present, and it will function perfectly. The SETVER facility lets you lie to an application about the DOS version number.

Setting Up SETVER

SETVER uses a version table which must be loaded into memory by
CONFIG.SYS during booting. DOS 5's SETUP automatically inserts the
following command into your CONFIG.SYS file:

```
DEVICE=path\SETVER.EXE
```

If it's not there and you need to use SETVER, insert the command into
CONFIG.SYS.

TIP	If you don't need to use SETVER, remove the DEVICE=SETVER command from CONFIG.SYS to save a little memory space.

TIP	If you need SETVER and your system is set up to take advantage of upper memory blocks (see Chapter 11 for details on this), change DEVICE to DEVICEHIGH so that the version table will be loaded into upper memory.

Setting a Version

The DOS documentation is not quite accurate on SETVER's format. The
correct format for adding an entry to the SETVER table is:

```
SETVER program-filename n.nn
```

The *program-filename* identifies the program to be lied to; include the
filename and extension, but not a path, as in GAVOT.EXE. The *n.nn* identifies the DOS version number to report. For example, suppose you have a
program named COMSPIN that requires DOS 3.3. You could enter this
command to tell COMSPIN that DOS 3.3 is present:

```
SETVER COMSPIN.EXE 3.3
```

The SETVER command merely adds or changes an entry in the version
table. You have to restart to load the changed table. Then you can try out
the application in question. If it works, good. If not, you'll have to solve the
problem some other way (such as upgrading the application software).

> **WARNING**
>
> Use extra caution when lying to an application with SETVER. The program could be fooled into accessing a disk incorrectly, and you could lose valuable data. For safety's sake, back up your hard disk drives before using SETVER with a program for the first time.

SETVER Options

Use the /DELETE or /D switch to delete an entry from the version table. For example, to delete the COMSPIN entry, you would enter this command:

```
SETVER COMSPIN.EXE /D
```

Add the /QUIET or/Q switch to suppress the confirmation message that is normally displayed when /D is used. (You can't suppress the long warning message that is displayed when you add or change an item in the table.)

Use the SETVER command without any parameters to list the current version table. You'll find that, in addition to your own entries, it has quite a few entries inserted by Microsoft.

A CLOSER LOOK
AT DOS SHELL

ntroduction

Don't be too quick to reject DOS Shell as child's play. It lets you do a number of things that the command-line interface doesn't, such as renaming directories and moving files by dragging them from one directory to another with a mouse. You can select a group of unrelated files to be processed by a single command; they don't even have to be in the same directory. On a somewhat larger scale, the Shell lets you start up several programs at once and switch among them using a facility called the *task swapper*. The Shell is also an excellent tool for setting up applications for easy access by people who don't have much PC or DOS experience.

> **N O T E**
>
> This book includes the menu name as the first word in menu commands. For example, **File Copy** refers to the **Copy** command on the **File** menu.

Starting DOS Shell

The Shell is started using the DOSSHELL command shown in Figure 2.1. This command (with no options) might have been inserted in AUTOEXEC.BAT by SETUP during installation. If not, and if you decide to insert it for yourself or another user, be sure it's the last command in AUTOEXEC.BAT, as any subsequent commands will not be executed until the Shell is terminated.

Figure 2.1.

DOSSHELL Command.

DOSSHELL

Starts up DOS Shell.

Format:

DOSSHELL [*switches*]

Switches:

/T[:*res*[*n*]]   Starts DOS Shell in text mode. *Res* specifies a screen resolution category of L (low), M (medium), or H (high). For monitors with multiple resolutions within resolution categories, *n* identifies the specific resolution.

/G[:*res*[*n*]]   Starts DOS Shell in graphics mode.

/B   Starts DOS Shell using a black-and-white color scheme.

Notes:

The graphics mode and resolution can also be controlled by the **Options Display** command once the Shell is started. You can see the entire list of options available for your monitor in the dialog box opened by that command.

Many more color schemes (including several monochrome versions) are available using the **Options Colors** command after the Shell is started. However, when you start DOS Shell with the /B switch, you cannot change color schemes with the **Options Colors** command.

The graphics mode, resolution, and black-and-white color scheme specified on the DOSSHELL command are not retained in DOSSHELL.INI and therefore do not affect future DOSSHELL startups.

The command switches control the screen appearance, which can also be managed from the **Options** menu after the Shell has been started. When you set it from the **Options** menu, DOS Shell saves the current screen setup in a file named DOSSHELL.INI and recalls it the next time, so once you have set up the screen the way you want it, it will stay that way for future DOS Shell sessions.

TIP	You can transfer your setup to other computers by replacing their DOSSHELL.INI files with a copy of yours.

Figure 2.2 shows a typical DOS Shell screen. This one is in graphics mode with 25 lines per screen. The **Options Display** command offers other setups that might be more compatible with your hardware, such as text mode and/or more lines per screen. The **Options Colors** command lets you select from a variety of color schemes, including several monochrome setups. You'll see how to define your own color schemes in Chapter 3.

Figure 2.2.

Typical DOS Shell Screen.

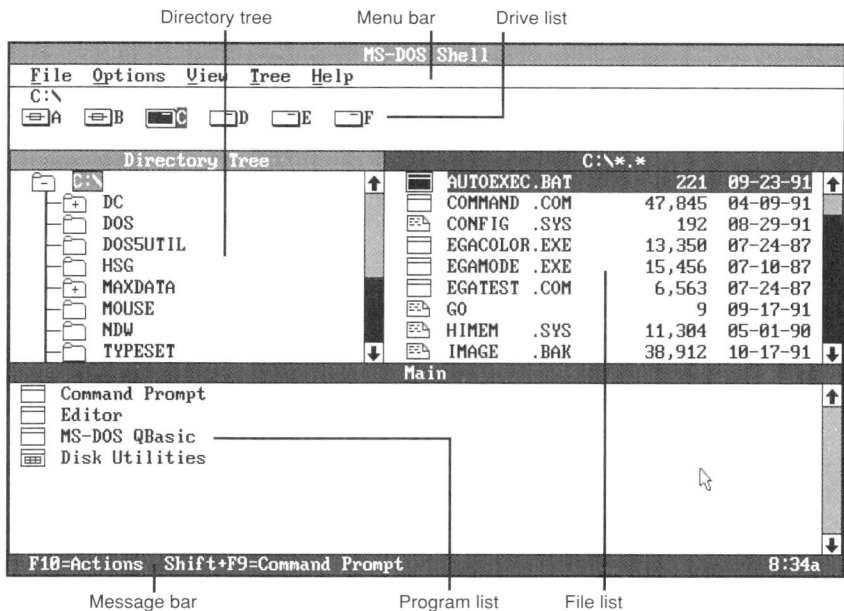

Controlling the Shell

At the basic level, the Shell works like most other graphic interfaces, and people who are experienced with other products will be able to start using it immediately. Beginners will master the basics quickly, as learning is fairly intuitive, especially for mouse users.

TIP	Show beginners how to access the Shell's help system. It provides on-screen reminders of mouse and keyboard actions and can be an important part of the early learning process.

Once you get beyond the basics, Shell manipulation becomes less intuitive, and even experienced people might find some maneuvers tricky. The following sections discuss some of the grayer areas in using the Shell.

Working with Menus

The **File** menu actually changes depending on which Shell area contains the cursor. Figure 2.3 compares the **File** menu when the file list is active to the **File** menu when the program list is active. If you can't find an expected item on the **File** menu, make sure the cursor is in the right Shell area and try again.

Figure 2.3A.

When the cursor is in the file list.

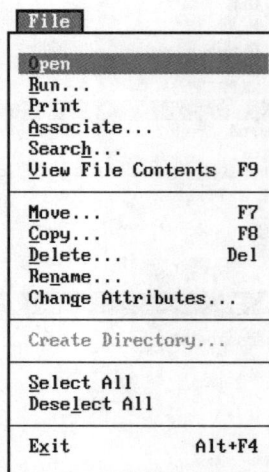

```
┌File────────────────────┐
│ Open                    │
│ Run...                  │
│ Print                   │
│ Associate...            │
│ Search...               │
│ View File Contents   F9 │
├─────────────────────────┤
│ Move...              F7 │
│ Copy...              F8 │
│ Delete...           Del │
│ Rename...               │
│ Change Attributes...    │
├─────────────────────────┤
│ Create Directory...     │
├─────────────────────────┤
│ Select All              │
│ Deselect All            │
├─────────────────────────┤
│ Exit             Alt+F4 │
└─────────────────────────┘
```

Figure 2.3B.

When the cursor is
in the program list.

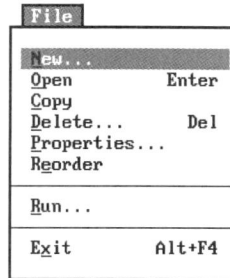

```
 File
┌──────────────────────┐
│ New...               │
│ Open          Enter  │
│ Copy                 │
│ Delete...     Del    │
│ Properties...        │
│ Reorder              │
│                      │
│ Run...               │
│                      │
│ Exit          Alt+F4 │
└──────────────────────┘
```

Hotkeys (such as F8 for **File Copy**) can be used to activate a menu command without pulling down the menu. It's traditional to list hotkeys next to the menu commands they replace, which is unfortunate in a way, because when the menu is showing, you don't need the hotkey. You have to memorize the hotkeys for commands you use a lot (or tape a list to your workstation). If you try a hotkey and it doesn't work, check to make sure the correct area is active and the right type of item is selected.

Working with the Drive List

The drive list shows all the drives currently available, including diskette drives, logical drives on a hard disk, RAM drives and other types of pseudo drives, and network drives. In graphics mode, each type of drive has its own icon.

Click a drive to select it. Or if you're using the keyboard, press Ctrl+d, where d is the drive letter, as in Ctrl+A or Ctrl+C. (Table 2.1 describes the keys that control the drive list.)

Table 2.1 Drive List Control Keys

When the cursor is anywhere on the shell screen:	
Ctrl+d	Selects drive d: (doesn't reread directory)
When the cursor is in the drive list:	
Left or Right arrow	Moves cursor in drive list
Enter	Selects highlighted drive (rereads directory)
Spacebar	Selects highlighted drive (doesn't reread directory)

The first time you select a drive after startup, DOS Shell reads and stores the drive's directory structure, which takes time. From then on, when you return to the Shell screen from some other screen, or when you select the drive again for any reason, DOS Shell displays the stored directory structure so that it doesn't have to reread the drive. But if you've made changes to the drive that DOS Shell isn't aware of—for example, if you've deleted files from outside the Shell—the display will be out of sync with the actual contents of the drive. In those cases you need to force DOS Shell to reread the drive by one of these methods:

➲ If the drive is already current, simply press F5, which is the hotkey for the **Options Refresh** command.

➲ To make the drive current and simultaneously reread it, double-click the drive name or highlight it and press Enter.

Working with the Directory Tree

The initial appearance of the directory tree shows only the root directory and the first level of subdirectories, as shown in the sample screen in Figure 2.2. You can rearrange the tree by expanding and collapsing branches. The **Tree** menu contains commands for expanding and collapsing branches, but every command can be accomplished more easily by mouse action or hotkey.

Branch Levels

A plus (+) sign (see the DC directory in Figure 2.2) indicates that a directory contains undisplayed subdirectories. You can click the plus sign or press + to see the next level of subdirectories for the current directory. To see all levels of subdirectories for the current directory, press *. To see all levels of subdirectories for all directories (that is, the entire tree), press Ctrl+*. This is one of the few areas in DOS Shell where you can do more from the keyboard than you can with a mouse, as there are no mouse equivalents for the * and Ctrl+* hotkeys.

A minus (−) sign (see the root directory in Figure 2.2) indicates that the directory is expanded and can be collapsed. Click the minus sign or press − to collapse it. There is no hotkey to collapse all directories; when you collapse the root directory, all subdirectories are collapsed into it.

TIP To select a directory without expanding or collapsing its subdirectories, click its name instead of its + or – sign.

When the cursor is in the directory tree, you can use **File** menu commands to create, delete, and rename directories. This is the only way to directly rename a directory in DOS. You can't move or copy directories directly with DOS Shell commands, but you can do it step-by-step: create a new directory, move or copy all the files to it, and remove the original one.

Locating a Subdirectory

When a large directory tree is expanded, the directory you want might not be showing in the tree window. A mouse user's natural instinct is to use the scroll bar to scroll to the right area in the tree. But it's faster to type the first character of the directory name, which automatically scrolls the window so that the next directory starting with that character is selected.

Working with the File List

The file list displays the files in the current directory, ready to be selected. You'll find there are several advantages to working with the file list under DOS Shell as opposed to managing files from the command prompt:

➲ You can select the exact files to be processed; their names don't have to match a global filespec as they do when you're working at the command prompt.

➲ You can select files from multiple directories to be processed with one command.

➲ You can move files from one directory to another with one command; you don't need to first copy, then delete them, as you do at the command prompt.

➲ DOS Shell will warn you when a copy or move operation will overwrite an existing file, and you can confirm or deny the overwrite. This feature alone makes the Shell worthwhile, as it can prevent expensive data loss.

Table 2.2 summarizes the keys that control the file list. The least intuitive procedure associated with the file list is selecting multiple files. To select multiple files with a mouse, press Ctrl while you click each filename. Pressing Shift while you click the mouse selects all files between the last one selected and the one you click on.

Table 2.2 File List Control Keys

character	Selects next filename beginning with *character*
Enter	Opens selected file
Del	Deletes selected file(s)
Ctrl+/	Selects all files
Ctrl+\	Unselects all files except highlighted one
Shift+Enter	Places highlighted program file on Active Task List
Shift+Cursor key	Adds file(s) to selection list
Shift+F8	Enters/exits ADD mode
Spacebar	(*In ADD mode only*) Adds highlighted file to or removes it from selection list
Shift+Spacebar	(*In ADD mode only*) Adds all files between the last one selected and the currently highlighted one to the selection list

To select several adjacent files from the keyboard, move the cursor to the first one, hold down the Shift key, and move the cursor to the last one (using any cursor movement method). You'll see the highlight expand to include all adjacent files as the cursor moves.

The procedure for selecting several nonadjacent files without a mouse is somewhat unusual because you must enter ADD mode by pressing Shift+F8. If you have a mouse (or plan to get one soon), you won't have to go through this cumbersome procedure; but if you're temporarily mouseless, at least you can continue to work with the file list until your mouse recovers.

The word "ADD" appears on the status line when ADD mode is in effect. You add a file to the list of selected files by moving the cursor to it and pressing Spacebar. If you press Shift+Spacebar, all the files between the last selected one and the current highlight are selected. When all the necessary files are selected, stay in ADD mode while you choose a command (such as **File Delete** or **File Move**) to process them. You can exit ADD mode by pressing Shift+F8 again.

Dragging Files

The easiest way to copy and move files is to drag them from one location to another using a mouse. Dragging is pretty straightforward, but here are some points that aren't explained in the DOS 5 documentation:

➲ The status of the Ctrl key determines the operation. If Ctrl is pressed, the selected files are copied, otherwise; they're moved. You can change operations in mid-drag by pressing or releasing Ctrl, because it's the Ctrl key status at the moment the mouse button is released that counts. Whenever the mouse pointer is over a legitimate target area, the message line indicates whether the files will be moved or copied.

➲ The shape of the mouse pointer indicates when it is over an invalid or valid destination. For valid areas, it indicates whether a single file or multiple files are being dragged. The message line also indicates when you are over a valid or invalid area and whether single or multiple files are being dragged.

➲ When dragging files to a directory on a different drive, use one of these techniques to reach the desired directory: (1) Make the desired destination directory the default directory on that drive, then drag the files to the drive icon. (2) Choose **View Dual File Lists** and use the second directory tree to display the destination directory.

➲ When dragging files to another directory on the same drive, use one or both of these techniques to bring the destination directory into view: (1) Choose **View Single File List** to give maximum space to the directory tree. (2) Expand and contract branches as necessary to bring the desired destination directory into view.

> **WARNING**
>
> When **Options Select Across Directories** is enabled, files aren't auto-
> matically deselected as you change directories, and it's easy to drag
> more files than you meant to. The confirmation dialog box doesn't
> list each filename individually, so you could end up copying or mov-
> ing files unintentionally. For safety's sake, keep **Options Select Across
> Directories** disabled except when you need it for specific operations.

Display Options

You can make the file list even more effective by taking advantage of the
Options File Display Options command, which opens the dialog box shown
in Figure 2.4. Suppose you want to delete all the BAK files in the current
directory. An easy way to do it is to specify *.BAK as the filename filter in
the **Name** box so that only BAK files are displayed in the file list. (The title
bar of the file list shows the current path and filename filter, which is *.* by
default.) Be sure to check **Display hidden/system files** if you want to include hidden and system BAK files in the list. When you get back to the file
list, use Ctrl+/ to select all files, press Del to delete them, and confirm the
deletions. Finally, select **Options File Display Options** again and restore the
default options.

Handling Files from Multiple Directories

DOS Shell gives you two ways to select files from multiple directories. **Options Select Across Directories** lets you select files in one directory, switch
directories and select more files, and so on until all the files you want are
selected. **View All Files** displays all the files on the drive in one file list so
that you can select as many as necessary regardless of directory. In either
case, once all the desired files are selected, you can process them with one
command, such as **File Copy** or **File Delete**.

Figure 2.4.

File Display Options
Dialog Box.

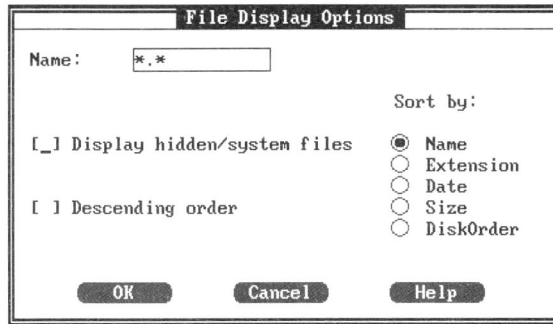

```
╔══════════════════ File Display Options ══════════════════╗
║                                                          ║
║   Name:    ┌───────────┐                                 ║
║            │ *.*       │                                 ║
║            └───────────┘                                 ║
║                                      Sort by:            ║
║                                                          ║
║   [_] Display hidden/system files    ◉ Name             ║
║                                      ○ Extension         ║
║                                      ○ Date              ║
║   [ ] Descending order               ○ Size             ║
║                                      ○ DiskOrder         ║
║                                                          ║
║         ( OK )        ( Cancel )         ( Help )        ║
╚══════════════════════════════════════════════════════════╝
```

In general, **View All Files** is a safer choice than **Options Select Across Directories**. You might forget that **Options Select Across Directories** is enabled (a diamond on the **Options** menu indicates that it's enabled, but you can't see it when the menu isn't pulled down), and you could accidentally delete or move files that you didn't realize were selected. But since **View All Files** affects the main DOS Shell screen, you're not likely to forget that it's selected, although you still might not see all selected files if the file list runs to more than one page.

Figure 2.5 shows what the **View All Files** screen looks like. There is no directory tree because files from all directories are included in the list. Instead, the left panel shows information about the drive and the selected files. Keep an eye on these two important sections:

⊃ The **Directory** section shows the location of the most recently selected or deselected file. Use it to find out what directory a file is in.

⊃ The **Selected** section indicates how many files are currently selected (**Number** field). Make sure it agrees with your opinion of how many files are selected before starting a delete or move operation.

You might see several identical file names in the all files view—notice that there are two 4201.CPI files in Figure 2.5. They are located in different directories, which you can see by highlighting each one and observing the directory name in the information panel.

Figure 2.5.

View All Files
Screen.

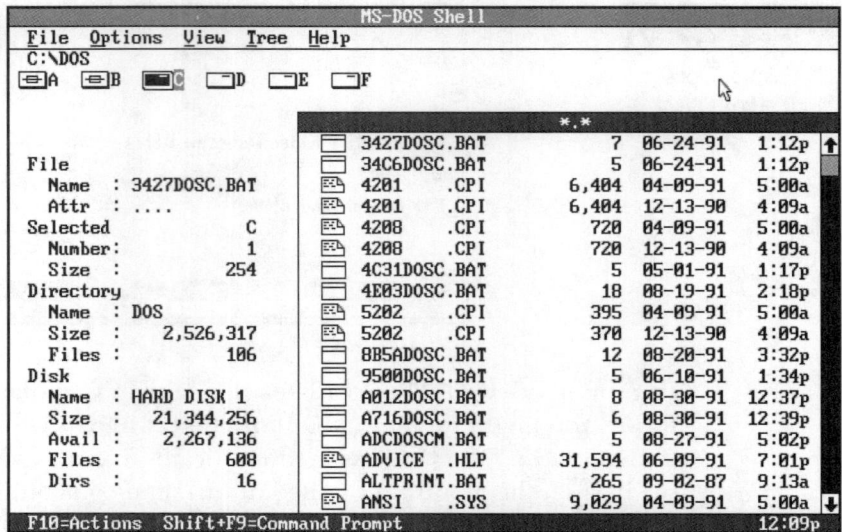

```
                                      MS-DOS Shell
    File  Options  View  Tree  Help
    C:\DOS
    ⊟A   ⊟B   ▇C   ⊟D   ⊟E   ⊟F                                    ⌐

                              ┌─────────────────────────── *.* ──────────┐
                              │ 🗋 3427DOSC.BAT      7  06-24-91   1:12p ↑│
    File                      │ 🗋 34C6DOSC.BAT      5  06-24-91   1:12p  │
      Name  : 3427DOSC.BAT    │ 🗋 4201     .CPI 6,404  04-09-91   5:00a  │
      Attr  : ....            │ 🗋 4201     .CPI 6,404  12-13-90   4:09a  │
    Selected        C         │ 🗋 4208     .CPI   720  04-09-91   5:00a  │
      Number:       1         │ 🗋 4208     .CPI   720  12-13-90   4:09a  │
      Size  :     254         │ 🗋 4C31DOSC.BAT      5  05-01-91   1:17p  │
    Directory                 │ 🗋 4E03DOSC.BAT     18  08-19-91   2:18p  │
      Name  : DOS             │ 🗋 5202     .CPI   395  04-09-91   5:00a  │
      Size  : 2,526,317       │ 🗋 5202     .CPI   370  12-13-90   4:09a  │
      Files :     106         │ 🗋 8B5ADOSC.BAT     12  08-20-91   3:32p  │
    Disk                      │ 🗋 9500DOSC.BAT      5  06-10-91   1:34p  │
      Name  : HARD DISK 1     │ 🗋 A012DOSC.BAT      8  08-30-91  12:37p  │
      Size  : 21,344,256      │ 🗋 A716DOSC.BAT      6  08-30-91  12:39p  │
      Avail : 2,267,136       │ 🗋 ADCDOSCM.BAT      5  08-27-91   5:02p  │
      Files :     608         │ 🗋 ADVICE  .HLP 31,594  06-09-91   7:01p  │
      Dirs  :      16         │ 🗋 ALTPRINT.BAT    265  09-02-87   9:13a  │
                              │ 🗋 ANSI    .SYS  9,029  04-09-91   5:00a ↓│
    F10=Actions   Shift+F9=Command Prompt                          12:09p
```

Locating Lost Files

The Shell offers two ways to locate a lost file when you know its name. One
way is to choose **View All Files** and limit the display with a specific or generic filename filter. Or you can choose **File Search**, which opens a dialog
box in which you can enter the specific or generic filename. You can
choose to search the entire current drive or just the current directory for
all files matching the specified filename. **File Search** produces a search list
from which you can select and process files just as if it were the file list.

Running Programs from the Shell

As you know, it's fairly easy to start up a program from the DOS command
prompt, especially if you set up a batch file to supply the details in response
to a one-word command. You can also set up the Shell for simplified program execution, with two very real advantages:

➲ You can use task swapping with programs started from the Shell.

➲ You can set up items in the program list that people can start by
   double-clicking. A program list item can display dialog boxes to

collect variable parameters such as directory paths and filenames during start-up. You can even give users their own program groups with individually tailored items and password protection.

There are five different ways to start up a program from the Shell screen, each with its advantages and disadvantages. These are explained in the next sections.

Opening a Program File

Perhaps the least convenient way to start up a program is to open its program file from the file list by double-clicking its filename or by highlighting it and pressing Enter. The program is started up, but you get no chance to enter any startup parameters. Many programs can't be successfully started up this way because they must have startup parameters. For example, FORMAT requires a drive name. Furthermore, you can't start up internal programs, such as DIR, because they're contained within COMMAND.COM and have no separate files to open.

If you really need to be able to start up programs from the file list, you can get around these limitations by creating batch files containing the desired commands and parameters and opening the BAT files from the file list. But as you'll see in the next sections, there are better ways to start programs from the Shell.

Opening an Associated File

Another way to start up a program from the file list is to open an *associated file*—a data file whose extension has been associated with a program or batch file. For example, when SETUP installs DOS 5, the extension BAS is associated with the command QBASIC /RUN and the extension TXT is associated with EDIT, the ASCII editor. If you double-click a file named README.TXT, EDIT is started up with the README.TXT file already open. This is a fast and convenient way to start up an application for a particular file, and you'll see how to associate file extensions with programs under *Associating Files* later in this chapter.

Using the File Run Command

The **File Run** command, which is available for all Shell areas, opens a dialog box where you can enter a command much as you do at the command prompt. Figure 2.6 shows the box filled in for formatting a bootable diskette on drive A. This method lets you enter internal or external commands, start up batch files, and include whatever start-up parameters are necessary. When the program terminates, you're asked to press a key to return to the Shell.

The DOS 5 documentation leaves out some important points about the **File Run** feature:

➲ You can enter multiple commands separated by semicolons (;) which must be surrounded by spaces. For example, to start up a program named SWITCHER from the D:\SWITCH directory, you could enter these commands in the **Command Line** field:

```
D: ; CD \SWITCH ; SWITCHER
```

➲ The **Command Line** field is 255 characters long, letting you enter twice as many characters as you can at the DOS command prompt. But only 127 characters per command (as delimited by semicolons) are recognized by DOS.

➲ You can use variable parameters (%1 through %9) in the command, much as you do in a batch file. DOS Shell will display a dialog box to collect the actual value for each variable parameter before executing the command.

Figure 2.6.

The Run Dialog Box.

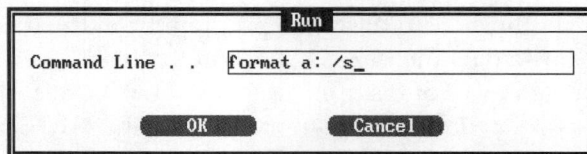

```
                              Run
 Command Line . .    format a: /s_


              OK                  Cancel
```

You probably won't need this last feature very often when entering a command in the File Run dialog box. You'll see it put to better use in Chapter 3, which explains how to define a new item for the program list.

Using a Secondary Command Prompt

Pressing Shift+F9 makes a temporary exit from the Shell to a command prompt, where you can continue entering commands (with as many startup parameters as necessary) until you have accomplished the task at hand. But you shouldn't start up any memory-resident (TSR) programs from this temporary command prompt. When you're ready to return to the Shell, you have to enter this command:

```
EXIT
```

TIP   If you enter any command at the command prompt that changes the directory structure, such as creating a new directory or deleting some files, you'll need to refresh the directory tree and file list by pressing F5 when you return to the Shell.

Opening a Program List Item

Perhaps the most convenient way to start up a program from the Shell is to open an item from the program list. The program list comes with a few predefined items, but you can modify or delete them and add others as needed. If you are setting up a system for other people, you'll probably want to set up the program list so that they can start up programs with a minimum of fuss.

When you open an item from the program list, its behavior depends on how it's defined. You might get a chance to enter variable start-up parameters in dialog boxes, or the start-up parameters might be predefined. Program termination might return directly to the Shell, or you might have to press a key first. You can even password-protect program items and prevent them from being used with task-switching. Chapter 3 examines the program list in more detail.

Associating File Extensions with Programs

It's fairly easy to set up file associations. Figure 2.7 shows how to associate the DOC extension with Microsoft Word by highlighting any DOC file in the file list, selecting **File Associate**, and filling in the command that starts up the program.

Figure 2.7.

Associate File
Dialog Box.

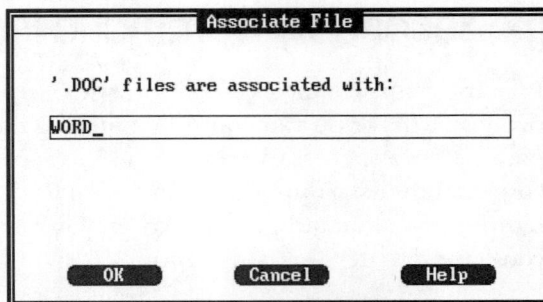

```
┌──────────────────────── Associate File ────────────────────────┐
│                                                                 │
│  '.DOC' files are associated with:                              │
│  ┌───────────────────────────────────────────────────────────┐ │
│  │ WORD_                                                       │ │
│  └───────────────────────────────────────────────────────────┘ │
│                                                                 │
│                                                                 │
│                                                                 │
│       ▐  OK  ▌        ▐  Cancel  ▌        ▐  Help  ▌            │
│                                                                 │
└─────────────────────────────────────────────────────────────────┘
```

When filling in the Associate File dialog box, keep in mind how DOS will use the command-text you place there. When you open an associated file, DOS creates a command like this:

    command-text filespec

You can include in the box whatever command-text is appropriate when starting up the desired program from the command prompt, such as a path, some switches, and other parameters. You can even combine commands with semicolons (surrounded by spaces) and include variable parameters (%1 through %9). DOS will display a dialog box for each variable parameter when you open an associated file, but each dialog box is blank—that is, it has no prompts to remind you what type of information is needed, which may not be desirable.

You can also create file associations from the program's perspective: highlight the program file, select **File Associate**, and fill in the name(s) of associated extension(s). When you do that, you have no opportunity to include parameters or switches in the command-text.

N O T E

A program can be associated with many extensions, but an extension can be associated with just one program. If you accidentally associate an extension with a second program, the first association is replaced with the second.

Task Swapping

One major reason for starting up programs from the Shell instead of the DOS prompt is so you can swap tasks, which has some real advantages. Suppose you start up your word processor, open a file, and edit it for a while. Now you want to do some spreadsheet calculations and copy the results into the current file. Without task swapping, you must close the current file, exit the word processor, and start up the spreadsheet application. When the calculations are done, you have to restart the word processor, reopen the file, and find your former place so you can continue working.

But the story is different when task swapping is in effect. You can switch to the Shell without terminating the word processor, start up and use the spreadsheet, and switch back to your word processor, which is in the same condition. In fact, the cursor is in the exact same location.

Let's clear up a common misconception: you can't execute programs simultaneously under the task swapper. When you switch from program A to program B, program A pauses and doesn't continue executing until you return to it. So you can't format a disk in a background task while you do other work in the foreground. If you would like to have that kind of capability, you'll need Windows, OS/2, or some other true multitasker.

DOS Shell has a few other limitations when compared with a multitasking program such as Windows. You can't see both your worksheet and your word processing file on the screen at the same time. And there is no clipboard, so you can't get the system to copy data from one program to the other; you have to do it manually. These disadvantages are offset by the fact the DOS Shell's price is right, it's relatively easy to install and use, and it doesn't take up a lot of disk or memory space when compared to a program such as Windows.

Setting Up Task Swapping

To enable/disable task swapping, select **Options Enable Task Swapper**. When a diamond (♦) appears next to this option, task swapping is enabled; no diamond means it is disabled. When task swapping is enabled, the active task list appears on the Shell screen in most views (you can see it in Figure 2.8), and every program you start up from the Shell is added to the list. In the example in Figure 2.8, three programs have been started: Hotshot, a secondary command prompt, and DOS's full-screen editor.

Figure 2.8.

DOS Shell Set Up for Task Swapping.

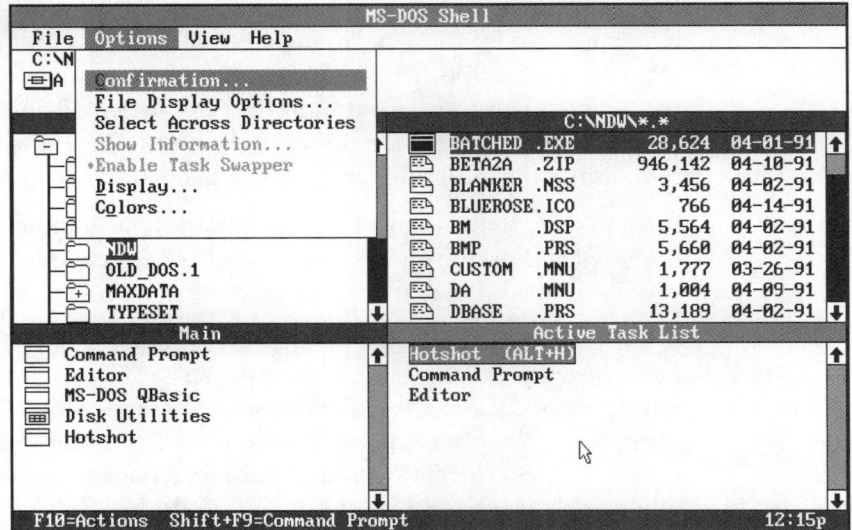

```
                              MS-DOS Shell
 File  Options  View  Help
 C:\N
 ⊟A  ┌Confirmation...──────────────┐
      │ File Display Options...     │              C:\NDW\*.*
      │ Select Across Directories   │  ▭ BATCHED .EXE      28,624  04-01-91 ↑
  ┌─┐ │ Show Information...         ├  ⊟ BETA2A  .ZIP     946,142  04-10-91
  ┌┤  │•Enable Task Swapper         │  ⊟ BLANKER .NSS       3,456  04-02-91
  ┌┤  │ Display...                  │  ⊟ BLUEROSE.ICO         766  04-14-91
  ┌┤  │ Colors...                   │  ⊟ BM      .DSP       5,564  04-02-91
  ┌┤  └─────────────────────────────┘  ⊟ BMP     .PRS       5,660  04-02-91
  ┌┤ NDW                               ⊟ CUSTOM  .MNU       1,777  03-26-91
  ┌┤ OLD_DOS.1                         ⊟ DA      .MNU       1,004  04-09-91
  ┌┤ MAXDATA                           ⊟ DBASE   .PRS      13,189  04-02-91 ↓
  └┤ TYPESET                  ↓
         Main                              Active Task List
 ▭ Command Prompt           ↑        Hotshot  (ALT+H)                    ↑
 ▭ Editor                            Command Prompt
 ▭ MS-DOS QBasic                     Editor
 ▭ Disk Utilities
 ▭ Hotshot                                        ▹
                            ↓                                            ↓
 F10=Actions   Shift+F9=Command Prompt                           12:15p
```

Swapping and the TEMP Variable

The task swapper needs at least 1M of disk space on which to store the current task when switching to another. It looks for an environment variable named TEMP to find the path of the directory where the swap data should be stored. (Environment variables are explained in Chapter 10.) To find out if TEMP has been defined for your system, enter the SET command, which displays all your environment variables something like this:

```
C:\>SET
COMSPEC=C:\DOS\COMMAND.COM
PROMPT=$P$G
PATH=C:\DOS;D:\NU;C:\;C:\MAXDATA;F:\WORD
TEMP=C:\DOS

C:\>
```

In this case, DOS would place the swap files on C:\DOS.

It's a good idea to define TEMP if there is no current definition. When there's no TEMP, DOS places the swap files in the current directory, which could cause swapping to fail if there's not enough room. SETUP inserted a command in your AUTOEXEC.BAT file to define TEMP unless it found one previously established by Windows (which also uses TEMP). Look in AUTOEXEC.BAT for a command in this format:

```
SET TEMP=path
```

If you don't find such a command, add one. Be sure to specify a drive that has at least 1M of free space; use a complete path, including the drive name, so DOS can find the directory no matter what drive or directory is currently active.

Switching Tasks

You can switch to a task on the active task list by opening it (double-click it or highlight it and press Enter). The task's screen—which is the normal screen of the program that owns the task, such as the DOS command prompt screen or a word processor's editing screen—replaces the Shell screen on your monitor. Once you're in the task, you must use a task-swapping hotkey (see Table 2.3) to switch to the Shell or another task.

Table 2.3 Task-Swapping Hotkeys

Ctrl+Esc	Switch to DOS Shell
Alt+Tab	Switch to the next task in the active task list
Alt+Shift+Tab	Switch to the previous task in the active task list
Alt+Tab,Tab,...	Cycle through programs in the active task list (forward)
Alt+Shift+Tab,Tab,...	Cycle through programs in the active task list (backward)

As you can see from the table, Ctrl+Esc takes you back to the Shell, where you can perform other functions or select another task. But you can also rotate among the currently active tasks without going through the Shell by holding down the Alt key while you press Tab. The first time you press Tab, the next task's screen appears on your monitor. But if you continue to hold down Alt and press Tab more times, only the names of subsequent tasks appear on your screen (including "MS-DOS Shell," which is considered one of the tasks even though it isn't listed in the active task list). Release Alt to select a task. To cycle backward through the tasks, press and hold Shift along with Alt while you press Tab.

Task Hotkeys

Some tasks have their own hotkeys listed next to them on the active task list, as Hotshot does in Figure 2.8. You can open that task by pressing the hotkey. You can also switch to directly to that task from another task by pressing the hotkey. If two or more tasks have the same hotkey, just keep pressing the hotkey until you reach the one you want.

Task List Order

You change the order of the active task list as you revisit tasks, because the currently open task is always placed at the top of the list. You can take advantage of this feature to place the two tasks you use most often in the top two positions so that Alt+Tab toggles between them. First open Task A; it takes over the top spot on the list. Then open task B; it assumes the top spot, shoving task A into second place. Every time you press Alt+Tab, the top two tasks switch places. Alt+Tab continues to toggle between them until you open another task, which changes the order of the list.

TIP	It's a good practice to save current data files before switching to another task. That way, if some task hangs up and you have to reboot, you won't lose much data.

Names on the Active Task List

The names that appear on the active task list depend on how the programs were started. If you open an item in the file list or program list, the item's name appears on the active task list. Suppose you double-click README.TXT, causing EDIT to start up; the active task list shows "README.TXT". When you choose **File Run** and enter a command in the resulting dialog box, the

entire text of the command, including parameters, appears on the active
task list.

Command Prompt Tasks

When swapping is in effect, Shift+F9 creates a command prompt task,
which you can swap with other tasks using the usual task-swapping hotkeys.
You can also open a command-prompt task by selecting "Command
Prompt" from the program list. The task will appear as "Command
Prompt" on the active task list no matter what program you start up from
its command prompt.

Duplicate Tasks

If you start up the same program twice, each version has its own task and
is considered a unique entity by the task swapper. You might have three
different Microsoft Word tasks at the same time, each with a different
document open.

If two or more items on the active task list have the same title, DOS Shell
places a single dot after the second one, two dots after the third one, and
so on, so that you can tell the difference between them.

Closing Tasks

When you terminate a program, its task is automatically closed and removed from the active task list. If a program hangs up and can't be closed
normally, avoid rebooting, which would abort all open tasks, possibly leaving files unclosed and changes unsaved. Instead, use Ctrl+Esc to get to the
Shell, if possible. Then highlight the stalled task and press Del to kill it.

WARNING

After you force a task closed with the Del key, the Shell should be
considered unreliable. Close all other tasks, exit the Shell, and reboot.

You have to close all tasks before you can disable swapping or exit DOS
Shell. But you can leave task swapping enabled when you exit. It will still be
enabled the next time you start up the Shell.

CHAPTER 3

SETTING UP
DOS SHELL

ntroduction

Your personalized program list can make a big difference in the effectiveness of the Shell. By adding to it the items you use often, especially those that are candidates for task swapping, you'll create a convenient, flexible, and fast way to start up programs. Items on the program list can be specific or generalized. For example, you might want to create several word processing items:

➲ One that starts up the word processor without identifying a filespec

➲ Several that start up the word processor for specific files that you edit frequently

➲ One that starts up the word processor for whatever file is currently selected in the file list

➲ One that asks you for a filespec when you open it

This chapter discusses the various options available when defining program items.

Program List Views

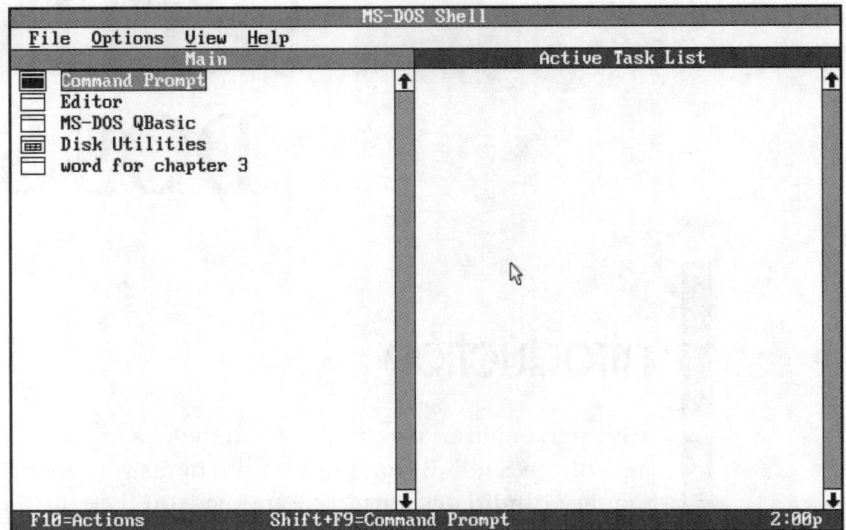

The program list appears in two of DOS Shell's five views, **View Program/File Lists** (the default view) and **View Program List**, which displays only the program list and the active task list, if task swapping is enabled, as you can see in Figure 3.1.

Figure 3.1.

Program List View.

```
                                    MS-DOS Shell
 File  Options  View  Help
                   Main                              Active Task List
   ▓ Command Prompt                  ↑                                        ↑
   ▤ Editor
   ▤ MS-DOS QBasic
   ▥ Disk Utilities
   ▤ word for chapter 3




                                    ↓                                        ↓
 F10=Actions           Shift+F9=Command Prompt                      2:00p
```

Structuring the Program List

The program list has a tree-like structure similar to a disk directory tree, but with *program groups* instead of subdirectories. At the top of the tree is the Main program group (which you can see in the title bar in Figure 3.1), with other program groups branching off from it and from each other. After installation, the Main group has one child, called Disk Utilities.

TIP

In graphics mode, you can tell the difference between program groups and program items in a list by their icons. In text mode, the names of program groups are enclosed in square brackets.

The Disk Utilities Group

Immediately after installation, the Disk Utilities group contains the items shown in Figure 3.2. You'll probably want to adapt the items, which are fairly generalized, to suit your hardware and to add more items. For example, if you have a 5 1/4-inch floppy-disk drive, a 3 1/2-inch floppy-disk drive, and two 40M hard drives, you might want to have the following items:

➲ FORMAT A: and FORMAT B:

➲ CHKDSK (any drive, with the current drive as the default)

➲ DISKCOPY A: and DISKCOPY B:

➲ BACKUP drive C and BACKUP drive D

➲ RESTORE (from A to C is the default)

➲ UNFORMAT (drive to be specified)

➲ UNDELETE (any path, but the current directory is the default)

➲ FC (filespecs to be provided)

➲ MIRROR (any drive, but the current drive is the default)

Figure 3.2.

Disk Utilities
Program Group.

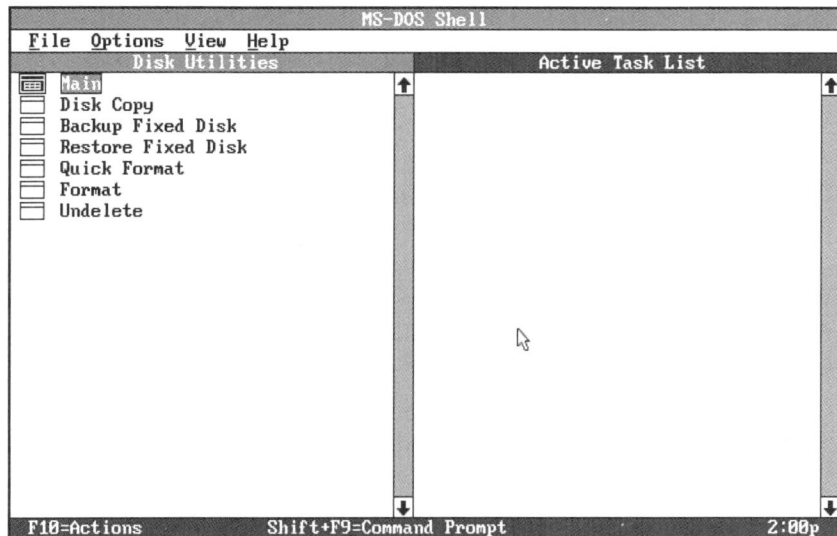

Defining New Program Groups

To define a new program group, place the cursor in the program list, open the group that will be the parent of the new group, and select **File New**. The first dialog box asks whether you want to define a program group or program item. When you select **Program Group**, the next dialog box that appears looks like Figure 3.3. You can enter up to 23 characters, including spaces, in the **Title** field, 255 in the **Help Text** field, and 20 in the **Password** field. Use **^m** (a caret followed by the letter m) to start a new line in the help text.

Figure 3.3.

Add Group Dialog Box.

```
┌─────────────────── Add Group ───────────────────┐
│                                                  │
│   Required                                       │
│                                                  │
│   Title . . . .      Davida's Group              │
│                                                  │
│   Optional                                       │
│                                                  │
│   Help Text . .      This group has been         │
│                                                  │
│   Password  . .      Captain Kirk                │
│                                                  │
│                                                  │
│      OK            Cancel           Help         │
│                                                  │
└──────────────────────────────────────────────────┘
```

Weak Password Protection

Don't expect a lot of protection from the password facility in the program list, either for program groups or for program items. When a password exists, DOS Shell requires the password to be entered in order to open or edit the group or item. But you can delete a group or item without knowing the password. Furthermore, as you'll see under *A Trip through DOSSHELL.INI* later in this chapter, anyone can find out passwords by viewing the DOSSHELL.INI file. So passwords prevent access only by people who don't know very much about DOS (and obviously haven't read this book).

Defining Program Items

Program items are easy to define and modify. Figure 3.4 shows the dialog box that opens when you indicate that you want to define a program item. The example in the figure defines a program item named Format A: that formats the diskette in drive A, then runs CHKDSK on the formatted diskette.

Figure 3.4.

Add Program
Dialog Box.

```
┌────────────────────── Add Program ──────────────────────┐
│                                                          │
│  Program Title . . . .  │Format A:                     │ │
│                                                          │
│  Commands  . . . . . .  │FORMAT A: ; CHKDSK A:_         │ │
│                                                          │
│  Startup Directory . .  │                              │ │
│                                                          │
│  Application Shortcut Key   │                          │ │
│                                                          │
│  [X] Pause after exit      Password . .  │            │ │
│                                                          │
│     ( OK )    ( Cancel )    ( Help )    ( Advanced... )   │
└──────────────────────────────────────────────────────────┘
```

Required Fields

You must enter a **Program Title** as you want it to appear in the program list (up to 23 characters, including spaces) and the **Commands** to be submitted to DOS when this item is opened, combining multiple commands with semicolons (remember the surrounding spaces). Replaceable parameters (%1 through %9) are permitted, along with any other parameters and switches that are appropriate for the command. Each individual command can have up to 127 characters, and the entire **Commands** field is limited to 255 characters.

Calling Batch Programs

Executing a batch file from a program item might require using the new CALL command. When you reference a batch file without CALL, DOS links to the batch file and never returns to the program item. There's no problem if the batch file is the only command in the **Commands** field or if it's the last in a set of combined commands. If TIMEOUT.BAT is a batch file, the following **Commands** field works perfectly:

```
DIR ; CHKDSK ; TIMEOUT
```

But if a batch file is followed by other commands, use CALL to force DOS
to return to the program item after the batch file terminates. In the following **Commands** field, the CHKDSK command would never be executed:

```
DIR ; TIMEOUT ; CHKDSK
```

To fix the problem, prefix TIMEOUT with CALL:

```
DIR ; CALL TIMEOUT ; CHKDSK
```

Optional Fields

Only the **Program Title** and **Commands** fields are required in the Add
Program dialog box. The remaining fields can be used if you want to take
advantage of special program item features.

Startup Directories

If you provide a **Startup Directory** (which can include a drive), DOS Shell
switches to that drive and directory before submitting the command. This
feature can save a few characters in the **Commands** field because you don't
have to include commands to change the drive and directory. But use it
only in cases where it's needed to get to the right directory. There's no
sense in changing directories unnecessarily; it's time-consuming and somewhat irritating. The program item defined in Figure 3.4 doesn't need a
startup directory because both programs are in the DOS directory, which is
in the search path, and no files from other directories are involved.

Application Shortcut Keys

You might want to define an **Application Shortcut Key** for programs with
task swapping potential—that is, programs that run continuously until you
intentionally exit them, such as editors, word processors, and database
managers, as opposed to programs that execute a specific function and
terminate themselves, such as FORMAT and CHKDSK. The shortcut key
acts as a hotkey to switch to a task after the program item has been started
up and appears on the active task list.

To define a hotkey, place the cursor in the **Application Shortcut Key** field and press any combination of Ctrl, Shift, and/or Alt plus a keyboard character. Any combination is acceptable except those listed in Table 3.1.

Table 3.1 Reserved Application Shortcut Keys

Ctrl+C and Shift+Ctrl+C	Emulate the Break key
Ctrl+H and Shift+Ctrl+H	Emulate the Backspace key
Ctrl+I and Shift+Ctrl+I	Emulate the Tab key
Ctrl+M and Shift+Ctrl+M	Emulate the Enter key
Ctrl+[and Shift+Ctrl+[	Emulate the Esc key

You may find situations where two or more items on the active task list have the same hotkey. Pressing the key combination switches to the next task in the list having that hotkey; you repeatedly press the hotkey until you reach the task you want.

Pause after Exit

Programs that terminate themselves frequently leave final messages on the screen that a user wants to read. FORMAT and CHKDSK both display disk statistics, for example, while DIR displays the requested directory entries. The **Pause after exit** option leaves program output on the screen, adding only the message "Press any key to return to MS-DOS Shell."

Without **Pause after exit**, DOS returns to the Shell immediately upon program termination, leaving no time to read final messages.

Pause after exit is checked by default. You'll probably want to uncheck it for any program that doesn't display a final message. It's a slight but frequent irritation to exit a program and then have to press another key to return to the Shell.

Advanced Options

The Advanced button opens a second dialog box, shown in Figure 3.5, where you define help text (up to 255 characters), memory requirements, and task switching limitations.

Figure 3.5.

Advanced Dialog
Box.

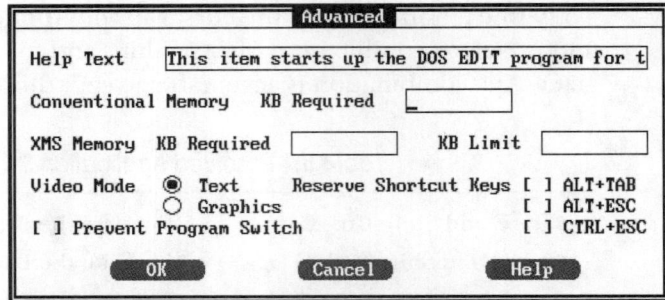

```
┌────────────────────────[Advanced]────────────────────────┐
│                                                           │
│ Help Text      │This item starts up the DOS EDIT program for t│ │
│                                                           │
│ Conventional Memory   KB Required   │_        │            │
│                                                           │
│ XMS Memory  KB Required  │        │    KB Limit │        │ │
│                                                           │
│ Video Mode  (●) Text      Reserve Shortcut Keys [ ] ALT+TAB│
│             ( ) Graphics                        [ ] ALT+ESC│
│ [ ] Prevent Program Switch                      [ ] CTRL+ESC│
│                                                           │
│      ( OK )           ( Cancel )           ( Help )        │
└───────────────────────────────────────────────────────────┘
```

Memory Requirements

The Advanced dialog box includes several items that specify memory requirements for the program item when task swapping is in effect. These
items are used only with task swapping.

Conventional Memory KB Required specifies the minimum amount of
memory that must be present for the program to be loaded; the default is
128K. Entering a figure here does not affect how much memory is allocated to the program when it's loaded; DOS always gives it all available
memory. But it does affect how much memory is saved on disk when you
switch to another task; that can be a key factor in how many tasks you can
start up under the task swapper as well as the amount of time it takes to
swap a task out or in. If you know that a program requires only 7K to run,
by all means enter a 7 under **Conventional Memory KB Required** so the
task swapper doesn't save the default 128K for this program.

When you start up DOS Shell, it requests all available extended memory
from HIMEM.SYS and does its own management of the extended memory
facility. The two extended memory fields, **XMS Memory KB Required** and
XMS Memory KB Limit, identify the minimum and maximum amounts of
extended memory that should be allocated to a program during task swapping. The defaults are 0 and 384K, respectively. When a task is swapped
out, its extended memory is held for it (unlike conventional memory,
which is swapped out to disk); no other task can access that area of extended memory. So the amount of extended memory that is set aside for

one task influences whether or not another task can be loaded. For this reason, do try to fill in these two XMS fields for all programs that require extended memory, if you can determine what their requirements are.

Video Mode affects how much memory is assigned to the video buffer. It should always be **Text** (even if the program uses graphics mode) unless you are using a CGA monitor and are having trouble switching to a program. The **Graphics** setting allocates more memory for the video buffer, which some CGA monitors need in some situations.

Task Switching Limitations

Some programs are not fully compatible with task swapping, and you can establish limitations in the **Advanced** dialog box. Check **Prevent Program Switch** to eliminate task swapping altogether for this program item. Once such an item is started, the user must exit it to return to the Shell screen or any other task. If you just need to reserve one or more task swapping hotkeys because the program uses them for other functions, all you have to do is check the pertinent keys under **Reserve Shortcut Keys**.

Replaceable Parameter Dialog Box

Whenever you include a replaceable parameter in the **Commands** field of the Add Program dialog box, DOS opens the dialog box shown in Figure 3.6. Here you define a dialog box to be displayed whenever the program item is opened so the user can enter a value for the replaceable parameter. The first three fields determine the text to be placed in the dialog box. The last field sets a default value for the replaceable parameter, if you wish. In addition to a fixed default value, such as the one shown in the figure, two special parameters are available: %F and %L. %F fills in as a default value the filename that is selected in the file list when the program item is opened. %L fills in the value that was used last time the item was executed. In any case, the user can overtype the default value when executing the program item.

Figure 3.6.

Defining a Program
Item Dialog Box.

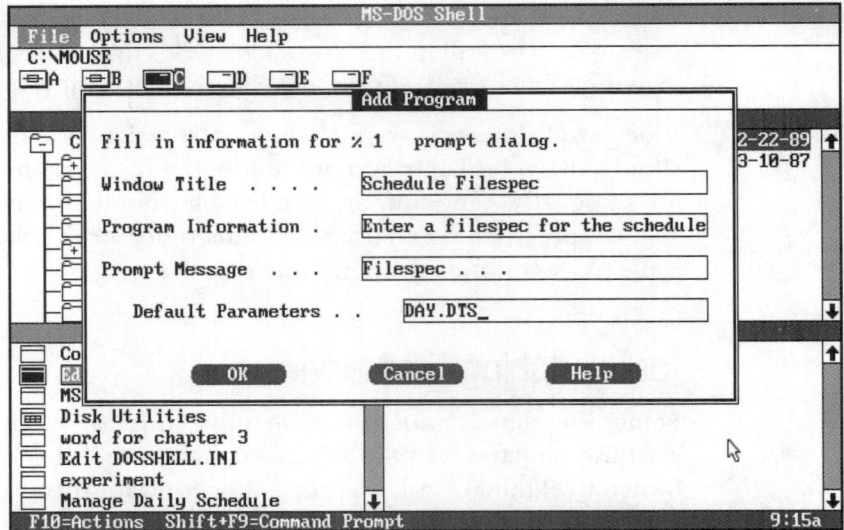

```
                                     MS-DOS Shell
  File  Options  View  Help
 C:\MOUSE
 ⊟A   ⊟B   ▭C   ⊟D   ⊟E   ⊟F
                              ┌──────── Add Program ────────┐
  ┌─ C                        │                             │          2-22-89  ↑
  ├─⊟                         │ Fill in information for % 1    prompt dialog.    3-10-87
  ├─⊟                         │                             │
  ├─⊟                         │ Window Title . . . .  │Schedule Filespec          │
  ├─⊟                         │                             │
  ├─⊟                         │ Program Information .  │Enter a filespec for the schedule│
  ├─⊟                         │                             │
  ├─⊟                         │ Prompt Message . . .  │Filespec . . .             │
  ├─⊟                         │                             │                          ↓
                              │   Default Parameters . .  │DAY.DTS_                 │
  ┌─ Co                       │                             │                          ↑
  │  Ed                       │    ┌──  OK  ──┐  ┌── Cancel ──┐  ┌── Help ──┐       │
  │  MS                       └─────────────────────────────────────────────────┘
  ▦  Disk Utilities
  ┌  word for chapter 3                                              ▷
  ┌  Edit DOSSHELL.INI
  ┌  experiment
  ┌  Manage Daily Schedule              ↓                                          ↓
 F10=Actions   Shift+F9=Command Prompt                                      9:15a
```

Modifying Program Group and Program Item Definitions

If you need to modify the definition for a program group or program item, highlight the object and choose the **File Properties** command. The same dialog boxes return so that you can edit them as needed.

Copying Program Items

When setting up a program list for several users, you can save some time by copying program items from one group to another with the **File Copy** command. When **File Copy** is chosen with a program list item selected, instructions on the message line tell you to open the desired destination group and press F2.

Transferring a Setup to Another Computer

The DOSSHELL.INI file contains all the setup information for the Shell screen, including program group and program item definitions. You can transfer a setup by copying DOSSHELL.INI from one computer to another.

If you want to use your computer to set up someone else's without losing your own setup, copy your setup as DOSSHELL.SAV (or whatever backup name you prefer). Then go ahead and change your setup as needed, copy the revised DOSSHELL.INI to a transfer diskette, and restore your former DOSSHELL.INI from DOSSHELL.SAV.

You might also find it handy to have multiple setups available. You could have setup files stored as SHELLA.INI, SHELLB.INI, and SHELLC.INI, for example. Rename whichever one you want to use now as DOSSHELL.INI before starting up the Shell.

A Trip through DOSSHELL.INI

Obviously, DOSSHELL.INI is the key to the Shell setup. The good news is: this very important setup file is designed to be edited by an ASCII editor such as DOS's EDIT. Figure 3.7 shows the beginning of the file (EGA/VGA version), which contains a significant warning: don't let your editor shorten the long lines or the file will no longer be valid. Here are a few more warnings for you:

⊃ Make a backup copy before viewing or modifying the file, just in case the editor damages it.

⊃ If you view or modify it with a word processor, be very careful that it gets saved in ASCII mode and does not get formatted in any way.

⊃ Don't modify any punctuation marks, especially brackets ([]) and braces ({}) unless you know exactly what you're doing. They're crucial to the structure of the file.

Savestate Section

The **savestate** section (see Figure 3.8) shows the status of various Shell parameters. You can see the direct relationship between parameters like **screenmode** and **displayhiddenfiles** and menu-controllable features such as the display mode (**Options Display**) and the file display options (**Display Hidden/System Files**).

Figure 3.7.

Beginning of DOSSHELL.INI.

```
 ile   dit   earch   ptions                                        elp
                          DOSSHELL.INI
EGA.INI/VGA.INI
***************** WARNING *********************
This file may contain lines with more than 256
characters. Some editors will truncate or split
these lines. If you are not sure whether your
editor can handle long lines, exit now without
saving the file.

Note: The editor which is invoked by the
            MS-DOS 5.0 EDIT command can be used
            to edit this file.
***************** NOTE ***********************
Everything up to the first left square bracket
character is considered a comment.
***************************************************
[savestate]
screenmode = graphics
resolution = low
startup = filemanager
filemanagermode = shared
sortkey = name
MS-DOS Editor  <F1=Help> Press ALT to activate menus        CN 00001:001
```

Figure 3.8.

DOS Shell Parameter Status.

```
 ile   dit   earch   ptions                                        elp
                          DOSSHELL.INI
[savestate]
screenmode = graphics
resolution = low
startup = filemanager
filemanagermode = shared
sortkey = name
pause = disabled
explicitselection = disabled
swapmouse = disabled
tasklist = enabled
switching = enabled
mouseinfo = 6.02,ignore
sortorder = ascending
displayhiddenfiles = enabled
replaceconfirm = enabled
deleteconfirm = enabled
mouseconfirm = enabled
crossdirselection = disabled
MS-DOS Editor  <F1=Help> Press ALT to activate menus        CN 00036:001
```

Programstarter Section: Program List Definitions

The **programstarter** section contains the definitions of the items on the program list. In Figure 3.9, you can see the definition of a program group titled Manage Daily Schedule, which has the Ctrl+D hotkey and executes this command:

```
SCHEDULE %1
```

```
 File  Edit  Search  Options                                    Help
                        ┌─────── DOSSHELL.INI ───────┐
    {
        help = This item is password protected. Do not attempt to use it.
        screenmode = text
        alttab = enabled
        altesc = enabled
        ctrlesc = enabled
        prevent = disabled
        shortcut = CTRL+D
        shortcutcode = 1056
        command = SCHEDULE %1
        title = Manage Daily Schedule
        password = BGXTASTGTJTBGORKE
        directory = C:\DTS
        pause = disabled
        dialog =
        {
            title = Schedule File
            info = Please identify the daily schedule file you want to work wi
            prompt = Filespec
            default = DAY.DTS
            parameter = %1
 MS-DOS Editor  <F1=Help> Press ALT to activate menus         CN 00207:001
```

Program Passwords in DOSSHELL.INI

This item's password was originally defined as "Barnum and Bailey." DOSSHELL.INI has slightly encrypted it by moving all lowercase letters up six letters in the alphabet and converting them to uppercase so that "a" becomes "G." (Uppercase letters are unchanged.) This is not enough encryption to fool anyone who really wants to access the password. Not only that, but the encrypted version will also work as the password to access the program item. You can see why the password protection offered by DOS Shell won't fool too many people.

Color Schemes

At the end of the **programstarter** section, each of the color schemes is defined (see Figure 3.10). You can edit this section to alter the predefined color schemes or add new ones. It doesn't take too much effort to figure out what each field represents on the screen and the correct format to define a new color scheme. It usually takes a bit of trial and error to put colors together that are effective under all circumstances.

The 16 available colors are white, red, brown, green, blue, cyan, magenta, black, and bright versions of each of these (brightwhite, brightred, etc.). Brightblack appears as gray on most screens, and brightbrown appears as yellow. White is grayish, while brightwhite is white.

Figure 3.10.

Screen Color
Definitions.

```
 File  Edit  Search  Options                                    Help
                              DOSSHELL.INI
color =
{
    selection =
    {
        title = Basic Blue
        foreground =
        {
            base = black
            highlight = brightwhite
            selection = brightwhite
            alert = brightred
            menubar = black
            menu = black
            disabled = white
            accelerator = cyan
            dialog = black
            button = black
            elevator = white
            titlebar = black
            scrollbar = brightwhite
            borders = black

MS-DOS Editor  <F1=Help> Press ALT to activate menus        CN 00224:001
```

File Associations

The final section of DOSSHELL.INI, which shows the file associations, comes in handy for discovering file associations that you weren't aware of. When you first install DOS, you can see the associations predefined by Microsoft (see Figure 3.11). Later on, you might want to review this section to see what associations are currently in effect.

Figure 3.11.

File Association
Definitions.

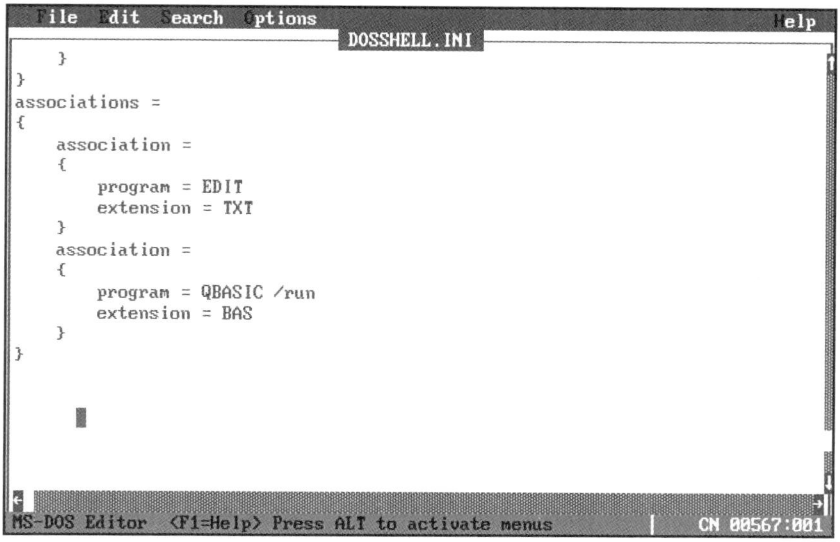

```
 File  Edit  Search  Options                                    Help
┌──────────────────────── DOSSHELL.INI ────────────────────────┐
      }
}
associations =
{
    association =
    {
        program = EDIT
        extension = TXT
    }
    association =
    {
        program = QBASIC /run
        extension = BAS
    }
}



        █


MS-DOS Editor  <F1=Help> Press ALT to activate menus        │   CN 00567:001
```

DOS AT YOUR COMMAND

ntroduction

The better you understand DOS commands, the more effective your PC work will be, whether you spend most of your time working at the command prompt or in the Shell. Better commands are more powerful commands, which in turn provide more powerful batch files as well as DOS Shell program items and file associations, putting the full power of DOS at your command.

Redirecting Input and Output

Most of the DOS utilities read input (if any) from the keyboard and send their output in the form of messages to the monitor. The TIME command is a good example:

```
                                               output to monitor
C:\>TIME
Current time is 12:32:07.88p
Enter new time: 4:13p
C:\>
                                       input from keyboard
```

Standard Input and Output

To be more precise, many DOS utilities request *standard I/O* services from DOS. When standard I/O is requested, DOS reads from or writes to a device that it calls CON (for *console*), which is usually defined as the keyboard and monitor. But you can redirect standard input and/or output from CON to files or to other devices using the symbols shown in Table 4.1.

Table 4.1 Redirection Symbols

< *source*	Redirects input to come from a specified file or device
> *destination*	Redirects output to a specified file or device; an existing file is overwritten
>> *destination*	Redirects output to a specified file or device; an existing file is appended
command1 ¦ *command2*	The output from *command1* becomes the input to *command2* (piping)

N O T E

The symbols shown in Table 4.1 are reserved by DOS and cannot be used in any names you create, such as filenames or directory names.

Not all I/O can be redirected. Redirection works with any programs that request standard I/O services from DOS, which include many of the DOS utilities and perhaps some of your applications. However, many applications use their own I/O techniques, not DOS's standard ones, when communicating with the keyboard and monitor; they are not affected by redirection.

Furthermore, not all DOS utility input and output can be redirected. For example, the TYPE and COPY commands don't use standard input, but since they are designed to read from a file or device, input redirection is not necessary. Similarly, the PRINT command's print output cannot be redirected to a file, because it does not use the standard I/O device. The only part of PRINT's output that can be redirected is the confirmation message that is normally displayed on the standard output device.

Standard Error Output

If a DOS utility encounters an error situation, such as a missing file, it sends the error message not to the standard output device but to a standard *error* output device, which DOS also displays on CON. Since redirection affects only standard output, not standard error output, error messages are not redirected.

The total output from a utility might include both types of output, as you can see here:

```
C:\>DIR BIMAX
 Volume in drive C is HARD DRIVE
 Volume Serial Number is 171D-78E4    } Standard output
 Directory of C:\

File not found                        } Error output
C:\>
```

If you redirected the above command, the screen would still show the error message:

```
C:\>DIR BIMAX > BIMAX.DIR
File not found
C:\>
```

Meanwhile the redirected file (BIMAX.DIR) would contain only the standard messages:

```
Volume in drive C is HARD DRIVE
Volume Serial Number is 171D-78E4
Directory of C:\
```

You might not always find this feature desirable, but knowing that it exists lets you take occasional advantage of it. Chapter 5 shows you how to turn a command in the above format into a macro that tells you when a file is not present without displaying all the usual DIR messages.

NOTE

You can redirect *all* keyboard input and monitor output by redefining CON using the CTTY command, a technique that's explained in Chapter 16.

Just to keep you on your toes, some programs use standard output to issue error messages (CHKDSK is one), and some programs use standard error output to issue standard messages (MORE is one). These aren't just flaky decisions by the program developers but are based on whether the messages in question are appropriately redirected when standard output is redirected. For example, if you redirect CHKDSK's output, the assumption is that you want to obtain a hardcopy or a file copy for documentation purposes and that you want error messages included in the documentation.

Redirecting Output to a File

Perhaps the most common use of redirection is to store the standard output of a command in a file. For example, you could store the complete directory listing of drive C: in a file called SAVECDIR with this command:

```
DIR C:\ /S > SAVECDIR
```

The C:\ parameter requests the root directory and the /S parameter causes all its descendents to be listed also. SAVECDIR will be a plain-vanilla ASCII file that can be viewed by TYPE, edited by EDIT, printed by PRINT, and so forth.

Overwriting vs. Appending

Both the > and >> symbols create a new file if the attached filespec is unique. The difference between these two symbols lies in what happens when the filespec identifies an existing file. With >, the existing file is replaced by the new output (without warning!), while >> causes the new output to be appended to the end of the existing file.

WARNING

The > redirection symbol will replace an existing file without warning. For safety's sake, use >> unless you're positive that you want an existing file replaced. Chapter 7 shows how you can test for the existence of a file and issue commands accordingly.

Suppose you want to write a batch job to create a file named SAVEDIRS containing the complete directories of drives C: through E:. Any previous version of SAVEDIRS should be replaced by the new file. The batch file could look like this:

```
DIR C:\ /S > SAVEDIRS
DIR D:\ /S >> SAVEDIRS
DIR E:\ /S >> SAVEDIRS
```

The first DIR command uses > to overwrite any previous SAVEDIRS. But the subsequent commands must use >> to append their outputs to the newly created file.

Redirecting I/O to Devices

You can also redirect standard I/O to devices using the names shown in Table 4.2. For example, the following command prints the complete directory of drive C:

```
DIR C:\ /S > PRN
```

Table 4.2 DOS Device Names

LPT1 through LPT3	Line (parallel) printers 1 through 3
PRN	The same as LPT1
COM1 through COM4	Communications (serial) ports 1 through 4
AUX	The same as COM1
CON	The user's console: the keyboard for input and the monitor for output (unless redirected via the CTTY command)
NUL	Nowhere (the data is simply dropped)

N O T E

The device names shown in Table 4.2 are reserved by DOS and cannot be used as names that you create.

LPT1 or PRN identifies the standard parallel printer, where DOS automatically directs all print output unless otherwise instructed. This is the default printer for the PRINT command and the Print Screen key.

N O T E

Chapter 18 explains how to redirect output from a parallel printer to another device using the MODE command.

Some Printer Incompatibilities

PostScript printers require special drivers, and DOS will not be able to print on them in their native modes. But most of these printers can be set to emulate a standard parallel printer (such as the Epson MX80) that DOS can handle, even if it can't take advantage of the printer's bells and whistles. Check your printer's documentation to find out how to force it to emulate a standard parallel printer.

NUL: The Road to Nowhere

You might find the NUL device occasionally useful to suppress the standard output from a command, because output directed to NUL simply disappears. For example, the following command would display a message only if the file was not found:

```
DIR CASEY.TXT > NUL
```

Such techniques can sometimes be useful in a DOSKEY macro or batch file to suppress messages that an inexperienced person is not prepared to deal with.

Redirecting Input

The < symbol tells DOS to redirect standard input to the specified file or device. For example, to read standard input from COM1 instead of the keyboard, you could enter this command:

```
SORT < COM1
```

One purpose of redirecting standard input is to automate commands so that you don't have to be at the keyboard while a command is executing. For example, if the file named C:\DOS\CR contains one blank line created by pressing the Enter key, the TIME command could be automated this way:

```
TIME < C:\DOS\CR
```

When DOS wants standard input, it reads from the CR file instead of the keyboard. The single carriage return causes it to retain the current time, terminate TIME, and display the command prompt. You could use the CR file to automate DATE and PRINT in the same way. When used with PRINT, it causes the print function to be initialized to the default print device (PRN).

Automating a simple command such as TIME or DATE might seem on the surface like more bother than it's worth. But it helps to make batch files run with less user interaction. (It also improves macros created by the DOSKEY feature, which is explained in Chapter 5.) And if you're careful, you can automate more complex commands that require a series of keyboard inputs. For example, a standard FORMAT interaction requires three inputs (if you don't include the /V switch in the command), which are underlined below:

```
C:\>FORMAT A:
Insert new diskette for drive A:
and press ENTER when ready...[Enter]

Checking existing disk format.
Saving UNFORMAT information.
Verifying 360K
Format complete.

Volume label (11 characters, ENTER for none)? [Enter]

    362496 bytes total disk space
    362496 bytes available on disk

      1024 bytes in each allocation unit.
       354 allocation units available on disk.

Volume Serial Number is 1035-0DE3

Format another (Y/N)?N


C:\>
```

You can automate the entire process by creating an input file containing two carriage returns and an N. To execute the automated command, enter a command like this:

```
FORMAT A: < C:\DOS\FMTIN
```

(where FMTIN contains the responses for the FORMAT command).

Each time DOS wants input from the keyboard, it reads the next line in the file.

WARNING

Automating commands such as FORMAT bypasses normal safety checks. Use automation techniques with caution and don't put them in the hands of inexperienced people. Also, if an error situation arises requiring an unusual response, the program will probably hang up waiting for valid input from the disk file. Ctrl+Break will kill the hung-up program and restore the command prompt.

TIP

In a batch file, it's often important to specify a complete path name when redirecting input so the command will work no matter what drive or directory is current.

Piping

Piping passes data from one command to the next using a temporary file called a *pipe*. The standard output from the first command becomes the standard input to the second. Piping is most often used with the DOS filters, and you'll see many piping examples when the filters are explained in the next section. But here's one quick trick you can do with piping. You have already seen how to automate a TIME or DATE command by redirecting the standard input to a file containing a carriage return. You can also pipe the carriage return to the TIME or DATE command. Here's one way to do it using the CR file that contains a single carriage return:

```
TYPE C:\DOS\CR ¦ TIME
```

The TYPE command sends the contents of the CR file to the pipe, and the TIME command reads it from the pipe. Thus, the carriage return contained in CR is passed to the TIME command.

NOTE

As with other forms of redirection, piping affects standard I/O only.

Using ECHO to Automate Commands

A more convenient way to pipe a value to a command uses ECHO instead
of TYPE. ECHO provides the value on the spot, so you don't need to have a
response file made up in advance. For example, to pipe a Y to a DEL *.*
command (to respond to "Are you sure (Y/N)?"), you could enter this
command:

```
ECHO Y ¦ DEL *.*
```

ECHO followed by a period with no space generates a carriage return that
can be used to automate commands such as TIME and DATE. Here's another way to automate the TIME command:

```
ECHO. ¦ TIME
```

This is the simplest way to automate commands that require single responses. It won't work with multiple response commands such as FORMAT,
however, since ECHO can provide only one value.

The Temporary Pipe Files

To pipe, DOS must create two temporary files, generating filenames such
as ABOABOBH and ABOABOBN. The temporary files are automatically
deleted after the command is completed or interrupted with Ctrl+Break,
but if you restart the computer or power it down during the command, the
temporary files will be abandoned on the disk. You can safely delete them.

> **N O T E**
>
> DOS uses the TEMP variable (explained in Chapter 2) to determine
> where to place the temporary pipe files. A piping command will fail if
> the TEMP disk doesn't have enough room or is write-protected.

The DOS Filters

DOS designates three of its utilities as *filters*—programs that read data from
the standard input device, manipulate the data in some way, and write it to
the standard output device. The three DOS filters are MORE, which breaks

standard output into display pages; SORT, which puts lines in order; and FIND, which locates lines containing text strings.

What's My Line?

The three filters operate on *lines* of data, as delimited by carriage returns. In an ASCII file, such as a batch file or CONFIG.SYS, the lines are obvious. But many word processors store a carriage return in a file only when you press the Enter key to end a paragraph. Even though the word processor breaks paragraphs into several lines on the monitor and in print, DOS sees each paragraph as only one line. An exception to this rule is when the word processor saves a file in ASCII format instead of its native format. Then DOS might insert carriage returns in each paragraph to turn the displayed line breaks into real ones. So when applying any of the DOS filters to files created by word processors the rule of thumb is: Be sure you know in what format the file is stored.

MORE in a Minute

The MORE command in its simplest form contains just the word MORE, which causes DOS to read input from the keyboard and display it on the monitor, pausing at the end of each page until you press a key to continue. Since that is rarely a useful function, MORE is almost always used with redirection or piping. Before EDIT was included in DOS, MORE was often used to display files page by page, but since EDIT lets you scroll around in files, it's the better choice for examining files.

If for some reason you want to view a file with MORE instead of EDIT, redirect the input to the file with a command in this format:

```
MORE < filespec
```

N O T E

When working with a file containing lines longer than the screen width, MORE formats the lines so that all data can be seen.

You'll find MORE most useful to page through command output via piping. The following command lists all the directories and files on the current drive, one page at a time:

```
TREE \ /F ¦ MORE
```

N O T E

It's hard to imagine why you would want to do so, but you can redirect MORE output to a file or device or pipe it to another command. The message — MORE — is not redirected; it still appears on the monitor to let you know when it's time to press a key to issue the next page.

It's Not My SORT

SORT's major reason for existence used to be to sort the output of the DIR command. But DIR's new /O options do a much better job of sorting directory information. SORT can still be useful on simple lists, such as an index with only one level of entries, but for any kind of complex job, you'll need a more sophisticated sort program.

Figure 4.1 shows the format of the SORT command. If you just enter the word SORT with no parameters or redirection, the utility reads from the standard input device, sorts the lines, and displays them on the standard output device. In case you ever find a need to do this, the sidebar explains how to enter data from the keyboard.

Figure 4.1.

SORT Command Reference.

SORT

Reads standard input, sorts it, and writes sorted standard output.

Format:

SORT [*switches*]

Switches:

/R   Reverses the order of the sort (from high to low).

/+n   Starts sorting in column *n*; default is column 1.

ENTERING FILES FROM CON

Most DOS utilities that read input from CON look for an individual key press, such as Y or N, or for a single line terminated by the Enter key. But the three DOS filters actually look for a complete *file* to be entered from CON if you don't redirect the input to a stored file. In addition, you can use CON as the source for a COPY command, which also requires a file. A file is one or more lines terminated by an end-of-file marker (**hex 1A**, which is depicted on the screen as ^Z).

Before EDIT, most experienced DOS users knew how to enter a file via CON, as that was a quick-and-dirty way to create a short ASCII file such as a simple batch file. It was also a character-building experience, somewhat akin to boot camp or freshman hazing, for you could work on only one line at a time and could not go back to modify or correct lines that were already entered without restarting the entire file from the top.

Now that EDIT is available, you never have to enter files via CON, but if you haven't installed EDIT or prefer doing it the hard way, here are the instructions:

1. After you enter the MORE, SORT, FIND, or COPY command, DOS will put the cursor at the beginning of the next line and wait for you to start inputting data.

2. Type each line carefully. Inspect and correct it before pressing Enter. Once you press Enter, there's no going back. (MORE and FIND will process the line immediately, then wait for the next line. The result is somewhat strange and probably not what you wanted or expected.)

3. When the last line has been entered, press F6 or type Ctrl+Z and press Enter to record the end-of-file mark. (FIND and SORT re-quire the end-of-file mark to be appear at the beginning of a new line.) DOS will then process the file.

Redirecting SORT I/O

Most of the time, you'll redirect the input to a file or receive the input from a previous command via piping. Output is frequently redirected to a file or piped to another command. For example, to sort the file called INDEX1 and display the output in pages, you could enter this command:

```
SORT < INDEX1 ¦ MORE
```

N O T E

The DOS 5 documentation indicates that you can specify an input filename without using redirection, but that's not true. You must use the < symbol to read SORT data from an input file.

To save the same output in a file called INDEX2 instead of displaying it on screen, you could enter this command:

```
SORT < INDEX1 > INDEX2
```

SORT Collating Sequence

SORT's collating sequence is determined by the current code page (code pages are explained in Chapter 17). Table 4.3 shows the collating sequence for the keys found on a standard 101-key keyboard using the English code page. (Read down the first column, then down the second column, and so on.) SORT ignores the difference between uppercase and lowercase letters.

Table 4.3 SORT Collating Sequence (Standard English Keys)

(space)	*	4	>	h	r	\
!	+	5	?	i	s	]
"	,	6	@	j	t	^
#	-	7	a	k	u	_
$	.	8	b	l	v	`
%	/	9	c	m	w	{
&	0	:	d	n	x	|
`	1	;	e	o	y	}
(	2	<	f	p	z	~
)	3	=	g	q	[	

SORT Limitations

Unfortunately, SORT is severely limited in function:

➲ It does alphanumeric sorts only, which produces erroneous results when sorting numeric values.

➲ It locates the beginning of the data to be sorted strictly by position. It cannot identify fields delimited by commas or tabs, the format used by many database and mail-merge files.

➲ Every line in the file is considered a separate record. There is no way to identify multiline records such as a name-and-address file might contain.

➲ It uses all the data from the beginning column through the end of the line as the sort key. You cannot limit the length of the sort key, and you cannot use primary and secondary sort keys.

Why You Can't Do a Two-Key Sort

This last point bears some extra discussion, because you might think you can accomplish a two-key sort by sorting first by the secondary key, then by the primary key. But a simple example shows why such a technique would work only by accident. Suppose you have some name-and-address records that you want to sort by name, and for those records with identical names, by city. A sample set of records might look like this after sorting by city:

```
JONES      MARY       45 PINE ST          GRAND RAPIDS, MI
ADAMS      PETER      2314 FIR ST         LAS VEGAS, NV
JONES      MARY       316 LOCUST ST       PITTSBURGH, PA
ADAMS      PETER      16 FOREST RD        SILVER SPRING, MD
ADAMS      PETER      5064 ELM ST         TULSA, OK
```

Now, if you *could* sort by the name in columns 1 through 20 only, the result would be as desired. Whenever identical names were encountered, the records would retain their city order:

```
ADAMS      PETER      2314 FIR ST         LAS VEGAS, NV
ADAMS      PETER      16 FOREST RD        SILVER SPRING, MD
ADAMS      PETER      5064 ELM ST         TULSA, OK
JONES      MARY       45 PINE ST          GRAND RAPIDS, MI
JONES      MARY       316 LOCUST ST       PITTSBURGH, PA
```

But that's not what happens in fact because SORT won't stop at column 20. It goes right on into column 21, 22, and so on to resolve identical records. The end result sorts the records by name, and for identical names, by *street address*, because that's the data that starts in column 21:

```
ADAMS       PETER       16 FOREST RD        SILVER SPRING, MD
ADAMS       PETER       2314 FIR ST         LAS VEGAS, NV
ADAMS       PETER       5064 ELM ST         TULSA, OK
JONES       MARY        316 LOCUST ST       PITTSBURGH, PA
JONES       MARY        45 PINE ST          GRAND RAPIDS, MI
```

There is no way to use SORT to order these records by name first and city second.

Using Other Sort Programs

As we said at the outset, SORT will do for small, simple jobs, but for anything complex, you'll need another sort program. You might already have a sort utility that will better meet your needs. All the major word processors include sort facilities, with WordPerfect's being especially full of features. Most word-processor sorters can be used on any file that is in the word processor's native format or in ASCII format. All database managers are capable of sorting their own databases, while spreadsheet programs can sort their own worksheets. However, the database and spreadsheet sorters probably can't be used on independent (that is, "not invented here") files.

What a FIND

The FIND command, shown in Figure 4.2, can help you locate individual lines from a file or from command output. When combined with the DIR command, it can even help you locate lost files that don't match a global filename.

Figure 4.2.

FIND Command
Reference.

<u>**FIND**</u>

Searches for a particular text string. Default output is a display of lines containing the string on the standard output device.

Format:

FIND *"string"* [*filespec...*] [*switches*]

Parameters and Switches:

"string"	Specifies the text to be located, which must be enclosed in quotes. (Use two quotes for quotes within the string, as in "An ""E"" for effort".)
filespec...	Identifies one or more files to be searched. If omitted, the standard input device is used. (Global filespecs are not permitted, but multiple filespecs are.)
/V	Displays lines that don't contain the string instead of the ones that do.
/C	Displays only a count of lines containing the string instead of the lines themselves.
/N	Displays line numbers with the displayed lines.
/I	Ignores case; if omitted, "a" is considered a different character from "A".

Locating Lines

Suppose you can't remember the name of the file containing a letter returning a defective compact disc. The current directory has three files that might be right: DISCLET, CDRETURN, and CDCOMP. You could find out which one includes the expression "compact disc" and the context of the expression with a command like this:

```
C:\>FIND "compact disc" /I DISCLET CDRET CDCOMP
---------- C:\DISCLET
---------- C:\CDRET
I have just received the enclosed compact disc, opened it,
and listened to it only once. Unfortunately, it skips in
several places. I am returning it to take advantage of your
"Full Replacement" guarantee. Over the last few years, I
have purchased more than 100 compact discs from your ser-
vice and this is the first problem I have ever encountered.
Keep up the good work!
---------- C:\CDCOMP
It will be some time before I can afford to add a CD ROM
drive. At the present, I have two high-density diskette
drives (one of each) and a 40M hard disk. By the time I can
afford a compact disc-style drive, maybe they'll be able to
write as well as read. Wouldn't that be great!
```

Although it looks like FIND displayed lines that don't contain "compact disc," remember that in text documents such as these, each paragraph is one line, so each paragraph that contains "compact disc" is displayed in its entirety. FIND wrapped the long paragraphs into shorter lines on the screen. You can see in this example that DISCLET does not mention "compact disc." The other two files do mention it, and it's clear which one is the desired letter. When doing a search like this, it's a good idea to include the /I switch (ignore case) so you'll match references to "Compact disc" and "Compact Disc" as well as "compact disc."

Searching All Files for a Text String

Unfortunately, FIND does not let you use a global filespec, so it's difficult to search all the files in a directory for a particular text string. It's even difficult to search all DOC or TXT (or whatever) files. You probably can't list all the filespecs in one command because you'll exceed the 127-character command limit. But take heart. Chapter 7 shows you how to accomplish it by combining FIND with the FOR command.

Locating Lines in Command Output

One common use of FIND is to select particular lines from command output. For example, suppose you want to display the current time or date without seeing the rest of the output from an automated TIME or DATE command. You could do it like this:

```
C:\>ECHO. ¦ TIME ¦ FIND "Current"
Current time is  7:31:30.18a
C:\>


C:\>ECHO. ¦ DATE ¦ FIND "Current"
Current date is Tue 10-01-1991
C:\>
```

There are many other applications of this particular technique. To see how much space is left on a disk:

```
C:\>DIR ¦ FIND "free"
                16189440 bytes free

C:\>
```

To see disk capacity:

```
C:\>CHKDSK | FIND "disk space"
  21387264 bytes total disk space
C:\>
```

To see how the TEMP variable is currently set:

```
C:\>SET | FIND "TEMP"
TEMP=C:\DOS
C:\>
```

Locating Files in a Directory Listing

The DIR command will display files that match a global filename or that have certain attributes. But how can you find all files created on April 1, or all files containing "RA" anywhere in their names (not just the first two letters)? Piping DIR output to FIND can help you satisfy these requirements. The following command lists all the files in the current directory that contain "RA" anywhere in their filenames:

```
C:\>DIR | FIND "RA"
COLDNEWS XRA       9103 08-30-91  11:52a
PIRATES  PCX      39625 08-30-91  11:52a
PRACTICE HSG      36478 08-30-91   3:15p
C:\>
```

> **TIP**
>
> Since FIND is normally case-sensitive, it's important to use all capitals inside the quotes when searching DIR output unless you use /L (for lowercase) with DIR or /I (to ignore case) with FIND.

Expanding this command to cover an entire branch or drive creates problems because of the way that DIR usually lists its output, with the directory name on a separate line from the filename. FIND would list only the file entries and you would have no idea what directories they belong to. But the /B switch causes DIR to list just filespecs. When /S is used with /B, the complete path is included with each filespec. Using /B and /S, you can find all the files in a complete branch whose names contain a particular text string:

```
C:\>DIR \ /S /B ¦ FIND "RA"
C:\VENTURA
C:\DOS\RAMDRIVE.SYS
C:\DOS\GRAFTABL.COM
C:\DOS\GRAPHICS.COM
C:\DOS\GRAPHICS.PRO
C:\HSG\GRAB.EXE
C:\>
```

You can't see the size, time, and date information, but at least you can see where to find each file. In the next chapter, you'll see how to turn this complex command, along with many of the other commands discussed in this chapter, into DOSKEY macros that can be executed by entering just a simple command at the command prompt.

CHAPTER 5

AT LONG LAST...DOSKEY

Introduction

DOS 5's new DOSKEY facility provides several major functions that DOS users have long wanted: the ability to combine several commands in one, edit the command line, recall former commands, and create command macros.

Getting DOSKEY Started

To take advantage of the DOSKEY functions, you must load the DOSKEY TSR using the command shown in Figure 5.1.

Figure 5.1.

DOSKEY Command Reference.

DOSKEY

Loads and controls DOSKEY; defines and displays DOSKEY macros.

Format: DOSKEY [*switches*] [*macroname=text*]

Parameters and Switches:

/HISTORY or /H	Displays all commands in the DOSKEY command history.
/MACROS or /M	Displays all current DOSKEY macros.
/REINSTALL	Installs another copy of DOSKEY (presumably with a different buffer size).
/BUFSIZE=*size*	Specifies the size of the buffer that stores the command history and macros; minimum is 256 bytes; default is 512 bytes.
/INSERT	Makes insert mode the default command editing mode; mutually exclusive with /OVERSTRIKE.
/OVERSTRIKE	Makes overstrike mode the default command editing mode (default); mutually exclusive with /INSERT.
macroname=text	Defines a macro.

When you enter DOSKEY with no parameters, the TSR is loaded with a 512-byte buffer—enough to hold about 50 commands and/or macros (of about 10 characters each). DOSKEY starts recording the command history as soon as it is loaded.

TIP   If your system is set up with EMM386.EXE so that you can load programs into upper memory blocks (explained in Chapter 11), use LOADHIGH to keep DOSKEY and its buffer out of conventional memory.

DOSKEY's Buffer

If no macros are defined, the command history will fill the buffer; then each new command overlays the oldest command(s) in the buffer. Each defined macro takes up permanent residence in the buffer, leaving less room for the command history. But DOSKEY limits the number of macros you can define in order to preserve about half the buffer for the command history.

> **N O T E**
>
> Macros are always placed at the beginning of the buffer, overlaying any commands in that position. Each time you define a new macro, you might lose part or all of your command history.

You can request a different buffer size with /BUFSIZE when you load DOSKEY. There's no way to change the buffer size after it's loaded; you must reinstall DOSKEY with a command similar to this (which changes the buffer size to 1K):

```
DOSKEY /REINSTALL /BUFSIZE=1024
```

The problem with this method is that it installs a new copy of DOSKEY, leaving the old DOSKEY (taking up about 3.5K plus the buffer size) in memory. The only other way to change the buffer size is to reboot to get rid of DOSKEY, then install it again with a larger buffer.

But How Can You Uninstall DOSKEY?

DOSKEY takes up memory space, of course, and if you can't load it into upper memory blocks, you might need to get rid of it to make room for a memory-hog. But have you noticed that you can't uninstall DOSKEY? The only way to get rid of it is to restart the computer, and if you've included the DOSKEY command in AUTOEXEC.BAT, you'll have to nullify it (insert REM at the beginning of the line) before restarting.

A History Lesson (DOSKEY Style)

Table 5.1 shows the keys used to recall commands from DOSKEY's command history. Use Up arrow, Down arrow, Page Up, and Page Down to search through the history list. To go directly to a command, type the first few characters at the prompt and press F8. Keep pressing F8 until you recall the command you want.

Table 5.1 Command History Keys

Up Arrow	Recalls the previous command in the list
Down Arrow	Recalls the next command in the list
Page Up	Recalls the oldest command in the list
Page Down	Recalls the newest command in the list
F7	Displays a numbered list of all the commands in the list
Alt+F7	Deletes all the commands in the list
F8	Recalls the next command in the list that starts with the characters on the command line
F9	Prompts for a command number, then recalls that command

N O T E

DOS's awkward old template editing keys, F1 through F5, still work when DOSKEY is installed, but on the most recently *recalled* command rather than the most recently entered one. Since they sometimes produce no effect at all, it's better to use the command history keys. In particular, if you're used to pressing F3 to recall the last command, learn to press Up arrow instead.

To see a numbered list of the entire command history, press F7. A long list is paged automatically. If you have just recalled but not yet entered a command, a pointer (>) indicates its position in the list. The Up and Down arrow keys go up and down from this point. The pointer is reset to the end of the list every time you enter a command. You can recall a command by number by pressing F9 and entering the number.

Another way to see the entire list (without numbers), is to enter this command:

```
DOSKEY /H
```

The output from this command is not automatically paged, so pipe it to MORE or press Pause to control it. This command comes in handy when you want to redirect the list to the printer or a file.

Here's a handy way to create a batch file. Suppose you've just executed five commands that you want to make into a batch called LISTEM.BAT. Enter the following command at the command prompt:

```
DOSKEY /H > LISTEM.BAT
```

You can edit LISTEM.BAT to remove unwanted commands from the list, insert comments and @ECHO OFF, and so on.

Clearing the command list with Alt+F7 is useful in two situations:

➲ It keeps other people from taking a peek at your work while you're away from your computer.

➲ It creates a blank slate in preparation for entering a series of commands that you want to save later as a batch file.

Command Line Editing: Now It's Easy

DOS users have struggled to edit the command line for years, using the F1 through F5 keys to recall characters from a hidden template. Now DOSKEY has changed all that, letting you edit the command line in a very natural style. You can see the command you're working on, move the cursor around in it without erasing characters, and insert and delete characters as needed. Table 5.2 shows the keys that edit the current command line. (It doesn't matter whether the line contains a new command or one that is recalled from the command history.) You can even move the cursor back to the first line of a two-line command, which you can't do without DOSKEY.

Table 5.2 DOSKEY Command Line Editing Keys

Left or Right arrow	Moves the cursor one character in the indicated direction
Ctrl+Left	Moves the cursor one word to the left
Ctrl+Right	Moves the cursor one word to the right
Home or End	Moves the cursor to the beginning or end of the command line
Esc	Clears the command line
Insert	Toggles insert mode on and off

continues

Table 5.2 Continued

Backspace	Deletes the character to the left of the cursor
Delete	Deletes the character at the cursor
Ctrl+Home	Deletes from the cursor to the beginning of the line
Ctrl+End	Deletes from the cursor to the end of the line

Use Left arrow, Right arrow, Ctrl+Left, Ctrl+Right, Home, and End to move the cursor around in the command line. Then delete, overtype, and insert characters as needed to correct or modify the command.

Insert vs. Overstrike Mode

DOSKEY lets you work in insert or overstrike mode, just as your word processor does. In insert mode, any characters you type are inserted into the command at the cursor position. In overstrike mode, new characters replace former ones. Press the Insert key to toggle back and forth between insert and overstrike mode.

One mode is the default, which takes over every time you start a new command line. The cursor becomes a flashing underline when the default mode is in effect. Whenever you change to the nondefault mode by pressing Insert, the cursor changes to a flashing rectangle.

Unless you have indicated otherwise, overstrike mode is the default. You can control which is the default mode by entering a DOSKEY command with the /INSERT or /OVERSTRIKE switch. You can include the switch on the command that loads DOSKEY, and you can change the default at any time by entering a command like this:

```
DOSKEY /OVERSTRIKE
```

or:

```
DOSKEY /INSERT
```

You don't have to reinstall DOSKEY to change the default insert/overstrike mode.

Two (or More) Commands for the Price of One

Another handy DOSKEY facility lets you combine two or more commands on one line by pressing Ctrl+T (which displays as ¶ on the monitor) to separate them. To display the directories of drives A and B, you could enter this command:

```
DIR A: ¶ DIR B:
```

Command combinations often make more useful entries in DOSKEY's command history. They also help to make more useful macros, which are explained next.

There is no implied relationship between the several commands combined with Ctrl+T. Data is not piped from one to the other, and if one fails, the next is executed anyway. To interrupt the entire set of commands, you have to press Ctrl+Break once for each remaining command on the line.

Macros

A macro is a command that you have created yourself, usually substituting a simple word or two for a much more complex command. For example, you might define a macro so that the word SPACE causes the following command to be executed:

```
DIR A: ¦ FIND "free" ¶ DIR B: ¦ FIND "free" ¶ DIR C: ¦
FIND "free"
```

Macros vs. Batch Files

A macro is somewhat like a batch file in that it executes a series of commands. But there are many points of difference. In some ways, macros are better than batch programs:

➲ Macros are stored in memory, so they are accessed faster and are available to all directories.

➲ You can replace the standard DOS commands, even internal ones, with macros.

But there are also several disadvantages to macros when compared to batch files:

➲ Macros are lost when you restart the computer, power it down, or press Alt+F10.

➲ A macro definition can include only one command line (although combined commands are permitted).

➲ ECHO OFF and the @ symbol do not suppress command echoing.

➲ You can't access environment variables from macros.

➲ You can't execute a macro from a batch file or from another macro.

➲ You can't branch in a macro as you can in a batch file.

➲ Macros are limited to 127 characters, whereas batch files can be any length.

Use macros because they're fast and don't take up any disk space. They're particularly good for temporary functions, but you could also save a set of permanent macro definitions in a batch file and make them available every time you boot.

Macro Definition

To define a macro, enter a command in the following format:

```
DOSKEY macroname=text
```

For example, to define a macro called FA that formats the diskette in drive A, you would enter this command:

```
DOSKEY FA=FORMAT A:
```

Special Characters

Table 5.3 lists some special characters you can use when defining DOSKEY macros. The first five ($G through $T) tell DOSKEY that redirection, piping, or combined commands are part of the macro. They're necessary to prevent DOS from identifying and processing redirection symbols when a DOSKEY command that creates a macro is entered. Suppose you enter this command:

```
DOSKEY SAVEDIR=DIR C:\ /S > C.DIR
```

DOS would recognize the > symbol and process it immediately, attempting to redirect the output of DOSKEY SAVEDIR=DIR C:\ /S to C.DIR. It would create the C.DIR file but, since the DOSKEY command has no standard output, the file would have a 0 size. But if you use the symbol $G instead of > in the above command, DOS bypasses the redirection symbol ($G), which is stored as part of the SAVEDIR macro and takes effect only when the macro is executed.

Table 5.3 DOSKEY Macro Special Characters

$G	Redirects output (equivalent to > in a regular command); the G stands for "Greater than"
GG	Equivalent to >> in a regular command
$L	Redirects input (equivalent to < in a regular command); the L stands for "Less than"
$B	Pipes output (equivalent to | in a regular command); the B stands for "Bar"
$T	Separates commands on the command line (equivalent to Ctrl+T in a regular command)
$1 thru $9	Replaced by the first through ninth command-line parameters (equivalent to %1 through %9 in a batch file)
$*	Replaced by all command-line parameters
$$	Displays a dollar sign

Sample Macro Definitions

You could convert some of the functions from Chapter 4 into DOSKEY macros.

To display the current date and time:

```
DOSKEY WHEN=ECHO. $B DATE $B FIND "Current" $T ECHO. $B
TIME $B FIND "Current"
```

To automatically format drive A:

```
DOSKEY AUTOFORM=FORMAT A: $L C:\DOS\FMTIN
```

To print the directory of the current drive:

    DOSKEY PDIR=DIR \ /S $G PRN

To delete all the files in the current directory:

    DOSKEY ADEL=ECHO Y $B DEL *.*

To see the entire tree of the current drive, one page at a time:

    DOSKEY PTREE=TREE \ /F $B MORE

To see all the files on the current drive that contain "RA" in the filename:

    DOSKEY RAFIND=DIR \ /S /B $B FIND "RA"

To see how much space is left on the disk:

    DOSKEY FREE=DIR $B FIND "free"

To see disk capacity:

    DOSKEY CAP=CHKDSK $B FIND "free space"

Replaceable Parameters

Many of the above macros would be more useful if they were more generalized. For example, rather than creating a macro to find all files with RA in their names, why not let a user enter the search string when the macro is executed? You can do that by using replaceable parameters, $1 through $9 and $*.

When a macro is executed, $1 through $9 are replaced by the first through ninth parameters from the executing command. For example, suppose a macro is defined to search for filenames containing the string specified by $1 in the directory specified by $2:

    DOSKEY FLOCATE=DIR $2\ /S /B $B FIND "$1" /I $B MORE

The name of the drive to be searched and the string to search for can both be specified when the macro is executed. To search drive D for all files containing JNF, you would enter this command:

    FLOCATE JNF D:

We made the drive name the second parameter so that it can be omitted when you want to search the current drive:

    FLOCATE DFF

This command would list all the files on the current drive containing the letters DFF in their filespecs.

Accessing All Parameters in a Macro

There may be cases where you want to insert not a specific parameter into a command but *all* the parameters, which you can do with the $* symbol. For example, suppose you want to create a DOSKEY macro to format the disk in drive A using whatever parameters are entered on the command line:

```
DOSKEY FA=FORMAT A: $*
```

To use FA to format a 360K diskette with the system files and a volume label of SMALL BOOT, you would enter this command:

```
FA /F:360 /S /V:"SMALL BOOT"
```

The command submitted to DOS after parameter substitution would be:

```
FORMAT A: /F:360 /S /V:"SMALL BOOT"
```

Generalized Macro Examples

Here are some other generalized macros:

To find out if a particular file is present ($1 is the filespec):

```
DOSKEY FILE?=DIR $1 $G NUL
```

To find out how an environment variable is set ($1 is the variable name):

```
DOSKEY SETVAR=SET $B FIND "$1" /I
```

To sort a file ($1 is the source filespec and $2 is the destination filespec):

```
DOSKEY FSORT=SORT $L $1 $G $2
```

Executing a Macro

To execute a macro, enter the macro name and any values for replaceable parameters at the command prompt. The macro name must be the first word of the command prompt. It can't be preceded by a space or by any other character. (This is unfortunate. It means you can't make a macro out of a complicated filespec and insert the macro in the middle of a command.)

Managing Your Macros

You can display all your macros with this command:

```
DOSKEY /M
```

To change the definition of a macro, simply enter another definition for the same macro name. You can recall the former definition from the history list and modify it. To delete a macro, enter a command like this:

```
DOSKEY macroname=
```

To delete all macros in the DOSKEY buffer, press Alt+F10.

Once you have developed a set of macros that you want to keep and reset every time you boot, you can save them in a batch file with this command:

```
DOSKEY /M > filename.BAT
```

The file will contain macro definitions in this form:

```
DELS=FOR %%F IN ($*) DO DEL %%F
FILE?=DIR $1 $G NUL
SETVAR=SET $B FIND "$1" /I
FSORT=SORT $L $1 $G $2
```

Turn it into a batch file by editing it to add the word DOSKEY in front of each definition. Every time you run the batch job, the macros will be redefined. You can call this batch program (don't forget to use CALL) from AUTOEXEC.BAT as long as the command that runs the batch job follows the command that loads DOSKEY.

WARNING

There is no way to turn off the echoing of a macro. If you include an ECHO OFF command, it turns off command echoing *after* the macro is echoed, with the overall result of suppressing the next command prompt. If this happens to you, simply type ECHO ON and press Enter to restore the command prompt.

Replacing DOS Commands with Macros

If you create a DOSKEY macro that has the same name as an internal or external command or batch file, the macro takes precedence over the other command. For example, suppose you create this macro:

```
DOSKEY DEL=DEL /P $*
```

This substitutes a macro for the DEL command so that whenever you enter DEL, the macro will be executed instead of the normal DEL. We've done this to force the use of the /P switch (which prompts for each filename to be deleted), a more cautious approach to deleting files.

You might want to set up similar replacements for other potentially destructive commands such as FORMAT, FDISK, and RECOVER. For example, you might define RECOVER like this:

```
DOSKEY RECOVER=ECHO Do not use this command! $T ECHO
Call R. James on ext. 499 for help in recovering
damaged data.
```

Once you have substituted macros for DOS commands, you can still execute the original commands if you know DOSKEY's loophole. Since a macro name must appear at the beginning of the line, if you type one or more spaces before the command name, you'll bypass the macro and reach the original command. To execute the above RECOVER macro, you would enter:

```
C:\>RECOVER
```

To execute DOS's RECOVER program (which nukes your disk directory structure—see Chapter 15), enter this command:

```
C:\>   RECOVER A:
```

BASICALLY
BETTER BATCHES

ntroduction

DOS's batch program facility lets you create your own programs out
of the commands you use every day plus a special set of batch commands. A relatively simple batch program lists one or more commands
to be executed in sequence, serving the primary purpose of conserving
keystrokes (and potential errors). You might create a batch program
called W that switches to a particular directory and starts up Microsoft
Word. The W batch program contains these lines:

```
E:
CD \WORDDOCS
WORD
```

Such programs can bypass problems in typing (or even remembering)
unfriendly commands. When Ventura Publisher installs itself, it creates a batch file called VP that starts up the desktop publisher with
these commands:

```
C:
CD \VENTURA\DICT
```

```
EDCODICT
DRTLCFG -M6 -B2 -E3 -AA -PC:\VENTURA\DICT\
DLOAD ENGLISH
CD \VENTURA
DRVRMRGR VPPROF %1 /S=SDFVGAH5.VGA/M=32
```

Imagine having to type these commands from scratch.

While a straight command sequence can be useful, the true power of batches becomes evident when you generalize them to handle a variety of situations and to process repetitive sets of data. This chapter and Chapter 7 explore advanced batch features.

A Quick Review of Batch Basics

A batch program must be stored in ASCII (unformatted) form and named in this manner:

> *filename*.BAT

Use EDIT or any ASCII text editor to create batch files.

TIP	You can create a batch file containing DOSKEY's current command history by entering a command in this format: DOSKEY /H > *filename*.BAT (DOSKEY is discussed in Chapter 5.)

To execute a batch program, enter the filename as a command. DOS will open the batch file and read and execute each command in turn. To interrupt processing and kill the batch job, press Ctrl+C or Ctrl+Break (they are equivalent). DOS asks:

> Terminate batch job (Y/N)?

If you enter Y, the entire batch job is terminated. If you enter N, only the current command is terminated and DOS goes on to the next command in the batch file.

TIP If you merely want to pause the batch job without terminating the current command, press the Pause key instead of Ctrl+Break. Pause suspends processing of any program (batch or not) until you press a key other than Pause.

You cannot use redirection in a command that executes a batch file. If you try, the redirection is ignored. But you can use redirection as normal on commands contained within a batch file.

TIP Chapter 10 describes a trick that lets you redirect the output of a batch job using the COMMAND command.

Batch File Contents

Any commands that can be entered at the DOS prompt can be included in a batch file, except for DOSKEY macros. In addition, the commands shown in Table 6.1 have been specifically designed for use in batch files.

Table 6.1 Overview of Batch Commands

CALL	Executes another batch program and returns to the current batch program
ECHO	Controls command echoing and displays messages
FOR	Repeats a command for a set of variables
GOTO	Transfers to another line in the batch file
IF	Tests whether a condition is true or false
PAUSE	Suspends execution until the user presses a key
REM	Inserts comments in the batch file
SHIFT	Permits processing of multiple command line parameters

What's in a Name?

In selecting a name for your batch file, it helps to understand how DOS searches for a program in response to a command. Suppose you want to execute the ROSE batch program:

1. If you enter ROSE as a command without the BAT extension, DOS searches for the program in this order:

   a. If DOSKEY is enabled, it looks for a DOSKEY macro named ROSE. (If the command name is preceded by one or more spaces, this step is bypassed.)

   b. Next it looks for an internal command named ROSE.

   c. Next it looks in the current directory for a file named ROSE.COM, ROSE.EXE, or ROSE.BAT, in that order. (If all three files exist, DOS finds and loads ROSE.COM and never notices the other two.)

   d. Next it looks in the first directory of the search path for ROSE.COM, ROSE.EXE, or ROSE.BAT, in that order.

   e. It continues to search each directory in the search path, in the order they are specified in the PATH command, until a program file is found.

2. To bypass DOSKEY macros, COM, and EXE files (but not internal commands) and search the current directory first, then each directory of the search path for ROSE.BAT, include the BAT extension in the command, as in:

   ```
   C:\>ROSE.BAT
   ```

Since BAT programs have the lowest priority, you should make their names unique unless you intend to take advantage of the program pecking order to achieve a special effect.

Bypassing COM and EXE Files

Chapter 5 shows you how to supersede a COM or EXE file with a DOSKEY macro of the same name. But DOSKEY macros are not as flexible as batch files. How can you supersede a COM or EXE file with a batch file when it has less priority? You do so by using DOSKEY to capture the command and call the batch file. For example, suppose you want to redirect RECOVER commands to a batch file, which prevents them from destroying a disk's directory structure. (Chapter 15 explains RECOVER.) The following command creates a DOSKEY macro that will do the trick:

```
DOSKEY RECOVER=RECOVER.BAT
```

Floppy Batches

DOS reads and executes one batch command at a time. When execution of one command is finished, DOS returns to the batch file to read the next command. This can cause some complications when executing a batch program from a floppy disk. If you change disks during the execution of a command, DOS must ask for the disk containing the batch file in order to continue the job. You'll see this message:

```
Insert disk with batch file
Press any key to continue . . .
```

This message appears even if there are no more commands in the batch file, because DOS doesn't know the batch file is empty until it tries to read a command and discovers the end-of-file mark.

If you remove the floppy disk containing the batch file without inserting another disk, you'll see the following message, which always appears when DOS tries to read an empty drive:

```
Not ready reading drive A
Abort, Retry, Fail?
```

When this message appears, insert the batch file disk in the drive and press R for "Retry."

Clobbering the Batch File

If you know, or even suspect, that a batch program will be executed from a floppy disk, watch out for commands that might process that same disk. Some commands, such as FORMAT, routinely give you the chance to change the floppy disk before starting to work, as long as the commands aren't automated. The REPLACE and XCOPY commands let you change the disk only if you include a /W switch (for Wait) in the command. Most of the commands that can affect a floppy disk or its files, including such commands as DEL *.* and RENAME, offer no opportunity to switch to another floppy disk. If such commands appear in a batch file on floppy disk and refer to the same floppy drive, the commands might destroy the batch file, which is probably not what was intended.

If you suspect that a batch program may be run from a diskette and has the potential for clobbering the batch file, be sure to include a warning message in the program and give the user a chance to change diskettes or cancel the program. The next section explains how to do this.

Message Control

You can do a lot more to control displayed messages from within a batch program than you can from the command prompt or a DOSKEY macro. In addition to redirecting standard output (which is explained in Chapter 4), you can suppress command echoing, display your own messages, and pause until the user responds by pressing a key.

TIP	The CLS command, which has no parameters or switches, is a good way to clear the screen of old commands and messages at the beginning of a batch program and perhaps at appropriate points during the program.

Command-Line Echoing

If left to its own devices, DOS displays each command line preceded by a blank line when processing a batch file. Suppose a batch file named DT.BAT contains these commands:

```
ECHO. | DATE | FIND "Current"
ECHO. | TIME | FIND "Current"
```

Executing DT looks something like this:

```
C:\>DT

C:\>ECHO. | DATE | FIND "Current"
Current date is Tue 10-22-1991

C:\>ECHO. | TIME | FIND "Current"
Current time is 6:47:23.76a

C:\>
C:\>
```

The first line shows the DT command being entered. The second line (not counting blank lines) echoes the first command from DT, and the third line shows its standard output. The fourth line echoes the next command from DT, and the fifth line shows its standard output. The two blank command prompts appear at the end of every batch job when command line echoing is not suppressed. The first one shows up when DOS tries to read another command from the batch file and discovers the end-of-file mark, signaling that the batch program is done. The second is the normal command prompt, which returns so you can enter your next command.

N O T E

When creating a batch file, if you type a carriage return at the end of the last command (which most people do) three (3!) blank command prompts are displayed at the end of the batch job.

This job would take slightly less time, take up less space on the monitor, and make a lot more sense to an inexperienced user if you could suppress the echoed command lines so that the entire job looks like this:

```
C:\>DT
Current date is Tue 10-22-1991
Current time is 6:47:23.76a


C:\>
```

You can suppress the echoing of any individual command (as well as the blank line preceding it) by prefixing the command with @, as in:

```
@ECHO. ¦ DATE ¦ FIND "Current"
@ECHO. ¦ TIME ¦ FIND "Current"
```

This revised version of the program still produces the extra command prompt at the end of the job, since you can't suppress the end-of-file mark with @:

```
C:\>DT
Current date is Tue 10-22-1991
Current time is 6:47:23.76a

C:\>
C:\>
```

The ECHO OFF command (see Figure 6.1 for the ECHO command format) turns off all future command echoing, including the blank line that precedes each command line, until an ECHO ON command is encountered or the batch file ends. Use @ to suppress the ECHO OFF command itself.

The following batch file has the desired effect of suppressing all command lines, all blank lines, and the extra command prompt(s) at the end of the job. In other words, only the command output is displayed.

```
@ECHO OFF
ECHO. ¦ DATE ¦ FIND "Current"
ECHO. ¦ TIME ¦ FIND "Current"
```

Figure 6.1.

ECHO Command
Reference.

ECHO

Controls command line echoing and displays messages.

Format:

ECHO [ON | OFF | *message*]

ECHO.

Parameters:

none   Displays ECHO status (ECHO IS ON or ECHO IS OFF).

ON   Turns command line echoing on.

OFF   Turns command line echoing off.

message Displays the specified message (up to 122 characters) as standard output.

Note:

ECHO. Displays a blank line (a carriage return).

This is the most common method of suppressing command echoing in batch jobs. @ECHO OFF is the first command in nearly every batch file.

N O T E

You might occasionally want to echo a command, which you can do by turning ECHO ON for that command, then turning it OFF again.

Echo Messages

You can also display your own messages during a batch file with commands in this format:

```
ECHO message
```

Use a command in the following format to display a blank line between messages (there must be no space between ECHO and the period):

```
ECHO.
```

We've been using ECHO. to generate a carriage return to pipe to the DATE and TIME command, but when the output isn't redirected, it causes the carriage return (i.e., a blank line) to be displayed on the monitor.

ECHO messages look strange when command echoing is on because you see the message in the ECHO command and then as output on the next line:

```
C:\>ECHO Let's format the diskette in drive A:
Let's format the diskette in drive A:

C:\>ECHO.

C:\>ECHO Insert the correct diskette in the drive.
Insert the correct diskette in the drive.
```

The messages look just right when command echoing is turned off:

```
Let's format the diskette in drive A:

Insert the correct diskette in the drive.
```

N O T E

You might think that ECHO followed by a space would display a blank line, but that causes DOS to display ECHO IS ON or ECHO IS OFF. ECHO followed by a space and then a period causes DOS to display a line containing a period. To generate a blank line, you have to use ECHO. with no space preceding the period.

Using ECHO in Batch Programs

When you're preparing a batch job for a user, make liberal use of ECHO messages to keep the user informed of what's going on. For example, suppose you are creating a batch program named VAULT to move a set of files from the hard disk to diskettes. You might do it like this:

```
@ECHO OFF
CLS
ECHO  **********************************************
ECHO  *                                            *
ECHO  *  This program moves all the DOC files      *
ECHO  *  from C:\WORD\DOCS to the diskette in      *
ECHO  *  drive A:.                                 *
ECHO  *                                            *
ECHO  **********************************************

REM First copy the files to drive A:
XCOPY C:\WORD\*.DOC A:

REM Then delete the files from C:
DEL C:\WORD\*.DOC

CLS
ECHO  **********************************************
ECHO  *                                            *
ECHO  *                All done!                   *
ECHO  *                                            *
ECHO  **********************************************
```

N O T E

When ECHO is ON, the REM command can also be used to display messages in a batch program. But when ECHO is OFF, REM commands produce no output and serve only to document the batch file itself.

Pausing

When you've automated the commands in a batch file and added your own messages, output lines might scroll off the screen before a user gets the chance to examine them. You can use the PAUSE command (see Figure 6.2) to suspend processing until a key is pressed.

Figure 6.2.

PAUSE Batch
Command
Reference.

> **PAUSE**
>
> Suspends processing until a key is pressed; displays the message "Press any key to continue . . .."
>
> **Format:**
>
> PAUSE [*message*]
>
> **Note:**
>
> A *message* is displayed only if the command is echoed (ECHO is ON). When ECHO is OFF, use ECHO to display instructions before pausing.

In the preceding batch program, you might want the program to pause after the first message to give yourself or another the chance to change diskettes, like this:

```
@ECHO OFF
CLS
ECHO *********************************************
ECHO *                                           *
ECHO *  This program moves all the DOC files     *
ECHO *  from C:\WORD\DOCS to the diskette in     *
ECHO *  drive A:.                                 *
ECHO *                                           *
ECHO *  Make sure the correct diskette is in     *
ECHO *  drive A: before continuing.              *
```

```
ECHO *                                         *
ECHO *******************************************
PAUSE

REM First copy the files to drive A:
XCOPY C:\WORD\*.DOC A:

REM Then delete the files from C:
DEL C:\WORD\*.DOC

CLS
ECHO *******************************************
ECHO *                                         *
ECHO *             All done!                   *
ECHO *                                         *
ECHO *******************************************
```

The pause also gives someone the chance to cancel the program using
Ctrl+Break after reading the preceding message. In fact, PAUSE can be
used to provide rather primitive input to a batch program. One unfortunate feature of DOS is that it provides no simple method of reading input
from a user during a batch job. But you can do something like this:

```
@ECHO OFF
CLS
ECHO *******************************************
ECHO *                                         *
ECHO *                  WARNING!               *
ECHO *                                         *
ECHO *    This program destroys any existing data *
ECHO *    on the diskette in drive A:. Make sure  *
ECHO *    you have the correct diskette inserted  *
ECHO *    before continuing. (Pull it out, look   *
ECHO *    at it, and replace it if necessary.)    *
ECHO *                                         *
ECHO *    To cancel this program:              *
ECHO *         1.  Press Ctrl+Break NOW!       *
ECHO *         2.  When you see the message    *
ECHO *             "Terminate batch job (Y/N)?" *
ECHO *             type Y and press Enter.     *
```

```
ECHO *                                        *
ECHO *  To continue with this program:        *
ECHO *         Press any key (except Ctrl+Break). *
ECHO *                                        *
ECHO ******************************************
PAUSE
```

N O T E

When DOS says "Press a key" or "Press any key," the locking keys (CapsLock, Scroll Lock, and Num Lock) and the shifting keys (Shift, Ctrl, Alt), when used by themselves, will not trigger the desired reaction. You have to press a character key or a cursor key to continue.

Offering Choices via Supplementary Batch Files

There is a roundabout way to let someone input one-word responses from the keyboard during a batch program. You ask a question and terminate the first batch program. The user enters a response at the command prompt (which you have altered for the purpose). You have batch files set up with the correct names to process the user's response (such as Y.BAT for a "yes" response and N.BAT for a "no" response). Here's an example in which we let the user decide whether or not to format a disk.

```
@ECHO OFF
CLS
ECHO ******************************************
ECHO *                                        *
ECHO *   This program reformats the diskette in  *
ECHO *   drive A:. All the data on the diskette  *
ECHO *   will be destroyed. Below is a listing    *
ECHO *   of the files currently on the diskette. *
ECHO *                                        *
ECHO ******************************************

ECHO.
DIR A:\ /S /W
```

```
ECHO.
ECHO *********************************************
ECHO *                                           *
ECHO *  If you would like to reformat this disk- *
ECHO *  ette, press Y to continue. If not, press *
ECHO *  N to stop. (Pressing Y will destroy the  *
ECHO *  data on the diskette.)                    *
ECHO *                                           *
ECHO *  Would you like to continue?              *
ECHO *                                           *
ECHO *********************************************
PROMPT (Y/N)?
```

That's the end of the first program. The normal command prompt has been replaced by the expression (Y/N)? The Y.BAT program looks something like this:

```
@ECHO OFF
FORMAT A: /U < FMT.IN
PROMPT $P$G
```

The last command restores the normal command prompt. The N.BAT program looks something like this:

```
@ECHO OFF
CLS
ECHO *********************************************
ECHO *                                           *
ECHO *  You chose not to format the diskette.    *
ECHO *                                           *
ECHO *              Goodbye.                     *
ECHO *                                           *
ECHO *********************************************
PROMPT $P$G
```

If you want several batch programs to ask yes and no questions, with different results, you can generate Y.BAT and N.BAT from within the program rather than storing them permanently on disk. Use a redirected ECHO command to store each line in the new batch file. The above program could be revised to look like this:

```
@ECHO OFF
CLS
ECHO *******************************************
ECHO *                                         *
ECHO *   This program reformats the diskette in *
ECHO *   drive A:. All the data on the diskette *
ECHO *   will be destroyed. Below is a listing  *
ECHO *   of the files currently on the diskette. *
ECHO *                                         *
ECHO *******************************************

ECHO.
DIR A:\ /S /W

ECHO.
ECHO *******************************************
ECHO *                                         *
ECHO *   If you would like to reformat this disk- *
ECHO *   ette, press Y to continue. If not, press *
ECHO *   N to stop. (Pressing Y will destroy the *
ECHO *   data on the diskette.)                 *
ECHO *                                         *
ECHO *   Would you like to continue?           *
ECHO *                                         *
ECHO *******************************************
PROMPT (Y/N)?

REM Create batch file to handle Y answer:
ECHO @ECHO OFF > Y.BAT
ECHO FORMAT A: /U >> Y.BAT
ECHO PROMPT $P$G >> Y.BAT

REM Create batch file to handle N answer:
ECHO @ECHO OFF > N.BAT
ECHO CLS >> N.BAT
ECHO ECHO ********************************************* >> N.BAT
ECHO ECHO *                                         * >> N.BAT
ECHO ECHO *   You chose not to format the diskette.  * >> N.BAT
ECHO ECHO *                                         * >> N.BAT
```

```
ECHO ECHO *                          Goodbye.                    * >> N.B
ECHO ECHO *                                                      * >> N.B
ECHO ECHO ************************************************** >> N.B
ECHO PROMPT $P$G >> N.BAT
```

Replaceable Parameters

A batch program becomes more generally useful if you set it up so that command specifics (such as filespecs) can be entered when the program is executed. You use the replaceable parameters (%0 through %9) for this purpose. The following SPACE.BAT program has limited usefulness because it displays the amount of space occupied by BAK files (a specific) on the current drive (another specific):

```
@ECHO OFF
ECHO The space occupied by *.BAK files on the current drive
is:
DIR \*.BAK /S ¦ FIND "file(s)"
```

The program becomes more generalized if you use %1 to represent the filespec and %2 to represent the drivename:

```
@ECHO OFF
ECHO The space occupied by %1 files on the %2 drive is:
DIR %2\%1 /S ¦ FIND "file(s)"
```

Now you can include a filespec and drive name when you execute the batch program. If you enter this command:

```
SPACE *.DOC D:
```

DOS substitutes *.DOC for %1 and D: for %2 everywhere in the batch file. The commands that are processed are:

```
@ECHO OFF
ECHO The space occupied by *.DOC files on the D: drive is:
DIR D:\*.DOC ¦ FIND "file(s)"
```

A Simple Application of Replaceable Parameters

The following two programs, named START.BAT and STOP.BAT might be used to track project work time. Whenever you start working on a project, enter START project at the command prompt. The date and time are recorded in the TIMETRAK file. When you stop working on the project, enter STOP project. TIMETRAK will be an ASCII file that you can edit, print, and delete as needed.

```
[START.BAT]
@ECHO OFF
ECHO Started working on %1 >> C:\TIMETRAK
ECHO. ¦ DATE ¦ FIND "Current" >> C:\TIMETRAK
ECHO. ¦ TIME ¦ FIND "Current" >> C:\TIMETRAK
ECHO. >> C:\TIMETRAK

[STOP.BAT]
@ECHO OFF
ECHO Stopped working on %1 >> C:\TIMETRAK
ECHO. ¦ DATE ¦ FIND "Current" >> C:\TIMETRAK
ECHO. ¦ TIME ¦ FIND "Current" >> C:\TIMETRAK
ECHO. >> C:\TIMETRAK
```

How Replaceable Parameters Work

DOS identifies the words on a command line by the spaces that separate them. The first word is always the command itself, which must be the name of a DOSKEY macro, an internal command, an executable program (COM or EXE), or a batch program (BAT). All subsequent words on the line are parameters. (A switch is a type of parameter.) After loading the requested program, DOS passes all the parameters to it.

However, when executing a batch file, DOS processes all replaceable parameters before executing a command. %0 is always replaced by the first word on the command line—the command that executed the batch file. You'll sometimes see %0 used in ECHO messages.

The symbol %1 is replaced by the first parameter on the command line, %2 by the second parameter, and so on up to %9, which is replaced by the ninth parameter. If you want to allow for more than nine parameters, you have to use the SHIFT command, which is explained under *SHIFT* later in this chapter.

Null Parameters

A missing parameter is replaced by a null value. In the SPACE batch file, if you omit the drive-name parameter, %2 is replaced by a null value, resulting in this batch job, which accesses the current drive as no drive is specified:

```
@ECHO OFF
ECHO The space occupied by *.DOC files on the  drive is:
DIR \*.DOC /S ¦ FIND "file(s)"
```

(Notice how carefully we worded the message so it reads all right when the drive name is null.) If you omit the filespec parameter too, %1 is also re-placed by a null value, resulting in this batch job, which reports on all files on the current drive:

```
@ECHO OFF
ECHO The space occupied by  files on the  drive is:
DIR \ /S ¦ FIND "file(s)"
```

Because DOS identifies parameters by position, you can omit parameters at the end of the command line only. In the SPACE example, there's no way to omit the filespec but include the drive name, as the first parameter on the command line will always be substituted for %1, whether it makes sense or not.

Keep this fact in mind when deciding which parameter in a batch job should be %1, which should be %2, and so on. The parameters most likely to be omitted should come last. In the SPACE example, there's a natural inclination to make the drive name %1 and the filespec %2, because that's the order in which they appear in the DIR command. But people fre-quently want to specify a filespec and omit the drive name, so we reversed the two replaceable parameters.

Also analyze how a command will function with null values for the replace-able parameters. The SPACE program provides a good example. Suppose you decide to include the colon from the drive name in the fixed text of the DIR command and replace %2 with the drive letter only. The batch file would look like this:

```
@ECHO OFF
ECHO The space occupied by %1 files on the %2: drive is:
DIR %2:\%1 /S ¦ FIND "file(s)"
```

To execute it for the TXT files on drive D:, you would enter:

```
SPACE *.TXT D
```

Both occurrences of %2 are replaced by the letter D, and the batch job works perfectly. But what if you omit the second parameter, trying to access the current drive? The commands to be processed after substitution are:

```
@ECHO OFF
ECHO The space occupied by *.TXT files on the : drive is:
DIR :\*.TXT /S ¦ FIND "file(s)"
```

The filespec :*.TXT is unacceptable to DOS and will cause the DIR command to fail. To avoid this failure, leave the colon out of the fixed text and enter it with the drive name.

It's not always possible to make every parameter replaceable by a null. When a batch job has required parameters, they should be the first parameters on the command line, and, of course, you should let others know which parameters are required and which are optional.

SHIFT

Nine replaceable parameters are more than enough for most batch files, but should you want more than that, the SHIFT command can be used to process an unlimited number of parameters. SHIFT, which has no parameters of its own, causes all the command-line parameters to be shifted down one position, so that the value that was formerly substituted for %1 is now substituted for %0, the value that was %2 is now %1, and so on. At the other end of the command line, the tenth parameter is now substituted for %9, which makes that parameter available for the first time.

Suppose you want to write a multiple-delete command called DELS.BAT that can accept up to 12 filespecs. One way to do it is shown below:

```
@ECHO OFF
ECHO Deleting %1
DEL %1
ECHO Deleting %2
DEL %2
ECHO Deleting %3
DEL %3
ECHO Deleting %4
DEL %4
ECHO Deleting %5
DEL %5
ECHO Deleting %6
DEL %6
ECHO Deleting %7
DEL %7
ECHO Deleting %8
DEL %8
ECHO Deleting %9
DEL %9

SHIFT
REM The 10th parameter is now %9
ECHO Deleting %9
DEL %9

SHIFT
REM The 11th parameter is now %9
ECHO Deleting %9
DEL %9

SHIFT
REM The 12th parameter is now %9
ECHO Deleting %9
DEL %9
```

Another way to accomplish the same result is:

```
@ECHO OFF
ECHO Deleting %1
DEL %1
```

```
          .
          .
          .
ECHO Deleting %9
DEL %9

SHIFT
SHIFT
SHIFT

ECHO Deleting %7
DEL %7
ECHO Deleting %8
DEL %8
ECHO Deleting %9
DEL %9
```

If a user enters fewer than 12 parameters, the DEL command will be executed with no filespec, causing an error message to be displayed. Chapter 7 includes a better solution to this problem.

Dumb Replacement

DOS applies no intelligence whatsoever to the parameter replacement process. It simply does a character-by-character substitution of %n with the characters in the parameter. No surrounding spaces are added. If the result doesn't make sense, DOS won't know it. Suppose the final command in DREK.BAT says:

```
%3%1 %2
```

What if you enter the following command line?

```
DREK R *.COM DI
```

After substitution, the final command in DREK.BAT looks like this:

```
DIR *.COM
```

Yes, it's a silly example, but it shows how you can apply a little creativity to make dumb replacement work for you, if necessary.

Escaping Replacement

Because of the way DOS handles the symbol % in a batch file, it ends up deleting every single occurrence of this symbol, even if it isn't attached to a digit to represent a replaceable parameter. You might occasionally need to use the % symbol in a batch file without having it deleted. For example, you might need to reference a file named TEN%ERS. Double a % to keep it from being deleted. For example, to print the file named TEN%ERS from within a batch file, use this command:

```
PRINT TEN%%ERS
```

DOS will replace the %% with % before processing the command.

CHAPTER 7

BATCH LOGIC

Introduction

A batch program can include commands to link to other batch programs, make decisions, and create loops for repetitive processing. For experienced programmers, the commands available in DOS will be familiar, if somewhat awkward when compared to the facilities available in, say, BASIC or C. This chapter introduces a touch of programming logic concepts (just the basics) for readers who have never programmed before.

Linking Batch Files

As batch programs get more complex, it's often convenient for one batch file to link to another. For example, suppose you have a program named FMT.BAT that automatically formats a diskette and handles all possible errors that can occur; it's over 100 lines long. Now you're creating a batch program that sets up diskettes with a new application; it must format several diskettes before copying files to them. You could copy the formatting routine into the new batch file, or you could link to FMT.BAT to do the formatting.

Linking offers some very real advantages:

⊃ You save disk space by not copying the 100+ lines into another file.

⊃ If you improve FMT.BAT, the improvements carry through to all programs that link to it.

The major disadvantages are that the link itself takes time, which slows down the program making the link; future modifications to FMT.BAT could make it inappropriate to some programs that link to it; and if you move, rename, or delete FMT.BAT, the link will no longer be valid.

Chaining vs. Calling

There are two ways to link to another batch program, as shown in Figure 7.1. When you *chain* to another program, you transfer completely to that program, causing the first batch program to be terminated. When the chained program ends (without chaining to another program), the batch job terminates and DOS resumes control. When you *call* another batch program, you transfer to it temporarily; when it's finished, you return to the original batch program, picking up with the instruction after the one that did the calling.

Figure 7.1.

Calling and
Chaining to Other
Batch Files.

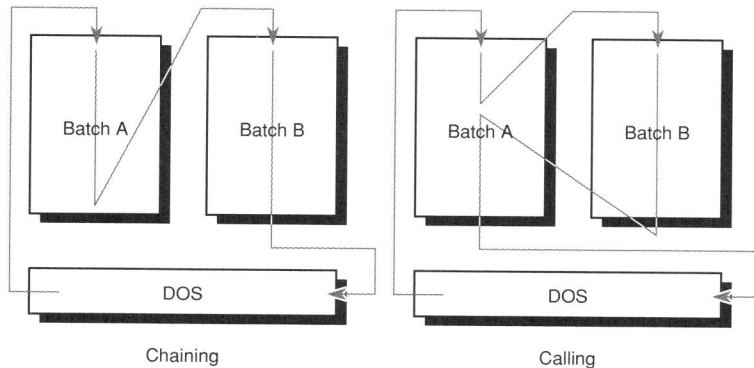

Chaining   Calling

Calling

To call another batch file, use a command in this format:

```
CALL batch-command
```

For example, this command calls FMT.BAT:

```
CALL FMT
```

When the FMT program ends, DOS returns to the command following this
CALL command.

Include whatever parameters on the CALL command that you would use
when executing the program from the command prompt. For example, if
FMT accepts an optional drive name and volume label as replaceable parameters, you could use this command:

```
CALL FMT A: TOTMASTER
```

N O T E

Redirection is ignored in a CALL command, as it is in any command
that executes a batch program.

Chaining

When you execute a batch file without the CALL command, DOS chains to it. For example, the following command chains to FMT.BAT:

```
FMT A: TOTMASTER
```

Let's be perfectly clear about this, because some people have a hard time believing it and can't figure out why their batch programs don't work. Any time you include a command in one batch program that executes another batch program without using CALL, a chain takes place and the first batch program is *automatically terminated*. For example, in the following batch file, the COPY command will never be executed because the FMT command chains to another batch program:

```
@ECHO OFF
ECHO Put the master diskette in drive B:
PAUSE
FMT B:
COPY C:\TOTDIR\*.* B:
```

You can correct the problem by inserting CALL in front of the FMT command.

N O T E

A batch program executes other types of programs, such as COM and EXE programs, without chaining. In the above batch program, ECHO, PAUSE, and COPY all cause programs to be executed without chaining. Only links to other batch programs cause chaining to take place.

Passing Replaceable Parameters

You can use replaceable parameters in the linking command; DOS will replace them before executing the link. For example, the following command passes two parameters from the calling program to FMT.BAT:

```
CALL FMT %3 TOTMASTER
```

As usual, the %3 will be replaced by the third parameter from the command line that executed the calling program; if that's A:, the CALL command as executed becomes:

```
CALL FMT.BAT A: TOTMASTER
```

The called batch program, FMT.BAT, treats the A: as %1 and TOTMASTER as %2. It has no awareness that the A: was originally %3 to the calling program.

Replaceable parameters are not automatically passed from the linking program to the linked program. You must include in the linking command any parameters to be passed to the linked program, and they must be in the correct order and format for the linked program, just as if you executed the same program from the command prompt.

Multiple Links

When you link to a second batch program, it might link to another. There's no limit to the number of links you can make in a batch job. Program A might chain to Program B, which calls Program C, which links to Program D, and so on. Your batch jobs will be easier to manage, revise, and debug if you limit them to a few links, however.

Recursion

A batch file can link to itself, creating a situation called *recursion*. The batch job will repeat endlessly until something interrupts it, such as a condition becoming true or someone pressing Ctrl+Break.

Killing a Batch Job with Links

If you press Ctrl+Break (or Ctrl+C) during a batch job involving links, DOS displays its usual message:

```
Terminate batch job (Y/N)?
```

If you enter Y, the entire batch job (including all linked programs) is killed. If you enter N, only the current command is killed.

Branching

DOS includes some commands that let you decide what to do next in a batch program based on a specific condition. Some typical conditions are:

- ⊃ Does the C:\AUTOEXEC.BAT file exist?

- ⊃ Did the preceding command succeed?

- ⊃ Does %1 equal "/S"?

Types of Branches

Branches can range from extremely simple to fairly complex (although not as complex as you can achieve in true programming languages such as BASIC or C).

Bypass Branch

Figure 7.2 illustrates the simplest kind of branch, in which you execute a routine if the condition is true but bypass it if the condition is false, or vice versa. We call this a bypass branch because only one path (either the true path or the false one) causes a routine to be executed. The other branch bypasses that and goes on to the next step. Notice that both branches end up at the same place eventually.

Figure 7.2.

Bypass Decision Logic.

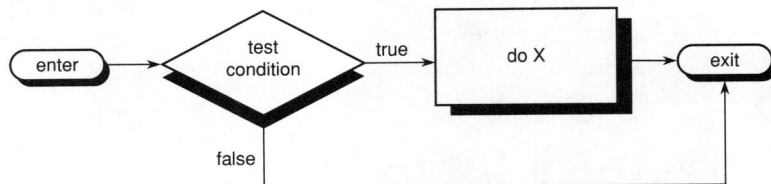

Some typical bypass decisions are:

- ⊃ If C:\AUTOEXEC.BAT exists, rename it as C:\AUTOEXEC.OLD.

- ⊃ If the preceding command failed, issue a warning message.

- ⊃ If %1 equals "SORT", sort the source file.

Alternative Branches

Another common type of branch has two paths, as illustrated in Figure 7.3. One routine is executed if the condition is true, while another routine is executed if it's false. Typical alternative branches are:

➲ If C:\AUTOEXEC.BAT exists, copy it to A:; otherwise, create a new A:\AUTOEXEC.BAT.

➲ If the preceding copy command succeeded, delete the source files; otherwise, display an error message and terminate.

➲ If %3 equals "/P", print the target file; otherwise, display it on the monitor.

Figure 7.3.

Alternative Decision Logic.

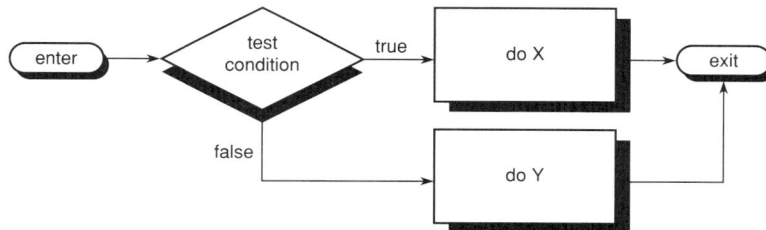

The IF Command

Figure 7.4 shows the IF command, which is used for decision-making in batch programs.

Figure 7.4.

IF Command Reference.

IF

Executes a command if (and only if) a condition is true

Format:

IF [NOT] *condition command*

Parameters:

condition	The condition to be tested, which must be one of the following:	
	ERRORLEVEL *n*	The condition is true if the preceding program's exit code equals or exceeds *n*.
	EXIST *filespec*	The condition is true if the specified file exists.
	string1==string2	The condition is true if the two text strings are equal.
command	The command to be executed if the condition is true.	

Note:

NOT negates the result of the condition so that the command is executed if the condition is false.

Exit Codes

Many programs set an *exit code* when they terminate. The exit code is a number between 0 and 255 that indicates whether the program achieved its function or what type of error occurred. There are no set meanings for exit codes; each program defines the exit codes it issues, although a 0 generally means that the program was completely successful. The FORMAT program provides a typical example of exit codes:

0	The disk was successfully formatted (no errors)
3	The user interrupted with Ctrl+C or Ctrl+Break
4	Some (unspecified) type of error occurred and the disk was not successfully formatted
5	A problem was identified and reported to the user, who chose to cancel the format

Unfortunately, not all of the DOS programs set exit codes, so it's not always possible to test for successful completion of an individual command in a batch file. Appendix A lists the exit codes set by the DOS utilities. If a DOS command isn't in the list, it doesn't set an exit code.

Your application programs and third-party utilities might also set exit codes. Check their documentation to find out.

The ERRORLEVEL Condition

The ERRORLEVEL condition tests the exit code of the preceding program. You specify a number, as in IF ERRORLEVEL 3, and the condition is true if the exit code equals or exceeds that number. The following commands format the diskette in drive A and, if that fails for any reason, display the message "Try again with another diskette."

```
FORMAT A:
IF ERRORLEVEL 1 ECHO Try again with another diskette
```

TIP	Since FORMAT doesn't use exit codes 1 and 2, you could just as easily say IF ERRORLEVEL 3. But it's common usage to say IF ERRORLEVEL 1 to discriminate between 0 (complete success) and all other exit codes.

You can include NOT in an IF command to negate the result of the condition; that is, the condition is true only if the exit code is less than the specified number. The following routine displays a message only if the format is successful:

```
FORMAT A:
IF NOT ERRORLEVEL 1 ECHO Remove the diskette from drive A:
```

It's easy to get tangled up in IF ERRORLEVEL logic, especially when you reverse it with NOT. A logic chart like the ones in Figure 7.5 can help you analyze a command, determine when it will be true and when false, and decide what's going to happen in each case.

Figure 7.5.

Sample IF Logic Charts.

condition	IF ERRORLEVEL 3	
exit codes	0, 1, 2	3, 4, ...
result	false	true
action	continue	kill program

condition	IF NOT ERRORLEVEL 2	
exit codes	0, 1	2, 3, ...
result	true	false
action	delete files	display message

The Short Life of the Exit Code

The exit code lasts only until another program changes it. Even if the next program doesn't set specific exit codes, the exit code might be reset to 0. Commands such as CALL and ECHO don't reset the exit code, but other commands (especially nonbatch commands) might. So if you're going to process an exit code, do it immediately.

The IF command does not reset the exit code. You can use several IF commands in a row to process various exit code possibilities after a command like FORMAT or XCOPY.

IF and Bypass Branches

The IF command is perfectly set up for a simple bypass branch. If the condition is true, it executes a single command, then goes on to the next line. If the condition is false, it simply goes on to the next line. If you want to execute more than one command when the condition is true, which is often the case, you can use CALL to execute another batch program, as in:

```
IF ERRORLEVEL 1 CALL BADFORM
```

All the examples you've seen so far are bypass branches. To accomplish alternative branches, you need to use the GOTO command, which is explained next.

Telling DOS where to Go

Suppose you're trying to accomplish an alternate decision like this: If the last command was successful, call GOODFORM; otherwise, call BADFORM.

The following program won't work:

```
IF NOT ERRORLEVEL 1 CALL GOODFORM
CALL BADFORM
```

It doesn't work because the CALL BADFORM command is executed in both cases.

The GOTO command (see Figure 7.6) is used to branch away from the current sequence of commands to another point in the program. To accomplish an alternative branch, you jump to another section of the program for the true path. Only the false path falls into the next line after the IF statement. For example:

```
IF NOT ERRORLEVEL 1 GOTO GOODFORM
REM If DOS reaches the next line, the FORMAT command
failed for some reason.
...
...    (commands to handle FORMAT error)
...
GOTO NEXTSTEP
```

```
:GOODFORM
...
...    (commands to handle a successful format)
...


:NEXTSTEP
...
...
...
```

Figure 7.6.

GOTO Batch
Command
Reference.

GOTO

Sends DOS to a line containing *label* in the same batch file.

Format:

GOTO *label*

Parameter:

label   Any character string; DOS jumps to the line in the batch file starting with :*label* (the same character string preceded by a colon).

Notes:

The label may be any length (for documentation purposes) but DOS pays attention to the first eight characters only, so make those characters unique within the batch file.

The label may contain spaces but not other separators (such as semicolons and equal signs).

Any line starting with a colon (:) is considered to be a label, even if no command in the program references that label. Unreferenced labels are ignored. Some batch programmers use : to create comment lines instead of REM.

In the preceding routine, if the condition is true, indicating that the exit code is 0, you branch to GOODFORM, which is a label in the same program, not a separate program. There might be several commands in the GOODFORM section. At the end, you fall into NEXTSTEP, which continues the batch processing. If the condition is false, the GOTO command is not executed and you fall through into the commands that process an exit code greater than 0. At the end of that false branch is an extremely important command: GOTO NEXTSTEP. This command branches around the GOODFORM routine. Without it, you would fall into GOODFORM after the false branch was completed, which is not desired when you're trying to create an alternate branch.

GOTO is also essential in creating multiple alternatives. For example, the following routine tries to display the exit code resulting from the FORMAT command:

```
FORMAT A:
IF ERRORLEVEL 5 ECHO Exit code is 5
IF ERRORLEVEL 4 ECHO Exit code is 4
IF ERRORLEVEL 3 ECHO Exit code is 3
IF ERRORLEVEL 0 ECHO Exit code is 0
```

Here's what the output looks like when the exit code is 4:

```
Exit code is 4
Exit code is 3
Exit code is 0
```

Because these IF commands come one after the other, DOS executes each one in turn, regardless of the outcome of the preceding one. IF ERRORLEVEL 5 is false, so that message is not displayed. But IF ERRORLEVEL 4 is true, and its message is displayed. And IF ERRORLEVEL 3 and IF ERRORLEVEL 0 are also true, so their messages are displayed as well. The result is not what we wanted.

The following routine completely processes the exit codes from the FORMAT command:

```
:FORMATSTEP
FORMAT A:
IF ERRORLEVEL 5 GOTO HANDLE5
IF ERRORLEVEL 4 GOTO HANDLE4
IF ERRORLEVEL 3 GOTO HANDLE3

REM If DOS reaches this line, the exit code must be 0
ECHO Exit code is 0
GOTO NEXTSTEP

:HANDLE3
ECHO Exit code is 3
GOTO NEXTSTEP

:HANDLE4
ECHO Exit code is 4
GOTO NEXTSTEP
```

```
:HANDLE5
ECHO Exit code is 5

:NEXTSTEP
```
[The program continues on from here.]

It's important to test from the highest exit code to the lowest so that the first true condition encountered is the one that equals the exit code.

Testing for Files

Sometimes it's handy to test for the presence or absence of a file before deciding what to do next. IF [NOT] EXIST is used for this purpose. The classic example prevents the COPY command from overwriting an existing file by testing the target filename first. The program named PCOPY.BAT (for Protected COPY) might look something like the following file. %1 is the source filespec and %2 is the target.

```
@ECHO OFF
IF EXIST %2 GOTO NOCOPY
COPY %1 %2
GOTO ENDING

:NOCOPY
ECHO The %2 file already exists. Please move, delete,
ECHO or rename it before trying this command again.

:ENDING
```

This routine fails if you omit the filespec for %2. It also produces an undesired result if you specify a drive and/or path for %2 but omit the filename, because the IF EXIST condition turns out to be false and the copy is made, even if the target directory does contain a file of the same name.

IF [NOT] EXIST can be used in bypass decisions too. The following command copies A:\AUTOEXEC.BAT to C:\ only if it doesn't already exist on C:\:

```
IF NOT EXIST C:\AUTOEXEC.BAT COPY A:\AUTOEXEC.BAT C:\
```

The following command renames C:\AUTOEXEC.BAT if it exists:

```
IF EXIST C:\AUTOEXEC.BAT REN C:\AUTOEXEC.BAT AUTOEXEC.OLD
```

Testing for a Directory

Suppose you want to find out whether the current directory has a subdirectory named TEMP. IF EXIST TEMP won't do it because EXIST doesn't identify subdirectories. But the special filename NUL is valid for every existing directory, so use this command to see if TEMP exists:

```
IF EXIST TEMP\NUL command
```

Comparing Text Strings

At first glance, comparing two text strings might seem totally useless. IF APPLES==APPLES is obviously true and IF APPLES==ORANGES is just as obviously false. But one or both of those text strings can be a replaceable parameter, giving you the power to check out the parameters that are entered on the command line.

The following batch program tests to see if the first parameter is /F; if so, it reformats the diskette in drive A before copying files to it. If the first parameter is anything but /F, including null, the diskette is not formatted.

```
@ECHO OFF
IF %1==/F FORMAT A:
COPY C:\MYAPP\*.* A:
```

Testing for Null Values

You can put quotes around *string1* and *string2*, but they're usually optional. If you use them, both parameters must be quoted. There's one case where they are needed, and that's in testing for a null parameter. To find out if %3 is null, use a condition like this:

```
IF "%3"=="" GOTO CONTINUE
```

Nested IFs

You can nest an IF command inside another IF command. That is, another IF command is executed when the IF command is true. The following GOTO command is executed if the current exit code is equal to or greater than 4 but less than 5; in other words, if it's 4:

```
IF ERRORLEVEL 4 IF NOT ERRORLEVEL 5 GOTO CODE4
```

The inner IF command is executed only if the outer IF command is true, and the GOTO command is executed only if *both* IF commands are true. The following GOTO command is executed if %1 is neither Y nor N:

```
IF NOT %1==Y IF NOT %1==N GOTO BADINPUT
```

Case is important in string comparisons. In the preceding command, a lowercase y or n would not be considered the same as Y or N and the GOTO instruction would be executed. You could adjust the command to permit users to enter either uppercase or lowercase letters this way:

```
IF NOT %1==Y IF NOT %1==y IF NOT %1==N IF NOT %1==n
GOTO BADINPUT
```

If there's any possibility that a user will omit the value, use quotes around the strings to avoid killing the program with a syntax error. For example, if someone omitted the Y or N when executing the above batch command, the resulting command would be:

```
IF NOT ==Y IF NOT ==y IF NOT ==N IF NOT ==n
GOTO BADINPUT
```

The condition ==Y is bad syntax and will kill the batch program. To avoid it, use this command instead:

```
IF NOT "%1"=="Y" IF NOT "%1"=="y" IF NOT "%1"=="N"
IF NOT "%1"=="n" GOTO BADINPUT
```

Now when the first parameter is omitted, the executed command is:

```
IF NOT ""=="Y" IF NOT ""=="y" IF NOT ""=="N"
IF NOT ""=="n" GOTO BADINPUT
```

This command has perfectly good syntax and will result in executing the GOTO BADINPUT command, since a null does not equal Y, y, N, or n.

Loops

A *loop* is a routine that can be executed more than once. Two types of loops are possible—open and closed. An *open loop* tests a condition and terminates itself when the condition becomes true. A *closed loop* simply repeats and repeats with no way out until someone interrupts it from outside, usually by pressing Ctrl+Break or by rebooting. Most closed loops are mistakes, but you might find occasion to use one on purpose.

Figure 7.7 diagrams the logic of an open loop. You perform an action (such as a FORMAT command), then test a condition (such as whether the exit code is 0). If the condition is false, you repeat the loop. When it's true, you exit the loop and go on with the program. In other words, the loop is executed until the condition becomes true. An open loop affects the condition in some way so that it may be true the next time it's tested.

Figure 7.7.

Loop Logic.

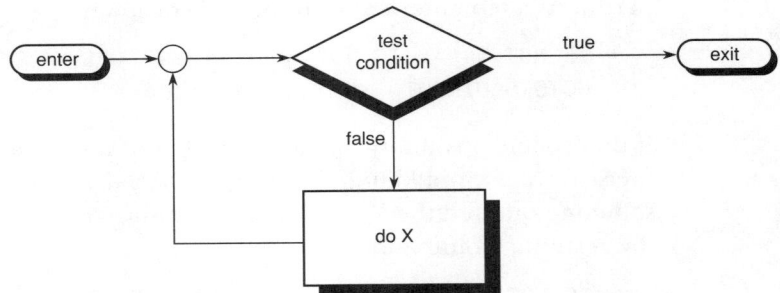

In some routines, it makes more sense to test the condition at the beginning of the loop instead of at the end. This allows for the possibility that the condition might be true from the start and the routine should never be executed.

Sample Loop

Suppose you want to execute FORMAT until it is successful. This type of loop is usually completed the first time, but if the first diskette is bad or some other problem occurs, then the loop will be repeated:

```
:FORMATLOOP
FORMAT A:
IF NOT ERRORLEVEL 1 GOTO ENDING

REM If DOS reaches this line, FORMAT was not successful

ECHO FORMAT failed for some reason. To try again
ECHO with another diskette, insert the diskette
ECHO and press any key except Ctrl+C or Ctrl+Break.
ECHO To quit now, press Ctrl+Break and enter Y
ECHO when you see "Terminate batch job (Y/N)?"
PAUSE
GOTO FORMATLOOP

:ENDING
```

Loops Involving SHIFT and String Conditions

Let's go back to the program to delete up to 12 filespecs (see page 111). It can be set up as a loop to delete *any number* of filespecs. The loop ends when no more parameters are left to process.

```
:DELLOOP
IF "%1"=="" GOTO ENDING
DEL %1
SHIFT
GOTO DELLOOP
:ENDING
```

Each loop starts by checking for a null value in the first parameter. If it's null, the program jumps to ENDING and terminates. If it's not null, a DEL command is issued for that filespec. Then all the parameters are shifted down, so the next one becomes %1, and the program returns to the beginning of the loop.

Using FOR to Create Loops

Another looping technique uses the FOR command (see Figure 7.8) instead of IF. Once you get used to its ugly duckling format, you'll discover there's a swan in there somewhere. One big advantage of FOR is that it can be used at the command prompt; it's the only way to create repetitive processing at the command prompt.

Figure 7.8.

FOR Command
Reference.

FOR

Repeats a command for every item in a set of items.

Format:

FOR %*x* IN (*item set*) DO *command*

Parameters:

%*x*   Any single character (except 0 through 9) preceded by a percent sign (%). This establishes a variable name that is used in the *command* and that will be replaced by each item in the *item set*.

item set   Any set of items, such as filespecs, drive names, or paths. Global filespecs can be used. If more than one item is specified, they are separated by spaces. The entire item set must be enclosed in parentheses.

command   The command to be executed. Use %*x* somewhere in the command to indicate where the items from the item set should be substituted.

Notes:

x must be a single character or a syntax error occurs.

If FOR is used within a batch program, use double percent signs (as in %%*x*) to prevent DOS from removing the percent sign from the command before processing it.

If a global filespec appears in the item set, DOS issues a separate *command* for every individual filespec that matches the global specification.

Command may not be another FOR command.

If *command* references a batch program (without CALL) DOS will chain to that program and never return to the original to process the next item in the item set. CALL eliminates this problem.

Redirection is ignored in *command*.

FOR repeats a specified command for a set of items. You could delete 12 filespecs this way:

```
FOR %%F IN (%1 %2 %3 %4 %5 %6 %7 %8 %9) DO DEL %%F
SHIFT
SHIFT
SHIFT
FOR %%F IN (%7 %8 %9) DO DEL %%F
```

The first FOR command above causes nine DEL commands to be issued. In each one, the F parameter is replaced by the next filespec from the item set, so the nine commands are:

```
DEL %1
DEL %2
```

```
        .
        .
        .
    DEL %9
```

When FOR is used at the command prompt instead of in a batch file, the second word takes the form of %x. You can use whatever character you like for x, as long as you use that same character in the command to be repeated. DOS replaces that character in the command with each item from the item set.

When FOR is used in a batch program, you must double the percent sign—%%x instead of %x—so DOS won't delete the % from the command.

Global Filespecs in the Item Set

When a global filespec appears in the item set, DOS issues a separate command for each matching filename. If 100 filenames match the global filespec, 100 separate commands are generated. Suppose you want to delete all the files in three different directories. You could do it this way:

```
C:\>FOR %X IN (C:\MYAPP\*.* C:\MYAPP\DATA\*.*
C:\MYAPP\PROGRAMS\*.*) DO DEL %X
```

This command could generate hundreds of DEL commands. It might not be the most efficient way to get the job done.

N O T E

This is a good place to remind you that any individual command line can have up to 127 characters.

FOR and FIND

Do you find it frustrating that FIND won't accept a global filespec? (Chapter 4 discusses FIND.) How can you search all the files in the current directory, or all the DOC and TXT files, when you can't use a global filespec in the command? The answer lies in combining FIND with FOR. FOR will turn the global filespecs in the item set into specific filenames and generate a separate FIND command for each one. The following command searches all the files in the current directory for the string "JNF":

```
FOR %%F IN (*.*) DO FIND "JNF" %%F
```

When you issue a command like this, be prepared to press Pause (or Ctrl+S) to page the output. Piping it to MORE won't help; redirection has no effect with the FOR command.

To check only the DOC, TXT, and BAK files, you would use a command such as this one:

```
FOR %%F IN (*.DOC *.TXT *.BAK) DO FIND "JNF" %%F
```

Using FOR with CALL

You can use CALL in a FOR command (even at the command prompt) to apply a whole program to the item set. For example, the following command invokes the batch program named RESTAMP for every file in the current directory:

```
C:\ORANGE>FOR %F IN (*.*) DO CALL RESTAMP %F
```

In each generated RESTAMP command, the individual filename is passed as the first parameter. (RESTAMP should use %1 to access this parameter.)

WARNING

If you reference a batch file without using CALL, the job will be terminated after the first execution of the batch file, defeating the purpose of the FOR command.

Using FOR with IF

Once you're comfortable with FOR, it provides a simple way to test a variety of different cases with the IF command. The following command jumps to GOODINPUT if %1 is Y, y, N, or n:

```
FOR %%X IN (Y y N n) DO IF "%1"=="%%X" GOTO GOODINPUT
```

CHAPTER 8

DIRECTORY MANAGEMENT

Introduction

DOS's directory structure and capabilities have grown since version 1, which handled only diskettes with one directory (the root directory). Now you can have many levels of directories with a handful of commands for creating and managing them. You can even fool older or poorly written programs into working with a directory structure they weren't designed to handle.

Review of Directory Basics

A directory is an index of the files on a drive. Every drive has a root directory, which is installed during formatting, always named \ (backslash). Space in the root directory is limited (the size is determined by the size of the disk and the program that formats it), but you can create subdirectories that are limited only by the size of the drive.

Subdirectories

A subdirectory is assigned a name much like a filename. Subdirectories of the root directory are considered to be the *children* of the root directory, which is considered to be their *parent*. Subdirectories may also have children, which in turn may have children, and so on until you run out of space.

The entire directory structure is called a *tree*, with the root directory at its head. The tree might contain many *branches*; a branch consists of all the descendents of one directory.

Managing Directories

You view the contents of a directory with the DIR command (discussed in Chapter 1). The MD command creates subdirectories, and you can switch to them with the CD command. The RD command removes a subdirectory, but only if it's empty—that is, it contains no files or lower level subdirectories. To remove an entire branch, you must start with the lowest level of subdirectories, because a parent can't be removed until its children are removed.

Paths

A directory is identified not simply by its name but by its *path*, which is a list of all the directories DOS must travel through to reach it. An *absolute path* starts at the root directory. For example, \JNFILES\WP\DOCS indicates that DOS must start at the root directory (\), find JNFILES, then find WP, then find DOCS. A *relative path* starts at the current directory by virtue of not starting with a backslash to indicate the root directory. For example, WP\DOCS indicates that DOS should start at the current directory, find WP, then find DOCS.

Special Directory Names

In paths, commands, and directory listings, a single dot (.) refers to the current directory and a double dot (..) refers to its parent. The first two entries in every subdirectory are for . and .., as that is how DOS keeps track of its directory structure. You can use the .. name in commands and paths to identify the parent of the current directory. For example, the path ..\RAFILES\ART tells DOS to start at the current directory's parent, find RAFILES, then find ART. The following command switches to the current directory's parent:

```
CD ..
```

TIP	You can access a grandparent using ..\.., a great-grandparent using ..\..\.., and so on.

Including Drive Names

If the directory you want is not on the current drive, you can include the drive name in the path. For example, the path D:\WORD tells DOS to start at the root directory of drive D: and look for the WORD subdirectory.

Default Directories

Every drive has a *default directory*—the one DOS will access when a directory is not specified in a command. Immediately after booting, every drive's root directory is its default directory (unless commands in AUTOEXEC.BAT change the defaults). You change the default directory with the CD command, which can affect a drive even though it's not the current drive. For example, the following command makes ESCROW the default directory on drive D: without changing the current drive:

```
C:\>CD D:\ESCROW
```

To see what directory is currently the default on a drive, enter the CD command with the drive name but no path, as in:

```
C:\>CD D:
D:\ESCROW

C:\>
```

If you omit the drive name also, the current drive and directory are displayed.

The default directory on the current drive is the *current directory*—the directory that DOS will access when neither a drive nor a directory is specified. Unless you have changed your prompt, the current drive and directory are displayed in your prompt.

Paths with Filespecs

To access a file that's not in the current directory, prefix its filename with its path—the result is called a *filespec*, which is short for "file specifier." A filespec looks a lot like a path; DOS can tell the difference when it locates the final element; if it's a file, the item is obviously a filespec, but if it's a subdirectory, the item must be a path. There's one situation where DOS might not be able to tell the difference, and it will ask you whether a path or file is intended. That happens with XCOPY and is discussed in Chapter 9.

If a desired file is located in the default directory on another drive, you can specify just the drive and omit the rest of the path. Be sure to leave out the backslash that indicates the root directory. For example, D:FRIENDS accesses the file named FRIENDS in the default directory on drive D:.

> **TIP**
> If you aren't sure what directory is current (which you wouldn't when writing a batch program), use an absolute path with filenames.

Paths with Command Names

Suppose you want to run the program named EXPLODE but it's not in the current directory. One way to access it is to attach the path to the command name so that DOS knows exactly where to find it. If it's in A:\, the command might look like this:

```
C:\>A:\EXPLODE TREEFILE
```

The specified path applies only to the EXPLODE command. DOS will look in the current directory for TREEFILE because no path is specified for it.

The PATH Command

It's inconvenient to have to change drives and directories or to specify a path for programs that you use frequently. The PATH command (see Figure 8.1) sets up a program search path—a list of directories that DOS will search when trying to find a program that has no path specified and isn't in the current directory. The following PATH command identifies three directories to be searched:

```
PATH C:\DOS;C:\WORD;C:\123
```

Figure 8.1.

PATH Command
Reference.

> ### PATH
> Creates, displays, and cancels a program search path. DOS searches the program search path when looking for a program that is not in the current directory and for which a path is not specified.
>
> **Format:**
>
> PATH[=][*path*[;*path*...]]
>
> PATH ;
>
> **Parameters:**
>
> none   Displays the current search path
>
> *path*   Identifies the path name of a directory; if multiple paths are specified, separate them with semicolons
>
> ;   When used by itself, cancels the current path
>
> **Notes:**
>
> If you enter the PATH command with one or more paths, the new path list supersedes the old one.
>
> To speed search times, paths should be listed in order from the most frequently used to the least frequently used.
>
> Use absolute path names, including drives, for each directory to be searched.
>
> DOS does not verify the paths when the PATH command is entered. If it encounters an invalid path name when searching the paths, the following message is displayed:
>
>   Invalid directory
>
> When PATH is entered with no parameters, DOS displays the current PATH in this form:
>
>   PATH=*path*;...

You probably have a PATH command in your AUTOEXEC.BAT file; it sets your search path while booting. Any major application that includes its own installation program probably adds its directory to your PATH command in AUTOEXEC.BAT automatically—maybe even putting itself first in the path. Review and adjust your PATH command periodically to make sure it still reflects the way you work on your computer.

PATH Recommendations

Be sure to use absolute filespecs in the PATH command so that DOS can find the directories no matter what drive or directory is current. For the fastest search times, the directories should be listed in order from the most frequently used to the least frequently used. That way, most searches will be resolved in the first few directories of the search path, and only occasionally will DOS reach the end of the search path.

Also, keep the search path as short as possible so that DOS doesn't have to search a long time to decide that a program file cannot be found.

Invalid Directory Message

If the PATH command references a path that doesn't exist, DOS won't notice or issue a warning until it is actually searching for a program and tries to access the missing directory. Then it displays the following message and goes on to the next directory in the search path:

```
Invalid Directory
```

When you see this message, review your PATH command and fix it if necessary. You might also get this message if your hard drive is starting to develop problems and DOS encounters difficulty finding a directory.

You'll also run into problems if you've included a diskette drive in the path. You'll get an error message if DOS finds the drive empty while traveling the search path.

Managing the Search Path

Enter PATH with a semicolon (as in PATH ;) to cancel the current path. Enter the following command to see your current PATH:

```
C:\>PATH
PATH=C:\DOS;C:\WORD;C:\123

C:\>
```

Notice that the message assumes the form of a legitimate PATH command. You can take advantage of that to preserve and restore the current path in a batch program that changes the path temporarily. In the following example, we save the current path in a file called SETPATH.BAT, then restore it by executing that batch file:

```
REM Save the current path in a batch file:
PATH > C:\SETPATH.BAT
.

.

.
REM Restore the former path:
CALL C:\SETPATH
DEL C:\SETPATH.BAT
```

Recommendations for Directory Structure

There are a number of things you can do to optimize your directory structure for ease of use and fast file access.

Put as few files as possible in the root directory, not only because space is limited but also because the UNFORMAT program might not be able to recover files in the root directory, as explained in Chapter 15. The root directory of the boot drive must contain the system files; CONFIG.SYS and AUTOEXEC.BAT must also reside in this directory, if they are used. You might also have some applications or utilities that require a file or two in the root directory of the boot drive. Other than that, try to keep files out of root directories.

To keep paths short, avoid creating more than three or four levels of subdirectories. The longer the path, the more chance of making a typing error. Also, DOS commands are limited to 127 characters, and you would run out of command space when trying to copy

```
C:\JNFILES\WP\DOCS\DOSBOOK\FIGURES\FIG3-1.PCX
```

to

```
D:\STORAGE\BACKUPS\JNF\DOCS\DOSBOOK\FIGURES\SAVE3-1.PCX
```

The time to access a file on your hard disk will be shortest if all your directories are located near the beginning of the disk (with the ones in the search path being the first ones), with the files you use most often (such as the DOS program files) coming immediately after. This means the read-write heads don't have to move very far to find a directory and then a desired file. But it's difficult to arrange your hard disk that way using only

DOS commands. If you notice your disk access time slowing down as you add more directories and files to your hard disk, you might consider getting one of the third-party utilities that reorganizes a disk for faster access.

| TIP | Another major factor in disk access speed is file fragmentation, which is discussed in Chapter 12. |

TREE

The DIR command is not the best way to view the directory structure on a drive. A graphic display like DOS Shell's is much more informative when you're interested in directory relationships. The TREE command (see Figure 8.2) displays a tree in graphic form, as shown below:

```
A:\>TREE

Directory PATH listing for Volume PCPA SAVE
Volume Serial Number is 171D-78E4
A:.
┌───PCPANEWS
│   └───ARTPCX
├───BROCHURS
│   ├───VITA
│   └───PHOTOS
└───FLYERS


A:\>
```

Figure 8.2.	**TREE**
TREE Command Reference.	Displays a directory tree in graphic format.
	Format:
	TREE [*path*] [*switches*]
	Parameters and Switches:
	none Displays the branch headed by the current directory
	path Displays the branch headed by the specified directory
	/A Uses text (ASCII) characters instead of graphics (extended) characters to depict the tree structure
	/F Lists filenames for each directory

If the tree is so big that it scrolls off the screen, you can pipe it to MORE.

Printing the Tree

The command prompt tree isn't interactive as the Shell's tree is; you can't move around in it, select a directory, expand and collapse branches, and so on. But it does have one big advantage over the Shell's tree—you can print it. Just redirect TREE output to PRN:

```
C:\>TREE > PRN
```

If your monitor or printer can't handle the graphics characters in the TREE display, include the /A (for ASCII) switch to force TREE to use text characters instead. When printing the tree structure for documentation purposes, you might want to include the filenames in the printout, which can be done with the /F switch. The output looks like this:

```
C:\>TREE /F

Directory PATH listing for Volume DRIVE C
Volume Serial Number is 171D-78E4
C:\
    ┌─AMC
    │     AMCDOC.STY
    │     APUP.DOC
    │     CRUP.DOC
    │
    ├─PROPOSAL
    │     MOREWORK.DOC
    │     MOREWORK.BAK
    │
    └─MYBUDDY
    .
    .
    .

C:\>
```

By default, TREE displays the branch headed by the current directory. To see another branch, include the path in the TREE command. To see the entire tree (that is, the branch headed by the root directory), first change to the root directory, or enter this command:

```
TREE \
```

Restructuring a Directory Tree

You might occasionally have to deal with some older software that recognizes drives A and B only, or doesn't accept path names. The SUBST and ASSIGN commands can help you out until you upgrade or replace the out-of-date software.

You also might sometimes find it convenient to create a search path for data files much as the PATH command does for program files. The APPEND command makes a directory available no matter what directory is current.

We've grouped these commands together because they all mask the true directory structure and must be approached with a great deal of caution—they can fool your software into accessing the wrong directory or files. Use them only when necessary and no longer than necessary. APPEND is never necessary, and most experts recommend that you never use it.

NOTE

Another directory-masking command, JOIN, is discussed in Chapter 17.

Many commands that work on drives and directories should not be applied to masked ones. They could end up producing erroneous (or even disastrous) results. Restricted commands are listed in the command reference figures and in your DOS documentation. Any time you use ASSIGN, SUBST, APPEND, or JOIN, keep a red flag at the back of your mind that commands such as FORMAT and BACKUP are dangerous.

ASSIGN

Suppose you're working with an early version of a program called LOCKOUT that expects its program files to be on drive A and its data files to be on drive B. You don't even have a drive B (although drive A can be addressed as drive B). But you have created two RAM drives, D and E, and copied the necessary files to them. The following batch program reassigns the drive names, runs the program, then restores the rightful drive names.

```
@ECHO OFF
ASSIGN A=D B=E
A:
LOCKOUT

REM The following restores the rightful drive names:
ASSIGN
```

ASSIGN solves a problem that has virtually disappeared, and Microsoft plans to phase it out in favor of SUBST, which can do more.

Figure 8.3 shows the format of ASSIGN along with a variety of caveats and warnings.

Figure 8.3.

ASSIGN Command Reference.

ASSIGN

Substitutes one drive name for another.

Format:

ASSIGN [*drive1=drive2* [...]]

ASSIGN /STATUS | /STA | /S

Parameters:

none	Cancels all drive reassignments
drive1	Identifies the drive to be reassigned
drive2	Identifies the drive to use in place of *drive1*
/STATUS	Displays all current drive reassignments; may be abbreviated as /STA or /S

Notes:

Do not reassign a hard drive.

Do not reassign a drive that is in use by a program.

Do not use the following commands on a reassigned drive: BACKUP, DISKCOPY, FORMAT, JOIN, LABEL, RESTORE, SUBST.

If both ASSIGN and APPEND are used during the same DOS session, APPEND must be used first, even if the commands apply to different drives.

SUBST

SUBST (see Figure 8.4) differs from ASSIGN in that it substitutes a drive name for a path instead of another drive name. The preceding LOCKOUT problem could also be solved this way:

```
@ECHO OFF
C:
SUBST A: D:\
SUBST B: E:\
A:
LOCKOUT

REM The following commands restore the rightful drive
names:
C:
SUBST A: /D
SUBST B: /D
```

We start by switching to drive C to make sure that neither drive A nor B is current, because the current drive cannot be redirected via a SUBST command. After the substitutions are made, any reference to drive A actually accesses D:\, and any reference to drive B: actually references E:\. The last two commands in the batch clear the substitutions so that A and B are normal again. It's necessary to switch to another drive before clearing them because you can't clear the substitution for the current drive.

Figure 8.4.

SUBST Command Reference.

SUBST

Substitutes a drive name for a path.

Format:

SUBST [*drive path*]

SUBST *drive* /D

Parameters:

none	Displays all the current substitutions
drive	Identifies the drive name to be substituted for *path*
path	Identifies the directory to be identified by *drive*
/D	Drops the substitution for the specified drive name

Notes:

Do not use the following commands on a substituted drive name: ASSIGN, BACKUP, CHKDSK, DISKCOMP, DISKCOPY, FDISK, FORMAT, LABEL, MIRROR, RECOVER, RESTORE, SYS.

Drive must be within the range of available drives for your system as defined by the LASTDRIVE command in CONFIG.SYS.

You cannot apply a SUBST command to the current drive.

SUBST also solves problems with programs that don't recognize paths. (For example, early versions of WordStar didn't.) Suppose you have a program named PLUS4 that recognizes only drive names, not paths. You want to use

PLUS4 with the C:\TODAY directory. You can assign it a fake drive name, called a *virtual drive name*, as in this batch program:

```
@ECHO OFF
SUBST F: C:\TODAY
PLUS4
C:
SUBST F: /D
```

When PLUS4 asks for a drive name, entering F: causes it to access the C:\PLUS4 directory.

Choosing a Drive Name for SUBST

In the PLUS4 example, we chose a drive name that didn't exist. We could have used a real drive such as A or B, but that would have made the real drive unavailable as long as the substitution was in effect. We didn't use a RAM drive name for the same reason.

Whatever drive name you choose must be available. Although DOS offers the potential of 26 drive names (A through Z), it doesn't automatically make all of them available. By default, DOS permits either five drive names (A through E) or the number of drive names that you actually have drives for (including RAM drives), whichever is larger. You must use the LASTDRIVE command in CONFIG.SYS (see Figure 8.5) to make more drive names available.

Figure 8.5.

LASTDRIVE
CONFIG.SYS
Command
Reference.

LASTDRIVE

Determines the number of drive names that DOS makes available to your system.

Format:

LASTDRIVE=x

Parameter:

x Identifies the highest drive name that your system needs; don't include a colon with this name

Notes:

The default number of drives is 5 (A: through E:) or the number of drives you actually have, including RAM drives, whichever is greater.

Suppose you have a common setup—two diskette drives (A and B) and one hard drive. The names D: and E: are available for SUBST and ASSIGN commands. But what if you have four hard disk drives (C through F)? By default, no virtual drive names are available for SUBST and ASSIGN commands. You can make two virtual drive names available (G and H) by inserting this command in C:\CONFIG.SYS:

```
LASTDRIVE=H
```

N O T E

CONFIG.SYS is processed only during booting. Any time you make a change to CONFIG.SYS, you have to reboot to put it into effect.

DOS maintains a drive name table in conventional memory, with each entry taking nearly 100 bytes. You can conserve valuable memory space by requesting only as many drive names as you actually need. If you make all possible drive names available by inserting LASTDRIVE=Z in CONFIG.SYS when in fact you need only four drive names, you're wasting a couple kilobytes of conventional memory space.

Switching Diskette Drives with SUBST

SUBST can also help you solve a problem that crops up occasionally. Suppose you want to install an application from 3 1/2-inch diskettes, which fit only in your B drive, but the application must be installed from the A drive. You can make the installation work by substituting B:\ for A: before starting up the installation program:

```
C:\>SUBST A: B:\

C:\>A:

A:\>INSTALL
```

After the installation program is finished:

```
A:\>C:

C:\>SUBST A: /D
```

TIP	If you need to boot from a diskette that fits only your B: drive, more drastic measures are called for. You'll have to switch the cables to your A: and B: drives and, for 286 or higher machines, run the SETUP program to redefine the drives. (See your hardware manual or your dealer for instructions on how to access and use SETUP for your machine.)

TRUENAME

When you've masked the true directory structure with SUBST or ASSIGN, you might be confused about what the current directory is or in what directory a file resides. DOS includes a (totally undocumented!) command called TRUENAME (see Figure 8.6) that shows the true path of a directory or file.

Figure 8.6.	
TRUENAME Command Reference.	**TRUENAME** Identifies the true location of a directory or file when the directory structure has been masked with ASSIGN or SUBST **Format:** TRUENAME [*drive* | *path* | *filespec*] **Parameters:** none Displays the true name of the current drive and directory *drive* Displays the true name of the indicated drive *path* Displays the true name of the indicated directory *filespec* Displays the true full filespec of the indicated file **Note:** TRUENAME doesn't check to make sure a file exists. It merely inserts the correct path for the substituted one.

To find out the true name of the current directory, enter TRUENAME with no parameters. The result looks something like this:

```
A:\>TRUENAME
C:\LOCKOUT\

A:\>
```

To find out the true location of a file, enter the filespec as a parameter:

```
A:\>TRUENAME LOCKOUT.DAT
C:\LOCKOUT\LOCKDATA\LOCKOUT.DAT

A:\>
```

This message would be displayed even if the current directory does not contain a file named LOCKOUT.DAT. All TRUENAME does is fill in the correct path; it doesn't check to see if the file exists.

APPEND for Your Thoughts

APPEND looks great on the surface—it makes the files in a specified list of directories available no matter what directory is current. It resembles the PATH command but applies to data files. But the fly lands in the ointment when you're modifying a file from an appended directory, as illustrated in Figure 8.7.

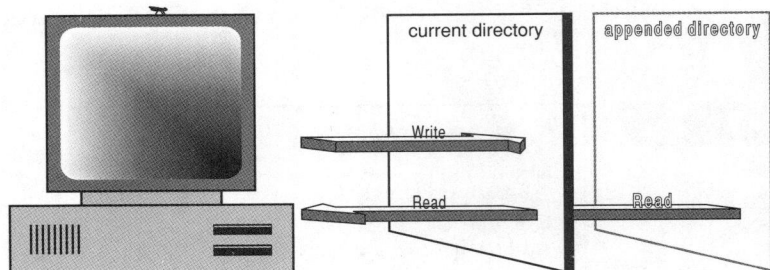

Figure 8.7.

Directory Mixups with APPEND.

The problem occurs when an application updates a file by saving a new copy instead of modifying the existing copy. To the application, the file appears to be in the current directory; only DOS knows about the appended directory. So the application saves the updated version in the current directory, and DOS doesn't know enough to reroute it to the appended directory. The overall result is that the new version is in the wrong directory, and the original version, in the right directory, has not been updated. Keep in mind that an application might not only update the data file you are working on, but support files that are essential to its functions (such as DOSSHELL.INI).

In case you think this is a rare problem, you should understand that *most* applications update files this way—all the major word processors, desktop publishers, graphics developers, text editors, spreadsheet programs, and so on. The most common exceptions are database managers, which tend to update files in place rather than save new copies.

The slight convenience that APPEND offers is not worth the dangers, and we'll assume you don't want to use it. We won't show you its format or discuss its uses.

COPYING FILES

ntroduction

DOS's copying commands have evolved from COPY, which has many limitations, to the much more sophisticated XCOPY and REPLACE. You might also need to use BACKUP to make a copy in certain cases.

Comparing DOS's Copying Commands

Table 9.1 compares advantages and disadvantages of the four copying commands. BACKUP is considered here only for its file copying abilities; it has a lot more advantages (and disadvantages) when used for backing up your hard disk, which is discussed in Chapter 13.

Table 9.1 Comparing DOS's Copy Commands

Command	Advantages	Disadvantages
COPY	Can concatenate files	Slower than XCOPY
	Can change the date/ time stamp on a file	Selects files by name only
	Can copy to and from nondisk devices	Handles only one directory at a time
		Doesn't set exit code
		Terminates when target disk is full
		Won't span a large file over two or more diskettes
		Has no prompt facility
		Will replace files of the same name on a target disk without warning
XCOPY	Faster than COPY	Terminates when target disk is full
	Will copy branch structure (including empty subdirectories, if requested)	Can't concatenate files
		Can't change date/time stamp
	Selects files by name, date, and/or archive attribute	Can't copy to/from nondisk devices
	Will turn off archive attributes of copied files, if requested	Won't span a large file over two or more diskettes
	Sets exit code	Will replace files of the same name on a target disk without warning

Command	Advantages	Disadvantages
	Will prompt you with names of files selected for copying	Sometimes has to ask whether the target is a file or a directory
BACKUP	Will cram files onto target diskette	Will destroy all files in root directory of target disk; might result in data loss
	Will span files over two or more diskettes	Target files are readable only by RESTORE
	Can select files by name, date/time stamp, and/or archive attribute	
	Sets exit code	
REPLACE	Finds and replaces target files having the same names as the source	Won't replace hidden or system files
	Can limit replacements to newer versions only	
	Will identify missing files on target and copy them from source	
	Will prompt you before adding or replacing a file, if requested	
	Will replace read-only files	
	Sets exit code	

COPY and XCOPY are the two commands that do garden-variety copies, and XCOPY is the command of choice for a number of reasons.

➲ When copying multiple files, COPY reads then writes one file at a time, while XCOPY reads as much data as memory will hold, then writes that much data, making this a faster method.

➲ COPY can select files by name only, but XCOPY can also select files by their archive attribute and time/date stamp. This feature lets you use XCOPY to back up your hard disk. (The advantages and disadvantages of XCOPY versus BACKUP as a backup tool are discussed in Chapter 13.)

➲ COPY can select files from one directory only, while XCOPY can copy an entire branch, creating subdirectories under the target directory as needed to duplicate the source branch.

➲ XCOPY will create the target directory if necessary.

➲ Sometimes empty files are created by an application. An empty file has a directory entry, including a name, but contains no data. COPY won't copy an empty file, but XCOPY will. Which is better? That depends on what you want.

➲ Unlike COPY, XCOPY sets exit codes (see Appendix A). This is an advantage when copying files in batch programs, especially if you plan to erase the source files after copying them.

There are a few things COPY can do that XCOPY can't, namely concatenate (combine) files, change the time/date stamp for a file, and copy to and from nondisk devices.

BACKUP's main advantage as a file copier is that it will span files over several diskettes. It keeps copying until the first diskette is completely full, pausing in the middle of a file if need be. Then it requests the next diskette and picks up copying where it left off. With BACKUP, there's no wasted space on the target diskettes. And it's the only way of copying to diskette a file that's larger than the size of a single diskette. The downside is that BACKUP automatically deletes any files in the root directory of a target diskette, and it concatenates all the files it copies into one big file called BACKUP.*nnn*, where *nnn* is the sequential number of the backup disk. You can't access individual files from BACKUP.*nnn* directly; you have to use the RESTORE command, which knows how to pull individual files out of BACKUP.*nnn* and how to reassemble a file that was spanned over more than one diskette.

REPLACE is also used only in special situations. It doesn't do everyday copying, but it will seek out and replace all the hard disk copies of a file with a newer version. This function is used primarily to upgrade software that might appear several times on your hard disk. REPLACE's other function will compare two directories and copy all missing files from the source to the target. This function can replace files that you accidentally deleted.

As you can see, the advantage is with XCOPY unless you need one of the special functions offered by COPY, BACKUP, or REPLACE.

XCOPY vs. DISKCOPY

It's often desirable to copy an entire diskette. The DISKCOPY command makes a track-by-track copy of one diskette to another diskette of exactly the same size. XCOPY can also be used to copy whole diskettes on a file-by-file basis, with these advantages:

➲ You don't need to use the same size source and target disks. You could copy a 1.2M diskette to a 1.44M diskette, for example.

➲ XCOPY doesn't copy the source diskette's formatting, which might not be accurate for the target disk. For example, DISKCOPY copies bad sector markings from the source to the target, blocking out sectors on the target diskette that aren't really bad.

➲ DISKCOPY fails if there are bad sectors on the target diskette; XCOPY doesn't.

➲ With DISKCOPY, if files are fragmented (split into separate parts) on the source, they'll have the same fragmentation on the target. XCOPY actually defragments files as it copies them, as long as the target diskette was empty to start with.

The XCOPY Command

Figure 9.1 shows the format of the XCOPY command (which some people call "ex-copy," some call "cross-copy," and some call "extended copy"). In its simplest form, it copies a file or set of files from one place to another. The following command copies all the DOC files from the current directory to the default directory on drive A, where they will have the same names they have in the current directory:

```
C:\PLAYS>XCOPY *.DOC A:
Reading source file(s)...
VOLUMES.DOC
ENCOUNTR.DOC
        2 File(s) copied
```

XCOPY

Copies files and subdirectories.

Format:

XCOPY *source* [*destination*] [*switches*]

Parameters and Switches:

source	Identifies the files to be copied.
destination	Identifies the location where the copy should be stored. If omitted, the current directory is used.
/A	Copies only files with a positive archive attribute. The archive attribute is not affected by the copy.
/M	Copies only files with a positive archive attribute. The source file's archive attribute is turned off after the copy is completed.
/D:*date*	Copies only files with a date stamp on or after the specified *date*.
/P	Prompts you for permission to copy each selected file.
/S	Copies subdirectories and their files to the target directory.
/E	Copies empty subdirectories. (If this switch is not included, only subdirectories containing at least one source file are copied.) This switch can only be used with /S.
/V	Verifies each copy.
/W	Displays the following message and waits for user's response:
	Press any key to begin copying file(s)

Notes:

Source can be a drive name, path, global filespec, or individual filespec.

Destination can be a drive name or path. If *source* is an individual filespec, *destination* can be an individual filespec, in which case the new copy receives the specified name.

A file can be copied to the same directory only if both the *source* and *destination* are individual filespecs, so that the copy receives a new name.

If *destination* identifies a directory that doesn't exist, XCOPY will create the directory and copy the *source* files to it.

Hidden and system files will not be copied, but empty files will.

All copies have their archive attributes set.

XCOPY sets an exit code (see Appendix A).

/A and /M are mutually exclusive.

Copying Branches

One of XCOPY's strengths is copying complete branches. Suppose you want to copy a branch from drive C to drive D. You don't even have to create the target directory first; XCOPY will do it for you. After turning off all hidden and system attributes (because XCOPY won't copy hidden or system files), use a command such as:

```
XCOPY C:\JNFSET D:\JNFSET /S /E
```

If the D:\JNFSET directory does not exist, XCOPY starts by asking this question:

```
Does D:\JNFSET specify a file name
or directory name on the target
(F = file, D = directory)?
```

In this case, you need to answer D for directory. XCOPY creates the directory and copies all files *and subdirectories* to D:\JNFSET so that it ends up being a duplicate of the JNFSET branch on the C drive.

TIP	You can avoid the "file or directory" question by putting a backslash after the destination path so that it can't be mistaken for a filename:

```
XCOPY C:\JNFSET D:\JNFSET\ /S /E
```

If D:\JNFSET already exists, XCOPY uses the existing branch, creating subdirectories only if they're missing from the target branch.

If you include a filespec with XCOPY and /S, only the specified files are copied to the destination. Without /E, directories that won't receive any files or subdirectories aren't created. With /E, all target subdirectories are created, whether they are empty or not.

Copying a File to the Same Directory

XCOPY can copy a single file to the same directory as long as you assign it a new name. In this case, XCOPY always asks the "file or directory" question, to which you answer F for file. (If you answer D, XCOPY creates a new directory and copies the file to the new directory using its old filename.)

Creating New Directories with XCOPY

One way to create a new directory is to copy some files to it with XCOPY. If the specified directory doesn't exist, XCOPY creates it.

Avoiding Disk Full Termination

One disadvantage that both COPY and XCOPY share is the irksome habit of terminating themselves when the target disk is full. Suppose you have indicated that all *.DOC files should be copied to drive A, and COPY or XCOPY copies about half of them before the disk is full. Then it quits, returning you to the DOS prompt. Now what do you do? If you insert another disk in the A drive and reenter the same COPY or XCOPY command, the same files will be selected and copied a second time because the program has no way of knowing that some of the files are not wanted. Your only recourse is to figure out which files have not yet been copied and copy them one by one.

There are several ways to avoid this problem. One is to use DOS Shell, which lets you continue a copy operation after changing the target diskette. Another solution uses BACKUP, but that probably has more problems than it's worth. Another solution uses the archive attributes with XCOPY. The drawback to this solution is that it alters the archive attributes of the source files, which can affect your backup system later on.

The XCOPY procedure works like this:

1. Turn on the archive attribute of every file you want to copy. (Also, turn off hidden and system attributes if you want to copy those files.)

2. Start XCOPY for those files using the /M switch to turn off the archive attribute of each successfully copied file.

3. When the current disk is full, insert a new disk and repeat step 2. The files that have already been copied will not be recopied because their archive attributes are now off.

A batch file for this procedure might look something like the one below. %1 is the filespec of the files to be copied. This procedure prints out the original attributes of the source files so they can be restored later if necessary.

```
@ECHO OFF
REM Record the current attributes in case we want to
REM restore them when the job is done.
ECHO Current attributes for the %1 files: > PRN
ECHO. > PRN
ATTRIB %1 /S > PRN
```

```
REM Turn on the archive attributes for all %1 files.
REM Also, turn off their hidden and system attributes.
ATTRIB %1 /S +A -H -S

:COPYLOOP
REM Copy all the %1 files that have positive archive
REM attributes. Turn off attributes as you copy:
ECHO Insert the next target diskette in drive A:
PAUSE
XCOPY %1 A: /S /M

REM Repeat loop if XCOPY terminated unsuccessfully
REM for any reason.
IF ERRORLEVEL 1 GOTO COPYLOOP

:ENDING
ECHO **************************************************
ECHO *                                                *
ECHO *  The archive, hidden, and system attributes    *
ECHO *  have been removed from the source files.       *
ECHO *  Check the printout and restore attributes as   *
ECHO *  needed.                                        *
ECHO *                                                *
ECHO **************************************************
```

You could make this job more useful by adding these features:

➲ Accept the target drive name or path as %2.

➲ Accept Y or N as %3 to indicate whether or not hidden and system files should be copied.

Pruning and Grafting

The tree surgeon's terms, *pruning and grafting*, are used in PCs to describe the movement of a directory or branch from one parent to another. If you don't have a third-party utility to prune and graft, you can do it using XCOPY, although the process is time-consuming. In the following list of steps, *path1* identifies the directory or branch to be moved and *path2* identifies the new parent.

1. Document hidden, system, and read-only attributes so they can be restored later if necessary:

   `ATTRIB path1\*.* /S > PRN:`

2. Remove these attributes:

   `ATTRIB path1\*.* /S -H -S -R`

3. Copy the entire branch to the new parent directory (which XCOPY will create if it doesn't already exist):

   `XCOPY path1 path2 /S /E /V`

4. After making sure the branch was copied correctly, remove each directory in the old branch following the steps below. Start with the lowest directories in the branch and work upwards:

   a. Delete all the files in a directory:

   `ECHO Y ¦ DEL path\*.*`

   b. Remove the directory:

   `RD path`

5. Using the printout from step 1, restore the hidden, system, and read-only attributes to each file as necessary:

   `ATTRIB filespec attribute(s)`

It's possible to make a batch file out of steps 1 through 3, but the last two steps can't be done in a batch program because you won't know the correct paths, filespecs, or attributes in advance. You could create a batch program to do a simple prune and graft, where the directory has no children and no hidden, system, or read-only files. But more complex jobs must be done manually.

Renaming Directories

The good news is: You *can* rename directories from the command prompt. The bad news is: The process is exactly the same as pruning and grafting. Copy the existing branch to a directory with the new name and remove the old branch. (You can do this much more easily using DOS Shell or a third-party utility.)

Verification

Mistakes can occur during a copy operation as a result of hardware failure, disk media failure, or power fluctuations. Mistakes are rare as long as your drive is healthy, but they do happen sometimes. By default, DOS does not verify copies. The /V switch forces each copy to be verified, which slows down the copy process, of course. You should be aware that this is not a 100-percent verification. It will catch most, but not all, errors. Verification methods, including a foolproof one, are discussed in Chapter 14.

Clobbering Files with XCOPY and COPY

Both COPY and XCOPY have one problem in common. They both will clobber an existing file without warning. For example, if you copy A:\MEMBERS.DB to C:\SFGROUP\MEMBERS.DB, but SFGROUP already contains a file named MEMBERS.DB, both COPY and XCOPY will replace the existing file with the copy, and you will not see any message that the replacement was made. You will not be able to rescue the clobbered file with DOS 5's UNDELETE, either.

Recovering a Clobbered File

If you do accidentally clobber a file during a copy, all is not necessarily lost. Both COPY and XCOPY replace the file entry in the directory (which is why DOS 5's UNDELETE can't find it) and mark the old file's space for reuse, but they don't actually overlay the data on the disk. A third-party recovery program that will access unallocated disk space, such as the Norton Utilities' UnErase, can recover the data.

However, you must recover the clobbered data immediately, as it's highly vulnerable sitting in reusable disk space. The next data you add to the disk might go into that space. In fact, if you simply start up an application such as a word processor, it might open a temporary file for itself during its startup routine and use the space you want to rescue. So once you realize that you've clobbered a file and that you need to recover it, *don't do anything* until you have recovered it.

But go ahead and try recovering even if you have added data to the disk. You might get lucky and be able to rescue all or at least part of the data.

Difficulties in Avoiding Clobbering

You might think you can write a batch program using IF EXIST to identify
an existing file with the same name in the destination directory, but a total
solution is not really possible because of the variety of ways that the source
and destination can be expressed in an XCOPY command. The following
routine works if the source (%1) is a single or global filespec referring
only to the current directory (with no path specified); the target (%2) is
the path of another directory; and no XCOPY switches (such as /S) are
desired.

```
REM Warn user about files that won't be copied:
FOR %%F IN (%1) DO IF EXIST %2\%%F ECHO %%F won't be
copied because a target version already exists

REM Copy files that won't clobber existing copies:
FOR %%F IN (%1) DO IF NOT EXIST %2\%%F XCOPY %%F %2
```

Burying the XCOPY command in the FOR command slows the copy procedure tremendously, but it's necessary to check only one file at a time with
IF [NOT] EXIST or the results could be wrong.

You could create a batch program using FOR, IF, and CALL that gives the
user the option of copying a file when a target version exists, but that
makes a complex job out of a function that's already available with the
REPLACE command, as you'll see at the end of this chapter.

Moving Files

Moving files involves copying them, then deleting the source files. You can
write a macro or batch program to do this easily as long as you want to assume that the copies were successfully completed. Most of the time, they
will be, but as you know, there is a chance that they might not be.

The following batch program (a macro can't do the same thing) uses IF
ERRORLEVEL to make sure all copies were successfully completed before
deleting the source files.

```
@ECHO OFF
XCOPY %1 %2
```

```
IF ERRORLEVEL 1 GOTO NOMOVE
IF "%2"=="" GOTO NOMOVE
DEL %1
GOTO ENDING

:NOMOVE
ECHO An error occurred during the copy
ECHO so the source files were not deleted.

:ENDING
```

The second IF command makes sure that a destination has been specified to prevent a special XCOPY error. If the source is in the current directory and no destination is specified, XCOPY terminates itself with the message "File cannot be copied onto itself" and, unfortunately, a 0 exit code. We don't want the source files to be deleted in this case, but the exit code won't prevent it. So we have to weed this case out separately. Unfortunately, it also weeds out commands where the source is not the current directory and it is safe to omit the destination directory, but we have no way to identify that situation. Better safe than sorry.

This program doesn't allow for any switches in the original command. You could revise the program to allow switches such as /A or /D, but you would have to weed out inappropriate switches such as /P (since all source files would be deleted whether they were copied or not) and /S (since DEL can access only one directory at a time).

The COPY Command

The COPY command has some features you can't find anywhere else in DOS:

⊃ It can *concatenate* files; that is, it combines two or more files into one.

⊃ It can update the time/date stamp on a file.

⊃ It can copy to and from devices.

Since XCOPY is more useful for day-to-day copies, we'll cover only these unique COPY features. Figure 9.2 shows the format of COPY for concatenating files only.

Figure 9.2.

COPY (for
Concatenation)
Command
Reference.

COPY (for concatenation)

Combines two or more files into one.

Format:

COPY [*switches*] *source* [+...] [*destination*] [*switches*]

Parameters and Switches:

source   Identifies the file(s) to be copied.

destination   Identifies the new file to be created.

/A   Uses ASCII mode for the copy.

/B   Uses binary mode for the copy.

Notes:

For the full COPY format, see your DOS reference manual.

For concatenation to occur, *source* must either be a global filespec or multiple filespecs connected by plus signs.

If *source* is a global filespec, all files matching the filespec are concatenated.

If *destination* is omitted, files are concatenated into the first source file that DOS locates.

The current time and date is assigned to the destination file, which also has a positive archive attribute.

The following special format updates the time/date stamp of an individual file:

COPY [/B] *filespec*+,, [*destination*]

The following special format concatenates files with identical filenames but different extensions:

COPY [*switches*] *.ex1* + *.ex2* [+...] [*.ex3*] [*switches*]

The /A or /B switch affects the filespec preceding it and all subsequent filespecs until it reaches a filespec that is followed by another /A or /B switch.

When /A is applied to a source file, the file is read up to, but not including, the first EOF mark (hex 1A). When /A is applied to a destination file, an EOF mark is added to the end of the file. When concatenating, COPY assumes the /A switch for both source and destination files by default.

When /B is applied to a source file, the file's size is determined by its directory entry and any embedded EOF marks are ignored. When /B is applied to a destination file, no EOF mark is added to it.

Concatenating Files

Suppose you want to combine three ASCII files named PART1, PART2, and PART3 into a new file named REPORT. The following command will do it:

```
C:\DOCS>COPY PART1 + PART2 + PART3 REPORT
PART1
PART2
PART3
     1 File(s) copied

C:\DOCS>
```

The message says "1 File(s) copied" because only one file was created (or replaced). The following command might or might not have the same effect:

```
C:\DOCS>COPY PART? REPORT
```

Since a global source filespec is used with a single target filespec, the plus sign is not necessary. COPY will concatenate all matching source files into the one target file. This might include more files than you intended. Furthermore, the order of the files will be as they appear in the directory. If PART2 appears first, it will be the first file copied to REPORT.

> **N O T E**
>
> When creating a new file, DOS places it in the first available directory entry, which might be the former entry of a deleted file. For this reason, the order of entries in a busy directory seems arbitrary. Even if you write PART1 first, PART2 next, and PART3 last, these three files could appear in any order in the directory.

Appending Files

Sometimes you want to concatenate files by appending them to an existing file. For example, suppose you want to append PART2 and PART3 to PART1 instead of creating a new file. All you have to do is omit the target filespec from the command, as in:

```
COPY PART1 + PART2 + PART3
```

> **N O T E**
>
> In this case, if COPY can't find PART1, it will concatenate PART3 into PART2 (if PART2 exists). When a target file is not specifically identified, COPY uses the first file from the left end of the command that it finds.

The following command is legitimate but might not have the same result, because a different set of files might be identified, and they might appear in a different order. The target file will be the first file in the directory that matches the PART? filespec:

```
C:\DOCS>COPY PART?
```

A variation on this command controls the target file by specifically identifying it:

```
C:\DOCS>COPY PART? PART1
```

This command could create a strange problem. Since PART1 is specified as the target file, COPY opens it and begins appending each source file to it. After the first file is appended, PART1 is irrevocably changed. If COPY then finds the PART1 entry in the directory and realizes that it matches the filespec for a source file, it also realizes that it cannot append PART1 to itself. The following message is displayed:

```
Content of destination lost before copy
```

This message looks devastating, but in fact it's perfectly normal. It means that, since the target file has already been changed, it cannot now be used as a source file. In fact, things are progressing just as they should. You can always ignore this message.

The Effect of Concatenation on Certain File Types

If PART1, PART2, and PART3 are ASCII (unformatted) text files, they'll concatenate with no problems. Other types of files are not so easy.

Application Data Files

Suppose PART1, PART2, and PART3 were created by a word processor and stored in its native format. They probably have header and trailer information surrounding the text itself. When you concatenate them, all three sets of headers and trailers are included in the file, creating a hybrid that can no longer be processed by the original word processor. The same problem exists with files created by most of today's applications: desktop publishers, spreadsheets, databases, graphics developers, and so on.

If you want to concatenate such files to be usable, don't use COPY; concatenate the files from within the application so that it can create (and remove) headers and trailers as appropriate.

Binary Files

As with application data files, you do not produce a usable product by concatenating binary files such as executable program modules. Concatenating two program modules not only will produce an invalid program module, it might create a monster that, if executed, will run amok inside your system. Here again, if you want to combine files, use the proper tools. For example, use a linkage editor to combine two executable program modules.

Updating Time/Date Stamps

When a file is copied by any of the DOS copying commands, the file's time/date stamp is unchanged, the theory being that the time and date identify the file's version. But when you concatenate files, the current time and date are assigned to the newly created file because it is a new version.

You can trick DOS into assigning the current time and date to a file by pretending to concatenate it with a command in this format:

```
COPY source-filespec+,, [destination]
```

Be sure to use a single source filespec, because a global one would cause a real concatenation to take place. So if you want to update the time/date stamp on all your *.TXT files, do them one at a time; you can use the FOR command to get it all done with one command. The two commas after the plus force DOS to stop concatenating. If the destination is included, the copy is made and only the target file has the new time/date stamp. If there is no destination, the source file receives the new time/date stamp.

The following batch program changes the time/date stamp to any value you wish on a group of files, where %1 is the new time, %2 is the new date, and %3 through %9 are optional filespecs, which can be global. (The /B in the COPY command is explained shortly.)

```
@ECHO OFF
TIME %1 > NUL
DATE %2 > NUL
FOR %%F IN (%3 %4 %5 %6 %7 %8 %9) DO COPY /B %%F+,,
ECHO The system time and date have been changed.
ECHO Please reset the correct time:
TIME
ECHO Please reset the correct date:
DATE
```

Matched Concatenations

COPY permits a special technique where it will concatenate files with matching filenames but different extensions. An example should make this clear:

```
COPY *.TXT + *.ADD *.NEW
```

This command causes COPY to concatenate FORM.TXT with FORM.ADD to create FORM.NEW, TEACH.TXT with TEACH.ADD to create TEACH.NEW, and so on. If the directory contains TEACH.ADD but not TEACH.TXT or vice versa, an error message is displayed and TEACH.NEW is not created.

Here are some variations on matched concatenations:

➲ You can specify more than two source files:

```
COPY *.1 + *.2 + *.3 + *.4  *.ALL
```

➲ You can omit the target filespec to concatenate into the first filespec:

```
COPY *.TXT + *.ADD
```

Copying to and from Devices

COPY lets you copy files to and from devices, using the device names shown in Table 4.2. A quick-and-dirty way to print a file without using DOS's PRINT (which loads a TSR into memory and formats the printout) is:

```
COPY filespec PRN
```

You can copy files to and from serial ports, but the result is unlikely to be satisfactory without a communications program acting as an intermediary.

N O T E

The sidebar on page 13 in Chapter 4 shows how to create a file by copying from CON.

You can concatenate files while copying to a device. The following command concatenates all .TXT files and prints the results:

```
COPY *.TXT PRN
```

The ABCs of /A and /B

The /A and /B switches can be important in copying and concatenating files, but in order to use them properly, you have to understand a bit about DOS file storage.

Clusters and Slack

DOS stores files in disk storage blocks called *clusters* or *allocation units*. Every disk has a fixed cluster size, which depends on the size of the disk and the program that formatted it. For example, a small-capacity (360K) floppy disk has 512-byte clusters, but a large-capacity disk, such as a 40M hard disk, might have 2048-byte clusters (or larger). The cluster size is set during formatting.

DOS allocates disk space to files in whole clusters. If a file doesn't use a complete cluster, the leftover space at the end of the cluster is called *slack*. On a disk with 2048-byte clusters, a one-byte file will occupy one whole cluster with 2047 bytes of slack. A 15K file will occupy eight clusters with 1K of slack at the end of the last cluster. Slack space is wasted space; it cannot be allocated to any other file. It might contain leftover data from a previous file (or files) that occupied more of the cluster.

Avoiding Slack when Accessing Files

When DOS reads a file for copying, printing, concatenation, or some other operation, it wants to read only the valid file data and ignore the slack. DOS has two methods of identifying the end of legitimate data in a cluster:

➲ The ASCII method depends on an end-of-file (EOF) mark—which is ^Z or hex 1A—appearing as the last character in the file. When using the ASCII method, DOS scans the data it reads and stops when it encounters hex 1A. (If a file has no EOF mark, DOS uses the file's size to decide when to stop reading.)

⊃ The binary method uses the file's size as recorded in its directory entry. If the directory entry says that the file is 3267 bytes, DOS will read exactly 3267 bytes from the disk. Any hex 1A characters in the data are read just like other data.

The problem with the ASCII method is that it works only with files that do not contain inadvertent EOF marks as part of their data, as might happen with binary files, worksheets, graphics files, and other application files. The only files that work reliably with the ASCII method are *true ASCII files*—files containing only ASCII character data and no formatting information.

DOS also has an ASCII and binary method of writing files. With the ASCII method, DOS adds the EOF mark to the end of the file. With the binary method, it doesn't.

Some DOS utilities (especially the older and more elementary ones) use the ASCII method while others use the binary method. Utilities that are designed to work with ASCII format files, such as TYPE and PRINT, use the ASCII method. Utilities that should work with any type of file, such as XCOPY and BACKUP, use the binary method.

COPY Methods

COPY sometimes uses one method and sometimes the other. It uses the binary method for most copy processes. But for processes that make sense only with ASCII files, such as concatenation and copying to CON or PRN, it uses the ASCII method. You can force it to use the other method with the /A and /B switches.

You can force COPY to use the ASCII method to read a source file by including the /A switch before or after the source filespec. You can force COPY to use the ASCII method of writing a file, which adds an EOF mark to the end of the copy, by including the /A switch after the target filespec. The EOF mark is never essential to DOS programs, but you might have some other software that requires it. (Most modern programs don't.)

You can force COPY to use the binary method to read a source file by including the /B switch before or after the source filespec. If you have a reason to concatenate binary files, you would have to use the /B switch to force COPY to read the source files in binary mode, since COPY concatenates in ASCII mode by default.

You can force COPY to write a file in binary mode, which omits the EOF mark, by placing a /B after the target filespec. You'll need this switch when concatenating binary files if you don't want DOS to add an EOF mark to the end of the new file.

Date Stamping Non-ASCII Files

You are most likely to need the /B switch when updating the time/date stamp on a non-ASCII file. If you don't use /B, the file might be truncated by the pseudo-concatenation; it will also receive an EOF mark. Specify a /B before the filespec to make sure the whole file is copied with the new time/date, but that no EOF mark is added. The following example updates the time/date stamp on the file named DEFRAG.COM:

```
COPY /B DEFRAG.COM+,,
```

Copying Files to a Device

Be sure to use /B when copying a non-ASCII file to a device, as COPY uses ASCII mode with many devices and any non-ASCII values in the file might not be handled correctly.

BACKUP and RESTORE as Copying Tools

BACKUP and RESTORE are fully discussed in Chapter 13. Here we show you how to use BACKUP and RESTORE to copy a large file to diskettes and back to a hard disk again.

WARNING

Use blank (or reusable) diskettes with BACKUP, which destroys any files in the root directory of the target diskette.

Start the backup with a command in this format:

```
BACKUP source-filespec target-drive
```

BACKUP will ask for diskettes as needed. Insert blank (or reusable) diskettes as requested. To keep the diskettes in order, label them as #1, #2,...#n as you remove them from the drive.

To copy the backed up file to another hard drive from the diskettes, you must first establish the same path on that drive. Then insert diskette #1 in drive A and enter a command in this format:

```
RESTORE drive filespec
```

RESTORE will request each diskette by number.

The backup files on the diskette are read-only. Use the following batch program to delete them:

```
@ECHO OFF
ATTRIB drive\*.* -R
ECHO Y ¦ DEL drive\*.*
```

The REPLACE Command

REPLACE has two special functions, both based on its ability to select files by comparing the contents of the source and target directories:

⊃ It will replace files that are present in the source directory but are missing in the target directory (*replace* is used here in the sense of restoring something that has been lost).

⊃ It will replace files that exist in both the source and target directories (*replace* here has the sense of substituting one item for another).

Figure 9.3 shows the format of the REPLACE command.

Replacing Missing Files

Suppose you deleted several files from C:\PROPS and now you have changed your mind. It's too late to undelete them, but you have backup copies on a floppy disk. (If the backups were made with BACKUP, this won't work.) If the files fit a generic filespec, you could restore them with an XCOPY command such as:

```
XCOPY A:*.DOC C:\PROPS
```

Figure 9.3.

REPLACE Command Reference.

REPLACE

Replaces destination files with source files of the same name or copies source files that are missing in the destination directory.

Format:

REPLACE *source* [*destination*] [*switches*]

Parameters and Switches:

source	Identifies the files to be copied to the destination. A filespec must be included.
destination	Identifies the directory to receive the copies. Must not include a filespec. If omitted, the current directory is assumed.
/A	Adds missing files to the destination directory. Do not use with /S or /U.
/P	Prompts for confirmation before replacing a file.
/R	Permits replacement of read-only files.
/S	Replaces matching files in destination subdirectories as well. Do not use with /A.
/W	Displays message and waits for user's response before beginning replacement.
/U	Examines time/date stamps of matching source and destination files and replaces (updates) only destination files that are older than the source files. Do not use with /A.

Note:

REPLACE terminates automatically if it is unable to replace a file because of the read-only attribute. Use the /R switch to avoid this type of termination.

Notice that this command could replace files that you didn't want. If a generic filespec or two won't select the desired files, then REPLACE might be the easiest way to restore them. The following command will select all files that exist on A: but do not exist on C:\PROPS:

```
REPLACE A: C:\PROPS /A /P
```

Because we used the /P switch, REPLACE will display each filespec and let us decide whether or not to copy it. This helps us avoid unwanted replacements.

Replacing Existing Files

Suppose you have installed an application several places on your hard disk. Now you receive an update. The following command seeks out and replaces all the files on the hard disk that have the same name as the files on the diskette in drive A:

```
REPLACE A: C:\ /R /S
```

REPLACE's /U (update) switch causes a file to be replaced only if its time/date stamp indicates that it is an older version than the matching source file. This comes in handy mostly with certain backup methods and is discussed in Chapter 13.

Using REPLACE with /P to Avoid Clobbering Existing Files

In our continuing effort to create a batch copy program that won't clobber existing files, let's see if REPLACE with the /P switch will do the trick. The following batch file uses REPLACE twice, first to replace existing files with permission, then to add missing files (no permission needed). The overall effect is to copy all files identified by %1 to the destination. (To avoid early termination of the first command, even read-only files are replaced in the destination.)

```
@ECHO OFF
REPLACE %1 %2 /P /R
REPLACE %1 %2 /A
```

This batch program can handle only one subdirectory at a time, so it lacks a lot of XCOPY's punch, and it's also extremely slow when compared to XCOPY, but it is a safe way to copy files from one directory to another.

10

DOS AND THE ENVIRONMENT

Introduction

DOS sets aside a memory buffer called the *environment* that it uses for storage of crucial variables such as the path and the prompt. Other programs might also store and access variables in the DOS environment. For example, Microsoft Windows uses the TEMP variable to locate its temporary files.

You can also create environment variables and access them in batch programs. In fact, you might find occasion to start up a second command interpreter just to obtain a new environment for a batch program.

Environment Variables

An environment variable has a name and a value. In the following example, TEMP is the variable name and C:\DOS is its value:

```
TEMP=C:\DOS
```

The name and value can be any length as long as they don't exceed the amount of space left in the environment. They can contain any characters, including spaces. DOS always translates and stores the name in uppercase letters, but the value will be stored exactly as entered.

Displaying Environment Variables

Figure 10.1 shows the SET command, which controls environment variables. SET with no parameters displays the full list of variables, as in:

```
C:\>SET
COMSPEC=C:\DOS\COMMAND.COM
PATH=C:\DOS;D:\NU;C:\WINDOWS;C:\WORD;C:\
PROMPT=$P$G
TEMP=C:\WINDOWS\TEMP
NU=D:\NU
```

Figure 10.1.

SET Command Reference.

SET

Creates, modifies, and deletes environment variables.

Format:

SET [*name*=[*value*]]

Parameters:

none   Displays all the environment variables

name   Identifies the variable

value   Assigns a value to the variable; if omitted, the variable is removed from the environment

There is no DOS command to display the value of a specific variable, but you can use the following batch program, where %1 is the name (or the value) of the variable you want:

```
@ECHO OFF
SET ¦ FIND "%1"
```

DOS's Environment Variables

DOS has a number of environment variables that it uses. Some of them are set automatically by DOS, while others are used by DOS if you set them.

PATH

The PATH variable is set when you enter a PATH command and shows your current search path. DOS accesses this variable whenever it must search for a program file. When there is no PATH variable in the environment, there is no search path.

PROMPT

The PROMPT variable is set when you enter a PROMPT command and shows the current format of the command prompt. DOS accesses this variable every time it displays the command prompt. If there is no PROMPT variable, DOS displays the default command prompt, which is just the current drive name (not the current directory) followed by a right angle bracket. The PROMPT command and the meaning of the symbols it uses are discussed in Chapter 16.

TEMP

The TEMP variable, which you must create with a SET command, tells DOS where to store temporary files (such as pipe files). If there is no TEMP variable, DOS stores temporary files in the current directory. Microsoft WINDOWS also uses the TEMP variable to locate its temporary files.

DIRCMD

The DIRCMD variable, which you must create with a SET command, establishes default parameters for the DIR command. DOS accesses DIRCMD whenever a DIR command is entered. When there is no DIRCMD variable, DOS uses the default DIR parameters and switches. DIR and DIRCMD are discussed in Chapter 1.

COMSPEC

The COMSPEC variable is automatically set by DOS to show the location of the command interpreter. DOS accesses this variable whenever it needs to reload the memory-resident portion of the command interpreter after some other program has overwritten it. You'll see how DOS decides on the value for COMSPEC later in this chapter.

Creating an Environment Variable

The following command creates an environment variable named TEMP and sets its value to C:\DOS:

```
C:\>SET TEMP=C:\DOS
```

Since both the name and the value can have spaces, make sure there is no space either before or after the equal sign unless you want that space included in the name or the value. DOS sees "TEMP" and "TEMP " (with a trailing space) as two different variables. When looking for the place to store its temporary files, it accesses "TEMP" but not "TEMP ."

The preceding SET command receives no confirmation messages unless the environment space is exceeded, in which case the following message is displayed:

```
Out of environment space
```

Modifying and Deleting Environment Variables

To change a variable's value, simply enter a SET command with the same name and the new value. To delete an environment variable, enter a SET command with the same name and nothing after the equal sign, as in:

```
SET TEMP=
```

NOTE

Rebooting deletes all environment variables except the ones DOS sets and those set in AUTOEXEC.BAT.

Accessing Environmental Variables

You can access environment variables from batch programs, much the same as you use replaceable parameters. Use a parameter in this format:

```
%variable-name%
```

For example, to switch to the directory defined as TEMP from within a batch program, use this command:

```
CD %TEMP%
```

NOTE

You cannot access environment variables from the command prompt or from DOSKEY macros.

Adding to the Path

The following command uses the PATH variable to add the C:\PROGS directory to the end of the current search path:

```
PATH=%PATH%;C:\PROGS
```

The %PATH% expression causes the current value of the PATH variable (that is, the current search path) to be filled into the command. Then

;C:\PROGS is appended to it. You could just as easily insert C:PROGS at the front of the search path.

Preserving and Restoring Environment Variables

If a batch program needs to reset the current prompt, you can preserve and restore the current one with commands like this:

```
REM Save the current prompt:
SET SAVEPROMPT=%PROMPT%

REM Make sure we didn't run out of environment space
IF %SAVEPROMPT%=%PROMPT% GOTO CONTINUE
.
. (commands to deal with inadequate environment space)
.
:CONTINUE
.
. (the remainder of the program)
.
REM Restore the previous prompt:
SET PROMPT=%SAVEPROMPT%

REM Remove unneeded variable:
SET SAVEPROMPT=
```

The same technique can be used to preserve and restore any environment variable.

Environment Variables vs. Replaceable Parameters

There are several advantages to using an environment variable instead of a replaceable parameter:

➲ You can use as many variables as you want (up to the size limit of the environment).

➲ An environment variable is more permanent than a replaceable parameter. It outlasts the batch job and can be accessed by other batch jobs.

Controlling the Command Interpreter and the Environment

The environment is established when the command interpreter is loaded during booting. To control the command interpreter and/or environment size, you must include a SHELL command (see Figure 10.2) in CONFIG.SYS.

SHELL

Loads a command interpreter.

Format:

SHELL=*filespec* [*parameters and switches*]

Parameters and switches depend on which command interpreter is indicated. The following are available for COMMAND.COM:

SHELL=[*path*]COMMAND.COM [*path*] [*device*] [/E:*nnnn*] [/P] [/MSG]

Parameters:

filespec	Identifies the command interpreter.
path	Identifies the location of the command interpreter if not in the root directory of the boot drive.
device	Identifies a device to be used for standard input and output; default is CON.
/E:*nnnn*	Identifies the size of the environment in bytes, from 160 to 32768; the default is 256.
/P	Establishes the command interpreter as the primary command interpreter.
/MSG	Requests that error messages normally stored on disk should be loaded into memory; use when the command interpreter is located on diskette.

When no SHELL command appears in CONFIG.SYS, DOS loads COMMAND.COM from the root directory of the boot drive. (If it's not there, the message "Bad or missing command interpreter" appears and booting is halted.) The default environment size is 256 bytes. You will quickly run out of environment space if you create and use your own environment variables in addition to those that DOS uses.

Use SHELL in any of these cases:

➲ You want to use a command interpreter other than DOS's COMMAND.COM.

➲ The command interpreter (including COMMAND.COM) is not located in the root directory of the boot drive.

➲ You want to use a nondefault environment size.

Environment Size

For a larger environment, you must include a SHELL statement in
CONFIG.SYS with the /E switch included in it. To use the default command interpreter and create a 1K environment size, use this command:

```
SHELL=COMMAND.COM /E:1024 /P
```

W A R N I N G

The environment is located in conventional memory, which is valuable space, so don't request more environment space than you need.

W A R N I N G

If you omit the /P switch and subsequently enter an EXIT command,
the system will hang up. If you include /P, EXIT is ignored.

Command Interpreter in Another Location

If the command interpreter is not in the root directory of the boot drive,
you must specify its location twice:

➲ You must include its path with the first parameter
(COMMAND.COM) so that DOS knows where to find the command
interpreter during booting.

➲ You must include the path again (without the filespec) as the second
parameter so that DOS knows where to find the command interpreter
when it needs to reload the transient part of it. This parameter causes
DOS to set the COMSPEC variable in the environment.

To use C:\DOS\COMMAND.COM as the command interpreter with the
default environment size, you would put the following command in
CONFIG.SYS:

```
SHELL=C:\DOS\COMMAND.COM C:\DOS /P
```

The second parameter causes DOS to create the following environment variable:

```
COMSPEC=C:\DOS
```

Using a Third-Party Command Interpreter

It's possible to use a command interpreter other than COMMAND.COM. For example, the Norton Utilities includes NDOS, with many more features than COMMAND.COM. The SHELL statement is used to establish an alternative command interpreter such as NDOS, in which case COMMAND.COM is not loaded.

Loading a Secondary Command Interpreter

Sometimes the best way to solve a problem is to start up a secondary command interpreter, even if it's another instance of COMMAND.COM. Among other things, this gives you a second environment to use.

The COMMAND command (see Figure 10.3) starts up COMMAND.COM as a secondary command interpreter. The parameters and switches are the same as those on the SHELL command when it references COMMAND.COM. The following command starts up a secondary COMMAND.COM with a 2K environment; since no other location is specified, the COMSPEC variable will be inherited from the parent environment.

```
COMMAND /E:2048
```

As long as you don't use the /P switch, the secondary command interpreter is a child of the primary one. The primary command interpreter is still in memory and will resume control when you terminate the secondary one. To terminate the secondary command interpreter and return to the primary one, enter this one-word command:

```
EXIT
```

COMMAND

Starts a new instance of COMMAND.COM.

Format:

COMMAND [*path*] [*device*] [*switches*]

Parameters and Switches:

none	Loads COMMAND.COM with a default environment size, the CON device, and the parent environment's COMSPEC variable.
path	Identifies location of the command interpreter if not in the root directory of the boot drive; this path is used to set the COMSPEC variable which DOS uses to reload the transient portion of COMMAND.COM when necessary.
device	Identifies a device to be used for standard input and output; default is CON.
/C *command-text*	Causes the new command interpreter to start up just long enough to execute the specified command, then terminate again.
/E:*nnnn*	Identifies the size of the environment in bytes, from 160 to 32768; the default is 256 or the size of the variables inherited from the previous command interpreter, whichever is larger.
/MSG	Requests that error messages normally stored on disk should be loaded into memory; use when the command interpreter is located on diskette; can be used only with /P.
/P	Makes this command interpreter the primary command interpreter.

Specifying COMSPEC

If you specify a location for COMSPEC, the new environment is empty except for the COMSPEC variable. You will have no PATH, PROMPT, or any other variable that existed in the parent environment. You should notice the difference immediately because your prompt changes to DOS's default prompt (that is, it shows only the current drive, not the current directory). You won't be able to start up programs from other directories until you establish a search path. One quick way to reset your path and prompt is to rerun C:\AUTOEXEC, but that could also load some TSRs for the second time, which may not be desirable.

Omitting COMSPEC

If you don't specify a location for COMSPEC, the secondary environment inherits the parent environment's variables. It can modify, add, and delete variables as desired without affecting those in the parent environment. When you return to the parent command interpreter, its environment is in exactly the same condition as when you left it. This is the main reason for starting up a secondary command interpreter. For example, suppose you must create a batch program that changes the prompt, the search path, and the TEMP directory. You want to restore the original parameters before ending the batch program. The easiest way to do it is this:

```
@ECHO OFF
REM Preserve current environment:
COMMAND
     .
     .      (remainder of batch program)
     .
REM Restore original environment:
EXIT
```

Suppose you are creating a batch program that needs a 2K environment. Starting a secondary command interpreter not only gives you the extra environment space temporarily, it also eliminates all extra environment variables automatically when you exit back to the parent command interpreter:

```
@ECHO OFF
REM Establish a larger environment:
COMMAND /E:2048
     .
     .      (remainder of batch program)
     .
REM Return to original environment:
EXIT
```

Dynamic Environment Allocation

The DOS 5 documentation does not correctly describe the way DOS handles the secondary environment space. DOS initially allocates the default or requested amount of environment space. But if you set variables in excess of that space and the adjacent memory area is available, DOS will dynamically allocate to the environment as many bytes as necessary to create the variables you request. You could set many thousands of bytes of environment variables this way, but keep in mind that you're removing available space from conventional memory, which could prevent programs from being loaded.

> **N O T E**
>
> While we're at it, the documentation also describes the default size of
> the secondary environment incorrectly. If /E is not specified, the size
> will be 256 bytes or the number of bytes necessary to inherit all the
> parent's variables, whichever is greater.

Starting COMMAND.COM when Another Command Interpreter is Primary

Suppose NDOS is loaded as the primary command interpreter and now
you need to run COMMAND.COM. To start it up as a secondary command
interpreter, enter this command:

```
COMMAND C:\ [switches]
```

It's necessary to specify the COMSPEC path so the COMMAND environment doesn't inherit NDOS's COMSPEC variable, which could lead to
trouble when DOS attempts to reload the transient portion of COMMAND
from the wrong directory. Because the COMSPEC path is specified, no
variables are inherited from the parent environment, so you might want to
set at least the path and prompt before continuing.

To return to NDOS again, enter this command:

```
EXIT
```

Loading a New Primary Command Interpreter

Suppose instead you want to replace the primary command interpreter
with COMMAND.COM. You need to include the /P (for primary) switch
like this:

```
COMMAND  C:\ [switches] /P
```

This has some effects similar to rebooting. AUTOEXEC.BAT is executed
from the root directory of the current drive. (If you're not on drive C:, you
probably won't have an AUTOEXEC.BAT available and the DATE and

TIME commands will be executed instead.) The EXIT command will not terminate this interpreter. Although you can't get back to the previous command interpreter, it continues to take up space in memory, which could cause a shortage of memory space. If memory is tight, it's better to modify the SHELL statement in CONFIG.SYS and reboot to get the command interpreter and environment you want.

Executing a Command with COMMAND.COM

The /C *command-text* switch causes COMMAND to start up a secondary command interpreter just long enough to run the indicated command, then exit to the parent command interpreter again. You'll use this feature primarily to redirect output that can't otherwise be redirected.

Recall that you can't redirect the output of a batch program or a FOR command. But you can redirect the output of COMMAND. Suppose you want to use the FOR command to print the output of CHKDSK for all your hard drives. Here's how you can do it:

```
COMMAND /C FOR %F IN (C: D: E: F:) DO CHKDSK > PRN
```

The redirection applies to COMMAND, not FOR, and therefore it works.

Suppose you want to redirect the output of a batch program called STYL-IST to a file named SAVESTY.TXT. The following command will do it:

```
COMMAND /C STYLIST > SAVESTY.TXT
```

Chapter 7 showed how to combine FIND with FOR to search a set of files for a specified phrase. But we were unable to pipe the output to MORE because FOR can't be redirected. Here again, COMMAND can be used to accomplish the redirection:

```
COMMAND /C FOR %F IN (*.DOC *.TXT) DO FIND "Carnival"
%F ¦ MORE
```

This command could result in a long pause while MORE builds a tempo-rary file of the entire output from the FOR command.

N O T E

If you redirect COMMAND output without the /C switch, all standard output of the secondary command interpreter is redirected until you exit back to the primary interpreter again. This includes the command prompt, which no longer appears on the monitor but is recorded in the redirected output. You can still enter commands and data, even though you can't see the command prompt.

CHAPTER 11

CIRCUMVENTING DOS'S MEMORY LIMITATIONS

ntroduction

Even though it's not much more than 10 years old, DOS has been suffering from a lack of memory for many years. DOS was originally designed for Intel's 8088 microprocessor, the chip installed in the original IBM PC and compatibles; it could accommodate up to 1M of memory, which seemed like a lot at the time. Intel (and Microsoft) decided to make 640K of that available for program use, providing 10 times as much space as any personal computer software of that day needed, and reserve the upper 384K for system needs.

As they say: That was then... this is now. Today's huge applications are bumping up against the 640K ceiling with increasing frustration. It's not uncommon to attempt to start up a program and receive the message "Not enough memory."

The 286 and later microprocessors that are used in modern personal computers are capable of accommodating huge memory areas, much larger than the original 1M. A 286-based computer, such as an AT, can access as much as 16M of memory, while a 386 or 486 can have as much as 4G (gigabytes)—that's more than four *billion* bytes. But poor old DOS is stuck with its original design and can still access only 1M, with 640K available for program use, even if the computer it's running on has several gigabytes of memory installed in it.

Why not just upgrade DOS to accommodate the larger memory capacities of today's machines? Because that would make it incompatible with earlier DOS versions and the thousands of programs designed to run under them. (OS/2 was an attempt in this direction which has been largely rejected by the personal computing public.) However, DOS 5 has added several new facilities to provide relief from the 640K barrier without changing its basic design, as you'll see in this chapter.

Memory Layout

When discussing DOS's memory layout, it's important to distinguish between memory address space and installed memory. Every byte in memory has a numerical address, which is used by programs to access that byte. Memory *address space* is a range of addresses set aside for memory, even if no memory chips have been installed for those addresses. The address space represents the computer's memory potential; it doesn't mean the computer has that much memory. For example, under DOS, the address space from 0H to A0000H (see sidebar for an explanation of why computer addresses are always stated in hexadecimal) is the 640K range that is available for running programs. Even if you install only 512K of RAM in your computer, DOS still reserves the entire 640K address range for that purpose, starting the system area at address A0000H.

THE HEXADECIMAL MYSTIQUE

Why do computers so often report addresses and other values in hexadecimal numbers instead of decimal? The answer is that it's partly a tradition and partly a necessity for programmers.

THE HEXADECIMAL MYSTIQUE

Internally a computer must store all data using the binary number system. With a base of 2, binary has only two digits, 0 and 1, which can be represented in an electronic circuit by a pulse or no pulse, on a disk by a magnetized spot or no spot, and so on. It takes a lot more binary digits (called *bits*) to represent a value. The number 20 in binary is 10100B; the number 500 is 111110100B.

When the computer displays or prints internal values, binary takes up too much room and is too difficult for humans to interpret at a glance. It's also easy for humans to skip or transpose digits when long strings of 1s and 0s are involved. So the computer uses a larger number system for display purposes.

Any number system whose base is a power of 2 has a direct relationship with binary, and it's easy to translate back and forth between the two. This makes octal (base 8) and hexadecimal (base 16) the most likely candidates for displaying numbers that are really binary. Over the years, hexadecimal has squeezed out octal and is now used almost universally. When you see a "hex" number, you're really seeing a binary number in "shorthand."

Since hexadecimal has 16 digits, we use the decimal digits 0 through 9 and the letters A through F to express hex numbers. Since 16 is the fourth power of 2 (that is, 2^4 =16), each hexadecimal digit represents four binary digits, from 0H=0000B to FH=1111B. The value 21C5H is actually 0010000111000101B.

Now for the $16 million question: Why not let the computer convert numbers into decimal? It's a lot better at calculations than we are. The answer is that programmers often need to see binary values to figure out what's happening internally. At one time, only programmers had to deal with hexadecimal output. With the advent of personal computers and nontechnical users, the conversions should be done (which is one reason the /C switch was added to MEM), but that doesn't always happen. It's a particularly strong tradition to display memory addresses in hexadecimal, as if decimal addresses aren't really valid. If this was a beginners' book, we'd translate the addresses to decimal. Since it's designed for advanced readers, we'll leave the addresses in hexadecimal because that's how they appear in other literature (such as the DOS 5 documentation).

Figure 11.1 shows the layout of DOS's total address space on a 286 or 386 computer. 8086/8088 machines have only the conventional and upper portions, not the extended. The following sections describe each type of memory in detail.

Figure 11.1.

Memory Layout.

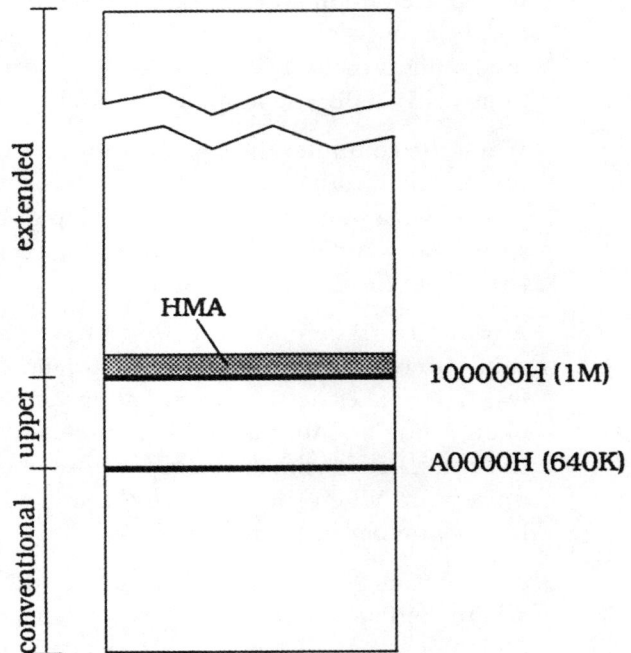

conventional   upper   extended

HMA

100000H (1M)

A0000H (640K)

Conventional Memory

The address space from 0H to A0000H is called *conventional memory*—the everyday workspace where most programs must be loaded to work under DOS. This is random-access memory (RAM), which can be written again and again. It's cleared when the power goes out and when you reboot.

DOS uses the first portion of conventional memory for system data. DOS itself resides in the next part (unless you use some of DOS 5's new commands to load it higher up). The remainder of conventional memory is available for other programs.

Most systems need to load at least a few device drivers—programs that control hardware such as the printer and the mouse. And most systems also start up some TSRs—programs that stay resident in memory after they're started up—such as DOS 5's PRINT and DOSKEY. The more drivers and TSRs you load into conventional memory, the less space you have to start up an application. In fact, you can put yourself into a situation where you can't start up some of your larger applications without removing some TSRs from conventional memory.

DOS 5 has some new features that can help free up conventional memory by letting you load drivers, TSRs, and DOS itself in other parts of memory, if you have the right setup.

Upper Memory

The address space from A0000H to 100000H, which is called *upper memory*, is reserved so DOS can access the memory built into controllers for devices such as a video monitor, keyboard, and printer. ROM BIOS and ROM BASIC (if present) are also accessed through this address space. Most systems don't have enough devices to fill the address space, and that provides a loophole through which DOS can access memory beyond the 1M limit.

Expanded Memory (EMS)

One way to provide extra memory in a PC is to add on a memory board and access it through upper memory just as if it is another external device. This early solution to the PC memory crunch, called *expanded memory*, can be used with any PC model. Expanded memory, like conventional memory, is RAM; it can be read and written, and it is cleared when the power goes out or you reboot. However, unlike conventional and upper memory, DOS cannot execute programs from expanded memory. It can be used for data storage only.

Figure 11.2 illustrates the methodology DOS uses to access and manage expanded memory. A memory manager uses some available address space in upper memory to create a *page frame*, which is divided into 16K pages. All of expanded memory is divided into pages of the same size. You can access any expanded memory page by allocating to it a page of address space from the page frame. The process of continually reassigning the address space in the page frame on an as-needed basis is referred to as *bank switching*. Notice that you can't access all of expanded memory at once. You can only access as many pages as there are in the page frame.

Figure 11.2.

Accessing
Expanded Memory.

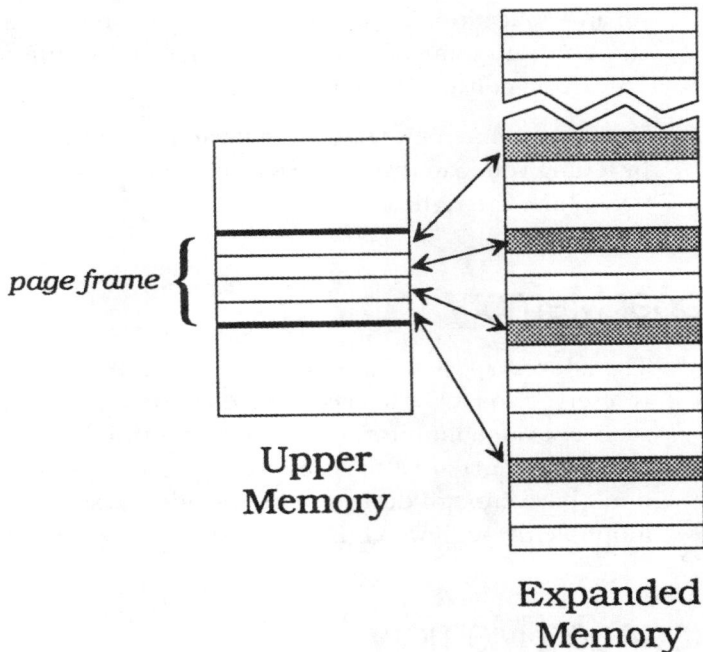

page frame {

**Upper
Memory**

**Expanded
Memory**

A program called an *expanded memory manager* keeps track of the pages, servicing the needs of all programs requesting expanded memory so that each program's data is protected from the others. Expanded memory boards usually come with their own management software, but you might find that you want to purchase a third-party manager with more features.

Chaos reigned in the early days of expanded memory management until Lotus, Intel, and Microsoft (LIM) created an Expanded Memory Specification (EMS), released as LIM 3.2 EMS. AST Research, Quadram, and Ashton-Tate developed an enhanced standard which was combined with the LIM 3.2 to produce LIM 4.0 EMS. Expanded memory that conforms to one of the LIM specifications is referred to as EMS memory.

Both LIM 3.2 and LIM 4.0 are in current use, and your expanded memory might conform to either one. LIM 3.2 limits the system to one 64K page frame with four 16K pages. LIM 4.0 permits any number of page frames, which may be smaller or larger than four pages and may appear in conventional as well as upper memory. LIM 4.0 also permits access to larger expanded memory areas (32M as opposed to 8M).

Extended Memory

A 286-based computer has a 16M address space, while a 386 or 486 has a 4G address space. Memory in the range above 1M is referred to as *extended memory* because it extends beyond the original PC's address space. As with conventional and expanded memory, any memory installed here is always RAM and is cleared when you reboot or lose power. And DOS can use it for data storage only (with one exception, which is explained shortly).

Some people order a 286 or higher machine with 1M of RAM thinking they won't have any extended memory because the first megabyte of memory will be used up by conventional and upper memory. That's not how it works. The first 640K of RAM becomes conventional memory, but the remaining 384K goes into the extended range. Since the address space from 640K to 1M is reserved for device and ROM BIOS memory, it is not filled in with general-purpose RAM.

If you have a machine with less than 640K of RAM, you still have upper memory. The memory included on device controller cards and ROM BIOS isn't included when you talk about how much memory your system has.

286 and higher machines have two basic modes of operation: protected and real. In *protected mode*, a program can directly address the entire memory range, from conventional through extended. (OS/2 runs in protected mode and programs designed to run under OS/2 can do this.) *Real mode* forces the more advanced computer to emulate an 8086/8088 so that it can run DOS and all the thousands of programs designed to run under DOS. In real mode, only conventional and upper memory can be directly addressed, with one important exception, which we'll get to shortly.

Some programs attempt to access extended memory under DOS by switching the machine into and out of protected mode on an as-needed basis, but this solution is difficult to program, difficult to manage, and can cause conflicts (and data loss) if two programs attempt it concurrently.

And now here's the loophole that provides DOS's *entre* to extended memory. Because of the way the memory addresses are handled in real mode (see the sidebar for details), DOS can actually access almost 64K of extended memory through the A20 address line. That area is called the *High Memory Area* (HMA) and is used to access and manage the rest of extended memory with a bank-switching technique similar to expanded memory's. It's not the ideal solution, but it's the best DOS can manage.

HOW DOS EXCEEDS THE 1M LIMIT WITH A 286 OR HIGHER MICROPROCESSOR

The 8086/8088 has 16-bit architecture, meaning that its registers and words are 16 bits (2 bytes) long. It would be natural if its memory addresses were 16 bits, too, since that's the size that can be stored in a register or memory word. But with 16-bit addresses you can access only 64K of memory, which simply isn't enough, so the designers had to come up with some other way of addressing memory.

The solution lay in dividing memory into 64K segments and having two 16-bit values for each address: a 16-bit segment address and a 16-bit offset within the segment. The 8086/8088 creates a 20-bit address by shifting the segment address to the left four bits and adding the offset to it. If the segment address is 5CH and the offset is 23H, the actual memory address is calculated this way:

```
    005C0H
+   00023H
    005E3H
```

The 8086/8088 has 20 memory address lines, named A00 through A19, to carry the 20-bit address from the microprocessor to the memory unit. With 20 bits, you can access an address range of 1M.

Now here's the loophole that lets DOS access more than 1M of memory on a 286 or higher machine. The maximum address that can be generated by the 8086/8088's addressing method is larger than 1M by almost 64K:

HOW DOS EXCEEDS THE 1M LIMIT WITH A 286 OR HIGHER MICROPROCESSOR

```
  FFFF0H  (largest segment address)
+ 0FFFFH  (largest offset)
  10FFEFH (largest address)
```

10FFEFH equals 1,114,095, which is 65,519 bytes more than 1M. But notice that it takes 21 bits to handle this number. (The high-order 1 in the range from 100000H to 10FFEFH requires the twenty-first bit.) Since the 8086/8088 has only 20 address lines, if such an address is generated, the twenty-first bit simply gets lost.

But the 286, 386, and 486 have more than 20 address lines. The twenty-first bit can be retained and used on line A20. And so DOS can actually address almost 64K over the 1M limit when operating on a 286 or higher machine operating in real mode. For convenience, we round this figure up to 64K.

A familiar group—Microsoft, AST Research, Intel, and Lotus—have released an extended memory specification (XMS) that standardizes control of extended memory through the A20 line in real mode, preventing conflicts in much the same way as LIM EMS does for expanded memory.

An XMS manager is not automatically provided when you install extended memory on your computer. Microsoft developed a manager called HIMEM.SYS for Windows; it is included in the DOS 5 package as well. Once again, however, you might find that you want to buy an XMS manager with more features.

DOS 5's Memory Facilities

DOS 5 includes a number of facilities to help you manage memory, free up conventional memory, and use upper, expanded, and extended memory:

➲ The MEM program displays a list of what's currently in memory. MEM helps you find out how much of each type of memory your system has, how much of it is currently available, and what programs are currently loaded where.

➲ The HIMEM.SYS XMS manager gives your 286 or higher machine access to extended memory according to the XMS standard.

➲ If XMS memory is present, the DOS command loads DOS itself into the HMA.

➲ If you have a 386 or higher with XMS memory, EMM386.EXE lets you convert some (or all) XMS extended memory to EMS expanded memory. It also lets you load drivers and TSRs into upper memory to free up conventional memory for applications.

Each of these features is discussed in detail in the following sections.

MEM

Figure 11.3 shows the format of the MEM command. When used without any switches, MEM displays a report similar to this:

```
C:\>MEM


   655360 bytes total conventional memory
   655360 bytes available to MS-DOS
   513328 largest executable program size


C:\>
```

Figure 11.3.

MEM Command Reference.

<table>
<tr><td colspan="2" align="center">MEM</td></tr>
<tr><td colspan="2">Displays current memory usage and availability.</td></tr>
<tr><td colspan="2">Format:</td></tr>
<tr><td colspan="2">MEM [switch]</td></tr>
<tr><td colspan="2">Switches:</td></tr>
<tr><td>None</td><td>Lists summary lines only.</td></tr>
<tr><td>/CLASSIFY or /C</td><td>Lists currently loaded programs and their sizes in both decimal and hexadecimal.</td></tr>
<tr><td>/DEBUG or /D</td><td>Lists the most detailed information about allocation of memory areas. Sizes and addresses are shown in hexadecimal only.</td></tr>
<tr><td>/PROGRAM or /P</td><td>Lists details of memory areas allocated to programs. Sizes and addresses are shown in hexadecimal only.</td></tr>
<tr><td colspan="2">Notes:</td></tr>
<tr><td colspan="2">Only one switch can be used per MEM command.</td></tr>
<tr><td colspan="2">When any switch is used, details are provided for conventional memory only unless EMM386.EXE is installed, in which case details for upper memory are also shown.</td></tr>
</table>

Extended and expanded memory availability are also summarized if they are present. Sometimes you want to find out exactly what programs are loaded. The /CLASSIFY or /C switch lists all programs in conventional memory, with their sizes shown in both decimal and hex, as in this example:

```
C:\>MEM /C

Conventional Memory :

    Name              Size in Decimal         Size in Hex
- - - - - - - - -     - - - - - - - - - - - - -     - - - - - - - - - - -
    MSDOS              15216     ( 14.9K)          3B70
    HIMEM               3040     (  3.0K)           BE0
    SETVER               400     (  0.4K)           190
    ANSI                4192     (  4.1K)          1060
    SMARTDRV           15840     ( 15.5K)          3DE0
    EGA                 3280     (  3.2K)           CD0
    COMMAND             2672     (  2.6K)           A70
    MOUSE              12192     ( 11.9K)          2FA0
    MODE                 464     (  0.5K)           1D0
    WORD              388576     (379.5K)          5EDE0
    COMMAND             2800     (  2.7K)           AF0
    FREE                  64     (  0.1K)            40
    FREE              206224     (201.4K)          32590
Total  FREE :         206288     (201.5K)

Total bytes available to programs :    206288   (201.5K)
Largest executable program size :      206032   (201.2K)

C:\>
```

You'll probably want to pipe the report to MORE so you can read it one page at a time.

The MEM /C display is not very detailed about exactly where each program and free block is loaded in memory. In particular, all free space tends to be shown at the end of the area, even though in reality, it's scattered around in memory. That's why the largest executable program size is smaller than the total free space. Also, MEM /C does not show the MEM program itself; it shows you what the situation will be like after MEM terminates, so you can decide whether another program could be loaded.

If you need more specific information, which you might when debugging a program, use MEM /P or MEM /D. They both show you exactly where programs and free space are, including MEM itself, but all numbers are in hexadecimal only. The difference between the two is that MEM /D includes more details about device drivers and TSRs.

HIMEM.SYS

HIMEM.SYS is DOS's XMS manager. When loaded, it takes over the HMA and permits other XMS-compatible software to use extended memory. It is loaded from CONFIG.SYS with a command like this:

```
DEVICE=C:\DOS\HIMEM.SYS
```

You will see messages similar to the following when HIMEM is installed properly:

```
HIMEM: DOS XMS Driver, Version 2.77 - 02/27/91
XMS Specification Version 2.0
Copyright 1988-1991 Microsoft Corp.

Installed A20 handler number 1
64K High Memory Area is available
```

If you have another XMS driver in your system, you must choose between it and HIMEM.SYS. If you decide to use HIMEM.SYS, remove the other driver's DEVICE command from your CONFIG.SYS file. (Just put REM in front of the command until you're sure that HIMEM.SYS is the program for you and you really don't want to use the other one. Then you can erase that command.)

With HIMEM loaded, the MEM summary will look like this:

```
   655360 bytes total conventional memory
   655360 bytes available to MS-DOS
   513328 largest executable program size

  1441792 bytes total contiguous extended memory
        0 bytes available contiguous extended memory
  1441792 bytes available XMS memory
```

In this example, the system has more than a megabyte of extended memory, but none of it is available directly because HIMEM has usurped it all. You can see that it all is available as XMS memory, which is controlled here by HIMEM.

It's important to place HIMEM's DEVICE command before any other command that uses extended memory (such as a command that installs a RAM drive or a disk cache in extended memory). If the other programs require an XMS manager, they won't be able to load without HIMEM being installed first. If they don't require an XMS manager and take over all or part of the HMA, HIMEM won't be able to start up. An error message during booting warns you when HIMEM can't be loaded.

If you have Microsoft Windows, you probably have two versions of HIMEM.SYS, one that came with Windows and one that came with DOS 5. Use whichever version is newest (check the time/date stamp in the directory entry).

Problems in Using HIMEM.SYS

If you find that HIMEM doesn't work for you in its default configuration—for example, if HIMEM.SYS won't load or other programs can't access extended memory—you might need some switches on HIMEM's DEVICE command. Figure 11.4 shows the switches and their settings.

The most likely problem is the /MACHINE switch, which identifies the driver that controls the A20 line. Microsoft includes several A20 handlers in HIMEM.SYS. The default handler is the most common one, handler number 1 or the AT handler. But your hardware might require one of the other handlers. There is additional information about A20 handlers in the README.TXT file provided with DOS 5.

N O T E

HIMEM's startup message tells you which A20 handler is installed.

TIP

If you're not sure which handler to use, it doesn't hurt to experiment. Your dealer or Microsoft's technical support folks might be able to help you find the right one.

Figure 11.4.

HIMEM.SYS
Configuration
Command.

<table>
<tr><td colspan="2" align="center">HIMEM.SYS</td></tr>
<tr><td colspan="2">Provides XMS extended memory management.</td></tr>
<tr><td colspan="2">Format:</td></tr>
<tr><td colspan="2">DEVICE=[path]HIMEM.SYS [switches]</td></tr>
<tr><td colspan="2">Switches:</td></tr>
<tr><td>/A20CONTROL:ON|OFF</td><td>With /A20CONTROL:ON (the default), HIMEM seizes control of the A20 line even if it was already in use. With /A20CONTROL:OFF, the line is seized only if it's not in use.</td></tr>
<tr><td>/CPUCLOCK:ON|OFF</td><td>With /CPUCLOCK:OFF (the default), HIMEM can affect your computer's speed. With /CPUCLOCK:ON, HIMEM can't change the speed, which slows HIMEM but might be necessary for your system.</td></tr>
<tr><td>HMAMIN=n</td><td>Specifies that a program must occupy at least nK in order to use the HMA. Range is 0 to 63; default is 0. A higher value prevents small programs from clogging up the HMA.</td></tr>
<tr><td>/INT15=xxxx</td><td>Allocates xxxx bytes of extended memory for the interrupt 15H interface. (This is for older programs that use an extended memory scheme based on the 15H interrupt.) Value must be 0 or 64 to 65535; default is 0.</td></tr>
<tr><td>/MACHINE:xxxx</td><td>Identifies the A20 handler. You can specify either the code or the number. The default is AT or 1. (The code table is listed under HIMEM.SYS in your DOS documentation.)</td></tr>
<tr><td>/NUMHANDLES=n</td><td>Specifies that n handles can be used simultaneously. Each block of extended memory allocated to a program requires a handle for identification purposes. Range is 1 through 128; default is 32.</td></tr>
<tr><td>/SHADOWRAM:ON|OFF</td><td>With /SHADOWRAM:OFF (the default in computers with less than 2M of RAM), RAM does not shadow ROM. With /SHADOWRAM:ON, RAM shadows ROM in systems with that capability.</td></tr>
<tr><td colspan="2">Notes:</td></tr>
<tr><td colspan="2">Some 386 and higher machines copy their ROM to a portion of RAM during booting since RAM is so much faster than ROM. Turning shadow RAM off slows down processing but avoids XMS conflicts.</td></tr>
</table>

Loading DOS into Extended Memory

Since the HMA is directly addressable by DOS, it is possible to run programs there. But HIMEM.SYS permits only one program in the HMA; the first one that loads itself there is the king of the hill. Most DOS 5 users load DOS itself in the HMA to get it out of conventional memory. If you don't do this, one of your other programs, such as Windows, may take up residence there.

You can load most of DOS into the HMA by including the following command somewhere following the XMS manager's DEVICE command in CONFIG.SYS:

```
DOS=HIGH
```

With most of DOS loaded into extended memory, MEM output will look something like this:

```
 655360 bytes total conventional memory
 655360 bytes available to MS-DOS
 613328 largest executable program size

1441792 bytes total contiguous extended memory
      0 bytes available contiguous extended memory
1376256 bytes available XMS memory
        MS-DOS resident in High Memory Area
```

The last line tells you that DOS has been loaded in extended memory. You should also see the difference in the amount of conventional and XMS memory available before and after DOS is loaded high.

Loading Programs in Conventional Memory with LOADFIX

When you move DOS into the HMA, other programs might be loaded into the low parts of conventional memory where DOS traditionally resides. A few programs don't work well when loaded in the first 64K of memory (DOS EDIT is one). If you receive the message "Packed file corrupt" when starting up a program, try inserting LOADFIX in front of the command, as in:

```
LOADFIX EDIT TRYME.BAT
```

LOADFIX forces the program to be loaded above the 64K line.

Using EMM386

Since expanded memory has been around longer and can be made available on any PC, many applications work with expanded but not extended memory. It's frustrating to have several megabytes of extended memory and have some applications that are suffering for lack of memory because they recognize only expanded memory. For 386 and 486 microprocessors with extended memory, EMM386.EXE has two functions:

⊃ It makes some or all of your extended memory emulate expanded memory.

⊃ It lets you load programs into upper memory instead of conventional memory.

Figure 11.5 shows the format of EMM386's DEVICE command, which must be placed somewhere after HIMEM's DEVICE command in CONFIG.SYS. If used without any parameters, it converts 256K of XMS extended memory into expanded memory but does not provide access to the upper memory area. Most of the parameters provide solutions to rare problems and can be ignored if you have no trouble emulating expanded memory or loading programs into upper memory. You might find use for the *memory-size*, RAM, and NOEMS switches, however.

Emulating Expanded Memory

If you have an application that wants expanded memory but your 386 or 486 has only extended memory, you might be able to use EMM386.EXE combined with HIMEM.SYS to provide the expanded memory you need.

TIP   Some programs, notably Windows 3.0, have their own emulators and don't work well with EMM386.

Suppose you have two megabytes of extended memory that is not needed by any of your applications. You also have an application that will use as much expanded memory as you can provide. The following CONFIG.SYS command will convert your entire range of extended memory into expanded memory:

```
DEVICE=C:\DOS\EMM386.EXE 2048
```

NOTE

Most drivers loaded with the DEVICE command have the SYS extension, but EMM386 has the EXE extension.

TIP   Although EMM386.EXE will not work with a 286, you can purchase third-party memory managers that will accomplish the same functions (and more) on a 286.

Figure 11.5.

EMM386.EXE
Configuration
Command
Reference.

EMM386.EXE

Emulates EMS (expanded) memory with XMS (extended) memory and makes upper memory blocks (UMBs) available for running programs.

Format:

DEVICE=[*path*]EMM386.EXE [*parameters*]

Parameters:

None	Provides 256K of expanded memory.
memory-size	Specifies the amount of expanded memory, which will be rounded down to the nearest 16K. If not enough XMS memory is available to create the requested amount of EMS, EMM386 lowers the amount as needed.
RAM	Provides access to both upper and expanded memory.
NOEMS	Provides access to upper memory and does not emulate expanded memory.
ON|OFF|AUTO	Specifies the beginning status of EMM386. ON is the default. If OFF, EMM386.EXE is loaded but is not activated until turned on by an EMM386 command. If AUTO, it's activated automatically when a program requests expanded memory.
W=ON|OFF	Enables/disables support for the Weitek coprocessor. Default is OFF.
M*x*	Specifies the page frame segment address using a numeric code: 1=C000H; 2=C400H; 3=C800H; 4=CC00H; 5=D000H; 6=D400H; 7=D800H; 8=DC00H; 9=E000H; 10=8000H; 11=8400H; 12=8800H; 13=8C00H; 14=9000H.
FRAME=*address*	Specifies the page frame segment address using the address itself. Range: 8000H through 9000H, C000H through E000H, in increments of 400H.
/P*address*	Same as FRAME=*address*.
P*n*=*address*	Specifies the beginning address of page *n*. Range for *n*: 0 through 255. Range for *address*: see FRAME=*address*. Note that pages 0 through 3 must be contiguous. If you specify the page frame address, you cannot specify separate addresses for pages 0 through 3.
X=*address1-address2*	Blocks out a range of upper memory addresses from being used in the page frame. Range: A000H through FFFFH. (You can specify more than one /X parameter.)
I=*address1-address2*	Includes an address range in the page frame. Range: A000H through FFFFH. X takes precedence over I if both are used and their ranges overlap. (You can specify more than one /I parameter.)
A=*n*	Specifies that *n* alternate register sets should be allocated for multitasking. Each alternate register set takes 200 bytes of conventional memory. Range is 0 through 254; default is 7.
B=*address*	Specifies lowest bank-switching address. Range is 1000H through 4000H; default is 4000H.
D=*n*	Reserves *n* kilobytes for buffered dynamic memory access (DMA). Range is 16 through 256; default is 16.
H=*n*	Specifies that *n* handles may be used simultaneously. Range is 2 through 255; default is 64.
L=*n*	Specifies at least *n*K must be left as XMS memory and not converted by EMM386.EXE.

Notes:

HIMEM's DEVICE command must precede this command in CONFIG.SYS.

For UMB access, the command DOS=UMB must also be specified in CONFIG.SYS.

The computer must have an 80386 or higher microprocessor and extended memory.

EMM386.EXE takes up a small amount of conventional memory (about 8K) for its own software; it cannot be loaded into upper memory. It also needs to borrow 64K from extended memory to create the upper memory page frame. And of course, it takes whatever extended memory is necessary to create the EMS memory. (If there isn't enough XMS to create the requested amount of EMS, it creates as much as it can, rounded down to the nearest multiple of 16K.)

With EMM386.EXE at work, a MEM summary looks something like this:

```
655360 bytes total conventional memory
655360 bytes available to MS-DOS
551744 largest executable program size

589842 bytes total EMS memory
196608 bytes free EMS memory

393216 bytes total contiguous extended memory
     0 bytes available contiguous extended memory
     0 bytes available XMS memory
       MS-DOS resident in High Memory Area
```

Notice that the total EMS memory (589824 or 576K) is much larger than you might expect—in fact, it's larger than extended memory. That's because MEM includes all 384K of upper memory in the figure, whether or not EMM386 is providing access to upper memory. Subtracting 384K from 576K leaves 192K, which is exactly the amount of free EMS memory shown in the report.

Turning Expanded Memory On and Off

Once you've installed EMM386 from CONFIG.SYS during booting, you can turn it on and off with the EMM386 command (see Figure 11.6) as long as it isn't currently in use. You might want to turn it off to make more extended memory available to an application, then turn it on again when you're ready to run an application that needs expanded memory.

In fact, you can load EMM386.EXE but turn it off (or place it in AUTO mode) by including the OFF or AUTO parameter in the CONFIG.SYS command that loads it. Then you can use the EMM386 command to turn it on when it's needed.

If you try to turn EMM386 off when it is providing access to upper memory blocks or when some program is using its expanded memory, you will see this message:

```
Unable to de-activate EMM386 as UMBs are being provided
and/or EMS is being used.
```

Figure 11.6.

EMM386 Command Reference.

EMM386

Turns expanded memory emulation off and on.

Format:

EMM386 [*parameters*]

Parameters:

None	Displays the same EMM386 status report that is displayed when EMM386.EXE is loaded.
ON|OFF|AUTO	Enables/disables EMM386 or sets it to be enabled and disabled automatically in response to program demand.
W=ON|OFF	Enables/disables Weitek coprocessor support.

Notes:

This command is valid only when EMM386.EXE has been installed via a DEVICE command in CONFIG.SYS.

EMM386 cannot be turned off when it is providing upper memory access or when any program is currently using expanded memory.

Using Upper Memory Blocks (UMBs)

WARNING

Trying to load programs into upper memory blocks can lock up your system. Make a bootable diskette and copy your current CONFIG.SYS and AUTOEXEC.BAT to it before trying the techniques in this section. Then if your system locks up while trying to boot from the hard disk, boot from the diskette until you can fix the problem.

Because various devices have fixed address ranges in upper memory, free space appears in chunks located here and there rather than in one contiguous piece. The free chunks are called *upper memory blocks* or *UMBs*. Of course, there is no RAM associated with UMBs unless you use a program like EMM386 to fill the address space with actual memory borrowed from extended memory.

Once UMBs have been associated with actual memory, you can load and run programs from UMBs just as you can from conventional memory. By loading drivers and TSRs in upper memory, you can free up conventional memory for applications.

To set up EMM386 to manage UMBs, you must use either the NOEMS or the RAM parameter on EMM386's DEVICE command. Use RAM if you want to use both of EMM386's functions; you'll get both EMS memory and upper memory access. Use NOEMS if you want upper memory access only and don't care to emulate expanded memory.

You must also include DOS=UMB somewhere in CONFIG.SYS. If you're already using DOS=HIGH, combine both commands in one like this:

```
DOS=HIGH,UMB
```

Remember—to make all this work, you have to have a 386 or 486 with extended memory and you have to include three commands in CONFIG.SYS:

```
DEVICE=C:\DOS\HIMEM.SYS
DEVICE=C:\DOS\EMM386 RAM (or NOEMS)
DOS=UMB (or HIGH,UMB)
```

You will find these as the first three commands in many CONFIG.SYS files. Don't forget that you have to reboot to put changes in CONFIG.SYS to work. EMM386.EXE displays a message similar to the following during booting:

```
MICROSOFT Expanded Memory Manager 386  Version 4.20.06X
   Copyright Microsoft Corporation 1986, 1990

EMM386 successfully installed.

   Available expanded memory . . . . . . . . . . 192 KB

   LIM/EMS version . . . . . . . . . . . . . . . 4.0
   Total expanded memory pages . . . . . . . . . 36
```

```
Available expanded memory pages . . . . . . .  12
Total handles . . . . . . . . . . . . . . . .  64
Active handles  . . . . . . . . . . . . . . .   1
Page frame segment  . . . . . . . . . . . . .D000 H

Total upper memory available  . . . . . . . .  31 KB
Largest Upper Memory Block available  . . . .  31 KB
Upper memory starting address  . . . . . . . .C800 H
```

EMM386 Active.

From this report, you can see how much expanded memory has been created and details about the expanded memory (the total expanded memory pages includes all 384K of upper memory—24 pages). You can also see that 31K is available in one upper memory block, starting at address C8000H. (Add a 0 to the end of all addresses in this report to find the actual addresses.)

N O T E

The upper memory starting address identifies the first address available for UMBs, not the first address in upper memory, which is A0000H.

Controlling the Page Frame Address

Most systems don't use upper memory starting at address E0000H for any hardware purpose, but EMM386 won't use this portion unless you tell it to. When you are using EMM386.EXE to access both UMBs and expanded memory, it pays to force the expanded memory page frame to start at E0000H, because this moves the page frame out of an area that EMM386 will use as an UMB, freeing up another 64K of UMB space.

You can force the page frame to start at E0000H several ways, all equally effective, but the easiest is shown below:

```
DEVICE=C:\DOS\EMM386.EXE M9 ...
```

Loading Programs into UMBs

Now that you've set up the UMBs, you can load programs into them. Device drivers and TSRs are the natural choice for a number of reasons. They are generally smaller than applications and can fit in the smaller spaces available in upper memory. And they're not transient, so they won't leave unusable "holes" in upper memory when they terminate.

Any driver that is normally loaded with the DEVICE command in CONFIG.SYS can be loaded into a UMB with the DEVICEHIGH command instead (except for HIMEM.SYS and EMM386.EXE, of course). DEVICEHIGH works just like DEVICE except it causes the driver to be loaded into a UMB if a large enough one is available. If DOS can't find a UMB large enough for the program, it loads the driver into conventional memory with no warning. After you set up your CONFIG.SYS with DEVICEHIGH commands and reboot, you can use MEM /C to see which programs were actually loaded into upper memory.

TIP	Rearrange your DEVICEHIGH commands to load programs from the largest to the smallest, giving large programs the first chance at the bigger UMBs.

TSRs can be loaded into UMBs using the LOADHIGH command, which is abbreviated LH. All you have to do is insert LH in front of the command that normally starts up the TSR, as in this command:

```
LH DOSKEY
```

TIP	Once you have set up CONFIG.SYS for UMBs, examine AUTOEXEC.BAT for TSRs. Insert LH in front of each command that starts up a TSR and rearrange the commands so that programs are loaded from the largest to the smallest.

Problems with UMBs

Not all programs work well in UMBs. Some try to expand themselves after loading and can't get the space to do so. Some make assumptions about where they're located in memory. If your system locks up during or after booting, boot from your safety diskette (you did make one, didn't you?) and see if you can figure out which program(s) caused the problem.

TIP	All TSRs and device drivers included with DOS 5 run from UMBs with no problems.

MEM and Upper Memory

MEM can't report details of what's in extended or expanded memory because it's not privy to the memory manager's tables. But it can show you what's in upper memory when EMM386.EXE is managing that space. Use MEM /C to determine what drivers and TSRs actually loaded into upper memory while you're trying to set up your system. A typical report might look like this:

```
C:\>MEM /C


Conventional Memory :

    Name              Size in Decimal            Size in Hex
  - - - - - - - -     - - - - - - - - - - -      - - - - - - -
    MSDOS             66608      ( 65.0K)        10430
    HIMEM              3200      (  3.1K)          C80
    EMM386             8400      (  8.2K)         20D0
    COMMAND            4704      (  4.6K)         1260
    FREE                 64      (  0.1K)           40
    FREE             572192      (558.8K)        8BB20

  Total  FREE :      572256      (558.8K)


Upper Memory :

    Name              Size in Decimal            Size in Hex
  - - - - - - - -     - - - - - - - - - - -      - - - - - - -
    SYSTEM           163840      (160.0K)        28000
    SETVER              400      (  0.4K)          190
    ANSI               4192      (  4.1K)         1060
    EGA                3280      (  3.2K)          CD0
    MOUSE             12368      ( 12.1K)         3050
    FREE              12400      ( 12.1K)         3070
```

```
Total  FREE :        12400        ( 12.1K)

Total bytes available to programs (Conventional+Upper):
                                   584656    (571.0K)
Largest executable program size :  572000    (558.6K)
Largest available upper memory block:  2400    ( 12.1K)

   589824 bytes total EMS memory
   196608 bytes free EMS memory

   393216 bytes total contiguous extended memory
        0 bytes available contiguous extended memory
        0 bytes available XMS memory
         64Kb High Memory Area available
```

You can clearly see from this report that four programs are loaded into upper memory. Use MEM /D or MEM /P to find out actual addresses. They don't clearly label the beginning of upper memory as MEM /C does, so remember that any address above A0000H is in upper memory.

Handling TSRs

A *TSR* (terminate-and-stay-resident) program is a program that stays in memory once it is loaded, whether it is active or not. Most TSRs lie nearly dormant in memory until you type a keystroke (called a *hotkey*) that triggers a particular function. DOSKEY provides a good example: Whenever you press Up arrow at the command prompt, it recalls the preceding command from the command history.

When you press a key with no TSRs installed, DOS sends the keystroke to its own keystroke handler for processing. When you load a TSR that responds to hotkeys (not all TSRs do this), the TSR inserts itself in the normal chain of keystroke processing so that it looks at the keystrokes first, keeps what it recognizes, and passes unfamiliar ones on to DOS's keystroke handler.

When you load a second TSR that responds to hotkeys, it inserts itself in the chain after the first one. The chain gets longer and longer as you load more TSRs. If you have loaded three hotkey-type TSRs, the chain would look like this:

```
TSR #1 → TSR #2 → TSR #3 → DOS's keystroke handler
```

It's this chain that prevents you from unloading any TSR except the last one loaded. If you were able to unload TSR #3 in the above chain, for example, the chain would be broken and your keystroke would never reach DOS's keystroke handler. In fact, the system would probably freeze up.

Not all TSRs behave as they should in the chain, and you may find that your system locks up anyway. Usually this is because two (or more) TSRs don't get along well together. Perhaps one is stealing the other's keystrokes or is not passing the correct information along. If this starts happening in your system, try installing your TSRs in a different order. (If you changed the order when you added LOADHIGH, go back to the order that worked before. MEM /C will show you the current order.) If that doesn't work, remove TSRs one at a time until you find the one that is causing the problem. Talk to its developers about how to load it with your other TSRs; they are probably aware of the problem and have found (or are working on) a solution.

Typical Startup Files

When you're using DOS 5's full memory facilities, your CONFIG.SYS file might look something like this:

```
DEVICE=C:\DOS\HIMEM.SYS
DEVICE=C:\DOS\EMM386.EXE 2048 RAM M9
DOS=HIGH,UMB
DEVICEHIGH=C:\DOS\SETVER.EXE
DEVICEHIGH=C:\DOS\ANSI.SYS
FILES=40
BUFFERS=15
DEVICEHIGH=C:\DOS\SMARTDRV.SYS 320
DEVICEHIGH=C:\DOS\EGA.SYS
```

The first three commands set up DOS to manage extended memory, provide 2M of expanded memory, provide access to UMBs, and kick DOS into the HMA. The first command must precede the second command and the second command must precede all those starting with DEVICEHIGH. The DEVICEHIGH commands load various device drivers into UMBs.

A typical AUTOEXEC.BAT might look like this:

```
@ECHO OFF
PROMPT $P$G
PATH C:\DOS;C:\NU;C:WORD
MIRROR /TC
SET TEMP=C:\TEMP
LH C:\MOUSE\MOUSE
LH DOSKEY
LH PRINT /D:PRN
DOSSHELL
```

The three LH commands load TSRs into upper memory blocks.

SPEEDING UP YOUR SYSTEM

ntroduction

When you consider how much more you can accomplish in a few minutes at your personal computer than you could with a typewriter, white paint, scissors, and paste, it's amazing that the computer sometimes seems so slow. You can do a lot of things to speed it up. Some of them are quite expensive, such as buying a newer system, installing math coprocessors, or adding several megabytes of extended memory.

But there are some things you can do with your present system and DOS that have a surprising impact on speed. All of them fall into the area of optimizing and buffering your hard disk to reduce access time as much as possible. (Although diskette drives are 10 times slower than hard disks, we don't use them as much, so their impact on system performance isn't as significant.)

Why So Slow?

A hard disk consists of a stack of metal platters with read-write heads that move between them. The heads are attached to an arm that must move in and out to position the heads at the various cylinders on the disk. (A cylinder is a vertical configuration of the same track on every surface on the hard disk. That is, cylinder 0 consists of side 0, track 0; side 1, track 0; side 2, track 0; and so on.) In most hard disks, all the heads are attached to one arm, which looks something like a rake or a comb; they all move together.

Anything mechanical moves at agonizingly slow speeds compared to the lightning quickness of solid state circuitry. If the microprocessor had to wait for the hard disk to find and read the data it requests or to locate a place to write data, system efficiency would plummet right through the floor! System architecture is designed to avoid most of the waiting and keep the microprocessor working, but there are some things the architecture can't do—and you can.

In general, your goal is to minimize the number and length of read-write arm movements. The more you can do that, the faster your hard disk access times will be, and the more efficiently *all* your programs will run. Disk-intensive programs, such as word processors and database managers, will benefit the most. There are two basic ways to minimize arm movements:

⊃ Organize the directories and data on your hard disk for optimum access.

⊃ Buffer disk access so that DOS reads as much from memory buffers as possible instead of from the disk. (Buffering involves the fine art of trading memory for speed. You'll have to decide which is more important to you.)

DOS offers a number of features to help you with the latter. The former requires some common sense and perhaps some third-party software.

How DOS Accesses a File

DOS can't read a file in one arm movement. It needs several movements, perhaps dozens. Figure 12.1 illustrates the process. First, DOS must find the directory entry for the file, which involves reading the root directory, then making several trips between subdirectories and the FAT until the desired subdirectory is found. When DOS finds the file's directory entry and knows the first cluster number, it must travel back and forth between the FAT and the file until all fragments are located and read.

Figure 12.1.

DOS Strategy in Accessing a File.

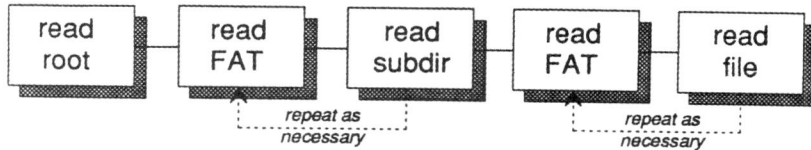

| read root | read FAT | read subdir | read FAT | read file |

repeat as necessary   *repeat as necessary*

As if all those arm movements weren't bad enough, some of them can be quite a long distance. Figure 12.2 diagrams the architecture of a hard disk. The first track contains only the partition table, which is accessed during booting but is not needed to locate or write files. The second track contains the remaining system data, so DOS can move between the root directory and the FAT with no arm movements. (DOS always uses FAT #1; the second FAT is a copy that is used to identify and fix problems in the first one.) All subdirectories and files are located in the data area, which starts on the third track. A subdirectory or file may be located anywhere in the data area. In order to locate a particular file, DOS might need to visit cylinder 227, the FAT, cylinder 412, the FAT, cylinder 7, the FAT, and so on.

Figure 12.2.

Hard Disk Layout.

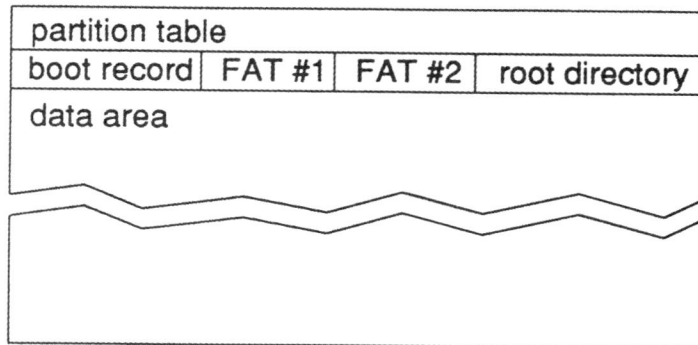

partition table			
boot record	FAT #1	FAT #2	root directory
data area			

Arm Movement Factors

Several important factors add to arm movements as you read and write files:

⊃ The length of a file's path: Remember that DOS must read every directory in a file's path every time it opens the file. The longer the path, the more subdirectories DOS must read.

⊃ The size of a subdirectory: The larger a subdirectory is, the more likely it is to be fragmented. The more fragments DOS must access, the more arm movements (perhaps long ones) are needed.

⊃ Subdirectory locations: When subdirectories are located all over the data area, DOS must move around more to follow a file's path.

⊃ File fragmentation: The more fragments the file is divided into, the more arm movements (perhaps long ones) DOS must use to read or write it.

⊃ File location: The farther a file fragment is located from the FAT, the farther the arm must move to access it.

⊃ Disk interleave factor: The arrangement of the segments around a track has a dramatic influence on access time. Interleave factors are explained in the next section.

You can control all these factors, partially with DOS, partially by setting up your disk and its subdirectories to facilitate access, and partially with third-party utilities.

Getting Your Disk Ready

Before setting up DOS to buffer your hard disk, it pays to optimize its structure. Some of these steps need to be performed only once, while some of them need to be repeated at regular intervals.

Setting the Interleave Factor

A disk's *interleave factor* determines how quickly data can be read from successive sectors. When the read-write head is positioned over a track, it must wait for the correct sector to roll around before starting to read. It reads one sector, transfers that to DOS, then waits for the next sector to arrive. Depending on the speed that the disk is spinning compared to the length of time before the system is ready for the next sector, the ideal location for the next sector might be immediately next to the current one, one sector away from it, two sectors away from it, or even farther away.

The spacing of the sectors on a track is known as the disk's interleave factor. With an interleave factor of 1, the sectors are located sequentially in the track. An interleave factor of 2 on a disk with 17 sectors per track means the sectors are arranged like this:

1   10   2   11   3   12   4   13   5   14   6   15   7   16   8   17   9

An interleave factor of 3 means they're arranged three apart, like this:

1   7   13   2   8   14   3   9   15   4   10   16   5   11   17   6   12

The interleave factor is established during the low-level format of the disk, which, for a hard disk, is usually done at the factory. You'd be surprised how often an inefficient factor is selected! The wrong interleave factor can double or treble the time it takes to access files on the disk. So it's worth finding out whether yours is correct.

DOS does not include any facility to analyze or correct the interleave factor. But you can get third-party utilities that test the interleave factor, find the ideal one for your hard disk, and set it up without destroying any of the data on your hard disk (very important, of course).

WARNING

Even if an interleave utility promises not to harm data, do a complete backup of your hard disk before trying it out.

WARNING

Don't spend a lot of money on an interleave utility until you're sure it can work with your hard disk. Some hard disks cannot be manipulated by interleave utilities.

Optimize the Directory Structure

It can be a long process, but reorganizing the directory structure to shorten paths and keep subdirectories to a reasonable length may be worth it. This is most easily done in DOS Shell, where you can see the whole directory tree and one or more directory listings all at once, and you can drag files around as necessary.

If you need to reorganize your directory structure, do it before the following steps, so that the new directory structure is used as you optimize your files.

Delete Unnecessary Files

It's amazing how quickly deadwood builds up on a hard disk. Not only do you forget to delete files that you don't need anymore, but your applications create backup and temporary files that aren't necessarily deleted.

While you're working with your directory structure in the Shell, question the files you find there. Delete any files you know you don't need any more. Table 12.1 lists DOS (and some Windows) files that can be deleted if you don't use their functions.

Table 12.1 Files to Delete

Filename	Description
HIMEM.SYS	Delete this if your system does not have extended memory. (If you use DOS's HIMEM.SYS, you can delete Windows' version.)
LOADFIX.EXE	Delete this program if you don't have extended memory or if you don't load DOS into the HMA.
EMM386.EXE	Delete this if your system does not have extended memory or if you do not want to convert it to expanded memory and/or provide access to upper memory blocks.
RAMDRIVE.SYS	Delete this if you don't want to use it to create RAM drives.
SMARTDRV.SYS	Delete this hard disk caching system if you don't want to use it, if your system has no extended or expanded memory, or if you use a newer version provided with Windows. (If you use DOS's version, you can delete Windows' version.)

Filename	Description
DRIVER.SYS	Delete this if you don't want to redefine or rename your diskette drives.
GRAFTABL.COM	Delete this if you don't need it to display graphics characters on your monitor.
GRAPHICS.COM GRAPHICS.PRO	These files let you print graphics screens under DOS and can be deleted if you don't need that function.
NLSFUNC.EXE KEYB.COM *.CPI COUNTRY.SYS DISPLAY.SYS PRINTER.SYS	Delete these files if you are in the U.S. and don't need international language support.
EXE2BIN.EXE DEBUG.EXE EDLIN.EXE LINK.EXE *.BAS (from the DOS directory)	Delete these if you are not a programmer.
MSHERC.COM	Delete this if you don't plan to use QBasic or if you don't have a Hercules graphics adapter.
*.TXT PACKING.LST (from the DOS directory)	Delete these documentation files when you don't need them any more.
DELOLDOS.EXE CLEANUP.*	You can delete these files after you have used one or the other to remove old DOS files after upgrading (or if you don't plan to use them).
FASTOPEN.EXE	Delete this if you don't plan to use it to cache hard disk directories in RAM.
SHARE.EXE	Delete this if you don't need it in a networking or multitasking environment.
DOSSHELL.* EGA.SYS	You can delete these files if you don't plan to use DOS Shell.

Every file you delete leaves room so you can move your active files closer to the system area, which helps to shorten arm movements. Repeat this procedure often to keep your hard disk optimized.

Recovering Lost Allocation Units

The next step in optimizing your hard disk is to recover any lost allocation units, decide what they are, save the ones you want, and get rid of the rest. A *lost allocation unit* is a cluster that contains valid data but DOS can't figure out to what file it belongs. Most lost allocation units belonged to files that were deleted; you can safely delete them once you know what they contain. Getting rid of the lost allocation units can free up thousands of bytes on your hard disk, giving you space to move active files closer to the directories and FAT. Chapter 15 explains in detail how to use CHKDSK for this process.

TIP   Repeat this procedure often to keep your hard disk optimized.

Defragment and Relocate Existing Files and Subdirectories

It is possible to defragment all your files and subdirectories and to relocate them so that all subdirectories come right after the FATs, your most-used files (probably your program files) come next, and your least-used files come last. This is the optimal organization for hard disk speed.

To do this using only DOS commands, you would have to back everything off the hard disk, reformat it so that it's blank, set up all the subdirectories (so they would be the first items in the data area), then copy files to the disk one at a time, starting with the ones you use most often. By the time you finished the process, the disk would be optimally organized. And you would be exhausted.

You can get third-party utilities that will do the entire job in much less time (although the job still might take a half hour or longer) simply by moving things around on the disk.

This is a task that you should repeat often to keep your disk functioning smoothly. You might want to defragment your files as often as once a week and relocate files once every few months, depending on how often you delete files from and add new files to a disk.

TIP	Chapter 15 explains how to use the CHKDSK command to examine file fragmentation on a disk.

Disk Caching

Once the hard drive has been optimized, you're ready to set up some systems that will speed it up even more. The single most important move you can make is to install a hard disk *cache* system, which stores hard disk data in memory so that you can substitute memory-to-memory transfers for disk reads and writes.

If you have extended or expanded memory, you can install DOS 5's intelligent caching system, SMARTDRV.SYS. (You might also have IBMCACHE.SYS available if you have an actual IBM machine with extended memory.) If not, you can install extra disk buffers to reap some of the benefits of caching.

SMARTDRV.SYS Features

SMARTDRV.SYS sets up a disk cache in either extended or expanded memory. Everything you read from or write to disk is copied to the cache. Whenever you read from disk, DOS looks in the cache first. If the desired material can be found in the cache, the disk access is avoided. You might be surprised how often the same sectors are reread; for example, imagine how many times an hour the root directory is accessed.

SMARTDRV.SYS also includes a *look-ahead* feature. When you read a sector from disk, SMARTDRV copies the next few sectors into the cache too. If you are reading data in sequence, as when loading a file, those are the sectors you will access next (as long as the file isn't fragmented).

SMARTDRV tracks your use of cached data. When the cache is full, it replaces the least-used data with the next read or write. This way, your most active data (such as that root directory) stays in the cache, and something you read only once, such as a program file, is soon replaced with something more useful.

SMARTDRV.SYS was developed for use with Windows, but the latest version has been included in DOS 5. Windows 3.0 interacts well with this version. In fact, Windows will borrow space from the cache to provide extended or expanded memory to its applications. When Windows terminates, the cache space is restored but won't contain any usable data.

N O T E

If you have both Windows 3.0 and DOS 5, you have two versions of SMARTDRV.SYS. Examine their date/time stamps and use the most recent one (which isn't necessarily the last one you purchased).

N O T E

The version of SMARTDRV.SYS included in DOS 5 does not work with Windows 386, version 2.

Installing SMARTDRV.SYS

You install SMARTDRV.SYS with either a DEVICE or DEVICEHIGH command (see Figure 12.3). The default cache size is 256K, but the bigger the cache is, the better, so give it as much space as you can. For example, if you have three megabytes of extended memory that is not used for any other purpose, install SMARTDRV with this command:

```
DEVICE=C:\DOS\SMARTDRV.SYS 3072
```

N O T E

SMARTDRV.SYS requires 20K for its software. It is an excellent candidate for loading into upper memory blocks if your system is set up for that.

If DOS is loaded into the HMA (DOS=HIGH), you have set up a 1M RAM drive in extended memory, and EMM386.EXE is providing access to upper memory blocks, you'll need to use MEM to find out how much XMS memory you have left. If the answer is only 128K, it's still worth your while to set up a cache. The following command will do it:

```
DEVICEHIGH=C:\DOS\SMARTDRV.SYS 128
```

Figure 12.3.

SMARTDRV.SYS
DEVICE Command.

SMARTDRV.SYS

Caches hard disk data in memory.

Format:

DEVICE=[*path*]SMARTDRV.SYS [*size*] [*minimum-size*] [/A]

Parameters and Switches:

none	Creates a 256K cache in extended memory; minimum size will be 0 bytes.
size	Specifies the size of the cache in kilobytes. Range is 128 to 8192; default is 256.
minimum-size	Specifies how much cache space cannot be borrowed by Windows 3.0. Default is 0.
/A	Places the cache in expanded memory

Notes:

Windows 3.0 will borrow cache space as needed to support its applications, as limited by the *minimum-size* parameter. Borrowed cache space loses its cached data. The space, but not the data, is returned when Windows terminates.

Extended vs. Expanded Memory Caches

If you have both extended and expanded memory, use the one that will give you the largest cache. But don't use expanded memory provided by EMM386.EXE; that will run slower than the original extended memory. Redo your EMM386 DEVICE statement to leave room for the cache in extended memory.

N O T E

If the specified cache size won't fit in the available extended or expanded memory space, SMARTDRV will adjust the cache size to fit the available amount of space.

Allowing Windows to Borrow Cache Space

Windows 3.0 functions most efficiently if you give it free rein to borrow as much cache space as it needs, even though it could decache your active data. Let the *minimum-cache* figure default to 0 unless you have a strong reason to do otherwise.

CONFIG.SYS Order

SMARTDRV's DEVICE[HIGH] command must follow the one that installs your XMS or EMS manager. Normally the order of other DEVICE[HIGH] commands isn't important, but if you load a program that usurps whatever extended or expanded memory space is left, be sure to load it after SMARTDRV.SYS.

Assessing the Effectiveness of SMARTDRV.SYS

Unfortunately, SMARTDRV doesn't provide any kind of results report, but you might want to set up a benchmark test of some kind to evaluate its impact. Following are some things you could try with and without SMARTDRV and time the difference:

⊃ XCOPY a large group of files

⊃ spell check a large file that has no spelling errors

⊃ back up the hard drive using BACKUP

⊃ convert a graphic from one format to another

These same benchmarks will come in handy in evaluating the effectiveness of other techniques discussed in this chapter.

IBMCACHE.SYS

If you have both SMARTDRV.SYS and IBMCACHE.SYS available, you'll have to decide which one to install. If you're using Windows 3.0, choose SMARTDRV. If not, you might find that you like IBMCACHE better. It lets you control the amount of data that is read ahead (but only on a limited basis), which SMARTDRV doesn't.

WARNING

Don't install two caching systems. Double-caching wastes both time and memory space.

To install IBMCACHE.SYS, insert the Reference disk that came with your PS/2 into drive A: and enter this command:

```
A:IBMCACHE
```

The installation program will tell you what to do next.

With IBMCACHE, the cache page size determines how far the system looks ahead when reading from disk. You have a choice of two, four, or eight sectors. Use the default value of 4 unless you know that you will be reading long, sequential, unfragmented files often, in which case 8 might be more appropriate. Use 2 if you know that most of your files are short, read randomly, and/or fragmented.

TIP	Third-party caching systems usually give you more control over caching parameters than either SMARDRV.SYS or IBMCACHE.SYS does. Most give you reports that let you assess the effectiveness of your cache and adjust parameters until you have found the best setup.

Disk Buffers

If you don't have extended or expanded memory, you can't use SMARTDRV.SYS or IBMCACHE.SYS. But you can set aside some disk buffering space in conventional memory to speed up disk access a little. Disk buffers are somewhat like a dumb cache.

DOS always reads from disk into a buffer before transferring the data to the program that requested it. Similarly, DOS always writes data from a program into a buffer before writing it to disk. If only one buffer is allocated, it must be used for all reads and writes, so it's unlikely that the data DOS wants next is already present in the buffer. But if 30 buffers are allocated, the probability of finding desired data in a buffer goes up dramatically. If 99 buffers are allocated (the maximum), the probability goes up even more, but in general, system performance goes down because DOS spends more time searching the buffers for desired data than it would take to access the disk.

If you also allocate some look-ahead buffers, DOS will read additional sectors when a program requests one. This increases the probability of finding the next desired sector in a buffer when unfragmented files are read sequentially.

Figure 12.4 shows the format of the BUFFERS command, which belongs in
CONFIG.SYS. If you don't specify the BUFFERS command, DOS allocates a
default number of buffers based on your system configuration. It's a sure
bet the default number is not what you want. If you are using a more intelligent caching system, cut the number of buffers back to about 15. If not, use
Table 12.2 to determine the number of buffers to allocate. Include some
look-ahead buffers if you tend to read unfragmented files in sequential
order.

Figure 12.4.

BUFFERS Configura-
tion Command
Reference.

BUFFERS

Specifies the number of hard disk buffers.

Format:

BUFFERS=$n[,m]$

Parameters:

n The number of read-write buffers. Range is 1 to 99; default (if BUFFERS command is
omitted) depends on your system configuration.

m The number of look-ahead buffers. Range is 1 to 8; default is 1.

Notes:

Buffers are created where DOS is loaded; that is, if DOS is loaded into the HMA, the buffers
are placed there, too. Otherwise, they are placed in conventional memory.

Each read-write buffer takes 532 bytes. Each look-ahead buffer takes 512 bytes.

Table 12.2 Buffer Allocation Recommendations.

disk size	number of buffers
< 40M	20
40M to 79M	30
80M to 119M	40
> 119M	50

FASTOPEN

If you open the same files repeatedly (a database manager or a language
compiler will do this), the FASTOPEN program can speed up disk access
considerably. FASTOPEN caches directory information for every file that is
opened. If you reopen a file whose directory information is in FASTOPEN's

cache, DOS does not have to wade through the directory system to find it; the time savings can be well worth the amount of space FASTOPEN takes.

FASTOPEN does not cache file data itself, just the directory entries necessary to reach the file. This is a different function than BUFFERS or SMARTDRV.SYS provides, and FASTOPEN can significantly improve the speed on systems that also use those features. However, your third-party caching system might include a fast-open feature, in which case you wouldn't want to double it up with FASTOPEN.

Installing FASTOPEN

Use the FASTOPEN command (see Figure 12.5) to install FASTOPEN. Once installed, you can't change or uninstall it without rebooting, so include all your hard drives in one command, as in:

```
FASTOPEN C:40 D:40 E:60 F:80 /X
```

Figure 12.5.

FASTOPEN
Command
Reference.

FASTOPEN

Caches directory entries in RAM.

Format:

FASTOPEN *drive*:[[=]*n*] ... [/X]

Parameters and Switches:

drive: Identifies drive to be cached by FASTOPEN, which must be a non-network hard drive. Up to 24 drives can be specified.

n   Specifies the number of entries to cache on the drive. Range is 10 to 999; default is 48. Each entry takes 48 bytes.

/X   Places the cache in expanded memory.

Notes:

The cache is placed in conventional memory unless /X is specified. FASTOPEN cannot access extended memory.

FASTOPEN can be specified only once after booting. To cancel FASTOPEN or change its parameters, you must reboot.

FASTOPEN can be started from CONFIG.SYS using an INSTALL command in this format:

INSTALL=[*path*]FASTOPEN.EXE *drive*:[[=]*n*] ... [/X]

WARNING

Do not run a disk-optimizing program when FASTOPEN is installed; if you do, FASTOPEN's cached entries will be out of sync with the new layout of the disk, and severe data loss can result.

You can install FASTOPEN from CONFIG.SYS using the INSTALL command, but there's little reason to do so. INSTALL saves a small amount of conventional memory (TSRs loaded with INSTALL are not allocated environment space) and lets you load a program even earlier in the TSR chain. The disadvantage is that you can't use LOADHIGH with INSTALL, and you should load FASTOPEN into upper memory if your system is set up to do so. (The FASTOPEN TSR takes about 5K.)

How Many Entries Should You Cache?

We can't predict how many cached entries will provide optimum performance; the answer depends on your hard disk size, the number of levels in its directory tree, the number of files you'll be opening repeatedly, and their positions in the directory tree. The rule of thumb is to cache one entry for every megabyte of hard disk space, but it wouldn't hurt to double that figure if you can kick the cache up into expanded memory. (It's worth using EMM386.EXE to create some expanded memory for this purpose, if you can. Each FASTOPEN cache entry is 48 bytes long.) Don't go much beyond 200 entries, however, or DOS might spend more time looking for a cached entry than it would using the directory structure.

RAM Drives

A RAM drive is a pseudo drive (often called a *virtual drive*) in RAM instead of on disk, with lightning-fast access times as a consequence. You can store directories and files on it just as you can on a real drive, but all its data disappears when you reboot or the power goes out—and that's the main drawback. Every time you start up your system, your RAM drive is empty; you have to load it with whatever files you want to access from it. When you're ready to shut down, you have to copy any modified files back to a real disk. Data files are simply lost if the power goes out or you have to reboot to kill a misbehaving program.

Even so, RAM drives can be a great boost to your system. Most people limit them to program files and keep data files on a real disk.

Creating a RAM Drive

DOS includes the RAMDRIVE.SYS driver (see Figure 12.6) to create and manage RAM drives. (This is called VDISK.SYS in some DOS versions.) It runs well in upper memory; use DEVICEHIGH if UMBs are available on your system.

Figure 12.6.

RAMDRIVE.SYS
DEVICE Command.

RAMDRIVE.SYS

Creates and provides access to a RAM drive.

Format:

DEVICE=[*path*]RAMDRIVE.SYS [*disk-size* [*sector-size* [*entries*]]] [*switch*]

Parameters and Switches:

none	Creates a 64K RAM drive with 512-byte sectors and 64 directory entries in conventional memory.
disk-size	Specifies the total size of the drive to be created. (System areas will be taken out of this space.)
sector-size	Specifies the size of sectors in the RAM drive. Allowable values are 128, 256, and 512; default is 512. If you specify *sector-size*, you must also specify *disk-size*.
entries	Specifies the number of 32-byte entries in the root directory. Range is 2 through 1024; default is 64. This figure is rounded up to fill a sector with entries. If you specify *entries*, you must also specify *disk-size* and *sector-size*.
1A	Creates RAM drive in expanded memory.
1E	Creates RAM drive in extended memory.

Notes:

If there is not enough memory space to create the specified RAM disk, RAMDRIVE.SYS will attempt to adapt the parameters to provide at least some RAM drive space. Watch boot messages to see what size RAM drive was actually created.

RAM drives are volatile; all data will be lost in a power outage or reboot.

Locating the RAM Drive

Stealing conventional memory for RAM drives is counter-productive, as you'll be short-changing application work space. In general, you should create a RAM drive only if you have the extended or expanded memory space available. Normally it doesn't matter which type of memory you use, but if your expanded memory is supplied by EMM386.EXE, placing the RAM drive in extended memory will make it run faster.

Determining RAM Drive Size

The bigger the RAM drive, the better. After determining what other programs need extended or expanded memory, give the rest to the RAM drive. But if you're considering robbing space from SMARTDRV.SYS, think twice.

In general, SMARTDRV.SYS gives you better performance improvement for the same amount of space.

Number of Directory Entries

If you want to be able to store more than 64 files in the RAM drive, you can either increase the size of the root directory or create subdirectories, which is done just as on any other drive. The space for the root directory and FATs is taken out of the RAM drive's total size. (A RAM drive doesn't have a partition table or boot record.)

Determining Sector Size

There's very little reason to use a sector size other than 512 bytes. Some people feel that you can save slack space if you use a smaller sector size, but DOS works best with the 512-byte size.

NOTE

You can create multiple RAM drives if you wish. Just include a separate DEVICE statement in CONFIG.SYS for each one.

Using the RAM Drive

The RAM drive is created when you boot. DOS assigns it the next available drive letter. A message during booting tells you the drive name.

TIP

You don't need to use LASTDRIVE to make a RAM drive name available. DOS automatically expands the number of available drive names to include RAM drives.

There's no need to format the RAM drive; in fact, you can't. Set up any necessary subdirectories, copy files to the RAM drive, and start using it. You might want to place the commands to set up the RAM drive in AUTOEXEC.BAT so it's ready to go when the command prompt first appears.

| TIP | Don't forget that XCOPY is faster than COPY and will create subdirectories as it goes. Chapter 9 explains this handy command. |

If you are placing temporary files and/or application support files in the RAM drive, be sure to let the application(s) know. You'll need some detailed knowledge about your applications to figure out how to do this.

Some applications depend on an environment variable to locate support and temporary files. For example, DOS and Windows locate their temporary files via the TEMP variable. If you want them to place temporary files in the root directory of RAM drive E (which will speed them up, by the way), include this command in AUTOEXEC.BAT:

```
SET TEMP=E:\
```

In some applications, you identify the location of support files by entering the path in a dialog box. For example, you tell Microsoft Word where to find its standard spelling dictionary through the **Customize** command on the **Utilities** menu, but you tell it where to find its document-specific dictionary through the spell check dialog box. (If you've ever waited for a word processor to load its spelling dictionaries or thesaurus, you'll appreciate what a RAM drive can do. But if you add words to a spelling dictionary in a RAM drive, be sure to copy the modified dictionary back to the hard drive before you lose it.)

Some applications need to be partially reinstalled to relocate their support files. For example, you have to run WSCHANGE to tell WordStar where to locate its dictionaries and other support files.

Some applications would have to be completely reinstalled in order to locate their support files in a RAM drive. After installing an application in a RAM drive, be sure to copy the entire directory or branch to hard disk for permanent storage. Copy it back to the RAM drive whenever you want to start it up.

WARNING

If you forget the switch to create the RAM drive in extended or expanded memory, DOS will try to create it in conventional memory. If it's too large for conventional memory, DOS issues the message "Configuration too large for memory" and freezes. You'll need to boot from a diskette until you can fix CONFIG.SYS. Be sure to have a bootable diskette available when adding a RAM drive to CONFIG.SYS.

CHAPTER 13

BACKING UP AND RESTORING FILES

ntroduction

Your files are the most valuable part of your computer system—not just software, but data files such as your customer database, your five-year plan, the proposal or thesis that's due next week, and your appointments calendar. Hardware and software can be replaced, but the loss of an important data file could be a real disaster. And yet, your files are extremely vulnerable—especially in this day of computer viruses. The next two chapters discuss techniques for preserving and protecting files so that you can recover smoothly from crises such as a hard disk crash or virus.

Backup Systems

The best—the absolute best—protection against data loss is a rigorous backup system. If you have up-to-date copies of all your valuable files stored on diskettes in a safe place, the loss of your hard disk, or even your whole computer, will be an expensive inconvenience rather than a major catastrophe. You'll be able to recover quickly.

A good backup system saves files painlessly and often so that your backups are always up-to-date. It is possible to buy backup systems involving software and/or hardware, such as tape drives, which are generally easy to use and require little work. If you can afford special hardware and software for backups, by all means use it. In this section, you'll see how to use DOS 5's backup tools, which aren't as convenient as a third-party system, but they are available to you right now, free of charge.

What to Back Up

You may not have to back up all files on your hard disk. Many, including the system and DOS files, can be restored from their original distribution diskettes. Applications such as Microsoft Windows, Ventura Publisher, Lotus 1-2-3, and dBASE IV take up lots of disk space and backup time. You don't have to back these up if you are willing to reinstall them when something goes wrong.

TIP	When you first acquire new software, use DISKCOPY to make a working copy of all its diskettes. The working copy serves as a backup of the installed version, and the original diskettes back up the working copy.

You may decide that other files need not be backed up. For example, previous versions of files saved by word processors, databases, and spreadsheet programs probably aren't needed once the newest version is backed up. Files downloaded from another computer could be downloaded again. Your personal notes and memos may not be worth saving. You will have to decide if it is worth the effort to bypass these files when backing up or whether it's easier to just go ahead and back them up.

TIP   Just before a backup is a good time to remove unneeded files from your hard disk. It helps keep your hard disk optimized and saves backup time and space.

It's possible to back files up to a second hard disk, especially one with removable cartridges. But the most common method uses floppy disks, and we assume that medium in this chapter. The techniques are the same if a hard disk is used.

A reasonably active personal computer should be backed up daily—especially if you constantly work on crucial files such as databases, worksheets, and appointment schedules. This chapter assumes that you will back up your files daily. If you don't want to be that rigorous, you might back up your files every two or three days; the techniques are the same even if the time lag is longer.

Backup Strategies

A good backup system requires planning to develop a consistent strategy. Catch-as-catch-can backups are not likely to serve your needs when it's time to restore one or more files. Two backup strategies are common:

➲ Daily full backups of the complete hard disk.

➲ Periodic full backups of the complete hard disk with daily supplemental backups of all files modified since yesterday.

Daily Full Backups

A full backup copies every file on your hard disk, except those that you intentionally skip. It ensures that a current copy of every crucial file is available in one set of backup disks.

It's wise to store two or three days worth of backup disk sets. You might not reuse Monday's disks until Thursday, for example. This way, you can fall back to an earlier version of a file that has become corrupted, you can recover a file that was deleted a few days ago, and you are partially protected if your most recent backup set gets damaged or lost. (We'll refer to previous day's backups as *fallback sets* because they let you fall back to earlier versions of files.)

The advantage of regular full backups lies in the ease of restoring. It's simple to locate the set of disks containing the file(s) to be restored, and the set contains only one version of each file.

But the disadvantages of this method outweigh the advantages for most people. After all, you don't have to restore files very often, but you do have to back them up every day. And a full backup takes a lot more time and disks than a supplemental one.

Daily Supplemental Backups

The supplemental method starts with a full backup. Then each day's modifications are backed up separately and added to the growing set of modified files.

This method is the easiest to handle on a daily basis. It requires the least amount of daily time and the fewest number of disks. But it requires the most work to restore from, as you might have to go through the entire set of disks to find the files you want to restore.

Storing Backup Diskettes

The best place to store your backup sets depends on your situation. Certainly they should be stored in a safe place, but that may be a bookcase, a safe, or even a freezer, depending on the security you need and the type of hazards you expect. You might want to store them off-site in case of fire, theft, or vandalism.

Working with Archive Attributes

DOS uses a file's archive attribute to indicate whether it needs to be backed up. When the attribute is off, theoretically a good backup of the current version exists and a backup is not needed. When the attribute is on, the file has supposedly been modified and needs to be backed up.

DOS turns on a file's archive attribute when it is created or modified. When you copy a file, DOS turns on the archive attribute for the copy. When a file is backed up with BACKUP, its archive attribute is automatically turned off. When it's backed up with XCOPY, the archive attribute is turned off only if the /M switch was specified. These automatic manipulations of the archive attribute help the attribute indicate the file's backup status.

But you can also manipulate archive attributes with the ATTRIB command. When you're ready to do a backup, you can turn on the archive attributes of files that you want backed up, and you can turn off the archive attributes of files that you don't want backed up. Both BACKUP and XCOPY will select files for backing up based on their archive attributes. (Other criteria are also available.)

Commands for Making Backup Files

DOS offers the BACKUP and XCOPY commands to help you back up data. If you find you need more features than these commands offer—such as data compression to conserve disk space—you'll probably have to turn to third-party software to find the system you want.

N O T E

XCOPY is covered in detail in Chapter 9. We'll examine its use only in backing up files in this chapter.

Comparing BACKUP and XCOPY

BACKUP and XCOPY each have advantages and disadvantages. They're different enough that you can't intermix them. You must choose one as your backup tool and stick with it. (You can change your mind if you're willing to start your system over with a full backup.)

BACKUP was designed for backing up files. It minimizes the number of floppy disks needed by filling each one as full as possible, spanning a file over two disks if necessary. It expects to work with multiple floppy disks and tells you when to insert each one. BACKUP automatically deletes all existing files from the root directory of each disk you feed it. It will format a new disk if necessary—a nice convenience.

BACKUP concatenates all the files it backs up into one read-only file. It remembers the path from which each file came. Only RESTORE can access individual files from the backup disks. RESTORE restores files to their original paths (although the drive can be different).

The major disadvantages of BACKUP are that you can't access the files in the backup set directly; you can't even see them listed in the disk's directory. Also, you could lose data from a floppy disk when BACKUP automatically deletes all the files in the root directory.

XCOPY was designed more for copying but has a couple of features that make it useful for backups. XCOPY's advantages are that it makes usable backups, which can be accessed directly on the backup disks. XCOPY lets you restore a file to any path, a minor convenience. And XCOPY doesn't delete anything, although it will overlay a file of the same name on the target floppy disk.

XCOPY's disadvantages are that it doesn't fill target disks or span files. Not only that but it quits when the target disk is full. And it doesn't copy hidden or system files.

Using the BACKUP Command

BACKUP destroys all files in the root directory of each target floppy disk, replacing them with two read-only files named CONTROL.*nnn* and BACKUP.*nnn*; the extension indicates the sequence number of the backup disk within the set. The BACKUP.*nnn* file contains the data from the files backed up on that disk, while the CONTROL.*nnn* file contains directory information for the files. These files aren't in ASCII format; you can't TYPE them or PRINT them. In order to delete them, you'll have to turn off their read-only attributes.

If a floppy disk contained subdirectories before the backup was run, each subdirectory and its files are untouched by BACKUP. Theoretically, you could keep other files on a backup disk, but in practice it's wiser to restrict your backup disks to backups only.

Figure 13.1 shows the complete format of the BACKUP command. The first parameter, the source, can include a drive, path, and/or a specific or global filename. The target must be a drive name only; it can be a floppy disk or a hard drive devoted to storing backups.

Figure 13.1.

BACKUP Command
Reference.

BACKUP

Copies the specified files to the destination drive in backup format.

Format:

BACKUP *source destination-drive* [*switches*]

Parameters and Switches:

source	Specifies where files are copied from. The *source* can include a drive, path, and/or filespec.
destination-drive	Identifies the drive that files are backed up to.
/S	Includes all subdirectories.
/M	Selects only modified files (with a positive archive attribute).
/D:*date* [/T:*time*]	Selects only files modified on or after specified date (and time).
/A	Adds files to earlier backup set.
/F[:*size*]	Formats diskettes (if needed) to specified size.
/L[:*filespec*]	Creates log file; if *filespec* is omitted, BACKUP.LOG is placed in the root directory of the source drive.

Notes:

Formatting of unformatted diskettes is automatic. The /F switch is needed only to format to a smaller size. Use the number of bytes: /F:360, /F:360K, and /F:360KB are all valid.

If you don't use /A, all previous files in destination root directory are deleted. Files in subdirectories are not harmed.

If the specified log file already exists, new log information is added to it.

The three DOS system files (IO.SYS, MSDOS.SYS, and COMMAND.COM or IBMBIO.COM, IBMDOS.COM, and COMMAND.COM) aren't backed up.

The exit code is set as listed in Appendix A.

It's common to run out of formatted disks in the midst of a backup. With earlier DOS versions, people sometimes had to cancel the BACKUP job so they could format more disks, then restart BACKUP from scratch. Now BACKUP handles unformatted disks automatically, calling on FORMAT to prepare them. You need to specify the /F switch only if you don't want new disks formatted to the drive's maximum capacity.

The /L switch controls a backup log, which lists the date of the backup, all files included in the backup, and the disk each file is on. The backup log compensates for the fact that you can't find out what files are contained on a backup disk by viewing its directory. The backup log is an ASCII file; you can view, print, and edit it.

Backup logs are essential to finding files for restoration, and you should always include the /L switch in a BACKUP command. You can specify the name and path of the log file, or you can let them default to \BACKUP.LOG on the source drive, which is a handy place to keep a backup log.

If a specified backup log already exists, the new backup information is appended to it. Otherwise a new file is created.

Daily Full Backup

Suppose you choose to do daily full backups of all files except COM, EXE, OVL, and SYS (but you do want to back up CONFIG.SYS, which is not a program file and is often modified). You can use archive attributes to select and bypass files, setting them every day so that new COM, EXE, SYS, and OVL files will be turned off, and all others turned on. The following batch program accomplishes this:

```
@ECHO OFF

REM Turn on all archive attributes:
ATTRIB C:\*.* /S +A

REM Turn off archive attribute for files to exclude:
ATTRIB C:\*.COM /S -A
ATTRIB C:\*.SYS /S -A
ATTRIB C:\*.EXE /S -A
ATTRIB C:\*.OVL /S -A

REM But make sure CONFIG.SYS is backed up:
ATTRIB C:\CONFIG.SYS +A

REM Back up archive files:
BACKUP C:\*.* A: /S /M /L
```

A batch program like this could be set up as a program item to be executed through the Shell.

The way you handle the log file depends on whether you keep fallback sets. If not, delete the old log file every day and create a new one. All you have to do is add this command to the program, preceding the BACKUP command:

```
DEL C:\BACKUP.LOG
```

If you do save fallback sets, you probably want to save their logs too. One way is to append new log information to the existing log file. The program as originally written will do this. It will eventually build a huge log file. You'll need to go in with EDIT and delete old log information from the file every so often.

Another way is to keep separate logs for the fallback sets, which you could name FALLBAK1.LOG, FALLBAK2.LOG, and so on. If you keep two fallback sets, you could insert these commands before the BACKUP command in the daily backup program:

```
DEL FALLBAK2.LOG
REN FALLBAK1.LOG FALLBAK2.LOG
REN BACKUP.LOG FALLBAK1.LOG
```

These commands move the existing logs back a day, deleting the oldest one. Then the BACKUP program creates a new BACKUP.LOG.

Daily Supplemental Backup

After a full backup, all archive attributes are off. As you add and modify files, their archive attributes are automatically turned on. The following command does a supplemental backup of all files with their archive attributes on, bypassing COM, EXE, OVL, and SYS files (except CONFIG.SYS). It adds the backups to the existing backup set and appends the current log:

```
@ECHO OFF

REM Turn off archive attribute for files to exclude:
ATTRIB C:\*.COM /S -A
ATTRIB C:\*.SYS /S -A
ATTRIB C:\*.EXE /S -A
ATTRIB C:\*.OVL /S -A

REM But make sure CONFIG.SYS is backed up:
ATTRIB C:\CONFIG.SYS +A

REM Back up files that have archive attribute on:
BACKUP C:\*.* A: /S /M /L /A
```

The /A switch is very important, as it causes the new backups to be appended to the existing set on the disk. If you forget the /A, the existing set would be wiped out by the new set.

You can run this job every day. It builds one set of backup disks containing each day's modifications. If one file is modified several times, all versions exist in the set. If you want to keep the full backup and all modifications in one set, insert the last disk of the full backup set when you run this job for the first time after the full backup. The modifications are appended to the end of the full set. Then subsequent days are added to that (as long as you always start with the last disk of yesterday's set).

Using the XCOPY Command

XCOPY (like COPY) doesn't select any files with the system or hidden attribute. Whether or not this is an advantage depends on what you want. To back up these files, turn off all system and hidden attributes with this command:

```
ATTRIB -H -S *.* /S
```

Figure 9.8 (in Chapter 9) shows the complete XCOPY format. Many of its switches are similar to BACKUP's.

Daily Full Backup

Suppose you want to do a daily full backup of all but the COM, EXE, OVL, and SYS files. As with BACKUP, you would need to use the archive attribute to exclude these files (except CONFIG.SYS). The archive attribute also makes it possible to continue the job after the disk is full, as explained in Chapter 9. The following program will do the desired backup:

```
@ECHO OFF
ECHO Please wait while I set attributes. . .

REM Remove all hidden and system attributes:
ATTRIB \*.* /S -H -S

REM Turn on all archive attributes:
ATTRIB \*.* /S +A

REM Exclude COM, EXE, SYS, and OVL:
ATTRIB \*.COM /S -A
ATTRIB \*.EXE /S -A
ATTRIB \*.SYS /S -A
ATTRIB \*.OVL /S -A
```

```
REM But include CONFIG.SYS:
ATTRIB \CONFIG.SYS +A

REM Copy all archive files to A:
:LOOP
ECHO Insert next diskette in drive A:
PAUSE
XCOPY \ A: /S /M
IF ERRORLEVEL 1 GOTO LOOP
```

This job does not format unformatted floppy disks, so you'll have to make sure you have a large enough supply before starting. Also, notice that it turns off hidden and system attributes without restoring them. If that's a problem in your system, add commands to the job to deal with it (Chapter 9 shows some sample solutions).

Daily Supplemental Backup

After the full backup above, all archive attributes are off. They're turned on automatically as files are added and modified. The following job backs up all files with positive attributes, excluding COM, EXE, OVL, and SYS (but including CONFIG.SYS).

```
@ECHO OFF
ECHO Please wait while I set attributes. . .

REM Remove all hidden and system attributes:
ATTRIB \*.* /S -H -S

REM Exclude COM, EXE, SYS, and OVL:
ATTRIB \*.COM /S -A
ATTRIB \*.EXE /S -A
ATTRIB \*.SYS /S -A
ATTRIB \*.OVL /S -A

REM But include CONFIG.SYS:
ATTRIB \CONFIG.SYS +A
```

```
REM Copy all archive files to A:
:LOOP
ECHO Insert next diskette in drive A:
PAUSE
XCOPY \ A: /S /M
IF ERRORLEVEL 1 GOTO LOOP
```

You can use new floppy disks each time you run this job, or you could reuse the previous day's disks. If you reuse disks, then new revisions might overlay previous versions of the same file. You might prefer that, or you might prefer to keep fallback versions.

Leaving Archive Attributes On

The /A switch selects modified files just as /M does, but it doesn't turn off the archive attribute. Use /A when you want to make an interim copy of modified files without affecting the archive attribute used in your regular backup system.

WARNING

If you haven't designed and implemented a backup system yet, do it now.

DIRE WARNING

If you don't, you'll regret it!

Restoring Files

As you work with DOS, a file may be accidentally deleted or replaced by a copy, a disk might be attacked by a virus or inadvertently reformatted. Data may be modified incorrectly or be damaged by malfunctioning hardware or by careless handling. Whenever you have a problem with a file or disk, your first recourse is the backup disk. With up-to-date backups, you will be able to recover the lost data without going through any heroic and heartrending measures.

Restoring XCOPYed Backups

When your backups are made by XCOPY, restoring files is simply a matter of locating the correct backup disks and copying the desired files to the hard disk.

Using REPLACE to Recover Missing Files

Suppose you accidentally deleted files using several global filespecs. RE-PLACE can be an interesting alternative for restoring. REPLACE will compare two directories and copy all the missing files from the source to the target. It will also display a prompt before each copy to let you approve or reject that file. The command below copies all files from the root directory of drive A that aren't present in the current directory of drive C:

```
REPLACE A:\*.* C: /A /P
```

This command is somewhat safer than XCOPY in this situation, since XCOPY might restore files you don't want, even overlaying modified files with earlier versions. The REPLACE command also gets the job done in one command, where XCOPY might take several. But when the /A switch is used, REPLACE handles only one directory at a time, whereas XCOPY will restore to an entire branch or tree.

N O T E

The UNDELETE command (covered in Chapter 15) can also be helpful in restoring deleted files.

Restoring BACKUP Files

If you used BACKUP to preserve files, you must restore them with the RE-STORE command (see Figure 13.2). Files must be restored to the same path from which they were backed up, although they can be restored to a different drive. RESTORE will create the directory structure if necessary, much as XCOPY does.

Figure 13.2.

RESTORE Command Reference.

RESTORE

Restores backed up files to a hard disk.

Format:

RESTORE *source target* [*switches*]

Parameters and Switches:

source	Specifies the drive on which the backed-up files are stored. May be a drive name only
target	Identifies the files to be restored. May include a drive, path, and/or filespec.
/S	Restores files in subdirectories as well.
/P	Displays a prompt if restored file will overlay a read-only or archive file.
/B:*date*	Restores only files stamped on or before this date.
/A:*date*	Restores only files stamped on or after this date.
/E:*time*	Restores only files stamped at or earlier than this time.
/L:*time*	Restores only files stamped at or later than this time.
/M	Restores file only if target has positive archive attribute.
/N	Restores file only if source file is not on target.
/D	Displays list of files to restore, but doesn't actually do any restoring.

Notes:

DOS cannot restore files to drives created by ASSIGN, JOIN, or SUBST, even if they were backed up from those drives.

If the DOS system files (IO.SYS and MSDOS.SYS) are on the backup disks, they will not be restored.

The RESTORE command sets an exit code as shown in Appendix A.

You can restore a single file, all those that match a filespec, all those in a directory or branch, or all the files in the backup set. You can even restore files last modified before or after a given date and time.

Most of the switches parallel those in the BACKUP command. Here they generally refer to the condition of the file on the target drive rather than the source. You may not want to replace read-only files or those that have been modified since the last BACKUP; in that case, include the /P switch to avoid overlaying files in the target drive that have the R or A attribute. If you omit /P, files are restored without question.

If a number of files have been accidentally deleted from the hard disk, you probably want to restore those files without affecting files that still exist. The /N switch lets you restore only files that are missing from the target. If several files on your hard disk are corrupted, you could delete those files, then restore them from the backup set using /N.

TIP	Restoring with /N might restore more files than you intended. Redirect RESTORE's messages to print or to a file for documentation so you can delete unwanted files after RESTORE finishes.

The /D switch lists the files that would be restored, but doesn't actually do any restoration. This affords a cautious approach for tricky situations where you're not sure what effect RESTORE will have.

Restoring Selected Files

Suppose you need to restore C:\CUSTS\CUST.DB and you use the daily full backup method. Suppose also that you don't have a backup log, so you don't know how to find this file in the backup set. RESTORE will locate it for you.

Decide which backup set you want to use—the most recent set or one of the fallback sets. Insert disk #1 from this set into drive A and enter this command:

```
RESTORE A: C:\CUSTS\CUST.DB
```

RESTORE will search through the entire set of backup floppy disks, looking for all versions of the specified file. It prompts you to insert each disk. You don't have to continue all the way to the end of the set. When you see a message that the correct file has been restored, you can press Ctrl+Break to kill the job.

WARNING

Since a file might be spanned over two floppy disks, always let RE-STORE examine the next disk before killing the job.

Now suppose you do have a backup log. Examine the log to determine which disk contains the file to be restored. When RESTORE asks for disk #1, insert the disk that contains the file you want to restore instead. You'll see this message:

```
WARNING! Disk is out of sequence
Replace disk or continue if OK
Press any key to continue . . .
```

Press any key to tell RESTORE to use the disk you inserted. After the file is restored, you can cut off RESTORE with Ctrl+Break.

Restoring from Supplemental Backups

When supplemental backups have been added to a backup set (with BACKUP's /A switch), several versions of the same files may exist in the backup set. If you let RESTORE run through the entire set, it will locate and restore each version. Each newer version will overlay the previous one, so the final result is the most recent version (unless you cut it off sooner with Ctrl+Break). You can also use the backup log to decide which backup disk contains the version you want to restore, and insert only that floppy disk (or two disks if the file is spanned).

Restoring Multiple Files

You can restore a set of files in much the same way as you restore an individual one, but use a generic filespec in the RESTORE command. RESTORE will search the entire set of backup disks for all versions of all files matching the filespec. In this case, it's wise to let RESTORE run through the entire set unless you're positive you know where all the desired files are.

Restoring the Entire Set

To restore an entire backup set, including all subdirectories, use a command like this:

```
RESTORE A: C: /S
```

If appropriate, you can use switches to limit the files restored to those last modified before or after a specific date or to those modified since being backed up.

If supplemental backups were appended to the full backup with /A, the RESTORE command above will restore the full backup, then continue through sequential disks restoring each supplemental backup in turn.

Exit Codes

Although the RESTORE command returns an exit code (see Appendix A), the exit code isn't as useful as for other commands. You might develop a batch program using BACKUP and RESTORE to copy or move a large file, in which case the exit code could come in handy. Using RESTORE in another type of batch program is unlikely.

CHAPTER 14

AN OUNCE OF PROTECTION

Introduction

Backing up your files isn't the only thing you can do to protect your data, although it's the most effective. DOS includes a number of other features to prevent data loss and facilitate data recovery. This chapter also discusses a couple of important tools that are missing from DOS and that you might want to get from some other source.

Format Protection

Before DOS 5, when you formatted a diskette with DOS's FORMAT program, any previous data on it was gone for good. Because every disk has to be formatted before it can be used, and reformatting is an effective way to remove data from a used disk, everyone sometimes reformats diskettes in error. Now FORMAT gives you protection even against itself.

The FORMAT Command

The FORMAT command (see Figure 14.1) prepares a new diskette for use. It also comes in handy to clear a used disk to hold other files.

Figure 14.1.

FORMAT Command Reference.

FORMAT

Prepares a disk for use or reuse.

Format:

FORMAT *drive* [*switches*]

Parameter:

drive   Identifies the drive to be formatted

Format type switches:

no switch   Does a safe format: On a used disk, clears the FAT and root directory but doesn't delete data; saves unformat information; checks for bad sectors. On an unused disk, does an unconditional format.

/Q   Does a quick format: Clears the FAT and root directory but doesn't delete data. Saves unformat information. Doesn't check sectors. This switch is valid for used disks only.

/U   Does an unconditional format: Lays out sectors and tests the surface for bad spots. Installs the boot record, root directory, and FATs.

Control switches:

/V:*label*   Records a volume label, which may be up to 11 characters. If this switch is omitted, FORMAT prompts you to enter label.

/S   Makes a system (bootable) disk.

/B   Reserves space for system files but does not install them; this switch is not needed in DOS 5.0

Disk size switches:

/F:*capacity* Specifies the capacity to format. Use number of bytes, as in 1200, 1200K, 1200KB, 1.2, 1.2M, or 1.2MB. Don't use any other size switches.

/T:*tracks*   Specifies number of tracks on disk; must be used with /S. Don't use with /F.

/S:*sectors*   Specifies number of sectors on disk; must be used with /T. Don't use with /F.

/1   Formats single side of diskette.

/4   Formats 360K (double-density, double-sided) diskette in a 1.2MB (high-density) drive. If used with /1, formats a 180K single-sided diskette.

/8   Formats a 5 1/4-inch diskette with 8 sectors per track instead of the more common 9 sectors (for DOS 2.0 and earlier). This type of diskette formatting can't handle a volume label, so don't use /V.

With DOS 5, diskettes can be formatted in three ways. Table 14.1 compares the effects of the three different format styles. An *unconditional format* (with the /U switch) does low-level formatting, which means that it lays out the sectors and tests the surface for bad sectors. This process obliterates any previous data on the disk. Then FORMAT installs a boot record, root directory, and two FATs, marking the FATs for any clusters that contain bad sectors. A disk formatted unconditionally is like a brand new disk; any previous data cannot be recovered. An unconditional format is the same as DOS's standard diskette format before DOS 5.

A *safe format*, which is the default, does an unconditional format on a new disk. But if the disk has been formatted before, all it does is zero the FAT, clear the root directory, and check the entire disk for bad clusters (without destroying existing data in the clusters). It takes a lot less time than an unconditional format, and any previous data can potentially be recovered with UNFORMAT.

A *quick format* (with the /Q switch) simply zeros the FAT and clears the root directory; it doesn't check for bad clusters. It's the fastest format process, but it can be used only on previously formatted diskettes, as it will not switch into unconditional mode for a new disk.

Saving Unformatting Information

As an additional aid in unformatting, both the safe and quick formats save a copy of the existing FAT and root directory before clearing them. The UNFORMAT program can use this information to recover the disk.

Table 14.1 Format Option Comparison

Function	Unconditional	Quick*	Safe
Clears FAT	✔	✔	✔
Clears root	✔	✔	✔
Redoes sector layout**	✔		
Checks bad sectors	✔		✔
Saves unformat info		✔	✔
Speed	slow	fast	medium

*Can be used only on previously formatted floppy disks.

**Redoing the sector layout deletes all previous data on the disk.

FORMAT saves unformatting information by calling on the MIRROR command (which is discussed next) to store a MIRROR.FIL file near the end of the disk. FORMAT then deletes that file, but UNFORMAT can find it if that becomes necessary.

The quickest way to reformat an old diskette is to combine the /Q and /U switches. FORMAT then doesn't check bad sectors (because of /Q) or save unformatting information (because of /U). It would be difficult to recover previous information reliably after running this command because there is no unformatting information. But if you're sure you don't want to recover previous data and you haven't any reason to suspect bad clusters (such as read or write errors), this is a safe combination of switches.

Unconditional FORMAT Guidelines

You should do an unconditional format if you have experienced any read, write, or "sector not found" errors when using an old diskette. Redoing the sector layout and blocking out bad clusters should clear up any problems. If the FORMAT summary shows too many bad clusters, throw the disk away. (If this happens very often, you should suspect that there is something wrong with your diskette drive or with the way you are handling your diskettes.)

Unconditional formatting also provides security when you are disposing of confidential or sensitive files; since the data is no longer present on the disk, no one can access it using normal means.

> **WARNING**
>
> There are ways to access old data from a disk after unconditional formatting. If you are trying to destroy highly confidential data, you need a government-approved data wiping utility. (Or you could completely trash the diskette.)

If you format a disk to a different capacity than it had before, you must do an unconditional format as the sectors have to be repositioned for the new capacity. If you try to do a safe format in this case, you'll be given a choice of canceling the format or continuing in unconditional mode. (A quick format will ignore the capacity change.)

Recoverable Formats

When you do a safe or quick format, you'll see these messages:

```
Checking existing disk format.
Saving UNFORMAT information.
```

The last line tells you that the disk will be recoverable. A quick format is fine for previously used diskettes that haven't had any problems. It is much quicker than a safe format, because the sectors aren't checked. But if you've had trouble reading or writing files, a safe or unconditional format is a better choice. (If you've encountered "sector not found" errors, choose an unconditional format.)

> **NOTE**
>
> Chapter 15 discusses techniques for rescuing data from a disk with bad sectors. If you don't have good backups, you might need to do this before reformatting the disk.

If a diskette is completely full, FORMAT won't be able to find space to write its unformat information. You'll see a message like this:

```
Checking existing format.
Saving UNFORMAT information.
Drive A error. Insufficient space for the MIRROR
image file. There was an error creating the
format recovery file. The disk cannot be
unformatted. Proceed with format (Y/N)?_
```

The problem is simply that the disk is full. If you are sure you won't want to unformat it, press Y and the format continues without recording the image file. If you aren't sure, press N. After you delete a file or two, you should be able to do a safe or quick format.

Protecting the Disk Structure

You've seen that FORMAT will save system information that makes recovery possible. You can also save system information without doing a format. This is particularly useful with hard disks, as it aids in recovering from system problems. The MIRROR command (see Figure 14.2) works at three levels to protect your data. It doesn't recover data, but it makes recovery more likely with UNDELETE and UNFORMAT.

Figure 14.2.

MIRROR Command Reference.

MIRROR

Saves system information as an aid in restoring damaged disks. Also tracks deleted files for more reliable undeletion.

Formats:

MIRROR /PARTN (To save partition information)

MIRROR [*drive*]... [/1] [/T*drive*[-*nnn*]]...

MIRROR /U (To unload the tracking TSR)

Parameters and Switches:

drive	Identifies the drive whose system information is to be saved.
/PARTN	Saves hard disk partition information (affects all hard drives).
/U	Unloads the MIRROR TSR from memory.
/1	Forces MIRROR to save only the current copy of system information; by default, the previous copy is saved as MIRROR.BAK.
/T*drive*	Specifies that deletions on the specified drive are to be tracked for later undeleting; this switch can be repeated.
nnn	Specifies the maximum number of deleted files to be tracked; the default depends on the drive capacity.

Notes:

Removing the MIRROR TSR with /U works only if no later TSRs have been loaded.

Drive system information is saved in a file in the root directory named MIRROR.FIL. (The previous version is saved as MIRROR.BAK.) Partition information is saved in a diskette file named PARTNSAV.FIL. Delete-tracking information is saved in a file in the root directory named PCTRACKR.DEL.

At the highest level, MIRROR saves information about your hard disk structure, including its partitioning and boot record, the information that makes it possible to boot the system and access the hard disk.

At the next level, MIRROR saves an image of the root directory and FAT, the same information stored by a quick or safe format. This information can help DOS unformat the disk and recover files.

At the third level, MIRROR works as a TSR that monitors file deletions to make undeleting easy and reliable.

Hard Disk Architecture (A Very Brief Overview)

A hard disk is organized in one or more partitions. Each partition functions as an independent logical drive. The first sector on each drive contains a partition table, even if the disk has a single partition. Each entry in the table contains information about one partition: where it starts, how many sectors it contains, what operating system owns it, and whether it is the partition to boot from. The information in this table is crucial to accessing data on the disk.

The partition table includes a master boot record, which identifies the sector size, the cluster size, and the location and size of the file allocation tables. It also includes a short program that executes when you try to boot from the disk. If the partition is bootable, the program loads the operating system into memory and turns control over to it. If not, the program displays a "non-bootable disk" message.

It is possible for the partition table to become corrupted, perhaps by a hardware problem, an editing error, or a virus. (Partition tables are a favorite target of viruses because, when damaged, the entire hard disk is inaccessible.) When you can't boot from your hard disk or even access data on it, you might suspect a corrupted partition table. When you boot from a diskette and enter the hard drive name at the DOS prompt, you might see the message "Invalid drive specification."

Saving Partition Information

MIRROR can save a copy of the partition table along with boot record information in a file on a different disk. This information should be stored on a diskette so it will be accessible when the hard disk fails. The UNFORMAT program uses that file to rebuild your partition table. To save the information enter this command:

```
MIRROR /PARTN
```

MIRROR reads the partition information from all of your hard drives. Then it asks you to insert a formatted diskette and type the letter of the drive that contains it. When you do, MIRROR writes a file named PARTNSAV.FIL to that diskette. Label it clearly and put it in a safe place. You won't have to rerun MIRROR /PARTN unless you repartition your hard disk or damage that diskette.

TIP You should always have a bootable diskette stashed away to use for rebooting in case you have hard-disk access problems. Have MIRROR write PARTNSAV.FIL to this bootable diskette. Copy the DOS files UNFORMAT.EXE and UNDELETE.EXE to it as well. You'll use UNFORMAT to rebuild the partition table, if necessary.

Saving Directory Structure Information

It's unlikely that you'll ever reformat a hard disk accidentally, as FORMAT displays dire warnings when you attempt it. But there are two good reasons to save root directory and FAT information for a hard drive, just as a safe or quick format does for a diskette:

⊃ It aids in recovering removed subdirectories using the UNFORMAT command.

⊃ It aids in recovering from an accidental RECOVER command.

Both UNFORMAT and RECOVER are explained in Chapter 15.

The MIRROR command saves a copy of the FAT and root directory in a file called MIRROR.FIL, which is stored near the end of the disk. UNFORMAT can use it to recover data that has been deleted or trashed by RECOVER.

If you change your directory structure, you want to make sure the MIRROR file has up-to-date information. If you have three hard drives, use a command like this in your AUTOEXEC.BAT file:

```
MIRROR C: D: E:
```

The MIRROR.FIL information is always saved on the disk being protected. If you change the directory structure significantly or alter many of your files, it is useful to run MIRROR again. You might want to have a DOSKEY macro, a batch program, or a Shell program item to run the command when you need it.

Delete-Tracking

When you delete a file, DOS doesn't get rid of the data right away. It overlays the first character of the filename with a special character, indicating that the directory entry can be reused. It also zeros the file's entries in the FAT, indicating that those clusters can be reused. But until other information is written there, you may be able to get the data back.

The UNDELETE command can recover deleted files if their directory entries and clusters have not yet been reused. But it might not be able to find all the data if a file was fragmented. The MIRROR command will track deleted files, keeping the information UNDELETE needs to restore the entire file (unless part of it has been reused by another file's data).

MIRROR with /T*d* saves information about deleted files on every specified drive. A file named PCTRACKR.DEL is placed in the root directory of each drive being tracked. Use a separate /T*d* switch for each drive, as in this command:

```
MIRROR /TC /TD /TE
```

The tracking TSR takes up less than 7K of memory no matter how many drives are being tracked. If your system is set up to use upper memory blocks (explained in Chapter 11), MIRROR is loaded there automatically; you don't have to use LOADHIGH.

TIP Any undelete operation is more likely to be 100-percent successful if you do it as soon as possible after the file is deleted. Once data from another file overlays a cluster, the old data is gone for good. Also, new deletions push old information out of PCTRACKR.DEL.

MIRROR has a default PCTRACKR.DEL file size for each size disk it works with (see Table 14.2). When this space is filled, new deletion information overlays the oldest information. You can tell MIRROR to allow for fewer entries (to save disk space) or more entries (to make undeletions possible for a longer time). Suppose you seldom delete more than a few files from a diskette, but delete a great many from your 120M hard disk. Here's how you might tell MIRROR to save space for only 10 files on drive A but allow for as many as 500 on drive C:

```
MIRROR /TA-10 /TC-500
```

Table 14.2 PCTRACKR.DEL File Size

Space	Entries	File size
360K	25	5K
720K	50	9K
1.2M	75	14K
1.44M	75	14K
20M	101	18K
32M	202	36K
>32M	303	55K

Combining Operations

To save partition table information, you must use only the /PARTN switch on the MIRROR command. But all the other switches can be combined into one command if you like. The following command might be included in an AUTOEXEC.BAT file:

```
MIRROR C: D: /TC /TD /TA-14
```

It updates the disk structure information and sets up the TSR to track file deletions on three drives.

Removing the TSR

If you are tight on memory or don't want a series of deletions to take up space in your PCTRACKR.DEL file, you can remove MIRROR from memory with this command:

```
MIRROR /U
```

If you haven't loaded any other TSRs since MIRROR was loaded, this should successfully unload the TSR. The PCTRACKR.DEL file remains available for UNDELETE to use, but additional deletions aren't recorded in it. When the TSR is loaded again, it uses the same file to track deletions.

NOTE

Other recovery utilities, including the Norton Utilities UnFormat and UnErase programs, will use MIRROR information if their own information isn't available. You don't have to do tracking with more than one program.

Verifying Files

DOS can verify that what is written to disk is a true copy of what is in memory. This provides still another form of data protection for you. Copying files is correct so often most of us don't even think about it. But you may want to have DOS verify all writes as an added measure of protection.

CRCs

In normal use, the drive controller performs a *cyclic redundancy check* (CRC) each time it writes a sector. It performs a calculation on all the bytes in the sector and stores the result in the sector control area immediately following the sector. Then it rereads the sector, recalculates the value, and compares it to the stored value. If they differ, the controller reports a write error to DOS. Later, when the sector is read, the CRC is performed again. If the calculated value doesn't match the stored value, a read error is reported. The CRC will catch all errors that occur after the data is transferred to the disk controller, but you might want to be even more exacting than that.

DOS's Verification

You can also ask DOS to verify each sector it writes. When DOS verifies, it makes sure that each sector is written correctly by comparing it to the data in memory. If verification fails, DOS reports a write error to you.

General Verification

Normally, DOS depends on the hardware's CRC verification and doesn't verify what it writes to disk. You can force it to verify all writes by using VERIFY ON at the command prompt. To find out the current state of verification, enter VERIFY (with no parameters). To turn verification off, enter VERIFY OFF.

General verification will slow down your entire system somewhat. You may prefer to verify only in specific instances.

Specific Verification

The COPY, XCOPY, and DISKCOPY commands let you use the /V switch to request verification for a single command. This switch works regardless of the setting of VERIFY, but it's redundant when VERIFY is ON. As with VERIFY ON, it takes a bit more time, but the delay may be worth it to you in some cases. For example, when you are backing up files, using either VERIFY ON or the /V switch is a good idea.

Comparing Files

Since DOS's verification compares the written file only to the memory version, mistakes can still creep in during a copy operation. The best protection is afforded by comparing the source and destination files. File comparison solves more problems than just ensuring that a copy is accurate. For example, if a program runs strangely, you could compare it to the original on its distribution disk. If they aren't identical, you could make a new copy from the original.

> **TIP**   You can't compare files backed up through BACKUP with the originals, since they are in a different format. You can compare files backed up with XCOPY, however.

Both the COMP and FC commands compare files, giving information about disparities in different ways. COMP is DOS's original file comparison command; it tells you quickly if two files are identical or different. The FC command tries to continue comparing the files after finding an unmatched area.

The COMP Command

The COMP command (see Figure 14.3) has been around since DOS 1 and is somewhat more primitive than FC; it terminates itself after identifying 10 mismatched bytes. The output is normally sent to the screen, but you can redirect it to a printer, a file, or MORE.

When two files are identical you see a message like this:

```
Files compare OK
```

If the files have different lengths, COMP won't compare them unless you force it to. You'll see a message like this:

```
Files are different sizes
```

If the files are different, each mismatched byte is reported in hexadecimal like this:

```
Compare error at OFFSET 22
file1 = 32
file2 = F3
```

Figure 14.3.

COMP Command
Reference.

> **COMP**
>
> Compares two files or sets of files and notifies you if there are any differences.
>
> **Format:**
>
> COMP [*filespec1*] [*filespec2*] [*switches*]
>
> **Parameters and Switches:**
>
> *filespec1*   Identifies the first file or set of files; may be a specific or global filespec.
>
> *filespec2*   Identifies the second file or set of files; may be a specific or global filespec.
>
> /D   Shows differences in decimal format.
>
> /A   Shows differences in ASCII format (characters).
>
> /L   Shows line numbers instead of offsets.
>
> /C   Ignores case differences.
>
> /N=*number*   Compares first *number* lines, even if files are not the same size.
>
> **Notes:**
>
> Default output is in hexadecimal format.
>
> COMP prompts for filespecs and switches if you omit them.
>
> COMP identifies the ends of lines in a file by the presence of carriage returns.

If COMP reports a difference and you want to know exactly what it is, you can specify that mismatch information is to be given in ASCII (/A) or in decimal format (/D) instead of the default hexadecimal. Don't tell COMP to ignore case (/C) if you want to know if the files are identical. Displaying the line number is useful only for certain files, because a line is defined by a carriage return. Binary files usually don't have carriage returns (except inadvertantly). In formatted text files, such as word processing documents, each paragraph is a single line, so a line number may or may not help you identify where the problem is. In ASCII (unformatted) files, each physical line ends with a carriage return, and the displayed line number can be useful.

Figure 14.4 shows screen output in which the first COMP command uses the default hexadecimal and the second uses ASCII with line-number reporting instead.

If you want to compare the first part of two files of different lengths, you have to use the /N switch to force COMP to compare them. To compare the first 300 lines of two files and show any difference in ASCII, use a command like this:

```
COMP C:\CHAPONE.DOC A: /A /N=300
```

```
C:\>
C:\>comp oldvp.bat temp\fixup.bat
Comparing OLDVP.BAT and TEMP\FIXVP.BAT...
Compare error at OFFSET 23
file1 = 44
file2 = 53
Compare error at OFFSET 24
file1 = 44
file2 = 53

Compare more files (Y/N) ? n

C:\>comp oldvp.bat temp\fixup.bat   /l /a
Comparing OLDVP.BAT and TEMP\FIXVP.BAT...
Compare error at LINE 3
file1 = D
file2 = S
Compare error at LINE 3
file1 = D
file2 = S

Compare more files (Y/N) ? n

C:\>
```

The FC Command

The FC command (see Figure 14.5) also lets you compare files, making up
for many of COMP's inadequacies. Most importantly, FC tries to continue
the comparison by locating matching data following a mismatch, so an
extra character early in the file doesn't throw off the whole comparison.

For binary files, FC gives much the same information as COMP but doesn't
stop after 10 mismatches. You may want to redirect the output to a printer
or a file or pipe it to MORE so that you can review it at your leisure.

When it does an ASCII comparison, FC is much more useful than COMP. It
compares two files line-by-line (a line is delineated by a carriage return).
When it finds a mismatch, it checks later lines trying to find a point where
the files match up again. If FC finds a rematch within a certain line limit,
the matching lines are used as the starting point for continuing the comparison.

A successful FC run displays this message:

```
FC: no differences encountered.
```

Figure 14.5.

FC Command
Reference.

FC

Compares two files or sets of files and informs you of any differences.

Format:

FC [*switches*] *filespec1 filespec2*

Parameters and Switches:

filespec1	Identifies the first file or set of files; may be a specific or global filespec.
filespec2	Identifies the second file or set of files; may be a specific or global filespec.
/B	Requests a binary comparison; this is the default if the file extension is .EXE, .COM, .SYS, .OBJ, .LIB, or .BIN (use no other switches).
/L	Requests an ASCII comparison; this is the default for other extensions.
/A	Abbreviates output to first and last lines of unmatched set.
/C	Ignores case.
/LB*n*	Specifies the number of lines in the compare buffer; default is 100.
/N	Displays line numbers during an ASCII comparison.
/T	Doesn't expand tabs to spaces; tabs are expanded by default, with tab stops every eight positions.
/W	Compresses white space: A sequence of spaces and tabs is treated as a single space in both files; spaces and/or tabs at beginning of each line are ignored.
/*nnnn*	Specifies the number of consecutive lines that must match before the two files are considered to be resynchronized. Default is 2.

Notes:

A binary comparison is done byte-by-byte with no resynchronization.

An ASCII comparison is done line-by-line with attempt at resynchronization until compare buffer is filled.

If files cannot be resynchronized within the size of the compare buffer, the comparison fails.

The output from an unsuccessful ASCII comparison displays the lines that don't match. If the /A switch is used, you'll see only the first and last line for each set of differences. By default, two successive lines must match before FC considers the files resynchronized. In the following example, the two files have a single difference—one file is missing a line.

```
C:\>FC AUTOEXEC.BAT AUTODIFF.BAT

Comparing files AUTOEXEC.BAT and AUTODIFF.BAT
***** AUTOEXEC.BAT
REM SET COMSPEC=C:\DOS\COMMAND.COM
VERIFY OFF
PATH C:\DOS;D:\WINDOWS;C:\WS5;C:\;C:\WORD
***** AUTODIFF.BAT
REM SET COMSPEC=C:\DOS\COMMAND.COM
PATH C:\DOS;D:\WINDOWS;C:\WS5;C:\;C:\WORD
*****
C:\>
```

Notice that the matching lines appear in the list of lines from each file. When looking for a matching set of lines after a mismatch, FC uses the contents of the compare buffer, which holds about 100 lines by default. If no match is found within the buffer, you'll be notified that the resynchronization failed. You can use /LB*n* for a larger buffer if necessary; if resynchronization fails repeatedly, try /LB200 and see if that works.

You can use the /*nnnn* switch to change the number of lines that must match to resynchronize the file. /1 sets the number to 1, so only one line must match; /5 requires five successive matching lines. You might see clearly identical lines identified as mismatches in the output if any number other than 1 is used. If one matching line isn't enough to resynchronize the file, those lines aren't considered a match.

Figure 14.6 shows part of the output from this command:

```
FC /C /W CHAP01.DOC A:BACK01.DOC
```

Figure 14.6.

FC Output.

```
Comparing files REMLINE.BAS and NEWLINE.BAS
***** REMLINE.BAS
'    the output lines in SUB GenOutFile. An example is shown in comments.
DEFINT A-Z
***** NEWLINE.BAS
'    the output lines in SUB GenOutFile. An example is shown in comments.
'    Set all default variable names to integer
DEFINT A-Z
*****

***** REMLINE.BAS
' Function and Subprocedure declarations
DECLARE FUNCTION GetToken$ (Search$, Delim$)
DECLARE FUNCTION StrSpn% (InString$, Separator$)
***** NEWLINE.BAS
' Function and Subprocedure declarations
' Declare statements inserted automatically
DECLARE FUNCTION GetToken$ (Search$, Delim$)
' Rest also automatic
DECLARE FUNCTION StrSpn% (InString$, Separator$)
*****


C:\DOS\QBASIC>
```

The comparison ignores any case differences and compresses white space. Two lines (the default) are required for resynchronization; notice that an apparently matching line appears in the middle of the second set.

The DISKCOMP Command

When you copy diskettes, you may want to make absolutely sure they are identical before storing or shipping the copies. The /V switch on the DISKCOPY command makes sure the data is written correctly from memory, but you need a command like DISKCOMP (see Figure 14.7) to make sure the data was both read and written correctly.

Figure 14.7.

DISKCOMP
Command
Reference.

DISKCOMP

Compares two diskettes of the same capacity on a byte-by-byte basis.

Format:

DISKCOMP [*drive1* [*drive2*]] [*switches*]

Parameters and Switches:

drive1	Identifies one drive for the comparison. Default is the current drive.
drive2	Identifies one drive for the comparison. Default is the current drive.
/1	Compares only the first side (even if double-sided).
/8	Compares only the first eight sectors per track, no matter how many sectors there are (for disks created under early DOS versions).

Notes:

You can't use DISKCOMP with hard drives.

Both diskettes must be the same type, although you can use /1 or /8 to make certain types of diskettes compatible.

To do the comparison using a single drive, name it (or imply it) as both *drive1* and *drive2*. You'll be prompted to insert diskettes as needed.

DISKCOMP sets an exit code as shown in Appendix A.

If you compare disks that were just DISKCOPYed and find errors, the problem may be the drive itself, a memory chip, or one of the disks. Hardware and media do wear out eventually.

Write Protection

Still another way to protect data is with write protection. It won't protect against sabotage, because any somewhat knowledgeable person can turn it off. It does protect against accidental overwriting, however.

A diskette can be write-protected by placing a write-protect tab over the notch (5 1/4-inch) or sliding the write-protect plastic tab to open the hole (3 1/2-inch). Hard disks can't be write-protected through DOS, although some third-party software allows this.

Files can be protected somewhat by setting the read-only or system attribute. A file with one of these attributes can't be changed or deleted by many programs that run under DOS. Anyone can change the attribute, however, then do what they will. And some DOS utilities, such as BACKUP and REPLACE, will overwrite or delete read-only or system files without warning.

Read-only files are listed in directory listings just like other files unless you exclude them with an /A*x* switch. System files aren't normally listed in directories, but you can include them with /A or /AS.

By default, the Shell includes read-only files but not system files in directory lists. You can include hidden and system files by choosing **Options File Display Options** and checking **Display hidden/system files**.

Read-only files and system files can be deleted through the Shell. A message warns you when a file is read-only and asks if you really want to delete it. If you choose Yes, DOS removes the read-only attribute and deletes the file. System files will be deleted without warning.

Additional Data-Protection Needs

A couple of important data protection functions aren't available through vanilla DOS. You may want to acquire third-party software to handle these.

Viruses (or Viri)

A virus is a program that hides in your system, waiting for something to trigger it. Then it starts up and destroys data or fills up empty spaces on your disk. Viruses usually arrive hidden in some seemingly innocuous software. They are generally created by programmers with an axe to grind (or a strange sense of humor).

Name-brand software in its sealed, original packaging should be virus-free. Viruses may creep into your system if you download files from a bulletin board or communications service or if you install freeware, shareware, pirateware, or some other type of alternative software. Problems can occur any time you share files or diskettes with someone who is less than scrupulous about where they come from. As always, your best protection from viruses is a good backup system so that you can recover your data.

Two types of anti-virus software are available: scanning and monitoring. Scanning software searches your disks for strings of data that appear in known viruses. This will tell you if any dormant viruses are stored in your system, although it might not be able to recognize all viruses. If a virus is detected, you can opt to have it removed.

A monitoring system takes the form of a TSR that constantly watches your system, detecting the types of behavior that indicate a virus at work. It will prevent the virus from writing to your hard disk and notify you of the problem. Virus monitoring will slow down your system, but the trade-off may be worth it, especially if you have made your system vulnerable by loading files not guaranteed to be virus-free.

Parking Your Disk Heads

When you turn off your computer, the hard disk stops spinning and the read/write heads have to settle somewhere. Many hard disks move the heads to a safe landing zone, but others just let the heads land wherever they happen to be, which can damage the disk surface over time. If your hard drive does not park its heads automatically (check its manual to find out), you should use a program to park the heads in a safe place before shutting down.

DOS does not include a parking program. Several third-party utility packages include one, or you may be able to get one from your dealer for a slight charge (make sure it's virus-free). If your system arrived with one already installed on the hard disk, be sure to use it.

A TON OF CURE

Introduction

No matter how careful you are or how many preventive measures you take, eventually you're going to lose some data. Whether it's from malfunctioning hardware or media, a virus, or a simple typo, you'll have to do your best to recover it.

DOS 5 includes a number of diagnostic and recovery tools that can help you respond to errors in the system areas and directory tree, bad spots on the disk media, accidentally deleted files, and accidentally reformatted disks. DOS's tools can handle most of your recovery needs. But you may need to turn to outside solutions in some cases.

Checking and Fixing Disks (CHKDSK)

The CHKDSK command (see Figure 15.1) identifies file and disk problems by analyzing the file allocation table (FAT) and directory structure. In some cases, it can correct problems. Or you might use other DOS commands to solve a problem or at least to save as much data as possible. Still other situations can't be easily solved within DOS, and you may need to resort to third-party data-recovery utilities or a disk repair specialist.

Figure 15.1.	
CHKDSK Command Reference.	**CHKDSK** Reports disk and file fragmentation status; diagnoses and repairs problems in the FAT and the directory structure **Format:** CHKDSK [*drive:*] [*filespec*] [*switches*] **Parameters and Switches:** None Displays summary report of current drive. *drive* Identifies drive to be checked; default is current drive. *filespec* Identifies file(s) to be checked for fragmentation; may be global. /F Fixes errors in FAT and directory tree wherever possible. /V Lists all files found on the disk. **Notes:** CHKDSK reports on errors even if you omit /F. It offers to make corrections but follows through only if /F was included. CHKDSK identifies pseudo-errors if run with files open; don't run under another program. CHKDSK doesn't work on drives formed by SUBST, JOIN, ASSIGN, or network drives.

WARNING

Some third-party recovery utilities require that they be run *before* you try CHKDSK with /F. They cannot function if CHKDSK has already tried to fix a problem.

Whenever you notice a disk or file access error or a general slowing of disk access, run CHKDSK (without /F) as a first step in determining the problem. Many people run it weekly or daily to head off potential problems. When you run CHKDSK without any parameters or switches, you see a summary report on the current drive similar to the following:

```
Volume FIXED DISK  created 03-27-1991 11:05a
Volume Serial Number is 16E8-7B6A

33462272 bytes total disk space
  327680 bytes in 11 hidden files
   69632 bytes in 24 directories
30998528 bytes in 1125 user files
    4096 bytes in bad sectors
 2062336 bytes available on disk

    2048 bytes in each allocation unit
   16339 total allocation units on disk
    1007 available allocation units on disk

  655360 total bytes memory
  551744 bytes free
```

The report shows information on the drive itself, including the size and number of allocation units (or clusters). This is followed by a report on conventional memory, a pre-MEM leftover.

The bad sectors shown are not a problem. They were detected when the disk was formatted, and the FORMAT program marked them in the FAT so no data is stored in them. Any problems identified by CHKDSK would be listed before the report summary.

TIP   All of CHKDSK's messages, even those indicating problems on the disk, are sent to standard output so that they can be redirected to print for documentation purposes.

The File Allocation Table

DOS locates a file by starting with its directory entry and continuing to its FAT entries. The directory entry tells DOS the size of the file and the first cluster it occupies. The FAT then locates the remaining clusters belonging to the file (if any), in the proper order.

The FAT is simply a table with one entry for every cluster on the disk. Each entry contains one of the following:

⊃ The number of the next cluster belonging to the same file.

⊃ An end-of-file indicator.

⊃ A 0, indicating the cluster is available.

⊃ A bad cluster indicator, which prevents DOS from ever using the cluster.

Examining the FAT

There are no clusters 0 and 1, so the FAT starts with an entry for cluster 2. Suppose these are the first 20 entries (for clusters 2 through 21) in a FAT:

```
         3    4    5 EOF    7    8
16    0    0 BAD EOF EOF   15 EOF
17   18   21 EOF    0 EOF
```

Suppose the drive's root directory indicates that the file named OLDMILL.DOC starts in cluster 2. The FAT entry for cluster 2 contains the value 3, indicating that this cluster starts a *chain* that continues with cluster 3. The entry for cluster 3 chains to cluster 4, which in turn chains to cluster 5. Cluster 5 contains an end-of-file indicator (EOF), so OLDMILL.DOC ends there; it is completely contained in four clusters. (The file's size, contained in the directory entry, should confirm that the file needs four clusters.)

Suppose another directory entry indicates that FAMILY.CRD begins in cluster 6. The FAT shows that the file chains to clusters 7 and 8, then jumps to 16, 17, and 18, and finally to cluster 21, which marks the end of the file. This file uses seven clusters in three fragments.

Entries for clusters 9, 10, and 20 contain 0s; these clusters are available, probably as a result of deleted files.

Cluster 11 was marked as bad by the formatting program (or possibly some other program, such as RECOVER which is explained later in this chapter). A bad cluster will never be used for data.

The EOF marks in clusters 12, 13, and 19 may represent one-cluster files or the last fragments of files begun elsewhere on the disk. We'd have to check the entire directory tree and FAT to know for sure. Cluster 14 starts (or continues) a file that ends in cluster 15.

Sample FAT Data

DOS itself doesn't let you look at the FAT, but Figure 15.2 shows a section of a FAT in the format displayed by some third-party utility programs. This FAT contains several allocation problems; we'll refer back to it later in this chapter.

Figure 15.2.

FAT Display.

		3	4	4	<EOF>	<EOF>	<EOF>
0	10	11	12	13	14	15	16
17	18	19	<EOF>	21	22	23	24
25	26	18	28	29	30	31	32
33	34	35	36	37	38	39	40
<EOF>	0	0	0	0	<EOF>	47	48
49	1	51					

Notice that the each line shows information for eight clusters. As always, clusters 0 and 1 don't exist.

By analyzing the directory structure and the FAT, CHKDSK can tell whether allocation units are in use but not connected to a specific file (*lost* allocation units), whether an allocation unit is assigned to more than one file chain (*cross-linked* allocation units), whether a file chains to an invalid allocation unit (such as 1), and whether the number of allocation units assigned to a file matches the recorded file size. It can also determine if the FAT itself has developed a bad sector and which, if any, files are fragmented.

Detecting and Fixing Errors

When you run CHKDSK without the /F switch, it detects and reports all errors. If CHKDSK could fix an error, you'll be asked if it should try. No matter whether you answer Y or N, however, CHKDSK won't make any change to the disk until you run it with /F. When CHKDSK terminates, you'll see a message something like this:

```
Errors found, F parameter not specified
Corrections will not be written to disk
```

Once you know an error was detected and whether or not CHKDSK can fix it, you can decide whether to let CHKDSK fix it or to try something else. If you want to let CHKDSK try, run the command exactly as before (use DOSKEY to recall it) with the /F switch added.

The next part of this chapter shows the errors that CHKDSK detects, what causes them, what CHKDSK can do about them, and other solutions you may want to try.

NOTE

Don't run CHKDSK with /F under another program, such as DOS Shell or Microsoft Windows. If any files are open (which they probably are), CHKDSK will detect and correct false errors.

Lost Allocation Units

CHKDSK's most common error message reports lost allocation units, which are clusters allocated to file data but not linked to a file directory entry. It isn't all that unusual to have several kilobytes involved in lost allocation units.

How Clusters Get Lost

Anything that interrupts DOS before it can finish closing or deleting a file could result in lost allocation units. Some of the more common causes are:

- ➲ shutting down or rebooting without waiting for the drive access light to go out

- ➲ having to reboot when a program hangs up

- ➲ power fluctuations

Lost clusters can also be the result of more serious problems, such as hardware malfunctions, media deterioration, or viruses. But in general you can assume that lost allocation units are normal unless you detect other symptoms of a malfunctioning system.

Handling Lost Clusters

However they occur, you deal with lost clusters in the same way. Suppose CHKDSK with no switches produces a report like this:

```
Errors found, F parameter not specified
Corrections will not be written to disk
    6 lost allocation units found in 2 chains
      12288 bytes would be freed
```

These messages tell you that 12K bytes on the disk are tied up in lost allocation units. Recovering them makes that space useful again. When you use CHKDSK /F, the message looks like this:

```
6 lost allocation units found in 2 chains
Convert lost chains to files (Y/N)?
```

At this point, you can't just ignore the situation; you must choose to convert the lost clusters to files or delete them. If you press Y (or Enter), each chain is converted to a file named FILE*nnnn*.CHK. You can examine the resulting files to see what data they contain. If the data is nothing you need to keep (the usual case), all you have to do is delete the files and the space is freed for future use. If you press N, the lost allocation units are zeroed in the FAT, freeing them immediately for future file data.

Overfilling the Root Directory

A root directory has a limited number of entries; the maximum depends on the disk size. CHKDSK may recapture hundreds of lost chains at once if you've allowed them to build up on your disk. Since they are all placed in the root directory, you might see this message:

```
Insufficient room in root directory
Erase files in root and repeat CHKDSK
```

It's time to examine and deal with all the FILE*nnnn*.CHK files that have been created so far. Delete as many as possible and copy the ones you want to keep to other directories. Then reenter the CHKDSK /F command to recover more lost allocation units.

Cross-Linked Allocation Units

The next most common problem identified by CHKDSK is a cross-linked allocation unit; this is an allocation unit that is assigned to two different files or to two different locations in the same file. The FAT in Figure 15.2 shows several cross-linkages, as shown in this CHKDSK report:

```
C:\STUDY.CHP
     is cross linked on allocation unit 4
C:\FOOLS.CAP
     is cross linked on allocation unit 18
C:\POSTSCRP.WID
     is cross linked on allocation unit 18
```

If only one file is cross-linked on an allocation unit, such as STUDY.CHP in the above report, the cluster is used twice in the file. Notice in Figure 15.2 that the FAT entries for clusters 3 and 4 both contain the value 4, causing the cross-linking problem. The file chain bogs down at that point because there's no indication of what cluster is next. (We can guess that cluster 4 is really supposed to chain to cluster 5, but neither DOS nor CHKDSK will make that kind of assumption. It's a good bet that cluster 5 in the example is a lost allocation unit.)

When two or more files are cross-linked on the same allocation unit, both files reference that cluster. In Figure 15.2, both FOOLS.CAP (which starts in cluster 9) and POSTSCPT.WID (which starts in cluster 20) chain to cluster 18. Here again, we can guess that the FOOLS.CAP chain is correct, while POSTSCPT.WID should chain to cluster 27. But DOS and CHKDSK aren't equipped for guessing. (The chain from cluster 27 to cluster 40 is probably lost.)

How Files Get Cross-Linked

Files become cross-linked in much the same way that allocation units get lost. Cross-linking is less common but more bothersome, since CHKDSK can't even try to fix it.

Dealing with Cross-Linked Allocation Units

If you have valid backups of cross-linked files, you have the ideal solution. Just delete the cross-linked files and restore them from the backups. If not, you have to deal with the problem some other way. CHKDSK has no way of knowing which file is correct and which is wrong; nor can it guess at how to fix the wrong one.

As you've seen in the examples, if you could view and edit the FAT, you may be able to guess at the correct way to resolve a cross-link. DOS has no facility for this but, as usual, you can buy third-party utilities that do. In fact, they let you view the contents of the clusters, too, so you can see whether your guesses are correct.

If you don't have access to such a utility and you want to try resolving the cross-link using DOS, you can try the procedures in the next section. They will be most effective with files containing text. It would be difficult for you to recognize the data in a worksheet, graphic, or program file, for example, simply by viewing it.

WARNING

Don't try to rescue a cross-linked program file. You could create an invalid program module that, when executed, could damage data on your hard disk. Always restore program files from their original distribution diskettes.

A Single Cross-Linkage

When a single file is cross-linked, two of its FAT entries chain to the same cluster. A loop is created, and the chain never reaches the end of the file. If you copy the file, DOS follows the chain until the right number of clusters are copied, but the result won't be correct. In all likelihood, the tail end of the file has been orphaned in the FAT. Converting lost allocation units to files will probably recover it for you.

Following these steps could recover all, or most, of the file:

1. Copy the file under a new name. The new file will not be cross-linked, although it probably won't contain the right data.

2. Delete the cross-linked file to get rid of the cross-linkage in the FAT.

3. Recover all lost allocation units into files.

4. Examine the new file under the application that created it, if possible. Eliminate duplicated data and decide what data is missing, if any.

5. Examine the FILE*nnnn*.CHK files to see which ones, if any, contain data belonging to the damaged file.

6. Use the file's original application to insert the desired CHK files into the damaged file, if possible.

7. Deal with the other CHK files, if any, as you do whenever recovering lost allocation units.

Multiple Cross-Linkage

When two files are cross-linked, a FAT entry for one of them contains a cluster number that really belongs to the other. When DOS tries to trace the FAT chains, both files end with the same cluster(s). One of the files is probably correct. If you don't have valid backups of the files, your problem is to discover which file is correct and recover as much as possible of the other file. The following steps might help for a text file:

1. XCOPY each file to a new name.

2. If the cross-linkage causes one file to be shorter than its directory entry indicates, XCOPY will go into a loop, endlessly repeating the file name on the screen. When this happens, press Ctrl+Break to end it. That's your problem file right there.

3. Delete the original, cross-linked files.

4. If you still don't know which file is damaged, examine each copy under the application that created it, if you can. You should be able to see which one is valid and which is damaged.

5. Call up the damaged file under the application that created it, if you can.

6. Delete any invalid data in the file.

7. If any data is missing from the damaged file, recover lost allocation units with CHKDSK.

8. Examine the CHK files and locate any data belonging to the damaged file.

9. Use the application to insert the desired CHK files into the damaged file, if possible.

10. Deal with the other CHK files, if any, as you do whenever recovering lost allocation units.

Invalid Allocation Units

A value in a file's FAT chain represents an invalid allocation unit if it is 0, 1, or larger than the number of allocation units on the disk. While 0s are valid for unused clusters, they should not show up in a file chain.

Figure 15.2 shows an invalid allocation unit in the file that starts in cluster 46; cluster 49 contains the value 1, which breaks the chain. In this case, CHKDSK knows the file has more clusters from the size in the directory entry, but it has no way to find the rest of the file's chain. (As always, it can't guess.)

Any other clusters that may have belonged to the file are orphaned; you may be able to find them among the lost clusters on the disk.

CHKDSK notifies you about invalid allocation units like this:

```
C:\BOOK1\CHAPTER.CPY
    First allocation unit is invalid, entry truncated
C:\BOOK1\STUDY.STY
    Has invalid allocation unit, file truncated
19 lost allocation units found in 4 chains
    38912 bytes would be freed
```

If the first allocation unit is invalid, no part of the file can be saved directly. At least one chain of lost allocation units probably belongs to this file, unless it was a one-cluster file. The invalid allocation unit in the second example is not the first cluster in the file, so at least part of the file can be found. Unless the invalid entry is at the end of the file, at least one lost chain should have data from this file.

How CHKDSK Fixes Invalid Allocation Units

If you can't restore the file from its backup and you use the /F switch, CHKDSK replaces an invalid entry with an end-of-file marker and adjusts the file size in the directory to match the number of clusters. When asked, type Y to tell CHKDSK to save any lost chains as files. Now you can access the file (if possible) and find out how much data you've lost, then examine the CHK files to recover what you can. As always, don't try to run a program file that has been treated this way.

Allocation Errors

CHKDSK reports a general allocation error when it detects that the size recorded for the file in the FAT doesn't match the number of allocation units assigned to it. You'll see a message like this one:

```
A:\NEWSTUDY.DOC
        Allocation error, size adjusted
```

If you haven't used /F, of course, the size in the directory entry isn't really adjusted.

How CHKDSK Fixes an Allocation Error

When /F is specified, CHKDSK fixes an allocation error by adjusting the file's size in the directory entry. The entire last cluster is considered as part of the file, since CHKDSK can't tell where the file ends and slack begins.

If the recorded size really was wrong and the number of allocation units in the FAT was correct, CHKDSK's repair may add slack (garbage) to the end of the file. If the recorded size was correct and the FAT included too few or too many allocation units for the file, the resulting file is incorrect; it is either too long or too short. Either the file now contains garbage at the end or there are some lost allocation units on the disk. But, at any rate, now you can access the file to figure out what to do next.

Dealing with Allocation Errors

WARNING

If CHKDSK detects an allocation error on a program file, delete the file and reinstall the program from its original diskettes.

When CHKDSK reports an allocation error in a file, and if you can't restore the file from its backup, run CHKDSK again with /F and let it adjust the file's size. Save any lost chains as files. When CHKDSK is finished, examine the damaged file under its original application, if you can. You may have to delete unwanted garbage at the end. Or you may have to locate and insert missing data from the CHK files created by CHKDSK.

Invalid Subdirectory Entry

Subdirectories are stored as files with a special directory attribute. They can be corrupted in many of the same ways that files can. If the .. directory entry shows the wrong cluster number for the parent, for example, DOS can't find the linkage from that subdirectory to its parent. If the parent's link to the child is corrupted, DOS won't be able to locate the subdirectory.

When CHKDSK detects an invalid subdirectory, the message depends on the severity. You might see this:

```
C:\BOOK1\CHAP03.DOC
    Invalid sub-directory entry
```

In this case, CHKDSK can fix the problem. It might be a corrupted entry for the backlink to the parent directory, for example. CHKDSK can search the tree, find the address of the parent that way, and fix the subdirectory entry. In this case, no files or allocation units are lost.

On the other hand, an invalid subdirectory entry message might be followed by some lines like these:

```
324 lost allocation units in 5 chains
   165888 bytes disk space would be freed
Convert lost directory to file (Y/N)?
```

This message usually indicates that you can't access anything in the subdirectory, and all its files appear to be lost chains, as do all its subdirectories and their files. CHKDSK can't do anything to fix the subdirectory entry.

What CHKDSK Does

If it doesn't ask about converting the subdirectory to a file, CHKDSK with the /F switch can find the information it needs. It quietly fixes the problem without losing any data.

But if CHKDSK asks and you type Y to convert a lost directory to a file, DOS makes the cluster that formerly contained the subdirectory into a file. Since they are no longer linked to the directory structure, allocation units for all files in the branch headed by that subdirectory are lost. You should respond with a Y when CHKDSK asks if you want to convert them to files.

Dealing with Invalid Subdirectory Entries

If you are offered the opportunity of converting an invalid subdirectory into a file, you might say yes for safety's sake, although there's very little you can do with the resulting file. But it is important to recover lost allocation units into files if you can't restore the branch from backups.

To restore the branch, remake all the subdirectories, then examine all the CHK files and copy them to their former subdirectories with their correct names. As a final step, delete any CHK files you don't need anymore.

Bad FAT Sectors

CHKDSK doesn't check for bad sectors or other surface problems on a disk. However, if the FAT itself has developed problems, you may see one of these messages:

```
Bad sector in FAT

Probable nonDOS disk
```

The "Probable nonDOS disk" message may reflect a bad spot in the boot record, rather than in the FAT. Either message reflects too major a problem for CHKDSK to handle.

If the problem is with a diskette and you have a valid backup, you'll probably just throw away the damaged one. But if the problem is on a hard disk, you might need to reformat it, repartition it, or get it repaired. In any case, you'll lose the current data on the hard disk and will need to restore it from your backups after the problem has been solved.

TIP | The Norton Utilities can do a surface analysis of a disk, giving you more information about bad spots and how to work around them.

Fragmentation

If you include a filespec in the CHKDSK command, CHKDSK tells you about file fragmentation. Fragmentation slows down disk access and lessens the chance of recovering files properly with UNDELETE and UNFORMAT.

This command checks all the files in the current directory:

```
CHKDSK *.*
```

Following the CHKDSK summary report, the fragmentation report looks something like this:

```
C:\STUDY.STY contains 6 non-contiguous blocks
C:\BATTERUP.COM contains 3 non-contiguous blocks
```

This message uses the word *block* to refer to a fragment (a group of contiguous clusters).

How Fragmentation Occurs

In normal, everyday use, you delete files from a disk and add other ones. When a file is deleted, DOS zeros its FAT chain. The next time DOS adds a file, it may reuse the clusters that were freed. If you erase six small files that are scattered about on your disk, then copy a large file to that disk, it may be divided into six or more fragments to fit into the available space. DOS will fragment a file even if there's a large enough space available later on the disk.

Defragmenting Files with DOS Commands

If a diskette is fragmented, you can clean it up by copying all the files (with COPY or XCOPY, not DISKCOPY) to an empty diskette. COPY and XCOPY both copy each file as a unit, so any fragments are brought together on the target diskette as long as there aren't any "holes" to fill in; that's why the target diskette must be empty. If you use DISKCOPY, however, the copy is made sector-by-sector, without regard to individual files, and any fragmentation on the source diskette is copied to the target.

Defragmenting is not so simple on a hard disk. You could, of course, do a complete backup, empty (or reformat) the hard disk, and restore all the files. But most people wouldn't dream of doing this; it takes too much time and effort. If you have several hard disks, you may be able to empty one of them, copy another hard disk to the empty one, empty the source, then restore it from the copies. (XCOPY is perfect for this job.)

N O T E

Chapter 12 discusses hard disk optimization in more detail, including third-party defragmenters that are much more efficient than XCOPY.

Undeleting Files

DOS doesn't remove a file's data from the clusters when it deletes the file. Instead, it overlays the first character in the filename with E5H, which displays as a lowercase sigma (σ), and zeros out the file's chain in the FAT.

These two actions make the directory entry and clusters available for reuse, but they do not actually delete the file's contents. As long as the file has not been overwritten by data for another file, DOS 5 can undelete the file. You may have to provide the first character of the filename, but that's all.

If you used MIRROR to set up delete-tracking, the MIRROR TSR program records the deleted file's directory entry and FAT chain in the PCTRACKR.DEL file. The UNDELETE program can use this information to undelete the file without asking for the first character of the filename. The PCTRACKR.DEL information also makes undeleting fragmented files more successful, because the exact chain is documented.

TIP	The best way to undelete a file is to restore it from its backup. Use UNDELETE only if you don't have a valid backup of the file.

Using UNDELETE

The UNDELETE command has several functions. You can use it to see what files are available for undeleting with or without the delete-tracking information. You can undelete a single file, a set of files that match a wildcard specification, or all the deleted files in a directory. You can't use UNDELETE to recover a subdirectory or to undelete a file in a directory that has been removed, however.

How DOS Undeletes a File

There are two different ways DOS can undelete a file; one uses PCTRACKR.DEL and the other uses deleted directory entries.

If delete-tracking information has been saved, the preserved directory entry and FAT chain tell DOS all it needs to know to restore the file as long as the clusters are still available. If there is no delete-tracking information, UNDELETE can search through the directory for deleted entries—those that start with the E5H character. Assuming the desired entry is found, it shows the file's size and the number of its first allocation unit. UNDELETE then checks the FAT; if the first allocation unit is still available (that is, its FAT entry contains a 0), UNDELETE recovers it and as many adjacent, available clusters as needed to make up the file's size. If enough contiguous clusters are not marked with 0s, UNDELETE recovers the available ones and warns you that the entire file could not be recovered.

WARNING

If you need to undelete files, try not to add any data to the disk, even if delete-tracking is in effect. DOS might overlay the very data you need to undelete. Don't even start up any program other than UNDELETE; it may create temporary files upon startup.

Problems in Undeleting Files

In some situations, UNDELETE will be unable to recover any part of a file:

- It can't recover a file whose first cluster has been reused.
- It can't recover a file that was replaced during a file copy.
- It can't find a deleted file if delete-tracking information is not available and the file's directory entry has been reused.
- It can't undelete a directory. You may be able to recover a deleted directory and its files with UNFORMAT, however.

In some situations, UNDELETE can recover only part of a file:

- If delete-tracking information is not available and a file was fragmented, UNDELETE can recover only the first fragment.
- If the first cluster of a file is available but later clusters have been re-used, UNDELETE offers you the choice of recovering a truncated file.

In some situations, UNDELETE will recover incorrect clusters into a file:

- If a deleted file was overlaid by a newer file that has also been deleted so that the clusters are available again, UNDELETE will be fooled into recovering the original file, but the recovered data will belong to the newer file.
- UNDELETE assumes that available clusters adjacent to the first cluster also belonged to that file. This assumption can be incorrect in the case of a fragmented file, in which case the wrong data will be recovered.

Occasionally, UNDELETE may report that files are available, then change
its mind. In the following example, the directory entry was present but the
first cluster was not:

```
MS-DOS directory contains   1 deleted files.
Of those,   1 files may be recovered.
```

```
Using the MS-DOS directory.
    ** ?MAGE    DAT    50688 10-05-91  10:33a  ...A
Starting cluster is unavailable. This file cannot be
recovered with the UNDELETE command. Press any key to continue.
```

TIP	The Norton Utilities can undelete files in cases where DOS's UNDELETE can't. It also includes a system to retain deleted files in a special directory for a few days so that the clusters cannot be overlaid.

Suggestions for Facilitating Undeletions

You can increase your chances of undeleting files by making these practices
a habit:

➲ Be careful when deleting files, especially when using a global filespec.
(Use/P to prompt for each selected file.)

➲ Always use delete-tracking.

➲ Increase the size of your delete-tracking file so that it can hold two or
three days' worth of deletions.

➲ Defragment files often.

➲ Undelete files as soon as possible after deleting them.

Using UNDELETE

Figure 15.3 shows the format of the UNDELETE command. Unless you tell
it not to, UNDELETE looks for a PCTRACKR.DEL file; it uses the directory
search recovery method only if PCTRACKR.DEL does not exist.

Figure 15.3.

UNDELETE
Command
Reference.

UNDELETE

Restores previously deleted files if the data is available

Format:

UNDELETE [*filespec*] [*switches*]

Parameters and Switches:

None	Selects all files deleted from the current directory.
filespec	Identifies file(s) to be undeleted; may be global.
/LIST	Lists files available for undeletion.
/ALL	Automatically undeletes all files (that match the filespec, if included).
/DOS	Ignores delete-tracking file and searches the current or specified directory for deleted file(s).
/DT	Searches delete-tracking file only.

Notes:

/LIST and /ALL are mutually exclusive. /DOS and /DT are mutually exclusive.

If you use /ALL with /DOS or /DT, you will be prompted for each individual undeletion.

By default, UNDELETE reports on files available for undeletion from both the delete-tracking file (PCTRACKR.DEL) and the current or specified directory, but it selects files from PCTRACKR.DEL only (unless PCTRACKR.DEL is not available). Specify /DOS to report on and select files from the directory only. Specify /DT to report on and select files from PCTRACKR.DEL only.

Suppose you deleted AUTOEXEC.BAT by accident and you want to undelete it. You start by entering this command:

```
C:\>UNDELETE AUTOEXEC.BAT
```

If you don't have delete-tracking set up, here's what you see on the screen:

```
Directory: C:\
File Specifications: AUTOEXEC.BAT

Deletion-tracking file not found.

MS-DOS directory contains    1 deleted files.
Of those,    1 files may be recovered.

Using the MS-DOS directory:
    ?UTOEXEC.BAT   215  9-15-91  4:07p ...A  Undelete
    (Y/N)?
```

Notice how many files are available for undeletion; there may be several that match the filespec. UNDELETE displays them one at a time, starting with the most recent one. Use the displayed directory entry (which shows the date and time the file was last modified) to decide whether this is the version you want to undelete. If you're not sure, you can undelete all versions until you have the chance to check them out, then delete the ones you don't want to keep.

If you press N, UNDELETE shows you the next available file. When there are no more files to undelete, UNDELETE terminates and the command prompt returns.

If you press Y to undelete a file, UNDELETE asks you:

```
Please type the first character for ?UTOEXEC.BAT:
```

After you type any valid character that doesn't cause the recovered filename to duplicate an existing name in the same directory, you'll see:

```
File successfully undeleted.
```

Then the next available file is displayed.

TIP
To cancel the command early, press the Escape key; it has the effect of bypassing the current undeletion and returning you to the DOS prompt.

If UNDELETE finds a PCTRACKR.DEL file, the same interaction will look something like this:

```
Directory: C:\
File Specifications: AUTOEXEC.BAT

Deletion-tracking file contains    1 deleted files.
Of those,    1 files have all clusters available,
             0 files have some clusters available,
             0 files have no clusters available.

MS-DOS directory contains    1 deleted files.
Of those,    1 files may be recovered.

Using the deletion-tracking file:
     AUTOEXEC.BAT   215  9-15-91  4:07p ...A  Deleted:
     9-30-91  4:54p
All of the clusters for this file are available.
Undelete (Y/N)?
```

In this case, the date of deletion is shown as well.

If you aren't consistent with the use of delete-tracking, an old PCTRACKR.DEL file may be present on the disk. If delete-tracking wasn't turned on when the file was deleted, the report may tell you no files are available. Just run the UNDELETE command again with the /DOS switch to find and undelete the file using the directory search method.

WARNING

Don't use UNDELETE to rescue files on disks formed by JOIN or SUBST. And if you use it with an ASSIGNed disk, do it before you ASSIGN the disk. Generally, UNDELETE is valid only on real drives and directories, although it works on RAM drives as well.

Undeleting All Files

The /ALL switch automatically undeletes all files that match the filespec. If you use it without /DOS or /DT, it immediately undeletes all files from PCTRACKR.DEL that match the filespec. Otherwise it undeletes all matching files using the directory search method. You don't even get to provide the first character of any filenames; UNDELETE supplies an arbitrary character, using # by default unless it creates a duplicate filename.

Listing the Available Files

You can use the /LIST switch to see a list of the files that are available for undeletion. It lets you know what files that match the filespec are available for undeletion by each method.

Rescuing Accidentally Formatted Disks

If you have never reformatted a diskette in error, you may be unique among your fellow computer users. DOS 5 includes an UNFORMAT program to rescue us from our mistakes. As long as the DOS 5 format wasn't done unconditionally, the format wasn't destructive and can be undone. How much of the data on the disk can be recovered depends on several factors:

⊃ whether the disk was formatted under DOS 5

⊃ whether the disk contains unformatting information

➲ whether any data was added to the disk after formatting

➲ whether the disk contained fragmented files

UNFORMAT can also be useful when a disk wasn't reformatted, as it can restore a directory tree destroyed by RECOVER, and it may be able to restore removed subdirectories.

When you use DOS 5's FORMAT in the safe or quick mode, you see the message "Saving UNFORMAT information" early in the process. An image of the FAT and root directory are stored in a MIRROR.FIL file, just as when you run the MIRROR command. This image file is deleted before the format is done, but UNFORMAT can find and use the saved information.

The UNFORMAT Command

Figure 15.4 shows the UNFORMAT command. The /PARTN switch is used only to rebuild the partition table on a damaged hard disk. All other switches are used to prepare for and unformat disks. UNFORMAT looks for an image file unless you specify /U, /L, or /P on the command.

Figure 15.4.

UNFORMAT
Command
Reference.

UNFORMAT

Restores a reformatted disk to its previous condition; restores a hard drive partition table; recovers removed subdirectories

Format:

UNFORMAT [*drive*] [*switches*]

Parameters and Switches:

drive	Identifies drive containing disk to be unformatted; this parameter must be specified unless /PARTN is specified.
/PARTN	Restores partition table; use no additional switches other than /L and /P.
/L	(Without /PARTN) Lists all directories and files found; suppresses use of image file. (With /PARTN) Displays partition table.
/P	Echoes messages on printer; suppresses use of image file.
/U	Unformats without using image file.
/TEST	Shows what files and subdirectories would be recovered without using image file; does not unformat.
/J	Verifies the image file without unformatting; do not use with any other switch.

Notes:

The image file may have been produced by MIRROR, FORMAT in safe or quick mode, or RECOVER.

To use the image file, enter UNFORMAT *drive:* with no switches. To bypass image file, use /U, /L, or /P following the drive name.

If you use /PARTN, you'll be prompted to insert a diskette containing PARTNSAV.FIL, created earlier with the MIRROR /PARTN command.

Disks formatted unconditionally cannot be unformatted.

The /J switch is used to verify the image information, while /TEST simulates UNFORMAT without image information. Neither switch actually unformats the disk.

Restoring Partition Information

It is possible for the partition table to become corrupted in several ways, perhaps by a hardware problem, an editing error on the disk, or a virus. When you can't boot from your hard disk or access data on it, you might suspect a corrupted partition table. If you boot from a diskette, then enter the hard drive name at the DOS prompt, you might see the message "Invalid drive specification."

Chapter 14 showed how to use the MIRROR /PARTN command to save partition table information on a diskette. UNFORMAT's /PARTN switch uses that diskette to restore the partition table. If you can boot from a diskette, you may be able to fix the hard disk partition table using UNFORMAT.

When you enter UNFORMAT /PARTN, you'll be prompted to insert the diskette containing the PARTNSAV.FIL file. When UNFORMAT is finished, try to access the hard disk before rebooting.

TIP	If you can now access the hard disk, copy any files that aren't backed up before you continue.

Now try to boot from the hard disk. If you still can't boot from it, you'll have to go further for a solution. Three possibilities are:

➲ Repartition the disk, reformat the drive(s), and restore all files from the backup set.

➲ Try a third-party hard disk repair utility.

➲ Call in a hard disk repair specialist.

Viewing Partition Information

UNFORMAT /PARTN with the /L switch shows you the current contents of the partition table. Figure 15.5 shows an example.

Figure 15.5.

Partition Table Display.

```
C:\>unformat /partn /l
Hard Disk Partition Table display.

Drive # 80h has 976 cylinders, 5 heads, 17 sectors (from BIOS).

The following table is from drive 80h, cylinder 0, head 0, sector 1:

                 Total_size        Start_partition   End_partition
   Type        Bytes   Sectors    Cyl Head Sector   Cyl Head Sector      Rel#
 ----------  ----------------  ---------------  ---------------  ---------
DOS16 Boot     32M     65518       0    1     1    770    4    17          17
EXTEND          9M     17425     771    0     1    975    4    17       65535

The following table is from drive 80h, cylinder 771, head 0, sector 1:

                 Total_size        Start_partition   End_partition
   Type        Bytes   Sectors    Cyl Head Sector   Cyl Head Sector      Rel#
 ----------  ----------------  ---------------  ---------------  ---------
DOS12           9M     17408     771    1     1    975    4    17          17

C:\>
```

The **Type** column identifies the operating system that owns the partition. **DOS12** and **DOS16** are DOS partitions with 12-bit and 16-bit FAT entries. (Smaller partitions can use smaller FAT entries because there aren't as many clusters on the partition, so the maximum number to be stored will fit in 12 bits.) You might also see **BIGDOS** or **HUGE**, which identify a partition larger than 32M. **EXTEND** identifies a DOS extended partition, which will have its own partition table displayed after the main one. **Boot** identifies the partition that is booted from. If your disk includes partitions owned by other operating systems or set up by a non-DOS disk manager, you'll see other names or undecipherable information in this column.

The **Total_size** columns show the partition's size in megabytes and number of sectors. The **Start_partition** and **End_partition** columns show where the partition starts and ends. The **Rel #** column identifies the beginning of the partition in terms of the number of sectors from the beginning of the disk. (The reason the first partition starts with sector 17 in the example is that the partition table occupies the entire first track, which contains 17 sectors on this particular disk.)

If the partition table is damaged, you might see error messages in this display that could help you (or a repair expert) diagnose the problem.

> **N O T E**
>
> FDISK also displays partition information, but it does not include the same details as this UNFORMAT display.

How Unformatting Works

UNFORMAT checks the specified disk to see if image information is available. (It will find deleted image files.) If more than one image file is found, you can choose which to use. Once you verify that UNFORMAT should use a particular image file, it replaces the system information on the disk with the saved data. The root directory and the FAT are both restored.

If no changes have been made to the FAT or root directory since the image information was saved, the restoration gives you complete and accurate access to all former files and subdirectories. No further restoration is necessary. If you have made a few changes to the disk after saving the image information, you might find discrepancies in some files. That may be preferable to losing all the former data.

When UNFORMAT doesn't use image information, it searches the disk for subdirectories and uses their backlinks (the .. entries) to locate their parents. By this means, it can rebuild the entire directory tree. When a subdirectory is recovered, its files are also recovered as much as possible. Like UNDELETE, UNFORMAT will find only the first fragment of any fragmented files.

When image information is not available, the biggest problem lies with the files in the root directory that have been cleared by a format program. Any files that were in the root directory cannot be recovered because their directory entries are gone. First-level subdirectories will be discovered in the data area, and UNFORMAT knows they belong to the root directory because they backlink to cluster 0, but there is no way of discovering their names. UNDELETE restores them to the root directory using generic names in the form SUBDIR.*n*. You can examine and rename them using the Shell. You won't be able to recover the files from the root directory, though, unless you use a third-party utility that lets you examine available clusters and make up files from them.

In some cases, UNFORMAT can be used to restore removed subdirectories on a disk that wasn't reformatted. If MIRROR was used before the subdirectories were removed, but no other changes were made to the disk structure, UNFORMAT will use the image file to restore them. If MIRROR wasn't used at the appropriate time (a more likely occurrence), you shouldn't use the image information. Then UNFORMAT searches the backlinks on the disk and restores the directory structure with generic names as needed. No files will be recovered because all files had to be deleted before the directory was removed. You can use UNDELETE to recover the files after the directory has been restored.

When it is not using an image file, UNFORMAT lists on the screen the complete path of any subdirectories it finds. It lists fragmented files and asks if each should be truncated or deleted. (If you include the /L switch, it lists all files fragmented or otherwise.)

> **WARNING**
>
> When recovering a removed subdirectory, UNFORMAT will truncate or delete *all* fragmented files on the disk, regardless of which directory they were in. Always back up all good files on the disk before using UNFORMAT to recover removed subdirectories.

UNFORMAT Using Image Information

If you have reformatted a disk in safe or quick mode, it can be restored. FORMAT saved unformatting information on the disk, so complete recovery is possible as long as you haven't added anything to the disk since the format.

Here's what you see on the screen when you enter UNFORMAT A: (with no switches) as the command:

```
Insert disk to rebuild in drive A:
and press ENTER when ready.
```

After you follow these instructions, the messages continue:

```
Restores the system area of your disk by using the
image file created by the MIRROR command.

        WARNING !!            WARNING !!
```

```
This command should be used only to recover from the
inadvertent use of the FORMAT command or the RECOVER
command. Any other use of the UNFORMAT command may
cause you to lose data! Files modified since the MIRROR
image file was created may be lost.

Searching disk for MIRROR image.

The last time the MIRROR or FORMAT command was used was
at 15:03 on 08-05-92.

The MIRROR image file has been validated.

Are you sure you want to update the system area of your
drive A (Y/N)?
```

At this point, UNFORMAT has examined the disk and discovered a valid image file; it hasn't yet made any changes to the disk. If it also finds a MIRROR.BAK file, the last few messages look like this:

```
The last time the MIRROR or FORMAT command was used was
at 15:03 on 08-05-92.
The prior time the MIRROR or FORMAT command was used was
at 13:03 on 08-03-92.

If you wish to use the last file as indicated above,
press L. If you wish to use the prior file as indicated
above, press P. Press ESC to cancel UNFORMAT.
```

Examine the dates and times carefully; using out-of-date information can be disastrous. If you haven't used the disk since it was reformatted, you want the latest file. If you ran MIRROR *after* the format, then the prior file is the one you want. Once you press L or P to select a file, you are asked if you really want to update the system area.

You can't tell UNFORMAT to ignore the image file if only one is available; you'd have to cancel and start over with the /U switch to do that. Once you tell it to continue, UNFORMAT restores the root directory and FAT from the image file. In a few minutes you see:

```
The system area of drive A has been rebuilt.
You may need to restart the system.
C:\>
```

Restarting the system is a good idea to clear any old directory information out of buffers and caches. After the disk is unformatted, the directories and FATs are back as they were when the MIRROR file was saved. If nothing was added to the disk since then, the directory and FAT entries will refer to the actual files. If not, some discrepancies may occur, but that might be preferable to losing all your previous data.

Missing Image Information

If UNFORMAT can't find image information in its normal location, you'll see messages like these:

```
Unable to find the MIRROR control file. If you want to
search for the MIRROR image file through the entire
hard drive, press Y, or press N to cancel the UNFORMAT command.
```

If you want, the rest of the disk will be searched. To run UNFORMAT without using the image file, press N here, then run UNFORMAT with /U, /L, or /P so it won't look for an image file.

UNFORMAT without Image Information

Unformatting a disk without image information might be necessary if:

⊃ You removed a directory or a branch, then changed your mind. (The disk was not reformatted.)

⊃ You reformatted the disk with a third-party format program that did not save image information.

⊃ The formatting program was unable to save image information because the disk was too full.

⊃ The image file is corrupted or missing.

Use UNFORMAT to recover removed subdirectories with a great deal of caution, as it will truncate all fragmented files on the disk. Back up all files before entering the UNFORMAT command. (UNFORMAT with the /TEST switch can tell you whether any fragmented files would be truncated.)

When image information is not available, you see these messages:

```
CAUTION !!

This attempts to recover all the files lost after a
format, assuming you've not been using the MIRROR command.
This method cannot guarantee complete recovery of your files.

The search-phase is safe: nothing is altered on the disk.
You will be prompted again before changes are written to the disk.

Using drive A:

Are you sure you want to do this?
If so, press Y; anything else cancels.
?
```

At this point, you can back out and nothing happens. If you enter Y, however, UNFORMAT begins searching the available clusters for subdirectories. The display shows you the percentage of the disk that has been searched and the number of subdirectories that have been found. When the search is finished, you'll see the number of files and subdirectories found in the root directory. It may find subdirectories that were removed long ago that you don't want; you can remove these with RD later. The messages look like this:

```
Searching disk...
n% searched.  n subdirectories found.
Files found in the root: n
Subdirectories found in the root: n
```

TIP	If you're trying to recover one or two removed subdirectories and you see that UNFORMAT has found the desired number of subdirectories, you can press Ctrl+Break to interrupt the search phase. UNFORMAT asks if you want to continue the search and gives you the choice of Yes (continue the search), No (discontinue the search and go on to the next phase), and Quit (terminate the UNFORMAT program). Press N to go on to the next UNFORMAT phase.

Next UNFORMAT checks the entire directory tree looking for files. Any first-level subdirectories that have been removed will have lost their names. You'll see the names UNFORMAT creates in the list:

```
Walking the directory tree to locate all files...
Path=A:\
Path=A:\SUBDIR.1\
Path=A:\SUBDIR.1\CHAPS\
Path=A:\SUBDIR.1\
etc.

Files found: n
Warning! The next step writes changes to disk.

Are you sure you want to do this?
If so, press Y; anything else cancels.
?
```

This is your last chance to back out. If you choose to go ahead, UNFORMAT begins recovering subdirectories and files. If only the first fragment of a file is available, you'll see messages like this:

```
Checking for file fragmentation...
Path=A:\
Path=A:\SUBDIR.1\
Path=A:\SUBDIR.1\CHAPS\
GETTY2.DOC    2560  9-25-91  11:32am  Only   512 bytes
are recoverable. Truncate or Delete this file?
```

You can decide whether UNFORMAT should save what it can (truncate) or just delete the file.

When UNFORMAT is finished, examine the directory tree. Your removed directories should be restored and you can now use UNDELETE to recover deleted files in the subdirectories.

Handling Image Files

The /J switch causes UNFORMAT to compare an image file to the current system area of a disk. Here's how the report looks when they don't match:

```
Restores the system area of your disk by using the
image file created by the MIRROR command.

    WARNING !!              WARNING !!

This command should be used only to recover from the
inadvertent use of the FORMAT command or the RECOVER
command. Any other use of the UNFORMAT command may
cause you to lose data! Files modified since the MIRROR
image file was created may be lost.

Searching disk for MIRROR image.

Just checking this time. No changes written to disk.

The last time the MIRROR or FORMAT command was used was
at 15:03 on 10-05-92.

The MIRROR image file has been validated.

The system area does not agree with the MIRROR image file.
```

If the image file does match the current system area, you'll see this message:

```
The system area of drive A has been verified
to agree with the MIRROR image file.
```

This facility can help you decide whether your image file is up-to-date or whether you need to run MIRROR. It can also tell you whether running UNFORMAT will make any changes on the disk.

Simulating an UNFORMAT

Sometimes you just want to know what UNFORMAT would do to a disk. You can't find out exactly what using the image file would do, but you can use the /TEST switch to find out what would happen if you ignore any image files. When you use /TEST, UNFORMAT performs the entire search phase, showing you what would be rebuilt as it lists the subdirectories and fragmented files. You can use this switch with /L and /P to get a hard copy of the information.

RECOVER

Occasionally, when DOS tries to read or write a file, it encounters a CRC error, indicating that a cluster within the file has developed a bad spot. Under normal circumstances, DOS won't access any part of a file that contains a bad cluster.

TIP	Some CRC errors are intermittent, so try several times before giving up.

How to recover from such a situation depends on whether the problem is on a diskette or hard disk and on whether you have a valid backup.

If you have a backup and the problematic file is on a diskette, copy other files to a new diskette. Restore the damaged file to the new diskette. Then get rid of the troublesome diskette.

If you have a backup and the damaged file is on hard disk, the best solution is to give the bad copy of the file a new name, then restore the desired file from its backup. Don't delete the bad file; if you do, DOS will reuse (or try to reuse) the bad cluster. There are several ways to prevent DOS from using that cluster again:

- ➲ Give the defective file a meaningful name (such as BADSPOT) and the system attribute, then just leave it on the disk.

- ➲ Reformat the drive to block out the bad cluster in the FAT so it won't be used again. Then restore all files from the backup set.

- ➲ Use RECOVER on the file containing the bad cluster. RECOVER will block out the bad cluster in the FAT without reformatting the disk.

If you don't have a recent backup, your best bet is the RECOVER command, which reads the file, omits the bad parts, and creates a new file of what is readable. If the file is smaller than one cluster in size, RECOVER won't be able to save any of it, since that cluster must be the one that has gone bad. RECOVER has some dangerous aspects, as you'll see, but sometimes it is the only way to get parts of a file back. We'll explain how to use it to fix individual files. Then we'll show you what can happen if you try anything else.

Fixing Individual Files

You can use RECOVER to fix an individual file. You won't be able to use a nontext file recovered this way since you can't restore the missing parts, but at least you'll block out the bad cluster.

> **WARNING**
>
> Never run a program that was rescued by RECOVER. It won't be complete and could damage data on your hard disk.

To get rid of a bad cluster within a file, use a command in this format:

```
RECOVER filespec
```

You can't use any wildcards in the filespec; it must refer to a single file by name. RECOVER then reads the file one cluster at a time, fixing the FAT so that any bad clusters are bypassed. For a text file without a valid backup, you could now edit it to restore the missing portion. Other types of files are best deleted.

TIP   A damaged spreadsheet or database file may not be readable by the software that originally created it. The Norton Utilities includes a utility to fix up such files so they can be worked on by their own applications once again.

Fixing Several Files

If you have several files with read errors, the disk may have been physically damaged by a head crash or a magnet. The first thing you should do is back up every file you can from the disk, if your backups aren't already up-to-date. If your hard disk is dying, you'll be able to restore a lot of data to a new or repaired disk from the backups.

If you don't have backups of the unreadable files, RECOVER each one individually and back those up. (Don't recover the whole drive! You'll see why not shortly.) When as many files as possible have been backed up, redo the low-level format, partitioning, and high-level format. (You might also want a disk repair specialist or special software to check out the hard disk.) Then you can put it back to work.

> **WARNING**
>
> RECOVER without a filespec will most likely leave the disk in worse shape than before!

Mushing an Entire Drive

If bad clusters appear in the root directory so that no files (or very few) are available on the disk, and if you have no other recourse, you may be brave enough to try to recover the whole disk yourself instead of calling in a specialist.

It's easy to start the recovery process; in fact, it's too easy. Just enter this command:

```
RECOVER drive
```

But before you try it, be sure you know what will happen. You'll see this message:

```
The entire drive will be reconstructed,
directory structures will be destroyed.
Are you sure (Y/N)?
```

RECOVER is going to recover every file it can into the disk's root directory and assign it a generic filename. You might end up with hundreds of files, named FILE0001.REC, FILE0002.REC, and so on, with no idea what they originally were or what directory they came from.

If you respond with a Y, you're given one more chance to change your mind:

```
Press any key to begin recovery of
the file(s) on drive d:
```

If you press a key other than Ctrl+Break, the RECOVER program goes to work. Eventually you'll see:

```
nn file(s) recovered
```

The first thing RECOVER does is make an image of the current disk structure, just as FORMAT does when it isn't doing an unconditional format. (This lets you run UNFORMAT if you got this far by accident!) RECOVER then ignores any directory information and starts working with file chains in the FAT, bypassing any clusters containing bad spots. Each recovered file is stored in the new root directory with a generic filename in the form FILE*nnnn*.REC.

NOTE

RECOVER doesn't restore previously deleted files. It works only with files that currently appear in the FAT.

RECOVER makes no distinction between program files, text files, and other types of files. You'll have to examine each recovered file (if you can), decide what it is (if you can), and rename it.

When the root directory is full, the RECOVER command terminates with an error message. If you want to keep going, copy those files to another disk, delete them from the root directory, and enter the RECOVER command again. Repeat this process until all files are recovered.

Recovering from RECOVER

Suppose you recover a disk accidentally. You now have a root directory full of generic filenames and no subdirectories. Is there any hope? Immediately try UNFORMAT, using the image information saved by RECOVER. The entire disk should be restored to its pre-RECOVER condition.

Sector Not Found Errors

Another sign of a disk in trouble is a "Sector not found" error. One such message could be a fluke, but when these messages appear with increasing frequency, the disk's low-level formatting needs to be redone.

Low-level formatting lays out the sectors on a disk, storing the sector's address and other information, such as the CRC value, in a few system bytes immediately following each sector.

With careless handling, sector information can be damaged. Specific sectors could be damaged by an unparked head landing on the disk surface. A little refrigerator magnet can do untold damage (not just to the sector information). But even when a disk is treated with respect, the low-level formatting can degrade over a period of time. For example, the read-write heads might shift slightly, making it hard to find the sector addresses and CRC value.

When the controller can't find a sector address requested by DOS, it reports back a "sector not found" error. DOS, in turn, refuses to access any part of the file. If this happens with only one file, you might be able to use RECOVER to rescue as much data as possible from the file. But if it's happening consistently on a disk, it's time to redo the low-level formatting.

WARNING

Many low-level formatting programs will destroy all data on a disk.

For diskettes, an unconditional FORMAT redoes the low-level formatting and will probably make the diskette usable again. DOS does not include a low-level formatting program for hard disks. If you did not receive one with your hard disk, you may be able to get one from your dealer or repair technician. Or you can buy one at your software store.

Your best bet for reformatting a hard disk is a utility that will redo the low-level formatting without damaging the data that's in the tracks. If you don't have access to such a utility, you'll have to do a destructive format, then repartition the disk, redo the high-level format for each drive, and reload the data from backups.

CONSOLE
CONTROL

ntroduction

The DOS command prompt screen, by default, is about as interesting as yesterday's blackboard: white text on a black background, 24 lines per screen, and no graphics. The keyboard types the characters shown on the keycaps and very little more. But you can do a lot to jazz up both the screen and the keyboard. You can add color and (somewhat limited) graphics to the screen, flash blinking messages at users, even splash a colorful banner across the top of the screen showing the date, time, and other useful information. You can redefine keys on the keyboard to type international characters such as Ü, graphics characters such as ╔, even complete macros such as "Peter Norton's Advanced DOS 5 Guide" or "CD\NORTH\ALASKA." The techniques in this chapter can make your own work, as well as the batch programs you create for others, more exciting and more effective.

DOS and Your Video Monitor

DOS supports several types of video: monochrome display adapter (MDA), color graphics adapter (CGA), extended graphics adapter (EGA), and the video graphics array (VGA). Other types of video adapters are usually compatible with one or more of these. A video adapter or monitor with more features than these basic types (such as more pixels or a two-page display for desktop publishing) is usually accompanied by software to help you take advantage of its features.

The CON Driver

DOS's command-prompt interface uses the built-in CON device driver to interact with whatever video adapter is installed. CON provides simple text-oriented services so that DOS can write messages to the command-prompt screen. CON uses functions built into the video controller to drive the hardware, which keeps DOS independent of the actual video equipment and lets the operating system function regardless of what display adapter is used. Unfortunately, the result is the dull-as-dishwater white on black (or whatever) screen that DOS users love to hate.

The Video Buffer

Every video adapter card has a memory area called the *video buffer*. Whatever will be displayed on the screen must first be stored in the video buffer. The video is said to be *memory-mapped* because every byte in its buffer is mapped to a specific location on the screen.

In text mode, the video buffer contains two bytes for each screen character position. The first byte contains the ASCII value of the character to be displayed, and the second byte contains its attributes (color, blinking, etc.). Figure 16.1 shows the beginning of a typical buffer. In this case, it contains the message "Sanity Reigns!" starting in the first character position on the screen. The first byte shows the ASCII value of the letter S. The next byte shows its attributes; 07H represents DOS's usual white-on-black style. The third byte shows the ASCII code for the letter "a"; the fourth byte shows its attributes.

Figure 16.1.

Figure 16.1.

Video Buffer in Text
Mode.

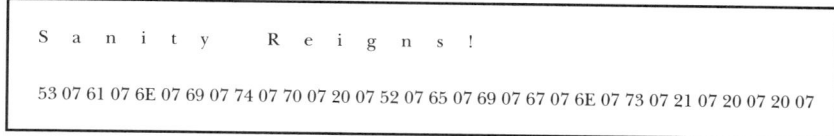

S a n i t y   R e i g n s !

53 07 61 07 6E 07 69 07 74 07 70 07 20 07 52 07 65 07 69 07 67 07 6E 07 73 07 21 07 20 07 20 07

On color systems, the attribute byte specifies the foreground and background colors, as well as the foreground intensity and blinking/steady status. On monochrome systems, the attribute can be used to specify intensity, underlining, blinking, and normal or reverse video in text mode. Programs that run in graphics mode handle their attributes differently; they work with smaller screen elements than text mode.

What ANSI.SYS Offers

The CON driver isn't able to use color. It just pokes ASCII codes into even-numbered (character) bytes of the video buffer and doesn't affect any odd-numbered (attribute) bytes, so the current attributes are never changed.

The ANSI.SYS device driver is sort of a super-CON; it gives you many more options to take advantage of your video and keyboard features. ANSI.SYS gives you a way to specify color and the other video attributes. It also lets you control the cursor position and clear the screen. It lets you use 43 or 50 lines if the monitor can handle that, and 40 columns instead of 80. Additional features let you manipulate the meanings of the keyboard keys.

Some programs depend on ANSI.SYS to provide enhanced video and keyboard services. Their documentation will advise you that ANSI.SYS must be loaded. Other programs use the PC's video BIOS, which contains even more efficient screen functions. Even a nonprogramming user, however, can use ANSI.SYS to spice up displays, the command prompt, and batch files. The results affect only the DOS command prompt screen (which includes EDLIN and DEBUG). It doesn't affect the Shell or EDIT screen or any commercial software that doesn't use the command-prompt screen.

The ANSI.SYS Device Driver

You load ANSI.SYS from the CONFIG.SYS file with a DEVICE or DEVICEHIGH command. Figure 16.2 shows the command format. Once ANSI.SYS is installed, it scans all standard output looking for its own commands.

Figure 16.2.

ANSI.SYS DEVICE Command.

> **ANSI.SYS**
>
> Allows control over the keyboard and screen components of the console.
>
> **Format:**
>
> DEVICE[HIGH]=[*path*]ANSI.SYS [*switches*]
>
> **Switches:**
>
> /K   Makes keyboard compatible with XT keyboard.
>
> /X   Maps duplicate keys separately.
>
> **Notes:**
>
> The /K and /X switches are mutually exclusive.
>
> If /K is specified, certain keys, including F11 and F12, are ignored. You must specify SWITCHES=/K in CONFIG.SYS as well. Do this only if some software has trouble responding reliably to your enhanced keyboard.
>
> If /X is not specified, any two keys of the same name, such as the two Up arrow keys, will be remapped the same if you remap either one.

You may want to use the /X switch if you assign different characters to keys that have duplicates, such as Up arrow, Home, and + (plus). If you don't specify the /X switch, two matching keys are mapped the same; for example both + (plus) keys will have the same effect. If you specify /X, you can assign different functions to each one. Key mapping is covered in detail later in this chapter.

Sending Commands to ANSI.SYS

When ANSI.SYS is installed, it remains in memory, taking about 4K. It continuously monitors all standard output, looking for *escape sequences*, which it recognizes as commands. An escape sequence begins with an Esc character followed by a left square bracket and ends with a specific terminator character. In between are the codes that make up the command. We'll cover the details of specific commands later, but the following is an example that sets a color screen to display cyan letters on a red background:

```
Esc[31;46m
```

The code 31 means a red background, while 46 means a cyan foreground. The terminator character "m" must be is used with all escape sequences that control color; it tells ANSI.SYS what function is desired. To set the colors back to the defaults, send Esc[m (without any color specification) to standard output.

N O T E

The case of terminator characters is significant. Using M instead of m to affect color won't work.

Typing the Escape Character

You can't just press Esc at the keyboard to start an escape sequence; it simply cancels the current command and starts another. How you enter Esc depends on how you decide to send the escape sequence to ANSI.SYS. The useful commands that produce standard output are PROMPT, TYPE, and ECHO.

Using PROMPT

In the PROMPT command, you can type normal text as well as special characters that represent untypeable items. Table 16.1 shows the complete set of PROMPT special characters, which can be typed in uppercase or lowercase. The command PROMPT PG establishes the familiar prompt that shows the current drive and path followed by the greater-than symbol.

Table 16.1 PROMPT Command Special Characters

$B		(bar or piping sign)
$D	Current date
$E	Escape
$G	> (greater-than sign)
$H	Backspace (to delete character)
$L	< (less-than sign)
$N	Current drive

continues

Table 16.1 Continued

$P	Current drive and path
$Q	= (equal sign)
$T	Current time
$V	DOS version number
$$	$ (dollar sign)
$_	↵ (Enter)

To use PROMPT to send an escape sequence, you use $E to specify the Esc character. Here are a few examples and their effects:

PROMPT $E[36;41m	Sets cyan text on a red background. At the same time, it removes the current prompt; you'll see only the cursor.
PROMPT $E[m	Restores the default white text on black background, with only the cursor as a prompt.
PROMPT $E[36;41m$P$G	Sets cyan text on a red background and displays the standard prompt.
PROMPT $E[36;41m$PGE[m	Sets cyan text on a red background, displays the standard prompt, then turns the color off so the default colors are restored for all except the prompt itself.

The disadvantage of using PROMPT to send commands to ANSI.SYS is that it eliminates your previous prompt unless you are careful to reset it. However, PROMPT is often the quickest way to try out escape sequences and see the effect right away.

TIP Follow the PROMPT command with CLS to set the entire screen to the new color scheme.

TIP Use DOSKEY to easily recall your PROMPT commands for editing.

Using a Text File

When you TYPE a file, DOS sends it to standard output. Any escape sequences are diverted by ANSI.SYS. You can create a text file containing one or more escape sequences, then TYPE it to put them all into effect.

You can use any text editor to create a file containing escape sequences as long as you know how to enter the Esc character into it. To TYPE correctly, of course, the file must be saved in ASCII form; DOS's EDIT program saves all files in this form. In EDIT, first press Ctrl+P, then press Esc to type an escape character. You'll see a left arrow on the screen, but it functions as the Esc character when you TYPE the file.

TIP	Pressing Ctrl+P followed by Esc also works in WordStar. In Microsoft Word, enter the ASCII code for Esc: hold down the Alt key and press 2 then 7 on the numeric keypad. When you release the Alt key, a left arrow appears on the screen. In WordPerfect, press Ctrl+V followed by Esc, which appears on screen as ^[.

The second character in every ANSI.SYS escape sequence must be a left square bracket, [. This is followed by the characters of the command itself, followed by the terminator letter. If you open a new DOS EDIT file named COLTEST, you could type these commands into it:

```
←[36;41m
CLS
```

After you save the file, enter the command TYPE COLTEST. The first escape sequence sets cyan text on a red background from the current cursor location; the second spreads the color scheme to fill the screen. To restore the default colors, TYPE a file containing these commands:

```
←[m
CLS
```

Using a Batch File

It's often useful to include ANSI.SYS escape sequences in batch programs. The ECHO command, which sends text to standard output, is more convenient than PROMPT because it doesn't reset the prompt. (Unfortunately, you can't use ECHO outside a batch file because it offers no method to type an Esc character.) For example, you might use red for error messages and yellow for informational messages. You can insert one escape sequence to set up the message, then another sequence later to restore normal colors. The following example displays the message "Sorting Records" in cyan on red, then restores normal colors:

```
ECHO ←[36;41mSorting Records←[m
```

Setting Screen Colors

A variety of ANSI escape sequences control different screen features. One set controls the color background and foreground as well as the text attributes. Another set controls cursor position and clears the screen. Still another set lets you control the graphics mode of your display.

The escape sequences for screen colors requires the use of numeric codes; we've been using the codes for red background (41) and cyan foreground (36) in our examples so far. Table 16.2 shows the complete set of attribute and color codes. Each color sequence requires the same terminator character: lowercase m.

Table 16.2 Color Display Codes

Attributes:

0	Normal text
1	High-intensity text
2	Low-intensity text
4	Underline on (monochrome only)
5	Blink on
7	Inverse on
8	Invisible text (foreground displays same color as background)

Color codes:

Color	Foreground	Background
Black	30	40
Red	31	41

Green	32	42
Yellow	33	43
Blue	34	44
Magenta	35	45
Cyan	36	46
White	37	47

Exactly how a color appears depends on the monitor; for example, normal yellow looks brown on many screens.

You can include as many codes as you need in each escape sequence; separate them with semicolons.

The attributes apply only to the foreground color on most systems. The high intensity attribute produces a brighter foreground color, quite different from the normal color, so 16 foreground colors are available. But in some systems attribute 5 causes a high-intensity background rather than a blink.

On some systems, low intensity produces still another color, but it's the same as high intensity on most systems. If you use attribute 8, the foreground color is stored as usual but foreground material is displayed using the background color.

TIP	If you are preparing a batch file for other users, check out the colors and attributes on their monitors if you can. They might be different from yours.

As you have seen, the command Esc[m resets the default attributes (none) and color (white on black). Suppose you want to have a blinking foreground of high-intensity yellow on a magenta background. This command, stored in an ASCII file and TYPEd to the screen, produces the result:

```
←[1;5;33;45m
```

Suppose a batch file displays the message "Sorting Members . . ." while it works. You could use this line in the batch file to make the message more noticeable:

```
ECHO ←[5;33;45mSorting Members . . .←[m
```

Screen and Cursor Control

By default, the cursor goes to the beginning of the next line when a command terminates. You can position it somewhere else through an ANSI command. The escape sequences for cursor position require a variety of special terminator characters as shown in Table 16.3. You might need to include row and/or column information. As always, the case of the terminator character is critical.

Table 16.3 Screen and Cursor Control Sequences

s	Save current cursor position
u	Restore saved cursor position
xxA	Cursor up xx rows
xxB	Cursor down xx rows
xxC	Cursor right xx columns
xxD	Cursor left xx columns
H	Cursor to upper left (0,0)
$xx;yy$H	Cursor to specified position
$xx;yy$f	Cursor to specified position
2J	Clear screen, cursor to upper left
K	Clear from cursor position to end of line
6n	Display cursor position in form ←[$xx;yy$R

When controlling the cursor position, be careful not to position it over (or before) existing text to avoid confusing users. Careful testing of cursor control changes is recommended.

Creating a Banner

You can use many of the cursor-positioning features in a PROMPT command to create a banner across the top of each screen. Figure 16.3 shows a screen with a sample banner. The command that produces this banner is shown on the screen. The banner is regenerated each time the prompt appears, so the time is kept reasonably up-to-date.

Figure 16.3.

Using PROMPT to
Create a Banner.

```
Path: C:\DOS      Ruth Ashley                  Wed 10-30-1991 @ 12:16
      114688 bytes in 42 directories
    29179904 bytes in 1293 user files
     3559424 bytes available on disk

        2048 bytes in each allocation unit
       16080 total allocation units on disk
        1738 available allocation units on disk

      655360 total bytes memory
      579136 bytes free

C:\COMMAND.COM Contains 2 non-contiguous blocks
C:\ADFIG1-1.SCR Contains 3 non-contiguous blocks
C:\TESTSORT.EXE Contains 4 non-contiguous blocks

=>>cd dos

=>>banner

=>>prompt $e[s$e[H$E[37;44m$e[KPath: $p       Ruth Ashley      $e[1;52H$d @ $t$h$h$h$
h$h$h$e[34;47m$e[u$q$g$g

=>>
=>>
```

This PROMPT command comprises a mixture of ANSI.SYS escape sequences, PROMPT special characters, and straight text. Each part is explained below:

$E[s	Saves the current cursor position
$E[H	Moves cursor to upper-left corner
$E[37;44m	Sets the banner to cyan on blue
$E[K	Erases the top line from cursor position
Path:	Displays the indicated text
$P	Inserts the current drive and path here
Ruth Ashley	Displays the indicated text
$E[1;52H	Moves the cursor to row 1 column 52
$D	Displays the current date
@	Displays the indicated text (@)
$T	Displays the current time
HHHHHH	Backspaces six times to remove seconds and hundredths from the time
$E[34;47m	Sets rest of screen to blue on cyan
$E[u	Restores the saved cursor position
QG$G	Displays the new prompt (=>>)

If you want to try a banner, be sure to load DOSKEY first if it isn't active; DOSKEY greatly simplifies modifying PROMPT commands.

Displaying a Message Box

You can also use ANSI.SYS to create a colored box containing a message. This makes an interesting, attention-getting display. Figure 16.4 shows a text file containing escape sequences to control the display of a red box with black text. This example uses a separate line for each sequence, but you can combine them if you prefer. You can also modify the commands, changing the position, color, size, and text to fit your needs. Use TYPE *filespec* in a batch file to produce the box. Alternatively, you can put the necessary escape sequences in ECHO commands in the batch file.

Figure 16.4.

Creating a Colored Message Box.

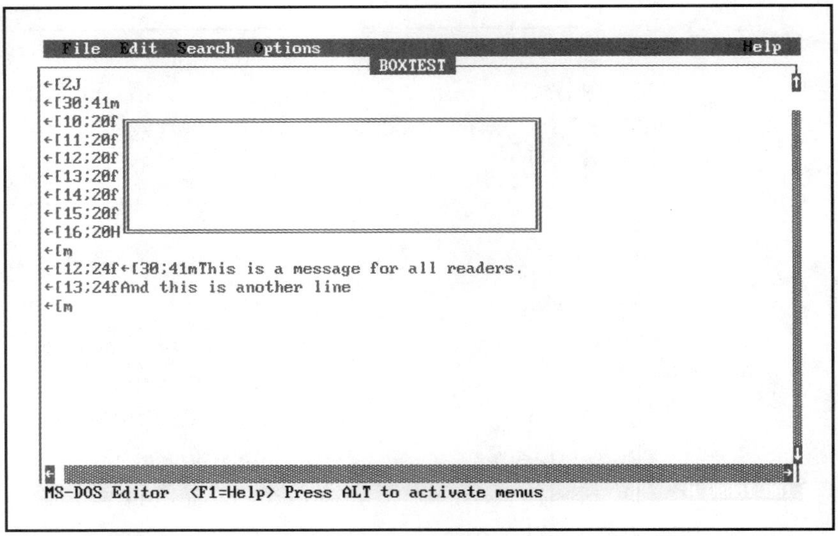

The box itself is drawn using the IBM extended character set (see Appendix B), which bears some explanation. A single byte, representing one text character on a monitor or printer, can hold a value from 0 to 255 (0FFH). The values from 0 through 127 are standardized as ASCII code, representing letters, digits, punctuation marks, and so on. The values from 128 through 255 have not been standardized so they can have different effects with different hardware and software setups. For example, DOS interprets these values according to the IBM extended character set, but Windows doesn't. When displaying a message from a DOS batch program using ECHO commands, you can count on the IBM extended character set to work.

Because a keyboard doesn't have keys for the extended characters, you can type one by holding down the Alt key and typing the byte's value on the numeric keypad. For example, to type the upper-left corner of the double-line box, press Alt+201. This method works for any byte value, not just the extended ones.

The escape sequences in the file shown in Figure 16.4 are explained below:

←[2J	Clears the screen with cursor in upper-left corner
←[30;41m	Sets the colors to black text on red background

The new colors affect only positions where text or spaces are typed. We limit that to the box itself by positioning the cursor for each line of text. The balance of the screen retains its former colors.

←[10;20f	Positions cursor at row 10 column 20; rest of line draws top of box
←[11;20f	Positions cursor at row 11 column 20; rest of line draws next line of box
(The next five commands draw box sides.)	
←[16;20H	Positions cursor at row 16 column 20; rest of line draws bottom line of box
←[m	Resets default colors
←[12;24f←[30;41m	Positions cursor and sets text color; rest of line displays a message in box
←[13;24f	Positions cursor; rest of line displays another message in box
←[m	Resets the colors

The cursor-positioning sequence using the f terminator is exactly the same as with H. If you omit the row and column values, f has no effect, while H defaults to the home (0;0) position.

Character Wrap

By default, when a command on the screen reaches column 80, characters wrap around to the next line. In earlier versions of DOS, characters were stacked up in column 80, so you could see only the most-recently entered character. Turning off character wrap hides characters at the ends of long lines. Use these commands to enable and disable the character wrap function:

←[=7h	to enable
←[=7l	to disable

Character wrapping affects not only the commands you type but also the output of commands that display long lines, such as FIND.

Screen Mode (Graphics)

Every video adapter and screen has a default mode. If you do any BASIC programming, you know that the screen mode can be changed to achieve different effects. Another set of escape sequences lets you change the screen mode using ANSI commands. The results might vary on different monitors. Table 16.4 lists the values you can use to specify screen modes; use terminator character h as in:

←[=modeh

Table 16.4 Screen Modes

Mode	Meaning
0	Monochrome text, 40 x 25
1	Color text, 40 x 25
2	Monochrome text, 80 x 25
3	Color text, 80 x 25
4	Medium-resolution graphics (4 color), 300 x 200
5	Same as 4, with color burst disabled
6	High-resolution graphics (2 color), 640 x 200

Mode	Meaning
13	Color graphics, 320 x 200
14	Color graphics (16 color), 640 x 200
15	Monochrome graphics, 640 x 350
16	Color graphics (16 color), 640 x 350
17	Color graphics (2 color), 640 x 480
18	Color graphics (16 color), 640 x 480
19	Color graphics (256 color), 320 x 200

If you change the screen mode to one not supported by your system, you may see a strange color pattern or the system may hang up. You'll have to reboot to restore normalcy.

ANSI Keyboard Control

ANSI escape sequences also give you control over your keyboard. You can switch the meanings of any two keys, for example. You can set up a key or key combination (such as Ctrl+D) to type an extended character or even a string of characters. Table 16.5 shows how to refer to some keys in ANSI.SYS commands. The ones in parentheses may not be valid on all keyboards. The complete list is included in your DOS 5 documentation in the discussion of the ANSI.SYS driver.

Table 16.5 Selected Key Codes

Key	Normal	Shift+	Ctrl+	Alt+
F1	0;59	0;84	0;94	0;104
F2	0;60	0;85	0;95	0;105
F3	0;61	0;86	0;96	0;106
F4	0;62	0;87	0;97	0;107
Home	0;71	55	0;119	
Up	0;72	56	(0;141)	
PageUp	0;73	57	0;132	

continues

Table 16.5 Continued

Key	Normal	Shift+	Ctrl+	Alt+
Left	0;75	52	0;115	
PrtSc			0;114	
Pause/Break				0;0
BkSp	8	8	127	(0)
Enter	13		10	(0;28)
Tab	9	0;15	(0;148)	(0:165)
(Grey keys)				
Home	(224;71)	(224;71)	(224;119)	(224;1051)
Up	(224;72)	(224;72)	(224;141)	(224;152)
PageUp	(224;73)	(224;73)	(224;132)	(224;153)
Left	(224;75)	(224;75)	(224;115)	(224;155)
(Keypad Keys)				
Enter	13		10	(0;166)
/	47	47	(0;142)	(0;74)
*	42	(0;144)	(0;78)	
-	45	45	(0;149)	(0;164)
+	43	43	(0;150)	(0;55)
5	(0;76)	53	(0;143)	
(Typeable characters)				
a	97	65	1	0;30
b	98	66	2	0;48
z	122	90	26	0;44
1	49	33		0;120
0	48	41		0;129
-	45	95	31	0;130
=	61	43		0;131

Assigning a value to a particular key *remaps* that key. Assigning a string of text to a key can be used to set up keyboard macros. The remapping affects only the DOS command prompt interface.

Remapping can be done in a PROMPT command, an ECHO command, or in a TYPEd text file, just as with other ANSI.SYS escape sequences.

Remapping Individual Keys

Many key combinations are unassigned. You can remap them to type extended characters. Or you might want simply to relocate a key. You could change a QWERTY keyboard to the more efficient Dvorak layout, for example.

To remap keys, use an ANSI command in this format:

```
Esc[key;new-valuep
```

The *h* identifies the key or key combination to be remapped; you can identify it by the current character it types, if any, placed in quotes, or by its key code (from Table 16.5). The *new-value* parameter identifies the new value for the key, which you can specify as a character in quotes or as a numeric code from 0 through 255. Appendix B shows the extended characters that result when you use 128 through 255. For example, to set Ctrl+F1 to type the upper-left corner of a double-line box, you could use either of these escape sequences:

```
←[0;94;"╔"p
←[0;94;201p
```

In both commands, 0;94 identifies the Ctrl+F1 key combination. The first command uses quotes surrounding the result of Alt+201, while the second uses the value 201 to specify the desired character.

You might want to assign the value ä (Alt+132) to Alt+A, for example, if you type that character very often, with one of these escape sequences:

```
←[0;30;132p
←[0;30;"ä"p
```

If you want to drive someone crazy, you could swap their "t" and "h" keys with commands like these:

```
ECHO ←["t";"h"p
ECHO ←["h";"t"p
```

An enhanced keyboard includes several keys that duplicate other keys. If you want the duplicates treated the same, don't do anything. If you want to give one of the set a different value, however, use the /X switch in the DEVICE=ANSI.SYS command. For example, this sequence makes the numeric keypad Home key respond with 7:

    ←[0;71;"7"p

This sequence makes the extra (gray) Home key respond with an asterisk:

    ←[224;71;"*"p

The two commands work only if ANSI.SYS was loaded with /X. On an enhanced, 101-key keyboard, the extra keys—such as gray cursor control keys—are the extended keys. These keys (and a few others) appear in parentheses in the key-code table. If you've disabled them with /K, or if you don't have an enhanced keyboard, then these keys are not available for remapping.

Assigning Strings to Keys

You can assign strings of text to keys. For example, you can assign complete commands, including the Enter key, so you can run a DOS command with a single key or key combination. You could establish a complete set of function key "macros" to run the commands you need most often. These commands aren't the same as DOSKEY macros—for example, you can't use replaceable parameters in them—but you could set them up to run DOSKEY macros for you.

To assign a simple text string, use a sequence in this format:

    Esc[*key*;"*string*"p

The sequence ←[0;84;"Imaginatronics, Inc."p causes the company name to be typed when you press Shift+F1. You can string together quoted values and numeric values, using semicolons to separate them. To cause the CD \ command to be issued when you press F12, use the sequence:

    ←[0;134;"cd \";13p

The value 13 sends the carriage return to enter the command, while the terminator character p ends the escape sequence.

You can't include replaceable parameters in an ANSI.SYS key assignment like you can in DOSKEY macros. But you can let the keyboard macro type the first part of the command, then type the variable information and press Enter.

If you use DOSKEY, you know that pressing F7 lists the stored command history. There is no comparable function key to list DOSKEY macros. You could set up F10 to list them like this:

```
←[0;68;"DOSKEY /MACROS";13p
```

We've overviewed some of the most useful ANSI.SYS functions here. You'll discover even more uses for these functions as you continue to apply them.

Controlling the CON (Console) Mode

You can change the number of lines and columns displayed on your monitor with a MODE command; the change affects EDIT, EDLIN, and DEBUG, but not the Shell. Figure 16.5 shows the MODE format for modifying the console, which includes the screen and the keyboard.

Identifying the Display Adapter

The MODE command lets you control a number of characteristics on your video display. You shouldn't have to use these features, but they are present for compatibility with earlier DOS versions.

If your normal text display isn't centered nicely on the monitor, however, you might want to shift it. To shift the display to the left, use this command:

```
MODE ,L,T
```

To shift it to the right, use this command:

```
MODE ,R,T
```

Specifying Lines and Columns

If you want to use more than the default 25 screen lines, you can use the LINES= parameter; ANSI.SYS must be loaded before you change the number of lines. A VGA screen can support 43 or 50 lines, while EGA can handle 43.

Figure 16.5.

MODE Command
Reference
(Console
Functions).

MODE

Configures system console devices.

Formats:

MODE [*display-adapter*] [,*shift*] [,T]

MODE CON[:] [COLS=*c*] [LINES=*n*]

MODE CON[:] RATE=*r* DELAY=*d*

Parameters:

none	Displays status of all devices.
display-adapter	Specifies an adapter mode; must be one of following values:

40 or 80	Sets number of characters per line.
BW40 or BW80	Selects the color adapter with color disabled and sets the number of characters per line.
CO40 or CO80	Selects the color adapter with color enabled and sets the number of characters per line.
MONO	Selects a monochrome adapter with 80 characters per line.

shift	Indicates whether to shift the screen to the left (L) or right (R).
T	Displays a test pattern for use in aligning screen.
COLS=*c*	Specifies the number of characters per line (40 or 80).
Lines=*n*	Specifies the number of lines per screen (25, 43, or 50).
RATE=*r*	Specifies the repeat rate of keyboard characters; range is 1 to 32, which is approximately 2 to 30 characters per second. Default is 20.
DELAY=*d*	Specifies the elapsed time in quarters of seconds before keyboard repeat starts; values are 1, 2, 3, and 4. Default is 2 (for .5 seconds).

Notes:

ANSI.SYS must be loaded in order to change the number of lines displayed.

To use 43 lines, the computer requires at least an EGA adapter and monitor. To use 50 lines, it requires at least a VGA compatible monitor.

If you specify either RATE or DELAY, you must specify the other as well.

You can also set up your screen for 40 or 80 columns. The larger characters (40 columns) can be read from farther away, but they can interfere with the layout of formatted output, such as a DIR /W listing.

Controlling Keyboard Response

PC keyboards have a *typematic* feature that causes keys to repeat when held down. If you hold any key down for more than half a second, the key starts to repeat at about 20 times per second. You may want to alter the typematic rate. The MODE command lets you modify both the DELAY, which sets the start of the repeat, and the RATE, which controls how fast it repeats. The following command causes the repeat to start after 0.25 second and to occur at the rate of 30 per second.

```
MODE DELAY=1 RATE=30
```

The following command causes a delay of one second, with only two repetitions per second. This gives more control to unskilled typists and slow thinkers.

```
MODE DELAY=4 RATE=2
```

Chapter 17 discusses additional ways to adapt the console and printer for use with international character sets.

17

ANOTHER COUNTRY HEARD FROM

Introduction

DOS-compatible computers are usually set up for the country in which they are manufactured or purchased. If you bought your system in the United States or Canada, your keyboard, monitor, and printer probably handle standard American English characters. Numeric values, dates, and times most likely appear in the traditional American formats. If you bought your system in some other country, its character set, numeric, date, and time formats should be standard for that country.

However, you may want to use your computer to prepare, read, or produce text for people from other countries who prefer, for example, to see the time and date in a more familiar form. You may have to prepare correspondence or reports for people in other countries or use characters common in other languages that are not on your keyboard.

This chapter covers various ways you can adapt DOS to deal with the problems of international communication.

Overview

DOS provides a gamut of commands that affect the way it deals with internationality. The KEYB command lets you emulate or interpret a country-specific keyboard. The COUNTRY command causes the system to use numeric formats of another country or region.

Your monitor and printer have *code pages* built into them. A code page is a table that tells the device what character corresponds to each one-byte code (from 0 through 255). With the standard English code page, code 66 is a "B"; code 123 is a "{"; code 156 is a "£" and code 168 is a "¿". Changing the code page tells DOS to use a different set of characters for the same codes for the monitor and/or printer.

DOS provides six software code pages, which can be downloaded to devices to replace the hardware (built-in) code pages. The first 128 values (from 0 to 127) are the same in each, since these are the values standardized as ASCII code. Table 17.1 shows some of the differences in the extended values (above 127) for the six code pages. The Appendix in your DOS documentation includes the complete list of characters for each code page.

Table 17.1 Selected Code Page Values

Name	Code page ID	Codes 145	156	157	164	228
United States	437	æ	£	¥	ñ	Σ
Multilingual	850	æ	£	Ø	ñ	Ō
Slavic	852			Ł		n
Portugal	860	À	£	Ù	ñ	Σ
Canada-French	863	È	£	Ù	¨	Σ
Nordic	865	æ	£	Ø	ñ	Σ

You may be able to use a different code page without much preparation with the COUNTRY or KEYB command. If you expect to change code pages often, however, it's best to set up the system so you can switch easily.

Using Special Characters

A code page includes 256 characters. Many of these cannot be typed directly, however. The default code pages built into your monitor and printer have many characters available that don't correspond to keyboard keys or key combinations. You can type any code by holding down the Alt key, typing the code on the numeric keypad (make sure NumLock is on), and releasing Alt. For example, suppose the standard English code page (437) is current and you have to type the character ä. Just hold down the Alt key and type 132 on the numeric keypad. When you release Alt, the character appears on your screen. It will even print on a standard printer.

With font-oriented software, such as word processors or desktop publishing software, the font controls the character set; characters may be different from the installed code page. For example, in Microsoft Word, Alt+210 produces a " ' ", "®", "❾", or "π", depending on whether the Courier, Symbol, Zapf Dingbats, or LineDraw font is used.

N O T E

A few monitors cannot display extended characters without help. If you don't see them on your screen, try the command GRAFTABL 437. If you use a different code page, specify it instead of 437.

You might want to set up a shortcut for extended characters you must type often using the ANSI.SYS features. The command below assigns the ä character to Ctrl+A so you can type it easily at the DOS prompt:

```
PROMPT $E[1;"ä"p$P$G
```

In creating the command, use Alt+132 to create the desired character. Chapter 16 covers the use of ANSI.SYS escape sequences in detail.

N O T E

Remapped keys are effective only on the DOS command-prompt screen; you can't use them in the Shell or in other software.

International Keyboards

If you use many non-English characters in your work, you may want to tell DOS you have a keyboard layout that lets you type those characters directly. You may even want to install different keycaps. The KEYB command lets you specify a different layout. DOS will then assign different codes to your keypresses, interpreting the characters according to the specified keyboard layout (regardless of what the keycaps say).

Table 17.2 lists the keyboard layouts available with DOS 5, along with the default code page and the alternate code page that can be used with each. The Appendix in the DOS documentation shows the exact layout of each available keyboard.

Table 17.2 Keyboard Codes and Code Pages

Country/Region	Code	Standard	Alternate	ID
Belgium	BE	850	437	
Brazil	BR	850	437	
Canadian-French	CF	863	850	
Czechoslovakia (Czech)	CZ	852	850	
Czechoslovakia (Slovak)	SL	852	850	
Denmark	DK	850	865	
Finland	SU	850	437	
France	FR	850	437	120,189
Germany	GR	850	437	
Hungary	HU	852	850	
Italy	IT	850	437	141,142
Latin America	LA	850	437	
Netherlands	NL	850	437	
Norway	NO	850	865	
Poland	PL	852	850	
Portugal	PO	850	860	
Spain	SP	850	437	
Sweden	SV	850	437	
Switzerland (French)	SF	850	437	
Switzerland (German)	SG	850	437	
United Kingdom	UK	437	850	166,168
United States	US	437	850	

> **TIP**   If you always use a nonstandard layout, put the appropriate KEYB command in your CONFIG.SYS or AUTOEXEC.BAT file so it becomes the default.

The KEYB Command

Figure 17.1 shows the format of the KEYB command. You can use it at the command prompt or install it from CONFIG.SYS. The two-letter keyboard code identifies which keyboard layout to use. If installed through CONFIG.SYS, KEYB must include the complete path if KEYBOARD.SYS is not in the root directory of the boot drive. When used as a command, you can depend on the established path to locate the KEYB.COM file.

Figure 17.1.

KEYB Command
Reference.

KEYB

Configures a keyboard for a different language character set, altering the meaning of some keys by loading a memory-resident keyboard handler that replaces the one in BIOS.

Format:

From the command prompt:

   KEYB [*xx*,[*yyy*],[*filespec*]] [/E] [/ID:*nn*]

From CONFIG.SYS:

   INSTALL=[*path*]KEYB.COM [*xx*,[*yyy*],[*filespec*]] [/E] [/ID:*nn*]

Switches and Parameters:

None	If a nondefault keyboard is installed, displays current keyboard code, related code page, and current code page used by CON. If the default keyboard is in use and no code pages have been installed, reports that neither KEYB nor a code page has been installed.
xx	Identifies the keyboard code; see Table 17.2.
yyy	Identifies an alternate code page for keyboard.
filespec	Specifies the location and name of the keyboard definition file if not KEYBOARD.SYS in a directory on the search path.
path	Specifies the location of the KEYB.COM file; default is in root directory of the boot drive.
/E	Indicates an enhanced keyboard is installed.
/ID:*nn*	Specifies the keyboard in use; needed only for countries with more than one layout (UK, France, Italy). See Table 17.2.

Notes:

An alternate code page is made active only if that code page has been installed with MODE.

If intervening values are omitted, commas are required. Trailing commas may be omitted.

KEYB sets an exit code. See Appendix A.

TIP	If your system is set up for it, use LH to load KEYB into an UMB. In this case, load KEYB from AUTOEXEC.BAT or the command prompt, not from CONFIG.SYS.

After KEYB has been installed, if you enter KEYB with no parameters, you'll see a message like this:

```
Current keyboard code:  LA    code page:  850
```

If a code page hasn't been downloaded, you'll see this line as well:

```
Active code page not available from CON device
```

You can still use the keyboard, but it reflects the built-in code page. Later in this chapter you'll see how to load different code pages.

Once a keyboard layout is installed, you can switch between it and the default (US) layout. Ctrl+Alt+F1 activates the built-in keyboard driver, while Ctrl+Alt+F2 goes back to the installed one. For example, suppose you load the Latin American keyboard with KEYB LA. When you press the semicolon key, you see ñ. If you press Ctrl+Alt+F1 and press the key again, the semicolon produces its usual; character. Typing KEYB with no parameters at this point indicates that the current keyboard code is still LA, even though the keyboard is set for the built-in mode. Use KEYB US to restore the default setup.

Some countries have a standard typewriter layout that differs from the keyboard layout; pressing Ctrl+Alt+F7 activates this layout.

Code Pages with Keyboards

When you change keyboard layouts, you might need to change monitor code pages as well, so that you can see all the characters you can now type. Each keyboard layout has a standard and alternate code page associated with it (see Table 17.2). For the best results, install the standard code page for the keyboard you want to use (covered later in this chapter). If you want to switch back and forth between keyboard layouts, code page 850 (the multilingual code page) might be your best bet, as it is the standard or alternate code page for every keyboard layout. You can get away with code page 437 (the English code page) for many layouts; it's probably your built-in code page, so you don't have to do anything to use it.

Any code pages other than 437 must be prepared first. If the code page has already been prepared when the KEYB command is entered, KEYB switches to it automatically. For example, suppose code pages 850 and 852 have been prepared. The following command switches to the Polish keyboard layout and monitor code page 852, the default for the Polish layout:

```
KEYB PL
```

The following command switches to the Polish layout and monitor code page 850:

```
KEYB PL,850
```

TIP   You may need to change printer code pages as well to print files containing international characters.

International Formats

The date, time, and numeric formats in other countries are frequently different from those in the United States. For example, the year may be first, a different currency symbol may be used, or the use of commas and decimal point characters in numeric values may be reversed. You can tell DOS to use formats that are specific to another region or country. (These formats affect the output of commands like DATE, TIME, and DIR.)

If a country uses characters like Ø and æ, they may be placed differently in the sort sequence than they are in a US-oriented code page. If you use these characters very often, you will want them sorted according to their country's standards. (The sort sequence affects commands like SORT and DIR.)

Table 17.3 lists the countries DOS supports, their codes, and the time and date formats they use.

Table 17.3 Countries and Formats

Country	Code	Date	Time
Belgium	032	05/01/1992	17:15:25,00
Brazil	055	05/01/1992	17:15:25,00
Canadian-French	002	1992-01-05	17:15:25,00

continues

Table 17.3 Continued

Country	Code	Date	Time
Czechoslovakia	042	1992-01-05	17:15:25,00
Denmark	045	05-01-1992	17.15.25,00
Finland	358	05.01.1992	17.15.25,00
France	033	05.01.1992	17:15:25,00
Germany	049	05.01.1992	17:15:25,00
Hungary	036	1992-01-05	17:15:25,00
International English	061	05/01/1992	17:15:25.00
Italy	039	05/01/1992	17.15.35,00
Latin America	003	05/01/1992	05:15:25.00p
Netherlands	031	05-01-1992	17:15:25,00
Norway	047	05.01.1992	17:15:25,00
Poland	048	1992-01-05	17:15:25,00
Portugal	351	05-01-1992	17:15:25,00
Spain	034	05/01/1992	17:15:25,00
Sweden	046	1992-01-05	17.15.25,00
Switzerland	041	05.01.1992	17,15,25.00
United Kingdom	044	05/01/1992	17:15:25.00
United States	001	01/05/1992	05:15:25.00p
Yugoslavia	038	1992-01-05	17:15:25,00

The COUNTRY Configuration Command

If format and sort sequence are the only changes you need, you can use the COUNTRY configuration command by itself to set them. Figure 17.2 shows the format of this command, which belongs in the CONFIG.SYS file.

The COUNTRY command must include the country code (see Table 17.3). The code is often (but not always) the same as the international dialing code for the country. Each country also has a default code page and an alternate one. If it is already available, the default code page for that country will be used automatically. If you want to use the alternate code page, you need the second parameter. Code page preparation is covered in more detail later in this chapter. As with the KEYB command, a different code page is not actually made available unless it has been installed.

Figure 17.2.

COUNTRY
Configuration
Command
Reference.

COUNTRY

Controls the time, date, and numeric (decimal point and thousands) formats, sort sequence, and currency symbol.

Format:

COUNTRY=*xxx*[,*yyy*] [,*filespec*]]

Parameters:

xxx   Specifies the country code (see Table 17.3); default is 001 (United States).

yyy   Specifies the alternate code page for the country; not needed for default code page.

filespec Identifies the location and name of the file containing country information; default is COUNTRY.SYS in the root directory of the boot drive.

Note:

If you omit *yyy* but include *filespec*, include two commas. (Trailing commas may be omitted.)

DOS must be able to find the COUNTRY.SYS file provided with DOS. If it is stored in the root directory of the boot drive, there is no problem. However, most people store all the DOS files in a \DOS directory, so the command must include a complete file specification.

The following command specifies the use of the Latin American formats:

```
COUNTRY=003,,C:\DOS\COUNTRY.SYS
```

The only way to change which country is specified is to edit the CONFIG.SYS file, change the COUNTRY statement, and restart your computer.

Using Code Pages

By default, your system uses the built-in (hardware) code pages for all text. You can set it up to use a code page arranged for a different language group by downloading a software code page. You can even set up several code pages and switch back and forth.

Several commands must be coordinated in order to use any code pages other than the built-in one. If either KEYB or COUNTRY needs a software code page, the code page must be prepared before it can take effect. The CONFIG.SYS file must install a device driver for the monitor (DISPLAY.SYS) and/or printer (PRINTER.SYS) in order to use the code page.

Once the environment is established, several commands are needed to handle the code pages. You can put these commands in AUTOEXEC.BAT if you use them every time, or you can enter them individually at the DOS prompt. The NLSFUNC command establishes National Language Support, which makes switching code pages easier. The MODE command installs specific software code pages preparing them for use by DOS. Additional MODE commands can change code pages or display the current status. The CHCP command uses National Language Support to switch code pages.

Monitor Code Pages

Standard monochrome and CGA monitors cannot use monitor code pages. However, all EGA, VGA, LCD, and more advanced types can. Before you can use software code pages on your monitor, you must load the driver DISPLAY.SYS (see Figure 17.3). As with most device drivers, you can use DEVICEHIGH instead to load the driver into upper memory if your system is set up for it. The following command loads DISPLAY.SYS for an LCD monitor:

```
DEVICE=C:\DOS\DISPLAY.SYS CON=(LCD)
```

The following command loads DISPLAY.SYS for an EGA monitor; it specifies the default code page, so the user can switch back to it, and allows for two code pages:

```
DEVICEHIGH=C:\DOS\DISPLAY.SYS CON=(EGA,437,2)
```

The code page information files, EGA.CPI and LCD.CPI, are part of the DOS 5 software. The *type* specifies which CPI file to use in loading the code page. If none is specified, DOS attempts to determine the console type internally.

If you omit the hardware code page in the command, you won't be able to switch back to it after loading a different one. This doesn't matter if you expect to install a software code page and use it all the time. The number of code pages determines the amount of memory reserved for switching code pages; it defaults to 1. If you want to switch back and forth between the hardware code page (437) and the multilingual code page (850), you need to store only one software code page. But if you want to switch back and forth between 850, 852, and 860, you need to store three code pages in memory.

Figure 17.3.

DISPLAY.SYS DEVICE Command.

DISPLAY.SYS

Identifies the monitor hardware code page and allocates buffers for software code pages.

Format:

DEVICE[HIGH]=[*path*]DISPLAY.SYS CON=(*type*[,*hwcp*],[*n*])

Parameters:

path   Specifies the location of the DISPLAY.SYS file, if not in the root directory of the boot drive.

type   Identifies the display adapter in use:

    EGA   EGA or VGA
    LCD   liquid crystal display

hwcp   Identifies the code page built into the monitor (usually 437); if omitted, you can't switch back to this code page.

n   Specifies the number of code pages in addition to the hardware code page, from 0 to 6. Maximum for EGA is 6, for LCD is 1.

Notes:

If you use a third-party console driver (such as VT52.SYS) in addition to DISPLAY.SYS, install DISPLAY.SYS last; the third-party one might disable DISPLAY.SYS if it isn't loaded first.

If you omit *type*, DOS attempts to determine the value internally; if you include any later parameters, include the comma to mark this parameter.

A final parameter, not shown above, specifies the number of subfonts to be used. Subfonts aren't generally available (or needed).

If any intervening values are omitted, be sure to include the comma; trailing commas may be omitted.

Printer Code Pages

You probably want to be able to print the same characters you see on the screen. To do this, use the same code page for the printer. Only specific printers (and compatibles) are able to handle the software code pages. Figure 17.4 shows the PRINTER.SYS DEVICE command format and lists the printers that use it. As with all DEVICE commands, you can use DEVICEHIGH instead to load the driver into high memory. The following command loads the PRINTER.SYS device driver for an IBM ProPrinter II on the default printer port:

```
DEVICE=C:\DOS\PRINTER.SYS LPT1=(4201)
```

The following command loads PRINTER.SYS into high memory for a ProPrinter XL24E, allowing it to switch back to the built-in code page; it can use two code pages:

```
DEVICEHIGH=C:\DOS\PRINTER.SYS LPT2=(4208,437,2)
```

Figure 17.4.	**PRINTER.SYS**
PRINTER.SYS DEVICE Command.	Tells DOS which code page is needed for the printer and reserves buffer space for software code pages.

Format:

DEVICE[HIGH]=[*path*]PRINTER.SYS LPT*n*=(*type*[,*hwcp*][,*n*]])

Parameters:

path   Specifies the location of the DISPLAY.SYS file, if it is not in the root directory of the boot drive.

LPT*n*   Identifies the printer port.

type   Specifies the type of printer:

4201	IBM Proprinter II and III (4201)
	IBM Proprinter II and III XL (4202)
4208	IBM Proprinter X24E (4207)
	IBM Proprinter XL24E Model (4208)
5202	IBM Quietwriter III Model (5202)

hwcp   Identifies the code page built into the printer (usually 437); if omitted, you can't switch back to this code page.

n   Specifies the number of code pages the system can support in addition to the hardware code page. The maximum is determined by the printer; default is 1.

Note:

A comma is required to mark the position of any omitted intervening values. Trailing commas may be omitted.

If you omit a value for *hwcp*, you won't be able to switch back to the built-in code page after loading a software code page. The number of code pages determines the amount of memory reserved for loading code pages; it defaults to 1.

Preparing Code Pages

Before any software code page can be used, it must be prepared. This process installs the code page in memory and makes it available to the system, including the COUNTRY and KEYB commands. Code pages must be prepared separately for each device using the MODE command. Figure 17.5 shows how MODE is used to reference code pages. Each command specifies one device followed by the word CODEPAGE followed by the action to be taken. The PREPARE format installs the code page. To install the multi-lingual code page for both the console and the printer, you would use these commands:

```
MODE CON CODEPAGE PREPARE=((850) C:\DOS\EGA.CPI)
MODE LPT1 CODEPAGE PREPARE=((850) C:\DOS\4201.CPI)
```

If the CPI file is located in a directory along the search path, you don't have to specify it here; the device driver has already let DOS know which file will be needed.

Figure 17.5.

MODE Command
Reference (for
Code Pages).

MODE

Prepares, selects, refreshes, or displays the numbers of the code pages for printers and monitors.

Formats:

To prepare a code page:
  MODE *device* CODEPAGE PREPARE=((*yyy* [...]) *filespec*)

To download or switch to a code page:
  MODE *device* CODEPAGE SELECT=*yyy*

To reload a code page:
  MODE *device* CODEPAGE REFRESH

To display code page status:
  MODE *device* CODEPAGE [/STATUS]

Switches and Parameters:

device   Identifies the device to use the code page; must be CON or LPT*n*.

yyy   Identifies a code page to prepare or download:

437	United States
850	Multilingual (Latin I)
852	Slavic (Latin II)
860	Portuguese
863	Canadian-French
865	Nordic

filespec   Specifies the location and name of the file containing the code-page information (extension CPI).

Notes:

Preparing a code page loads it into memory. You can prepare as many monitor code pages as you allocated buffers in the DISPLAY.SYS DEVICE command and as many printer code pages as you allocated buffers in the PRINTER.SYS DEVICE command. Code pages must be prepared before they can be downloaded or refreshed, or before KEYB or COUNTRY can install them.

Separate MODE commands are needed to handle monitor and printer code pages.

The files named EGA.CPI, LCD.CPI, 4201.CPI, 4208.CPI, or 5202.CPI must be available when MODE CON or MODE LPT*n* is executed.

CODEPAGE can be abbreviated CP. PREPARE can be abbreviated PREP. SELECT can be abbreviated SEL. REFRESH can be abbreviated REF. /STATUS can be abbreviated /STA.

If you specified the hardware code page in the device driver configuration command, you can switch back and forth between it and an installed code page. If you install several code pages in one or more MODE commands, you can switch among them.

Switching Code Pages

When you switch to a different console code page, the device uses the new code page table to translate one-byte code values into displayed characters. Some characters already on the screen may switch to the new character set. The console code page does not affect the printer. When characters are sent to a printer, they are interpreted using the currently active printer code page.

If you change to a different code page while a program is running, there may be an internal conflict. To avoid this problem, make sure all programs are terminated before changing code pages.

TIP   If you are using the task swapper, don't switch code pages while any task is active. It causes more problems than it is worth.

DOS provides several ways to switch code pages. The KEYB command can switch to an installed code page. Another method uses a MODE command similar to the one you use to install the code page.

The CODEPAGE SELECT format of the MODE command makes the prepared code page active for the specified device. This command makes the multilingual code page active for the console:

```
MODE CON CODEPAGE SELECT=850
```

To make the default code page active again, use this command:

```
MODE CON CODEPAGE SELECT=437
```

If you didn't specify the hardware code page in the device driver command, you won't be able to return to it once you select a different code page.

Complete Code Page Example

Suppose you need to use the Portuguese keyboard and formatting conventions some of the time, using the alternate Portuguese code page (860). Since you work in English as well and need the built-in code page (437), you want to be able to switch between the two code pages.

Put these commands in your CONFIG.SYS file:

```
COUNTRY=351,860,C:\DOS\COUNTRY.SYS
DEVICEHIGH=C:\DOS\DISPLAY.SYS CON=(EGA,437)
DEVICEHIGH=C:\DOS\PRINTER.SYS LPT1=(4201,437)
```

The COUNTRY command establishes the numeric and other formats for country 351, which is Portugal. We specified its alternate code page. The DEVICE commands reserve memory for one software code page for an EGA monitor and *Proprinter* printer. They also define 437 as the hardware code page so you can switch back to it as needed.

Since we aren't sure which keyboard or code page to use first, we'll leave those commands for the DOS prompt. These commands go into AUTOEXEC.BAT:

```
MODE CON CODEPAGE PREPARE=((860)C:\DOS\EGA.CPI)
MODE LPT1 CODEPAGE PREPARE=((860)C:\DOS\4201.CPI)
```

Each MODE command installs the software code page for the specified device.

Once the AUTOEXEC.BAT file has been executed, you are set up to switch between your keyboards and your code pages. You can type these commands at the DOS prompt to manage the keyboard and monitor code pages:

`[LH] KEYB PO`	(switches to Portuguese layout; doesn't switch the code page since the default 850 hasn't been prepared)
`KEYB US`	(switches to US English layout and code page 437)
`MODE CON CODEPAGE SELECT=860`	(switches console to code page 860)
`MODE CON CODEPAGE SELECT=437`	(switches console to code page 437)
`MODE LPT1 CODEPAGE SELECT=860`	(switches printer to code page 860)
`MODE LPT1 CODEPAGE SELECT=437`	(switches printer to code page 437)

If you use these commands or similar ones, at the keyboard, you may want
to set up DOSKEY macros to make them easier to use. The following batch
file contains four DOSKEY macro definitions:

```
DOSKEY C8=MODE CON CODEPAGE SELECT=860
DOSKEY C4=MODE CON CODEPAGE SELECT=437
DOSKEY P8=MODE LPT1 CODEPAGE SELECT=860
DOSKEY P4=MODE LPT1 CODEPAGE SELECT=437
```

You could map the commands to key combinations if you prefer. For example, this command sets up Shift+F1 to switch to monitor code page 860
and restores the usual prompt:

```
PROMPT $E[0;84;"MODE CON CODEPAGE SELECT=860"p$P$G
```

You can switch between keyboards using Ctrl+Alt+F2 to access the memory-
resident one (Portugal) and Ctrl+Alt+F1 to return to the built-in one.

National Language Support

DOS's National Language Support feature makes code-page switching
easier, both internally and externally, although you still use MODE to install the code pages. In order to use National Language Support, you must
load NLSFUNC as a TSR. Figure 17.6 shows the command format. You
don't have to specify the filespec if it's in the COUNTRY command; otherwise it defaults to COUNTRY.SYS in the root directory of the boot drive.

The NLSFUNC program can be loaded at the DOS prompt or through the
CONFIG.SYS INSTALL command. Using INSTALL lets you make sure the
TSR is loaded before COMMAND.COM. This can help if the language
support functions don't seem to work. If you use the INSTALL method, it
must follow the DEVICE commands that load DISPLAY.SYS and
PRINTER.SYS.

Once National Language Support is installed, you can use the CHCP command (see Figure 17.6) to change code pages for printer and monitor at
once. CHCP without a parameter displays the number of the active code
page, even if NLSFUNC hasn't been loaded.

Figure 17.6.

NLSFUNC
Command
Reference.

NLSFUNC

Loads country-specific information for National Language Support (NLS); enables you to use CHCP to change code pages for all devices with one command.

Format:

From the command prompt:

  NSLFUNC [*filespec*]

From CONFIG.SYS:

  INSTALL=[*path*]NSLFUNC.EXE [*filespec*]

Parameters:

filespec Specifies the location and name of the file containing country-specific information. Not needed if specified in COUNTRY command or if COUNTRY.SYS is in the root directory of the boot drive.

path Specifies the location of NSLFUNC.EXE program, if it's not in the root directory of the boot drive.

Notes:

The country file isn't accessed until requested by CHCP; no error message occurs if it isn't available at boot time.

If the language support doesn't seem to work when loaded from the command prompt, load it through CONFIG.SYS. This lets NLSFUNC load before COMMAND.COM. Be sure the INSTALL command follows DEVICE=DISPLAY.SYS and DEVICE=PRINTER.SYS if they are used.

Figure 17.7.

CHCP Command
Reference.

CHCP

Changes to another prepared code page associated with your country setting.

Format:

CHCP [*nnn*]

Parameters:

None Displays number of current code page even if NLSFUNC hasn't been run; default is 437.

nnn Identifies the prepared code page to change to.

Notes:

Before CHCP can change a code page, NLSFUNC must have been run to place CHCP in memory.

CHCP downloads a code page to all eligible devices at once (if it has been prepared and NLSFUNC is in memory). It will affect only prepared devices and code pages.

Another Code Page Example

Suppose you want to use National Language Support in the Portuguese example presented earlier. The same commands are needed in your CONFIG.SYS file:

```
COUNTRY=351,860,C:\DOS\COUNTRY.SYS
DEVICE=C:\DOS\DISPLAY.SYS CON=(EGA,437)
DEVICE=C:\DOS\PRINTER.SYS LPT1=(4201,437)
```

The same commands to install the code pages can be placed in the
AUTOEXEC.BAT file, but you also need the NLSFUNC command:

```
LH NLSFUNC
MODE CON CODEPAGE PREPARE=((860)C:\DOS\EGA.CPI)
MODE LPT1 CODEPAGE PREPARE=((860)C:\DOS\4201.CPI)
```

Once the AUTOEXEC.BAT file has been executed, you are all set up to
switch between your keyboard layouts and your code pages. You can enter
these commands at the DOS prompt to manage the keyboard and monitor
code pages:

KEYB PO   (switches to Portuguese layout; doesn't change the code page)

KEYB US   (switches to US layout)

CHCP 860   (switches both devices to code page 860)

CHCP 437   (switches both devices to code page 437)

The CHCP command loads the specified code page to all prepared devices,
simplifying the task.

Manipulating Code Pages

Occasionally, DOS may lose track of a code page. This may happen if a
printer is turned off, for example. In that case, use the MODE command to
refresh the code page. The command below reinstates the last active code
page for the printer:

```
MODE LPT1 CODEPAGE REFRESH
```

The console code page may also be reinstated after a monitor problem, but
if the monitor has locked up, you'll probably have to reboot to free it. In
that case, the commands in your CONFIG.SYS and AUTOEXEC.BAT files
are processed again. Then you can switch code pages at the keyboard with
a MODE command or with CHCP (if NLSFUNC was loaded).

Displaying Code Page Information

Several commands give you information on the status of your system; you
can use any of these at the DOS prompt or through the Shell as needed.

The KEYB command with no options displays the current keyboard information in this format:

```
Current keyboard code: BE   code page: 850
Current CON code page: 850
```

The messages give you both the keyboard layout and the code page in effect. If KEYB has not been used, you'll see a message like this instead:

```
KEYB has not been installed
Active code page not available from CON device
```

The CHCP command with no options displays just the current code page in this format:

```
Active code page: 850
```

The report is produced even if NLSFUNC isn't in memory.

The MODE command with no parameters displays information on all the attached devices and any current code pages. It provides lots of information, so you'll want to use MODE | MORE or redirect the output so you can see it all.

The /STATUS switch of the MODE command gives you information on a specific device. For example, the command MODE CON CODEPAGE /STATUS gives this output:

```
Active code page for device CON is 850
Hardware code pages:
  code page 437
Prepared code pages:
  code page 850


MODE status code page function completed
```

In most cases, the /STATUS switch is optional; you get exactly the same information whether or not you use it. (In Chapter 18, you'll see the one situation where /STATUS is required.)

18

PRINTING THROUGH DOS

ntroduction

When you print a file from an application, such as a word processing document or a worksheet, the application provides its own printer driver. The developers of print-oriented applications put a lot of effort into their printer drivers so the applications can make the best use of the popular printer models.

DOS is hardly print-oriented, but it provides some primitive printing services so that you can capture screen prints with the PrintScreen key, print ASCII text files (such as README files), redirect standard output to the printer, and echo the monitor in print. Although DOS assumes you have a very basic printer attached to LPT1, there are ways of getting it to use other types of printers, including a laser printer attached to a serial port.

Printer Types

DOS uses only the most basic printer capabilities. For this reason, it can print on almost any PC-compatible printer.

Most modern-day printers can emulate a basic printer of some type. If DOS doesn't seem to communicate with your printer, check its documentation and find out how to emulate an IBM, Hewlett-Packard, Epson, or Diablo printer; DOS handles these types very well.

DOS cannot communicate directly with PostScript laser printers, but most PostScript printers will emulate one of the above printers. You may have to set a switch on the printer itself to make it emulate an Epson (or whatever). Don't forget to return the printer to its normal setting when using it with software that has a PostScript driver.

> **TIP**
>
> If you try to print something using a PostScript driver and the printer spews out page upon page of apparently meaningless phrases, the printer is in an emulation mode. The text being printed is PostScript control information.

DOS expects a parallel printer and uses LPT1 as the default printer port; device PRN refers to the same port. When you use echo printing or screen printing, the output is sent to PRN. You can redirect a parallel port to a serial port using a MODE command, as explained later in this chapter.

DOS Print Features

There are several different ways to print material through DOS. Redirecting standard output to the printer is one method. For example, you could use a command like this to print a directory:

```
DIR > PRN
```

The standard output appears on the printer instead of the monitor. But any error messages and the next DOS prompt appear on the monitor.

Printer Control Commands

You can also use redirection to control the printer. Printer control commands are often specific to the printer; its documentation should detail the commands to which it responds. The signal generated by pressing Ctrl+L will eject a page on most printers. The following ECHO command sends a Ctrl+L signal to the printer; pressing Ctrl+L displays the ^L in the command. You can enter this command at the DOS prompt; it doesn't have to be in a batch file:

```
ECHO ^L > PRN
```

The following command creates a DOSKEY macro named PAGE to eject a printer page:

```
DOSKEY PAGE=ECHO ^L $G PRN
```

The following command remaps the F1 key to eject a page:

```
PROMPT $E[0;59;"ECHO ^L > PRN";13p$P$G
```

NOTE

Details on creating DOSKEY macros are included in Chapter 5. Details on remapping key assignments appear in Chapter 16.

The macro or the remapped key is particularly useful with laser printers, as they often don't eject a printed page until the page is full. (Some will time out after a minute or so and eject a partially full page.) But the page eject command forces the printer to print the page now, even if it has only one or two lines on it.

The following batch program prints the entire hard disk directory, including hidden and system files, ejecting the last page. For a laser printer, this causes the last page to be printed. For a continuous form printer, it rolls the last page up so it's ready to tear off:

```
@ECHO OFF
DIR C:\ /S /A > PRN
ECHO ^L > PRN
```

You could use the same technique to print the results of CHKDSK, TREE, FIND, and other verbose commands.

Echo Printing

Echo printing has a more lasting and inclusive effect than redirection. It copies everything that crosses the screen to the default printer: prompts, commands, error messages, and command output. You might use it to print a series of directory lists or diagnostic reports, for example, or to document a work session. It affects only commands and messages that cross the command-prompt screen. If you start up some other program while echo printing is in effect, echo printing resumes when that program terminates.

To start echo printing, press Ctrl+PrintScreen or Ctrl+P. All DOS commands and messages from that point on are echoed to the printer. If no printer is attached or redirected to LPT1, the system hangs up; make the printer available or reboot to continue. Once echo printing is in effect, press Ctrl+PrintScreen or Ctrl+P again to cancel it.

NOTE

You cannot turn echo printing on or off from within a batch program or DOSKEY macro. Ctrl+P or Ctrl+PrintScreen must be pressed at the command prompt.

Text Screen Printing

Echo printing must be turned on before the text you want to capture crosses the screen. If the text is already displayed, you can capture it with a screen print. Just press the PrintScreen key (Shift+PrintScreen on some keyboards) and all the text on the screen is printed on the default printer. Printing graphics screens requires the GRAPHICS command, which is explained later in this chapter.

WARNING

If you press PrintScreen with no printer available on LPT1, your system might just beep or it might hang up waiting for a printer. If it hangs up, either make the printer available or reboot.

Configuring a Printer

Every printer has a standard vertical spacing measured in lines per inch (lpi), and horizontal spacing, measured in characters per inch (cpi). Most printers use 6 lpi and 10 cpi by default. You can modify the spacing with a MODE command (see Figure 18.1). For parallel printers, you can set the vertical spacing at 6 or 8 lpi and the horizontal spacing at 80 or 132 cpi. If you use the words to identify the parameters (as in COLS=132), they can be in any order. If you omit the words, the parameters must be entered in the order shown. The following command sets LPT1 to print the maximum amount per page:

```
MODE LPT1 COLS=132 LINES=8
```

Figure 18.1.

MODE Command
Reference
(Parallel Printer
Configuration).

<u>MODE</u>

Configures a parallel printer to use specific vertical and horizontal spacing and retry action.

Formats:

MODE LPTn [COLS=c] [LINES=l] [RETRY=r]

MODE LPTn [c],[l],[r]

Parameters:

LPTn Identifies the parallel port: LPT1 to LPT3. You can use PRN instead of LPT1.

c Specifies the number of columns per line: 80 or 132.

l Specifies the number of lines per inch: 6 or 8.

r Specifies the retry action action if a time-out error occurs. Valid values are:

    E   return an error
    B   return "busy"
    P   continue retrying until printer accepts output
    R   return "ready"
    N   no retry value (default)

Notes:

If the parameter names are used in the command (as in the first format), they can be in any sequence. If only the values are used (as in the second format), they must be in the order shown. If intervening values are omitted, their commas must be included. (Trailing commas may be omitted.)

The parameter RETRY=B has the same effect as the P parameter in previous DOS versions.

The RETRY parameter tells DOS how to react if DOS senses the printer, but it isn't ready to receive signals. By default, it simply gives up. The P parameter tells it to continue trying until the printer becomes available. This can cause your system to hang up when you try to print something and the printer is turned off, out of paper, off-line, or some other problem exists. To break out of the loop, make the printer available or press Ctrl+C to break out of this loop.

Once you configure the printer with MODE, it applies to all uses of that printer, including all applications that use DOS's printing services. Some software may override the configuration, but it will be restored when that application terminates.

Using Serial Printers

To use a serial printer for printing directly under DOS, you must first tell DOS the communications characteristics of the device. And if the serial printer is your only printer or you want to use it as DOS's PRN (default) device, you must redirect LPT1 to it.

Configuring the Serial Port

A serial port, also known as a communications port, might be attached to a printer, a mouse, a modem, or some other device. Each device could have different communications characteristics (baud rate, parity check, and so on). To use a serial port with DOS, you must define its communications characteristics with a MODE command (see Figure 18.2). This section shows how to use MODE to set up a serial port for a printer. The same parameters are used to set it up for any device.

The parameters can be used in any order if the labels are attached (as in BAUD=96). If you omit the labels, the parameter values must be in the order shown in the format, and the commas must be included. These two examples both configure a serial printer the same way:

```
MODE COM1 BAUD=96 PARITY=N DATA=8 STOP=1 RETRY=P
MODE COM1 96,N,8,1,P
```

The configuration affects all uses of the COM port until another MODE command changes it.

You can't guess at the communications characteristics. You must use the correct values for the attached device. In most cases, the device's documentation tells you exactly how to write the MODE command.

Figure 18.2.

MODE Command
Reference
(Configuring
Serial Ports).

MODE

Configures a serial (COM) port for use by a device such as a serial printer.

Formats:

MODE COM*n* [BAUD=*b*] [PARITY=*p*] [DATA=*d*] [STOP=*s*] [RETRY=*r*]

MODE COM*n* [*b*],[*p*],[*d*],[*s*],[*r*]

Parameters:

COM*n* Identifies the serial port: COM1 to COM4.

b Specifies the baud rate. You can use the full baud rate (e.g., 9600) or just the first two digits (e.g., 96). Supported baud rates are:

110	1,200	19,200 (on some computers)
150	2,400	
300	4,800	
600	9,600	

p Specifies the type of parity the system should check for. Supported values are:

N none
E even (default)
O odd
M mark (on some computers)
S space (on some computers)

d Specifies the number of data bits in a character. Range is 5 to 8; default is 7.

s Specifies the number of stop bits that define the end of a character. Values are 1, 1.5, and 2; default for 110 baud is 2; for other baud rates, default is 1. (1.5 is not supported on all computers.)

r Specifies the retry action if a time-out error occurs. Valid values are:

E return an error
B return "busy"
P continue retrying until device accepts output
R return "ready"
N no retry value (default)

Notes:

If the parameter names are used in the command (as in the first format), they can be in any sequence. If only the values are used (as in the second format), they must be in the order shown. If intervening values are omitted, their commas must be included. (Trailing commas may be omitted.)

Don't use a RETRY value on a network; use RETRY=P only on a printer.

This MODE command format can be used to set up a communications port for telecommunications, but many communications programs handle this themselves.

Resident Portion of Mode

Some of MODE's functions require a small (.5K) TSR to be installed. Configuring a serial port is one of these memory-resident functions. Whichever MODE command installs the TSR results in this message:

```
Resident portion of MODE loaded
```

The TSR needs to be loaded only once, then all of MODE's memory-resident functions can use it.

N O T E

This TSR cannot be loaded in upper memory blocks. DOS ignores
LOADHIGH when applied to a MODE command.

Redirecting a Serial Printer

If you want DOS to use a serial printer as PRN (for screen prints, echo
printing, and so on), you must redirect LPT1 to it using a command like
this:

```
MODE LPTn=COMn
```

For example, `MODE LPT1=COM1` tells DOS that any data directed to LPT1
should be sent to COM1 instead. Of course, you can specify any valid serial
(COM) and parallel (LPT) ports in the command. But to use the serial
printer as PRN, the default printer, you must redirect LPT1.

N O T E

This MODE command format redirects parallel ports to serial ports
only. It cannot be used to redirect a serial port, nor can it redirect a
parallel port to any other type of port.

Many applications depend on DOS's printing services, so you may need to
redirect LPT1 even if you don't plan on screen prints or echo printing.
The MODE command that sets the COM port's characteristics must precede the redirection command, or DOS won't be able to use the port.

To undo a redirection, enter `MODE LPTn` (*without* the `=COMn`). You'll see a
message like this:

```
LPT1: not rerouted.
No retry on parallel printer time-out
```

Viewing Redirection Status

The MODE command with no parameters displays status information for
all the devices it controls. In addition, MODE generally displays status

information for a device when you enter MODE followed by the device name and no other parameters. Here are some examples:

```
MODE CON      (Displays status information about the console)
MODE COM1     (Displays status information about the first serial port)
MODE LPT1 CODEPAGE (Displays status information about the printer
                   codepages)
```

But the following command will not display status information about the indicated parallel printer. Instead it will undo any redirection applied to the printer:

```
MODE LPT1
```

To see status information for parallel printers, you must include the /STATUS switch (which can be abbreviated /STA), as in:

```
C:\>MODE LPT1 /STA
Status for device LPT1:
-----------------------
LPT1: rerouted to COM1:
Retry=NONE

Code page operation not supported on this device

C:\>
```

The /STATUS switch may be used with the other device names, but it is not necessary.

The PRINT Command

Once a printer is attached (and configured, if necessary), DOS can print files on it using the PRINT command. PRINT lets you print the contents of ASCII files, one at a time or in a queue. It works in the background, so you can continue with other DOS work in the foreground. The first PRINT command in a session loads a TSR (about 5.5K) and configures background printing for the session. You'll have to reboot to change its configuration.

N O T E

If you have redirected a parallel printer to a serial printer, you can print to either the COM port or the redirected parallel port.

Identifying the PRINT Device

Figure 18.3 shows the format of the PRINT command. The first PRINT command after booting results in this question:

```
Name of list device [PRN]:
```

Whatever you enter here becomes the PRINT device until you reboot. To use the default PRN, just press Enter. To use another device (such as LPT2 or COM1), type the device name and press Enter.

You can avoid the question-and-answer interaction by including the /D switch on the first PRINT command after booting. Many people include a PRINT command with no filespec in AUTOEXEC.BAT to load the TSR and establish the print device, something like this:

```
PRINT /D:PRN
```

If you want to print from DOS Shell, you must initialize the print device before starting the Shell. Placing the above command in AUTOEXEC.BAT (before the DOSSHELL command) does the trick nicely.

Configuring PRINT

You may want to configure other PRINT features in the initializing command. You can control such features as print-buffer size, print-queue size, and the balance between background and foreground processing.

N O T E

PRINT can be configured only on its initializing command. It cannot be reconfigured without rebooting.

Figure 18.3.

PRINT Command
Reference.

PRINT

Configures PRINT TSR and prints text files in the background.

Format:

PRINT [*configuration switches*] [*filespec...*] [*control switches*]

Parameter:

filespec	Identifies the file(s) to be printed; can include a path; can be repeated; can use wildcard characters.

Configuration Switches:

/D:*device*	Specifies the name of the print device. Any parallel or serial port can be named.
/B:*size*	Sets the size of the print buffer in bytes; the default (and minimum) is 512; maximum is 16384. Increasing the print buffer speeds printing but reduces available conventional memory.
/U:*ticks*	Specifies the maximum number of clock ticks to wait until printer is available; if not available then, the PRINT command is aborted. Range is 1 to 255; default is 1. Raising this number may slow foreground processing.
/M:*ticks*	Specifies the maximum number of clock ticks to print a character. Range is 1 to 255; default is 2. If printing is too slow, DOS may abort the command and display an error message. Raising this number slows foreground processing.
/S:*ticks*	Specifies the number of clock ticks in one background time slice. Range is 1 to 255; default is 8. Raising this number speeds printing but slows foreground processing.
/Q:*size*	Specifies the number of files allowed in the print queue. Range is 4 to 32; default is 10.

Control switches:

/T	Terminates printing and removes all files from the queue. Don't include filespecs with this switch.
/C	Removes individual files from queue; this switch affects the filespec preceding it as well as all those following until another switch takes effect.
/P	Adds files to the queue; this switch affects the filespec preceding it as well as those following it until another switch takes effect.

Notes:

The configuration switches can be specified only the first time PRINT is used after booting. You must reboot to restart PRINT with other configuration values.

Each filespec can be up to 64 characters long.

Print only text or ASCII files.

There are approximately 18 clock ticks per second.

The /B switch sets the size of the print buffer; a larger buffer speeds up printing but decreases the amount of available conventional memory. (You cannot kick PRINT or its buffer upstairs.)

The rest of the configuration switches control how DOS does time-slicing when PRINT runs in the background. A clock tick is about 1/18 of a second. Normally, DOS will abort the PRINT command if the printer isn't available within one clock tick; if you want more time, increase it with the /U parameter. The /M parameter specifies how many clock ticks are allowed for printing one character. If you have an extremely slow printer and PRINT often aborts with an error message, you might want to specify a higher value here. The /S switch specifies how much background printing is done before DOS checks for a foreground action. If you increase this value from the default 8, print speed is increased but your foreground work may be impeded.

Controlling the Print Queue

Normally, the print queue holds up to 10 files. Each new file is placed at the end of the queue; if the queue is empty, the file is printed immediately. You can include several filespecs separated by spaces or even a global filespec to queue several files at once. A message warns you when the queue is full.

The /Q switch, which belongs on the initializing command, sets the size of the print queue; if you often need to queue up more than 10 files, you might want to specify a larger number.

You can see the current queue by entering PRINT with no parameters. The /T switch, with no filenames, terminates the queue immediately, right in the middle of the current file.

N O T E

When /T is entered, PRINT stops shipping data to the printer, but the printer will keep printing until its own buffer is empty. A printer with a large buffer might print several pages before stopping. You can stop the printer and empty its buffer immediately by turning it off.

You can cancel files from the queue by issuing another PRINT command with the /C switch before or just after the filename to be removed. All filenames following /C are removed from the queue; if a filename precedes it, that one is removed as well. To add files to the queue in the same command, use /P. Just like /C, it applies to all filenames following it and the one immediately before it. Files named in a PRINT command without either /P or /C are added to the queue. For example, the following command cancels ACT.1, ACT.2, and ACT.3 and prints PART.1, PART.2, and PART.3:

```
PRINT /C ACT.1 ACT.2 ACT.3 PART.1 /P PART.2 PART.3
```

You can't directly change the order of files in the print queue. To force a later file to be printed quickly, you would have to cancel any files preceding it in the queue, then add them to the queue again following that file.

Printing GRAPHICS Screens

DOS normally cannot print graphics screens that can be displayed by CGA, EGA, and VGA monitors; it might try to convert them to text characters. There are several third-party software programs that you can use to capture to disk, print, and even modify graphics screens. On occasion, however, you may want to print a graphics screen from a CGA, EGA, or VGA monitor using PrintScreen. The GRAPHICS command might make this possible. DOS can't handle video modes that aren't supported by the BIOS; many SuperVGA graphics can't be handled, for example. And some applications reprogram the VGA display to a different mode; these displays can't be printed under DOS.

How GRAPHICS Works

The GRAPHICS command loads a TSR that lets DOS print supported graphic screens on several types of printers. Once GRAPHICS is loaded, the signal generated by the PrintScreen key is intercepted. If the screen is in text mode, the request is passed back to the BIOS for standard text-screen printing. If the screen is in graphics mode, however, GRAPHICS takes over. It scans each pixel on the screen, translates it for the printer, and prints it. Both the number of pixels (screen resolution) and the number of dots per inch (printer resolution) affect the result. Some graphic displays are printed sideways for best effect.

Your DOS directory includes a file called GRAPHICS.PRO that includes printer profiles for the printer types DOS supports, including details on translating different video formats for printing. This is an ASCII file; you can examine it with EDIT or print it with PRINT.

The GRAPHICS Command

Figure 18.4 shows the format of the GRAPHICS command. GRAPHICS with no parameters is equivalent to GRAPHICS HPDEFAULT; DOS prepares to print graphics screens on a printer that recognizes the PCL (page control language) commands used by most Hewlett-Packard printers. Table 18.1 shows a complete list of the available printer type parameters.

Figure 18.4.

GRAPHICS
Command
Reference.

GRAPHICS

Permits the PrintScreen key to produce printed copies of graphic screens from CGA, EGA, and VGA monitors.

Format:

GRAPHICS [*type*] [*filespec*] [*switches*]

Parameters and Switches:

none	Loads the TSR in its default configuration.
type	Identifies the type of printer. See Table 18.1 for valid values.
filespec	Specifies the name and location of the file that contains information about supported printers. If omitted DOS looks for a file named GRAPHICS.PRO in the current directory and in the directory that contains GRAPHICS.COM.
/B	Prints the background in color. Valid only for COLOR4 and COLOR8 printers.
/R	Prints the image with white characters and symbols on a black background. By default, the screen is printed as black characters and symbols on a white background.
/LCD	Prints the image using the LCD aspect ratio rather than the CGA aspect ratio; has the same effect as /PB:LCD.
/PRINTBOX:*size*	Specifies the aspect ratio as STD or LCD. This must match the specification in the GRAPHICS.PRO file. Abbreviate as /PB:*size*.

Notes:

You can't print a graphics screen to a PostScript printer via DOS.

After GRAPHICS is loaded, press Shift+PrintScreen or PrintScreen (depending on keyboard) to print the screen. Number of shades of gray depends on both monitor and printer. If the monitor is 640x200 or better, the screen will be printed sideways.

To change profile files, the new one must be smaller than the existing one. If it is larger, reboot and load GRAPHICS again.

Table 18.1 GRAPHICS Printer Types

Type	Printers Included
COLOR1	IBM PC Color Printer with black ribbon
COLOR4	IBM PC Color Printer with RGB ribbon
COLOR8	IBM PC Color Printer with CMY ribbon (cyan, magenta, yellow)
HPDEFAULT	any Hewlett-Packard PCL printer (the default)
GRAPHICS	IBM Personal Graphics Printer, Proprinter, or Quietwriter; also most Epson dot-matrix printers

Type	Printers Included
GRAPHICSWIDE	any GRAPHICS printer with a wide carriage
LASERJET	Hewlett-Packard LaserJet printer
LASERJETII	Hewlett-Packard LaserJet II printer
PAINTJET	Hewlett-Packard PaintJet printer
QUIETJET	Hewlett-Packard QuietJet printer
QUIETJETPLUS	Hewlett-Packard QuietJet Plus printer
RUGGEDWRITER	Hewlett-Packard RuggedWriter printer
RUGGEDWRITERWIDE	Hewlett-Packard RuggedWriter Wide printer
THERMAL	IBM PC-convertible Thermal printer
THINKJET	Hewlett-Packard ThinkJet printer

To find out how the GRAPHICS command works on your printer, choose the printer option that seems closest to your printer. If it emulates one of the listed types, specify that type. Most dot-matrix printers emulate the Epson; the GRAPHICS option works on most of them. Use GRAPHICSWIDE if your printer has a wide carriage. Many laser printers emulate one of the Hewlett-Packard models. Don't try printing a graphics screen on a PostScript printer, however, unless it emulates a printer DOS can handle. It will just hang up and you'll have to turn off the printer and reboot your system.

If GRAPHICS.PRO isn't in the same directory as GRAPHICS.COM or the current directory, you'll have to tell DOS where it is in the *filespec* parameter.

GRAPHICS Switches

Normally, screens are printed with a white background; this is easy on a printer because the background is simply ignored. The average screen, however, is displayed on the monitor with a dark background. If you want the screen print prepared with a dark background, use the /R switch; the result will more closely match the displayed screen. (Most printers don't do a very good job of solid black areas, however.)

When you print to a color printer, GRAPHICS also uses white for the background by default. The /B switch tells it to use a color; this is valid only for COLOR4 and COLOR8 printers. If you examine the GRAPHICS.PRO file following these two headings, you'll see listings of how each displayed color is printed.

Aspect Ratio

The aspect ratio of a screen is different on an LCD monitor than on a standard one. Normally, you can trust GRAPHICS to choose the correct one, as they are specified in GRAPHICS.PRO for each printer as the PRINTBOX value. If you find that the ratio is not quite right on a printed graphics screen (if circles come out as ellipses, for example), check GRAPHICS.PRO to see if your monitor can handle both LCD and STD; the values follow the word PRINTBOX for each screen resolution. Either /LCD or /PB:LCD specifies the LCD aspect ratio. Use /PB:STD to specify a standard one.

You may have to reboot to replace the GRAPHICS profile. If the new profile takes less space in memory, it can be loaded over the existing one. If not, you'll see an error message, and you'll have to reboot and start over.

TIP	Once you decide on the correct GRAPHICS command for your system, load it through AUTOEXEC.BAT so it is always available. If you can't load it in upper memory and can't afford the conventional memory space on a regular basis, make a batch program or DOSKEY macro to load GRAPHICS as you need it.

CHAPTER 19

CONFIGURING DISKS AND NETWORKS

Introduction

In every computer's life, a little change must fall. If you change the type of hardware attached to a system, particularly the disk drives, you may have to tell DOS what you did so it can handle the new drives properly. The DRIVPARM command and the DRIVER.SYS device driver let you redefine your disk drives. You can even set up extra logical drive names for floppy disk drives to make certain processing more convenient. You'll learn when and how to use these configuration commands in this chapter.

Attaching a PC to a network requires both hardware and software changes. The network operating system handles most of the software needs, but there are a few DOS features you have to consider in running DOS under a network. They are covered in this chapter.

Configuring Physical Disks

A *block device* is a device that reads and writes more than one character at a time. It may be a floppy disk drive, a hard disk drive, or a tape drive. DOS senses block devices during booting and creates a table of parameters (number of heads, number of tracks, and so on) that tell it how to access the device. This procedure works most of the time, but DOS may be fooled by newer devices. Then you have to use DRIVPARM to define the device. If DOS has difficulty accessing a new block device, especially in formatting it, try DRIVPARM to correct the problem.

DRIVPARM

The DRIVPARM configuration command (see Figure 19.1) lets you change internal device parameter tables so that DOS accesses the drive correctly. Include the DRIVPARM command in your CONFIG.SYS file with the correct switches and DOS will always use valid drive parameters.

Figure 19.1.

DRIVPARM
Configuration
Command
Reference.

DRIVPARM

Specifies new parameters for an existing physical drive.

Format:

DRIVPARM /D:*drive* [*switches*]

Switches:

/D:*drive*   Specifies the physical drive number; 0=A, 1=B, 2=C etc.; this switch is required.

/F:*type*   Identifies the type of drive. Valid values are:

    0   360K or less
    1   1.2M
    2   720K (default)
    3   eight-inch single-density
    4   eight-inch double-density
    5   Hard disk
    6   Tape drive
    7   1.44M
    8   Read/write optical disk
    9   2.88M

/H:*heads*   Specifies the number of heads (or sides).

/S:*sectors* Specifies the number of sectors per track.

/T:*tracks*   Specifies the number of tracks.

/C   Indicates that the drive has change-line support.

/N   Indicates a nonremovable drive.

/I   Indicates an electronically compatible 3 1/2-inch drive.

Notes:

When you use /F for a diskette drive, the defaults shown in Table 19.1 apply. To specify any other parameters, use /H, /S, and /T.

Change-line support means the drive can detect when the door is open.

Notice that DRIVPARM can accommodate almost any type of block device. Each type of device has its own set of defaults for heads, sectors, and tracks. Table 19.1 shows the defaults for standard diskette types. If you are installing a different device type, specify the correct values from the device documentation if you aren't sure what the defaults are. If you specify wrong or inconsistent values, DOS will do erratic or bad formatting on the drive.

Table 19.1 Standard Floppy Diskette Parameters

Capacity	Heads	Sectors	Tracks
160K	1	8	40
180K	1	9	40
320K	2	8	40
360K	2	9	40
720K	2	9	80
1.2M	2	15	80
1.44M	2	18	80
2.88M	2	36	80

WARNING

If you specify your boot drive in the DRIVPARM command and give it the wrong parameters, you might not be able to start up your system. Or it might start up as usual, then destroy the root directory when it writes to the disk. Be sure you have a valid backup and a recovery disk handy before redefining the boot drive.

Suppose you plug in a 720K drive to replace an old 360K drive on B and DOS has difficulty recognizing the new drive. You would include this command in CONFIG.SYS:

```
DRIVPARM /D:1 /F:2 /C
```

This sets the parameters for drive 1 (the B drive) to match type 2 (720K) and says that the drive has change-line support.

Change-Line Support

A *change line* is a mechanism that lets DOS know that a drive door has been opened, signaling that a diskette may have been changed. Most 360K and below diskette drives do not have this feature. If DOS thinks there is change-line support, it saves time by referring to a cache of the directory instead of rereading the directory itself.

A malfunctioning change-line mechanism could threaten the integrity of data on your floppy disk. If DOS accesses one floppy disk using another floppy disk's directory, data could be read from or written to the wrong clusters. If you suspect this is happening, repair or replace the drive or use DRIVPARM to tell DOS that the drive does not have change-line support.

Configuring Logical Floppy Disks

The DRIVER.SYS device driver creates a logical floppy disk drive based on a physical one. It assigns a new drive letter, the next one in sequence. Two major uses of DRIVER.SYS are:

⊃ To force DOS to recognize and assign a logical drive name to an external diskette drive.

⊃ To assign an alternate logical drive name to a diskette drive.

NOTE

To create a new logical drive name for a hard disk, use the SUBST command.

Figure 19.2 shows the switches you can use with the DRIVER.SYS device driver. Notice that you can use DEVICE or DEVICEHIGH to load the driver. You can use more than one DRIVER.SYS command to define multiple logical drives. Each loaded driver takes about 240 bytes in memory.

Figure 19.2.

DRIVER.SYS DEVICE
Command.

DRIVER.SYS

Creates a new logical drive corresponding to a physical diskette drive.

Format:

DEVICE[HIGH]=[*path*]DRIVER.SYS /D:*drive* [*switches*]

Parameters and Switches:

path	Identifies the location of DRIVER.SYS if it is not in the root directory of the boot drive.
/D:*drive*	Specifies the number of the physical diskette drive; 0=first, 1=second, up to 127.
/F:*type*	Identifies the type of drive:

0	360K or less
1	1.2M
2	720K (default)
7	1.44M
9	2.88M

/H:*heads*	Specifies the number of heads (or sides).
/S:*sectors*	Specifies the number of sectors per track.
/T:*tracks*	Specifies the number of tracks.
/C	Indicates that the drive has change-line support.

Notes:

This command applies the next available drive letter to the newly created logical drive.

When you use /F, the defaults shown in Table 19.1 apply. To specify any other parameters, use /H, /S, and /T.

Change-line support means the drive can detect when the door is open.

Creating an Alternate Drive Name

Many computers these days have drives of two different types, such as 1.2M and 1.44M. If you want to copy files from one diskette to another of the same type, you can't do it directly, since DOS rejects a command such as:

```
XCOPY A:\*.* A:
```

You can use DRIVER.SYS to assign a second logical drive name to a physical drive so that you can do copies from one diskette to another in that drive using COPY or XCOPY commands. This command sets up a second drive letter for the second diskette drive (with a 360K capacity):

```
DEVICE=C:\DOS\DRIVER.SYS /D:1 /F:0
```

Be sure to notice what drive letter is set up. A message like this appears when the driver is loaded:

```
Loaded External Driver for Drive D
```

With the logical drive created in this example, you could use this command
to copy files:

```
XCOPY B:\*.* D:
```

You'll be prompted to insert one diskette at a time (starting with the target
diskette so DOS can check it out). The messages look something like this:

```
C:\>XCOPY B:*.* D:
Insert diskette for drive D: and press any key when ready
Insert diskette for drive B: and press any key when ready
Reading source file(s)...
Insert diskette for drive D: and press any key when ready


A:CHAP02.CHP


   ...


A:APPP.CHP


Insert diskette for drive B: and press any key when ready
        7 File(s) copied

Insert diskette for drive D: and press any key when ready

C:\>
```

TIP   When you are copying more than one file, use XCOPY rather than
COPY. You'll have to do a lot less disk swapping because XCOPY fills
memory with files before writing any, while COPY handles each file
separately.

Setting Up Two Alternate Drive Names

Suppose your computer has two diskette drives, 1.2M and 1.44M, and two
hard drives. You might include these commands in your CONFIG.SYS file:

```
DEVICE=C:\DOS\DRIVER.SYS /D:0 /F:1
DEVICE=C:\DOS\DRIVER.SYS /D:1 /F:7
```

When the system boots, you'll see these messages on the screen:

```
Loaded External Disk Driver for Drive E
Loaded External Disk Driver for Drive F
```

You can refer to drives E and F as needed during your DOS work; they have exactly the same characteristics as drives A and B. Most importantly, you can copy files from drive A to drive E (which is the same physical drive) and from drive B to drive F.

NOTE

DOS keeps track of which logical drive name was used last. If drive E is in effect and you enter this command:

```
DIR A:
```

you will see this message:

```
Insert diskette for drive A: and press any key when ready
```

Adding an External Floppy Disk Drive

If you add a drive that DOS doesn't recognize automatically, either DRIVPARM or DRIVER.SYS can be used to tell DOS that you have added the drive to your PC. For example, this command specifies a 1.2M external drive as the third diskette drive:

```
DEVICE=C:\DOS\DRIVER.SYS /D:2 /F:1 /C
```

If you want to be able to copy files in that drive, you'll need a second, identical DEVICE command to set up a second logical drive. It will have the next drive letter.

DRIVER.SYS or DRIVPARM

If you use DRIVER.SYS to change the parameters of a physical drive, a new logical drive name is assigned to the drive. It is better to redefine drive characteristics with DRIVPARM, which lets you continue to use the drive's original name. Also, DRIVPARM takes up less space in conventional memory.

Adding an Unsupported Drive

If you add a diskette drive that is not supported by the BIOS, a driver supplied with it may not work. For example, suppose you get a 2.88M drive at a swap meet for your drive A and your BIOS doesn't support it (most older ones don't). As a first step, add this DRIVPARM command to CONFIG.SYS:

```
DRIVPARM /D:0 /F:9 /C
```

If you still have access problems, try using DRIVER.SYS to define it; then two logical drive names will refer to the same diskette drive. Use a configuration command like this:

```
DEVICE=C:\DOS\DRIVER.SYS /D:0 /F:9 /C
```

It's possible that you may need both commands.

Running DOS on a Network

A network is a set of two or more computers linked to each other via some hardware and software; the details differ from network to network. The hardware includes network adapter cards in each computer, cables, and a network drive. The software includes the network operating system and a file server, which manages file access. It may also include other servers to handle printers and communications.

Each computer in a network is often called a workstation or node. The workstations can range from a simple keyboard and monitor to a full-fledged 486 computer; some PC networks can handle Macintosh computers as well. In any network, each node can access at least one network disk (network drive) and peripheral devices on the other nodes. They can transfer files among nodes, access a central database, send messages to each other, and share the same printer.

Special network commands set up the system when it is turned on. Some DOS commands, such as ASSIGN, JOIN, and SUBST, may be used to set up the required access paths for the network. While these commands are valid, they should not be used on a network for any purpose other than what is required to establish the network, as they can cause trouble within DOS, as explained in Chapter 8.

Each workstation can still operate independently of the network, using most DOS commands. Neither the processing nor the commands differ while the programs and data are contained within the operative computer. However, time does become a factor when transferring data across connections, particularly if several users are doing it at once.

One or more drives may be set up as network drives rather than drives belonging to a particular computer.

DOS Command Limitations

Most DOS commands work the same under a network as on an independent computer. However, some DOS commands cannot be used over a network connection. Other commands can't be used to refer to network drives. Table 19.2 lists these commands.

Table 19.2 DOS Command Network Restrictions

Do not use on network drives:
CHKDSK
DISKCOMP
RECOVER
SYS

Do not use across network connections:
FASTOPEN
FORMAT
LABEL
UNFORMAT

A command that can't be used on a network drive can be used to refer to personal drives on a networked computer, as long as those drives are not specified as network drives. Any DOS command that cannot be used across network connections can be used to refer only to drives on an individual computer.

Logical Drives

The network operating system establishes logical names by which people can access data on network drives and drives on other computers. Each node includes the LASTDRIVE command in its CONFIG.SYS file to allow for enough drive names. (See Chapter 8 for LASTDRIVE details.)

Another DOS command that is very useful when you work on a network is TRUENAME (see Chapter 8 for details). TRUENAME sees actual filespecs across a network, so it can give the complete, actual drive and path of a given file.

Sharing and Locking Files

When working on a network, it is possible that two people might try to access the same file at the same time. They might even try to make simultaneous changes to the file. Large databases accessed by everyone are frequently stored on network drives. Most network file servers prevent this problem. But you might need the SHARE command to allow only one person at a time to access a file. Figure 19.3 shows the command format.

The SHARE command specifies the amount of space reserved for storing file specifications and a maximum number of files that can be locked at a time. If your network requires SHARE, it was probably placed in your AUTOEXEC.BAT file when the network was installed.

Special Considerations

Some LANs have special features or problems that affect DOS usage. For example, PC LAN has a command named APPEND. If you happen to use the DOS APPEND command, you may get unexpected results. If your computer is connected to a PC LAN network, the DOS APPEND program may have been renamed or removed.

Figure 19.3.

SHARE Command
Reference.

SHARE

Installs file locking and sharing functions on a hard disk; usually used in a network or multitasking environment. Once SHARE is installed, it validates all read and write requests.

Format:

From the command prompt:

SHARE [*switches*]

From CONFIG.SYS:

INSTALL=[*path*]SHARE.EXE [*switches*]

Parameters and Switches:

path   Identifies the location of the SHARE.EXE file if it is not in the root directory of the boot drive.

/F:*space*   Specifies the space (in bytes) for recording file sharing information; default is 2048.

/L:*locks*   Specifies the number of files that can be locked at once; default is 20.

Notes:

Each open shared file requires space for the full file specification; the average length is 20 bytes.

SHARE can be loaded high from the command prompt.

20

UPGRADING
TO QBASIC

ntroduction

QBASIC is a more advanced language than many earlier forms of
BASIC, including GW-BASIC and BASICA, which were supplied with
earlier versions of DOS. With QBASIC you can create structured programs that not only execute more efficiently but also are easier to
code and debug. QBASIC is an interpretive version of Microsoft
QuickBASIC; unlike the full QuickBASIC, it has no compiler. Any
programs you create under QBASIC can be compiled and run under
QuickBASIC. QuickBASIC source code will run under QBASIC.

There are many differences between the earlier supplied forms of
BASIC and QBASIC. The major differences concern the user interface, data types, line numbers, and new statements that let you create
control structures. This chapter is not designed to teach QBASIC programming. Instead, it is intended for BASIC programmers and discusses only the major differences between QBASIC and unstructured
versions of BASIC.

QBASIC's Interface

The QBASIC programming environment is provided by the same full-screen ASCII text editor that is accessed by DOS 5's EDIT command. But EDIT starts up the editor in its document mode, whereas QBASIC normally opens the editor in its programming mode (see Figure 20.1), which is quite a bit different. You can start up QBASIC in document mode by adding the /EDITOR switch to the QBASIC command.

Figure 20.1.

QBASIC Editor
Screen.

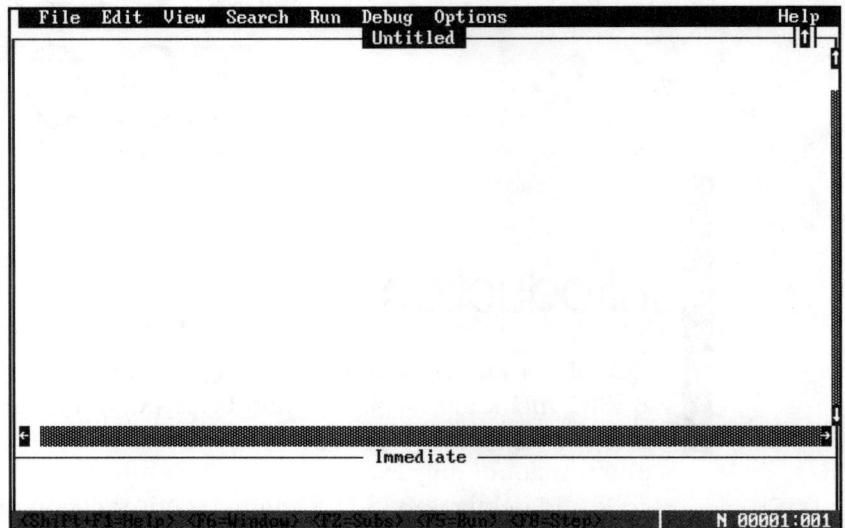

The QBASIC Editor

The QBASIC menus assist you in creating, testing, and debugging QBASIC programs. The **File** menu lets you open and save files as well as exit QBASIC. The **Edit** menu includes commands to cut and copy text and create subprograms and functions. The **View** menu lets you view and edit any procedure of the current program, split the screen so you can see two parts of the same program, and switch immediately to the output screen. **Search** menu commands will find and replace text strings. **Run** menu commands execute all or part of a program. The **Debug** menu offers several tools, such as tracing and stepping through a program. The **Options** menu includes commands to modify the display and set the status of Syntax Checking.

The screen includes two windows. The larger window is the standard program-editing area. Its title bar shows Untitled unless the currently loaded program has a name. The smaller window, called the Immediate window, holds one line at a time, which is executed as soon as you press Enter. You can use the Immediate window to test parts of your program as you work.

The status line shows the position of the cursor as well as some of the function keys that you can use. Once the window contains statements, pressing F1 gets context-sensitive help on the QBASIC word containing the cursor. Table 20.1 includes a complete list of the hotkeys when the editor window is active. Different hotkeys are available when you aren't in edit mode.

Table 20.1 Hotkeys in QBASIC Editor

Key	Unshifted Key	Shift+Key	Ctrl+Key
F1	Help	Using Help	
F2	View SUBs	Next Procedure	Previous Procedure
F3	Repeat Find		
F4	Output Screen		
F5	Continue	Run Start	
F6	Next Window	Previous Window	
F7	Execute to cursor		
F8	Step		
F9	Breakpoint		
F10	Procedure Step		Zoom
Del	Clear	Cut	
Ins	Overtype/Insert	Paste	Copy

Smart Editor Effects

The editor begins to work on your program lines as soon as you type them. Once you press Enter or move the cursor to another line, any QBASIC words are converted to uppercase and spaces are inserted around equal signs and operators. If **Options Syntax Checking** is turned on, you'll be informed immediately of any syntax errors. You can press F1 to view the correct format of the current statement. The editor automatically keeps the capitalization pattern of names consistent by converting all to the layout of the latest typed one. If a reference is made to a different procedure, the editor inserts the required DECLARE statement at the beginning of the program. If the main program includes a DEF*type* statement, the editor includes it automatically at the beginning of other procedures.

You can copy or cut lines by selecting them and using the **Edit** menu or the hotkeys. Copied or cut lines are stored in the clipboard until another copy or cut replaces them; you can paste the clipboard contents as often as you need. You can even copy or move lines to another program or procedure, since the clipboard is unaffected by anything except another cut or copy or exiting QBASIC.

Converting a GW-BASIC or BASICA Program

QBASIC stores programs in ASCII format, so if your existing programs are stored in GW-BASIC's or BASICA's default binary format, you'll have to convert them. Start up the other BASIC editor, call up the program, and save it in ASCII format with the BAS extension. Here's how to save a GW-BASIC file as OLDPAY.BAS in ASCII form:

1. Start up GW-BASIC.

2. Load the file.

3. Enter this command:

```
SAVE "OLDPAY.BAS",A
```

4. Type SYSTEM to exit GW-BASIC.

Now you can start up QBASIC, use the **File Open** command to open the program, and run it from within the QBASIC editor.

Running Programs

The easiest way to run a loaded program under QBASIC is to press F5. Alternatively, you can choose **Run Start**. A program converted from a different form of BASIC should run with no problems unless it uses any of the few features not supported by QBASIC (see Table 20.2). If your program uses any of these features, you'll have to modify it to run under QBASIC.

Table 20.2 QBASIC Incompatibilities

Statements not supported:

DEF USR

EXTERR(n)

LIST

LLIST

MERGE

MOTOR

USR

Major features not supported:

CALL (*offvar,var1...*)

CHAIN (ALL, MERGE, DELETE, *linenumber*)

CLEAR (,n)

DRAW (*var=;*)

PLAY (*var=;*)

VARPTR (#*filename*)

Other possible problems:

QBASIC has additional reserved words

PEEK and POKE in Data Segment may have different effects

A message prompts you to press F1 for help if a syntax error occurs.

Line Numbers

In QBASIC, line numbers are not required, but they are permitted. If you use GOTO to transfer control, you can reference a line number if you like; just number the target line as in other BASICs. If you prefer, you can use a label, which is a QBASIC word followed by a colon. For example, the statement GOTO ERRORLINE transfers control to a line beginning with ERRORLINE: and continues from there. Any string of up to 40 letters and digits that is not a QBASIC reserved word and is not used for another purpose in the program can be used as a label. The trailing colon tells QBASIC that the string is a label.

Removing Line Numbers

A program named REMLINE.BAS is supplied with QBASIC. This program removes unused line numbers from BASIC programs stored in ASCII format. It prompts you for input and output filenames, then strips out any line numbers that aren't actually referenced.

The REMLINE program is set up to handle programs of up to 400 lines. You can modify the program to increase this number; when you view the program, the comments at the beginning tell you how to modify it.

If the first thing on a line is a number, it is treated as a line number. If your program has lines that wrap around, you may find that numbers at the beginning of wrapped lines disappear. You might scan your program first to see if this looks like a problem. Or you could have REMLINE create a new file (keeping the BAS extension), so you'll be able to go back to the original, if necessary. If you don't supply a new name to REMLINE, the original program is saved with extension BAK.

New Constant and Variable Types

You have more choices for constants and variables in QBASIC than in GW-BASIC or BASICA. The names can have up to 40 characters, in any combination of uppercase and lowercase letters, digits, and the period. If the same string of characters is used, however, QBASIC assumes it is the same name even if the capitalization is different. The editor helps you be consistent by converting all strings of the same characters to the same capitalization format. If you use FIRSTNAME$, then later type Firstname$, all other occurrences of FIRSTNAME$ are converted to the last typed configuration.

As in the earlier forms of BASIC, you can use the DEF*type* statement to specify names as string (DEFSTR), integer (DEFINT), single-precision (DEFSNG), or double-precision (DEFDBL) numbers. Any DEF*type* statements you use in the main program are automatically copied to any procedures you create later. If you add a DEF*type* statement to the main program after creating procedures, the procedures aren't updated, however. Data type suffixes on names override the DEF*type* statements.

Constants

You can create named constants with a CONST statement, which looks much like an assignment statement:

```
CONST ConstantName=value
```

The *ConstantName* and the *value* must be of the same type. You can use CONST Logo$ = "IBM" or CONST TotalLines% = 400, for example. The value can't include a variable name or function, but it can include expressions and other constant names if necessary.

QBASIC won't let you change the value assigned to a constant. If you define CONST Rate=.0935, you can't specify Rate=Rate+.01 later in the program. Of course, you can use literal constants of any type just as in other forms of the BASIC language.

Numeric Variables

In addition to the standard numeric variable types, QBASIC provides the long integer, which can handle values between –2,147,483,648 and 2,147,483,647. (Standard integers must be between –32,768 and 32,767.) The long integer is stored in four bytes of memory, while the standard integer takes only two bytes. Even though the long integer takes as much space as a single-precision value, it is stored in two's complement form and allows for more efficient execution of the program.

You can use the DEFLNG statement to reserve initial letters for a long integer or use the type character & at the end of the name. Once declared by its appearance in a statement, a long integer is used just like other integers.

String Variables

String variables can be declared and used much as in earlier forms of BASIC. In QBASIC, you can also define fixed-length string variables using a form of the DIM statement. Here's the format:

```
DIM StringName AS STRING * n
```

The following statement defines a 30-character variable named Fullname:

```
DIM Fullname AS STRING * 30
```

It overrides any DEFSTR statement; in addition, you can't use the $ type character on the name. Fixed-length strings are useful in many file and database applications. If you want an array of fixed-length strings, include the array dimension following the *StringName*. The following statement defines an array of 50 string variables, each 30 characters long:

```
DIM Fullname(50) AS STRING * 30
```

When data is placed in a fixed-length string variable, it is left-justified and padded with blanks on the right. If a value is too long for the variable, it is truncated on the right with no warning.

Additional String Functions

QBASIC supports the standard string functions, as well as several new ones. The UCASE$ and LCASE$ functions change the string's letters to all uppercase or all lowercase. The following statement converts the value in Fullname (a string variable) to all uppercase and assigns it to the variable Fixname$ (a variable-length string).

```
Fixname$=UCASE$(Fullname)
```

In this case, the resulting value in Fixname$ is as long as the fixed-length string variable.

The LTRIM$ and RTRIM$ functions let you remove leading or trailing spaces and/or tabs from a string. The following statement removes any number of trailing spaces from the string Fullname and assigns the result to Fixname$:

```
Fixname$=RTRIM$(Fullname)
```

The resulting value in Fixname$ has no trailing spaces, so it may be shorter than the fixed-length string that provided the value.

Array Variables

Arrays can be defined and used just as they are in unstructured BASICs. Alternatively, you can specify the subscript range in a TO clause. The following statement sets up a 12-element array with the specified subscripts:

```
DIM MONTH(1 TO 12)
```

The following statement sets up a 61-element array with subscripts ranging from 1940 to 2000:

```
DIM YEAR(1940 TO 2000)
```

You can define arrays that contain several different data types in one element by using the user-defined or record data type, described below.

Record Data Type

QBASIC supports a user-defined data type called a *record data type*, which is defined with the TYPE block and creates a record. It can contain any combination of existing data types, so that the result can contain several values. The record data type is especially useful in defining an array that contains several data types in each element or in defining a record of mixed data for use in files. Here's the format:

```
TYPE usertype
     element1 AS typename1
     element2 AS typename2
     ...
END TYPE
```

The *usertype* is a standard QBASIC name that is not used for any other purpose in the procedure. Each *element* is a data item within the record; each can be accessed individually by the program. The *typename* specifies the type (and hence the length) of the individual element; it can be INTEGER, LONG, SINGLE, DOUBLE, STRING * *n*, or another already-defined *usertype*. For example, the following block defines user data type GPA to contain three different elements:

```
TYPE GPA
     StudentNumber AS STRING * 6
     StudentHours AS INTEGER
     StudentPoints AS SINGLE
END TYPE
```

The *usertype* defines a data type, not a variable name, so it can't be used directly in statements. It can be used only as a *typename* in its own definition or as an element in another TYPE block. To use data in the defined format, declare a variable as that data type. For example, after defining the data type above, you could use the following statement to define Student as a 12-byte variable; six bytes for the string, two bytes for the integer, and four bytes for the single-precision value:

```
DIM Student AS GPA
```

To reference a part of the record, join the variable name with the element name, connecting them with a period as in this example:

```
Student.StudentHours = Student.StudentHours + NewHours
```

Records in Arrays

A variable of a user-defined data type can be used in an array. The following statement sets up an array of 180 elements, each 12 bytes long.

```
DIM Student (180) AS GPA
```

Student(25).StudentNumber refers to the six-character string in the twenty-fifth occurrence of the array.

The following example defines *datatype* Employee and uses it for the array variable Worker:

```
TYPE Employee
     EmpNumber AS STRING * 9
     EmpSalary AS SINGLE
     EmpDependents AS INTEGER
END TYPE
DIM Worker(240) AS Employee
```

The program refers to elements of the record by connecting them to the variable name with a period. For example, Worker(Next%).EmpSalary refers to the EmpSalary element of the array component indicated by the value of Next%.

Records in Files

Record data types can be used instead of FIELD variables in QBASIC programs. This allows you to create and modify file data much more easily, without all the restrictions on FIELD variables. For compatibility, QBASIC supports the FIELD statement, of course.

New Flow of Control Facilities

In earlier forms of BASIC, a program had an essentially linear form with branching. The single-line IF statement handled decision making, and GOTO statements and line numbers let you create a morass of decision-based loops. The WHILE...WEND statement allowed some looping control. QBASIC provides more techniques and statements to handle flow of control in your program in a structured, efficient manner.

Expanded IF Statement

QBASIC can handle all the earlier formats of IF, including the one-line IF...THEN and IF...THEN...ELSE statements. It's hard to read these IF statements, much less debug them. So QBASIC includes an expanded, multiline IF block that conforms to structured programming principles. Here's the format:

```
IF condition THEN
    statements to be executed if condition is true
[ELSE
    statements to be executed if condition is false]
END IF
```

The line beginning with IF starts the block; it must include the conditional expression and the word THEN. When the condition is true, statements on all lines down to ELSE are executed; if there is no ELSE statement, statements on all lines down to END IF are executed. When the conditional expression is false, statements on all lines between ELSE and END IF are executed; if there is no ELSE statement, control passes to the statement following END IF. The following example executes several commands if the condition is true:

```
IF TotalBill! >= CreditLimit! THEN
    PRINT OverLimitMessage$
    OverFlag$ = "Y"
    CALL warningflash
END IF
```

The following example executes only one set of statements, depending on the condition's value:

```
IF ApplicantAge% < 21 THEN
    PRINT MinorMessage$
    AgeProblem$ = "Y"
ELSE
    PRINT NoProblemMessage$
    AgeProblem$ = "N"
END IF
```

Another QBASIC option makes it easier to code complex nested IFs. You can include the ELSEIF element, as shown here:

```
IF condition THEN
    statements to be executed if condition is true
[ELSEIF condition-n THEN
    statements to be executed if condition-n is true]...
[ELSE
    statements to be executed if all conditions are false]
END IF
```

The following example uses ELSEIF to include a second condition and allow execution of one of three possible sets of statements:

```
IF ApplicantAge! < 21 THEN
    PRINT MinorMessage$
    AgeProblem$ = "Y"
ELSEIF ApplicantAge% > 65
    PRINT SeniorMessage$
    AgeProblem$ = "Y"
ELSE
    PRINT NoProblemMessage$
    AgeProblem$ = "N"
END IF
```

You can use as many ELSEIF elements as needed to fully create the desired branches.

TIP   You can optimize processing time by arranging the IF and ELSE conditions from the most-likely to least-likely to occur.

Using a Case Structure

You may be familiar with using ON...GOTO or ON...GOSUB to handle multiple branching situations. While such situations can often be handled with a nested IF or ELSEIF, QBASIC provides a special statement block that is designed for just such situations. The SELECT CASE statement lets you name a variable, then execute specific blocks of statements based on its value; the entire block sets up a case structure. Here's the simplest format:

```
SELECT CASE variable
    [CASE valuelist
        statements to execute if variable =
    any value in valuelist]...
    CASE ELSE
        statements to execute if variable <> any
    value in valuelist
END SELECT
```

When the SELECT CASE block is executed, the CASE variable has a single value. One CASE block or CASE ELSE block is processed, then control jumps to the END SELECT statement and continues from there. You can include as many values as you like (separated by commas) in each *valuelist*, and as many CASE blocks as you need. The CASE ELSE block specifies statements to be executed if the value of the CASE variable is not equal to any of the specified values in any of the CASE statements.

For example, suppose you have a menu or multiple-choice question to display. The input value is a single character, supposed to be A through D. A different subprogram is executed for each situation. Here's how you could handle it in a CASE block:

```
SELECT CASE MenuChoice$
    CASE "A", "a"
        CALL DoSubA
    CASE "B", "b"
        CALL DoSubB
    CASE "C", "c"
        CALL DoSubC
    CASE "D", "d"
        CALL DoSubD
    CASE ELSE
        CALL DoBadChoice
END SELECT
```

This example lets you enter either uppercase or lowercase letters. If a character that is not in the desired range is typed, subprogram DoBadChoice asks you to try again. If you prefer, you can include a set of statements, as many as needed, following each CASE statement.

Actually, SELECT CASE doesn't limit you to a single variable and valuelist for each case. Here's the complete format:

```
SELECT CASE variable
    [CASE expressionlist
        statements to execute if any expression is
            true]...
    CASE ELSE
        statements to execute if no expressions are true
END SELECT
```

The *expressionlist* lets you use more than a single value or list of values to determine which block is executed. To include a condition, assume the variable name and type the word IS followed by the rest of the relational operation. You might use CASE IS > 65 or CASE IS <= 20, for example. To specify a range, use the TO keyword, as in CASE 1 TO 5 or CASE "X" TO "Z". You can even combine expressions, as in CASE 0, 18 TO 20, IS > 65. Just make sure each individual value or expression is valid, and separate them with commas.

Loop Structures

In earlier forms of BASIC, loops are created with FOR...NEXT, with GOTO statements, and with WHILE...WEND statements. While these forms are still available for consistency, QBASIC's DO statement blocks allow easier structuring and clearer code than WHILE...WEND. A DO block begins with a DO statement and ends with a LOOP statement. All statements in between are executed during the loop. The block includes either a WHILE or an UNTIL element, added to either the DO or the LOOP statement. A DO WHILE...LOOP block is equivalent to a WHILE...WEND block.

The WHILE or UNTIL element includes a conditional expression. The expression is tested at the beginning of the loop if it is included on the DO statement, at the end if it is included on the LOOP statement. The loop is executed repeatedly as long as the condition is true when WHILE is used

or until the condition becomes true when UNTIL is used. Here's the DO
format to use if you want the condition to be tested before the block is executed the first time:

```
DO [WHILE¦UNTIL] condition
    statements to be executed
LOOP
```

Here's the format to use if you want the block to be executed at least once,
regardless of the truth of the condition:

```
DO
    statements to be executed
LOOP [WHILE¦UNTIL] condition
```

Contents of Loop

Any statements can be used within a DO...LOOP block. You can use IFs,
FOR...NEXT, WHILE...WEND, nested DOs, even subprogram references.
Nested DO loops can be of any type; inner loops don't have to match the
outer loop's structure. The only rule is that an inner loop of any kind (even
FOR...NEXT) must end before its outer loop does.

In the following example, the condition is tested before the loop begins:

```
X! = 0
INPUT "Enter a value to be exponentiated: ",Xin!
PRINT "Powers of ",Xin!
DO UNTIL X! = 10
    X! = X! + 1
    PRINT X!; Xin! * X!
LOOP
```

The value of X! is set before the loop begins and tested in the UNTIL condition on the DO statement. The loop then processes the entered value 10
times. Then control falls through to the end of the loop.

In the next example, the decision on repeating the loop occurs within the
loop, so the condition belongs on the LOOP statement.

```
Xend$ = "N"
DO
      INPUT "Enter a value to square: ", Xin!
      PRINT Xin!, " Squared is ", Xin! * Xin!
      INPUT "Press Y to do another: ", Xend$
LOOP UNTIL Xend$ = "Y" or Xend$ = "y"
```

If you must terminate a loop before the condition causes it to end, use an EXIT DO statement. When EXIT DO is executed, control passes immediately to the statement following the LOOP statement that marks the end of the current DO block.

Modular Programming

Earlier versions of BASIC are essentially linear; statements are executed in sequence unless a branch directs execution to another location in the program.

QBASIC lets you work with modules. Execution of a program always starts and ends in the main module. The program can include as many procedure modules as you need, either subprograms or functions. Each procedure is a separate, named entity, called by the main module.

When a subprogram is created, you give it a name. Using that name as a statement or including it in a CALL statement starts its execution. After the statements in the subprogram are executed, control returns to the statement following the one that called it, much like a GOSUB procedure.

A user-defined function is also given a name. You then use it just like you use the built-in functions. Defining a QBASIC function has much the same effect as the DEF FN statement, but it allows more than one program line.

NOTE

For compatibility with other versions, GOSUB and DEF FN both work in QBASIC. You can reference a label in a GOSUB statement instead of a line number.

A subprogram or function is a separate procedure, so variables in the main module (or any other procedure) have no effect in other procedures unless you make them global (COMMON SHARED). You can pass specific values to either a subprogram or a function in an argument list. (Global variables and passing values are covered later in this chapter.)

Examining a Structured Program

The REMLINE.BAS program supplied with QBASIC is a modular program. It has a main module, along with several functions and subprograms. When you open the program file, you can examine the main module in the editing window. If you press F2 or choose **View SUBs**, you can select another procedure to view and edit in the window. You can use Shift+F2 to see the next procedure directly or Ctrl+F2 to see the previous one without going through the SUBs dialog box again.

Creating a New Procedure

To create a new subprogram or function, choose **Edit New SUB** or **Edit New Function**. If the cursor rests on text, you'll see the current word in the dialog box like the one in Figure 20.2. You can accept that as the procedure name or type in a name and choose OK. The resulting window is an editing window for the procedure. QBASIC puts in the first line (SUB or FUNCTION) with the name you provided followed by an empty set of parentheses and the last line (END SUB or END FUNCTION). You can add whatever you need between these two lines. If you used any DEF*type* statements in the main program, they are copied to the beginning of each procedure when you start creating it.

TIP	Type `SUB ProcedureName` in a program and press Enter. You'll get to the editing window for the new procedure immediately.

Figure 20.2.

New Procedure
Specification
Dialog Box.

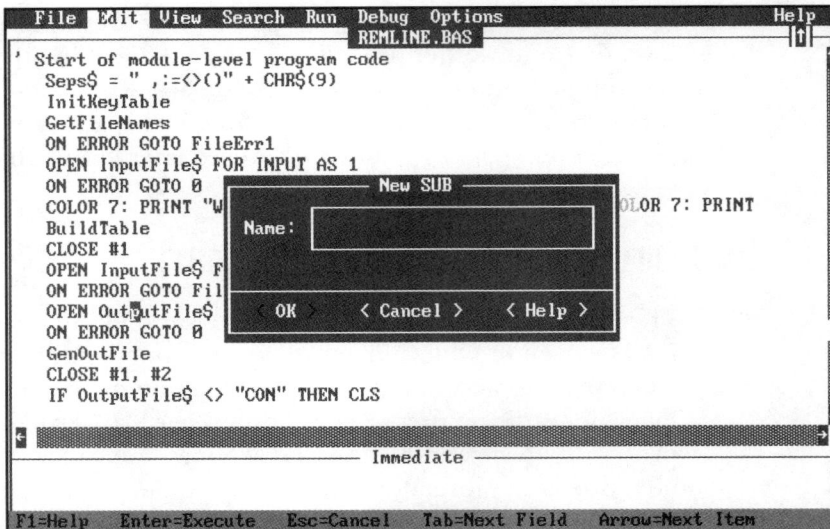

```
 File  Edit  View  Search  Run  Debug  Options                    Help
                          REMLINE.BAS
' Start of module-level program code
  Seps$ = " ,:=<>()" + CHR$(9)
   InitKeyTable
   GetFileNames
   ON ERROR GOTO FileErr1
   OPEN InputFile$ FOR INPUT AS 1
   ON ERROR GOTO 0                ┌──── New SUB ────┐
   COLOR 7: PRINT "W              │                 │   OLOR 7: PRINT
   BuildTable                     │ Name:           │
   CLOSE #1                       │      ┌──────────┐│
   OPEN InputFile$ F              │      └──────────┘│
   ON ERROR GOTO Fil              │                  │
   OPEN OutputFile$               │ < OK >  < Cancel >  < Help > │
   ON ERROR GOTO 0                └──────────────────┘
   GenOutFile
   CLOSE #1, #2
   IF OutputFile$ <> "CON" THEN CLS


──────────────────────────── Immediate ──────────────────────────

 F1=Help   Enter=Execute   Esc=Cancel   Tab=Next Field   Arrow=Next Item
```

Once a procedure has a name and has been saved, you can view or edit it
by choosing **View SUBs** or by pressing F2. The resulting dialog box, like the
one shown in Figure 20.3, lets you choose from all the procedures for the
current program. You can even delete them if necessary. When the program is saved, a DECLARE statement for each new procedure is generated
and added to the beginning of the main module.

Figure 20.3.

View SUBs
Dialog Box.

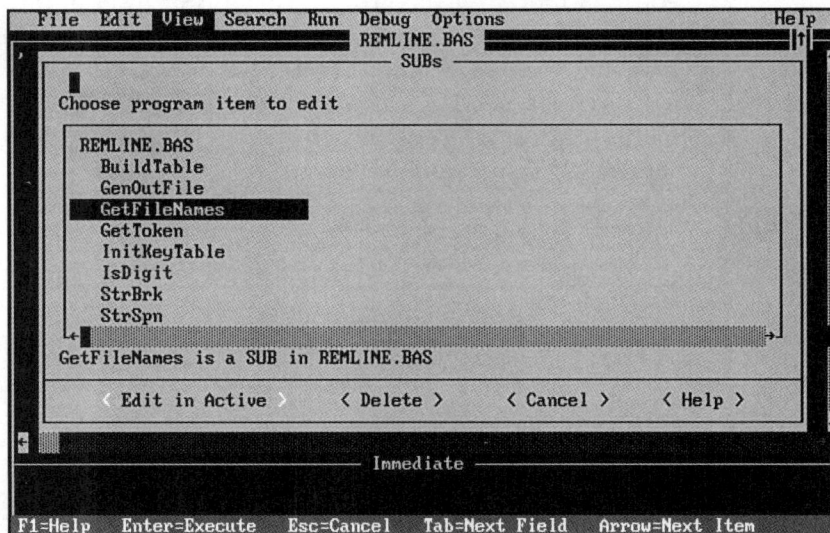

```
 File  Edit  View  Search  Run  Debug  Options                    Help
                          REMLINE.BAS
'                              ──── SUBs ────

  Choose program item to edit

   ┌──────────────────────────────────────────────────────────┐
   │  REMLINE.BAS                                               │
   │     BuildTable                                             │
   │     GenOutFile                                             │
   │     GetFileNames                                           │
   │     GetToken                                               │
   │     InitKeyTable                                           │
   │     IsDigit                                                │
   │     StrBrk                                                 │
   │     StrSpn                                                 │
   └──────────────────────────────────────────────────────────┘
  GetFileNames is a SUB in REMLINE.BAS

   < Edit in Active >    < Delete >    < Cancel >    < Help >

──────────────────────────── Immediate ──────────────────────────

 F1=Help   Enter=Execute   Esc=Cancel   Tab=Next Field   Arrow=Next Item
```

Global Variables

By default, all variables used in a procedure are local variables; they apply only to the procedure in which they appear. A variable named TaxRate in the main program has no effect on a variable named TaxRate in a subprogram or function unless you make special arrangements. You can tell QBASIC up front to make certain variables available to all procedures; these are called *global variables*.

Global variables must be declared in the main program in a COMMON SHARED statement, with this format:

```
COMMON SHARED VariableList
```

You can include as many variables as needed, separating them with commas. Multiple COMMON SHARED statements may be used.

TIP	Use one COMMON SHARED statement for all variables used together for easier program maintenance.

Suppose your main program includes this statement:

```
COMMON SHARED PrimeRate!, CreditLimit!
```

If the value of PrimeRate! is set in one procedure, it is the same in every procedure used by the program. If the variable were local, the value would apply only in the procedure in which it was set.

Subprograms

A subprogram is a block of code between SUB and END SUB statements. When you choose **Edit New SUB**, these lines are included automatically. If you type a SUB statement as part of the main module, the smart editor assumes you want to create a new subprogram and puts you in a new editor window to create it; the effect is the same as choosing **Edit New SUB**. Once defined, subprograms can be called by the main module or by other subprograms. When execution reaches the END SUB statement, it returns to the statement following the one that started the subprogram.

Here's the general format for a subprogram:

```
SUB subprogramname [(parameters)]
        [local variable or constant declarations]
        statements to be executed
END SUB
```

Subprograms can be used to handle many complex operations. You might use a subprogram to print headers on each page of a printed report. Another subprogram might print footers.

Here's an example of a subprogram that plays "Happy Birthday":

```
SUB birthday
' Play a tune
PLAY "L4 C8C8DCFE2 C8C8DCGF2"
PLAY "C8C8>C<AFED2 B-8B-8AFGF2"
END SUB
```

A subprogram is invoked by naming it in a CALL statement or by using its name as a statement in the main program or another procedure. If the subprogram has no parameters, you can use CALL or omit it. The subprogram above could be run by either of these statements:

```
CALL birthday
birthday
```

Each time a subprogram is invoked, any local variables in it are reset to their default values. Any global variables maintain their current values. If you want the subprogram to hold its local values between executions, add the word STATIC to the first line.

The following statement causes local variables in taxwithholding to keep their values when the subprogram ends and use them again the next time it is executed:

```
SUB taxwithholding STATIC
```

The main program finds out about subprograms through DECLARE statements, which must precede any executable statements in the program. When you create a subprogram, QBASIC generates an initial DECLARE statement for the program using information currently available in the SUB statement. Here's the format:

```
DECLARE SUB subprogramname (parameters)
```

If there are no parameters, an empty set of parentheses is used. If you change the content of the parameter list later, be sure to change it in the DECLARE statement as well.

Passing Values

Sometimes a subprogram has to use specific values passed from the calling program. If you use the CALL statement, the values to be passed must be enclosed in a single set of parentheses. If you omit the word CALL, you also omit the parentheses around the value list.

You can pass constants in the form of named constants, quoted strings, numeric values, or expressions. You can also pass local variables or expressions by including them as arguments. Every passed local variable can be changed in the subprogram, and the changed value will be available back in the calling procedure. If you want to prevent a passed variable from being changed, create an expression by enclosing it in an *individual set of parentheses* in the calling statement.

In the following example, changes to Taxrate won't affect the calling program when control returns:

```
CALL taxwithholding (Gross, Dependents, (Taxrate))
```

Any changes to variables used only in passed expressions won't be carried back to the calling procedure.

The arguments are received by the subprogram into a parameter list; every parameter is represented by a variable name. Arguments are passed to parameters by position, not by name. That is, the first argument is passed to the first parameter, the second argument to the second parameter, and so on. Because of the positional relationship, any that are skipped must be represented by a comma. The matched items must be of the same data type. That is, a string argument must be paired with a string parameter, an integer argument must be paired with an integer parameter, and so forth. Here are some examples of valid sets:

Calling statement:

```
MakeMailingLabel Name$, Address1$, City$, State$, Zip$
```

Subprogram:

```
SUB MakeMailingLabel (Line1$, Line2$, City$, State$, Zip$)
```

Calling statement:

```
CALL FigureTax (Total#, TaxRate!, TypeTax$)
```

Subprogram:

```
SUB FigureTax (BaseAmount#, CurrentRate!, TaxType$)
```

FigureTax can refer to BaseAmount#, CurrentRate!, and TaxType$ but not
to Total#, TaxRate!, or TypeTax$. When control returns to the main mod-
ule, however, Total#, TaxRate!, and TypeTax$ contain the values the corre-
sponding variables held when control exits the FigureTax subprogram.

Functions

Functions calculate and return a single value, much like the DEF FN statement of GW-BASIC and BASICA. The difference is that a function name
need not begin with FN and the FUNCTION procedure can use as many
statements as it needs.

Like the subprogram, each function must be defined by a DECLARE statement. When you begin a new function through QBASIC, the appropriate
DECLARE statement is generated and positioned in the main program
automatically. You have to keep the parameter list up-to-date yourself if you
change it later.

Creating a New Function

To create a new function, choose **Edit New FUNCTION** or type a FUNC-
TION statement and press Enter. Once QBASIC has a name for the function, you'll be placed in an editor window for defining the function.

The format of a function is:

```
FUNCTION functionname [(parameters)]
    [local variable or constant declarations]
    statements to be executed
    functionname = expression
END FUNCTION
```

Here's an example of a function that calculates a random integer between
1 and the value of the integer argument:

```
FUNCTION RANDINT%(N%)
     RANDOMIZE TIMER
     RANDINT% = INT(RND*N%)+1
END FUNCTION
```

This function could be invoked by a statement such as this:

```
CurrentValue = RANDINT%(GUESS%)
```

Debugging Innovations

QBASIC offers several features that help in debugging files. When a program terminates with an error, you see the critical program line highlighted in the editor document window. You can see the line in context; it may even give you information you need to fix the problem. More likely, you will have to do more in the way of debugging.

The Immediate Window

The Immediate editor window not only lets you check statements during program entry, but it also permits variable checking when a program ends with an error. You can enter PRINT statements in the Immediate window to find the current values of crucial variables.

Tracing a Program

The **Debug** menu includes three commands that control tracing. **Trace On** is a toggle that turns it on or off; a dot next to the command indicates trace is on. When tracing is in effect, the program runs in slow motion; the statement being executed is highlighted. By watching the screen, you can see if the statements are processed in the order you expect. You can use Ctrl+Break to interrupt the trace and pause the program. The Immediate window is available to check values, and you can press F4 to see the any screen output. Pressing F5 resumes the trace.

Debug Step sets up a process whereby execution pauses after each statement is executed. Choosing **Debug Step** or pressing F8 executes the next statement. If the statement produces screen output, you can press F4 to see the result on the output screen; any key returns you to the program window. At any time, you can use **Run Start** to start over.

The **Debug Procedure Step** command (F10) is similar, but it executes each function or subprogram as a single instruction. This will speed the stepping process when all your functions and subprograms have already been debugged.

Breakpoints

A breakpoint is a spot where you want execution to pause. You can insert breakpoints in a program at points where you want to check to see how the program is progressing. For example, you might insert a special PRINT command, then flag it as a breakpoint. When you run the program, the output will be generated and the program will pause.

To set a breakpoint, position the cursor in the line, then press F9 or choose **Debug Toggle Breakpoint**. The line will appear in red or inverse video, depending on your monitor. You can set as many breakpoints as you wish. To remove a breakpoint, place the cursor on the line again, and press F9 or choose **Debug Toggle Breakpoint**. To clear all breakpoints when debugging is complete, choose **Debug Clear All Breakpoints**.

A

EXIT CODES

M any DOS commands set an exit code when they terminate. You can access these codes only if the command was run as part of a batch program. In most cases, an exit code of 0 means that the command functioned correctly and the operation was successfully completed. Any other exit code means the operation was not completed correctly. The IF ERRORLEVEL command lets you test the code and take action depending on what it is.

Command	Exit Code	Meaning
BACKUP	0	All requested files backed up; normal exit
	1	No files found to back up
	2	Not all files backed up; sharing conflicts
	3	User pressed Ctrl+C to stop
	4	Error; program stopped at some point
DISKCOMP	0	Disks are the same; normal exit
	1	Disks are not the same
	2	User pressed Ctrl+C to stop command
	3	Hardware error (such as no floppy disk)
	4	Initialization error
DISKCOPY	0	Disk copied successfully; normal exit
	1	Not a success; nonfatal read/write error during copy
	2	User pressed Ctrl+C to stop command
	3	Fatal hardware error
	4	Initialization error
FORMAT	0	Disk formatted successfully; normal exit
	3	User pressed Ctrl+C to stop command
	4	Error; program stopped
	5	User pressed N in response Proceed with Format (Y/N)
GRAFTABL	0	Character table loaded; normal exit
	1	Character table replaced former table
	2	Not loaded; file error
	3	Nothing done; incorrect parameter
	4	Nothing done; not DOS 5
KEYB	0	Keyboard file loaded; normal exit
	1	Bad keyboard code, code page value, or syntax
	2	Bad or missing keyboard definition file
	4	CON device error
	5	Requested code page not prepared

Command	Exit Code	Meaning
REPLACE	0	Specified files replaced or added; normal exit
	2	No files affected; source files not found
	3	No files affected; source or target path not found
	5	Read/write access denied; at least one file not replaced; use ATTRIB to change access
	8	Not done; not enough memory to run command
	11	Not done; bad parameter or invalid format
RESTORE	0	Files restored; normal exit
	1	No files found to restore
	3	User pressed Ctrl+C to stop the command
	4	Error occurred; command interrupted
SETVER	0	Mission accomplished; normal exit
	1	Not done; invalid switch
	2	Not done; invalid filename
	3	Not done; not enough memory
	4	Not done; wrong version-number format
	5	Not done; entry not found in version table
	6	Not done; DOS system requested not found
	7	Not done; invalid drive
	8	Not done; too many parameters
	9	Not done; missing parameter
	10	Not done; error reading SETVER.EXE file
	11	Not done; version table in SETVER.EXE is corrupt
	12	Not done; specified SETVER.EXE file doesn't support version tables
	13	Not done; no space left in version table
	14	Not done; error writing to version table
XCOPY	0	Specified files copied; normal exit
	1	No file found to copy

continues

Command	Exit Code	Meaning
	2	User pressed Ctrl+C to stop command
	4	Not enough memory or disk space, syntax error, or initialization error
	5	Write-protected disk or other write error

IBM EXTENDED
CHARACTER SET

128	Ç	150	û	172	¼
129	ü	151	ù	173	¡
130	é	152	ÿ	174	«
131	â	153	Ö	175	»
132	ä	154	Ü	176	▓
133	à	155	¢	177	▓
134	å	156	£	178	▓
135	ç	157	¥	179	│
136	ê	158	℞	180	┤
137	ë	159	ƒ	181	╡
138	è	160	á	182	╢
139	ï	161	í	183	╖
140	î	162	ó	184	╕
141	ì	163	ú	185	╣
142	Ä	164	ñ	186	║
143	Å	165	Ñ	187	╗
144	É	166	ª	188	╝
145	æ	167	º	189	╜
146	Æ	168	¿	190	╛
147	ô	169	⌐	191	┐
148	ö	170	¬	192	└
149	ò	171	½	193	┴

194 ┬	217 ┘	240 ≡
195 ├	218 ┌	241 ±
196 –	219 █	242 ≥
197 ┼	220 ▄	243 ≤
198 ╞	221 ▌	244 ⌠
199 ╟	222 ▐	245 ⌡
200 ╚	223 ▀	246 ÷
201 ╔	224 α	247 ≈
202 ╩	225 β	248 °
203 ╦	226 Γ	249 ·
204 ╠	227 π	250 ·
205 =	228 Σ	251 √
206 ╬	229 σ	252 η
207 ╧	230 μ	253 ²
208 ╨	231 Υ	254 ■
209 ╤	232 Φ	255
210 ╥	233 Θ	
211 ╙	234 Ω	
212 ╘	235 δ	
213 ╒	236 ω	
214 ╓	237 φ	
215 ╫	238 ∈	
216 ╪	239 ∩	

INDEX

Symbols

SORT collating sequence key, 72

$ SORT collating sequence key, 72

$$ DOSKEY macro special character, 87

$* DOSKEY macro special character, 87

$1-$9 DOSKEY macro special character, 87

% SORT collating sequence key, 72

% symbol, 114

& SORT collating sequence key, 72

(SORT collating sequence key, 72

" SORT collating sequence key, 72

' SORT collating sequence key, 72

* SORT collating sequence key, 72

/ALL switch UNDELETE command, 294

< source redirection symbol, 60

> destination redirection symbol, 60

> redirection symbol, using warning, 63

>> destination redirection symbol, 60

2.88M diskette, formatting, 4, 6

A

/A switch
BACKUP command, 243
COMP command, 265
COPY command, 170
DIR command, 14-17
FC command, 267
REPLACE command, 247
RESTORE command, 250
TREE command, 143
using XCOPY command, 246

A20 handlers, 201

absolute
filespecs, using in PATH command, 140
path, 136

accessing
all parameters in macros, 89
correct drive, 370-371
environment variables, 179
extended memory, High Memory Area (HMA), 196
files, strategy, 217

active task list, 40, 49

Add Group dialog box, 46

ADD mode, 28

Add Program dialog box, 47-48

adding
external floppy disk drives, 375-376
variables, environment, 184

address spaces
memory, 190
reassigning, 194

allocation
errors, 284-285
for file storage, 169
invalid, 277, 283
of bytes to environment dynamically, 185
units
cross-linked, 277, 280-281
lost, 277- 279
recovering lost, 222

Alt+F7 key combination, 83

Alt+Shift+Tab key combination, 39

Alt+Shift+Tab,Tab,... key combination, 39

Alt+Tab key combination, 39

Alt+Tab,Tab,... key combination, 39

alternate code pages, 336-337

alternative branching, linking batch files, 121, 124-125

ANSI.SYS device driver, 313-314

anti-virus software, 271
APPEND command, 150
appending
    files, 165
    versus overwriting, 63
application data files, concat-
    enating, 166
Application Shortcut Key field,
    48
architecture of hard disks, 217
archive attributes, backing up
    files, 238
arm movements, read-write,
    216-218
array variables (QBASIC),
    388-389
/AS switch, 270
ASCII
    avoiding slack when access-
        ing files, 169
    non-ASCII files, updating
        time/date stamp, 171
    editors
        EDIT, 3, 10-11
        editing setup files, 53
        EDLIN, 10
    files, 109
aspect ratio of screens, 368
ASSIGN command, 144-145,
    377
assigning
    fake drive name, 147
    strings of text to keys, 328
associate file dialog box, 36
associated files, opening from
    Shell, 33
AT handler, 201
ATTRIB command, 5
    manipulating archive at-
        tributes, 239
attributes, archive, backing up
    files, 238
AUTO parameter in
    CONFIG.SYS command, 207
AUTOEXEC.BAT file, 22, 39,
    81, 179, 214, 232, 260
automating commands, 65-68

AUX device, 64
/Ax switch, 270

B

/B switch
    COPY command, 170
    copying non-ASCII files to
        devices, 171
    GRAPHICS command, 368
    PRINT command, 363
backup
Backspace DOSKEY command
    line editing keys, 84
BACKUP command, 5,
    151-154, 238-240, 242-245,
    406
    avoiding disk full termina-
        tion, 158
    warning, 171
BACKUP.nnn file, 240
backups, 237
    daily
        full, 237
        supplemental, 238
    disks, storing, 238
    fallback sets, 237
    files
        assessing value, 236
        compression of data, 239
        conserving disk space,
            239
        warning, 246
    frequency, 237
    logs
        files, 241-242
        fullback sets, 243
    restoring
        entire set, 250
        multiple files, 250
    strategies, 237
    supplemental, restoring
        files from, 250
    systems, 236
    XCOPY command, 244-245
bad sectors, 277

BADFORM command, 124
bank switching, 194
banner, creating, 320
BAS (from DOS directory) file,
    221
batch files, 47-48, 90-95
    accessing environment
        variables, 179
    commands, 95
    controlling displayed mes-
        sages, 98
    creating, 83, 99
    displaying value of specific
        variable, 177
    dumb replacement param-
        eters, 113, 114
    executing from floppy disks,
        97-98
    for selecting and bypassing
        files for backup, 242
    linking, 116-119
        branching, 120
        by alternative branching,
            121
        by bypass branching,
            120, 124
        by calling another pro-
            gram, 116-117
        by chaining to another
            program, 116-118
        killing jobs, 119
        multiple, 119
    naming, 95
    null parameters, 110-111
    preparing for other moni-
        tors, 319
    priorities, 96
    pruning and grafting, 160
    recursion, 119
    replaceable parameters,
        108-113
    supplementary, 105-108
    suppressing command-line
        echoing, 98-100
    termination of, 118
    TIMEOUT.BAT, 47
    versus macros, 85-86

binary
    files, concatenating, 167
    method of avoiding slack
        when accessing files, 169
    number system, 191
block devices, 370
branches, 136
    copying complete, 156
    displaying, 13-14
    moving, 159-160
branching
    alternative, 121, 124-125
    bypass, in linking batch
        files, 120, 124
    linking batch files, 120
breakpoints, 404
buffers
    disk, 227
    DOSKEY's, 80-81
    look-ahead, 227
    memory, 175
    video, 312
BUFFERS command, 8, 228
bypass branching, linking
    batch files, 120, 124

C

/C command-text switch,
    output redirection, 187-188
/C switch
    COMP command, 265
    MEM command, 199,
        210-211
    PRINT command, 364
caches
    entries, 230
    size, 225
    space, borrowing in Win-
        dows 3.0, 225
    systems, 225
        IBMCACHE.SYS, 223
        IBMCACHE.SYS, warn-
            ing, 226

SMARTDRV.SYS, warn-
    ing, 226
    third-party, 227
CALL batch command, 95
CALL command, 47-48,
    117-118
CALL statement, 401-402
CALL with FOR commands,
    combining, 134
calling another program
    linking batch files, 116-117
cartridges, tape, for backup,
    237
case structure (QBASIC pro-
    gram), 393-394
CD command, 136
CGA monitor, 51
chaining to another program,
    linking batch files, 116-118
change line mechanism, 372
changing
    environment variable, 179
    time/date stamp for files,
        154

characters
    extended, 409
    per inch (cpi), 357
    set, extended, 322
    typing code page charac-
        ters, 335
    wrapping, 324
CHCP command, 351
CHKDSK command, 5, 274,
    277-278, 283-285
CHKDSK/F, 278
choosing drive names, 147
/CLASSIFY switch, MEM com-
    mand, 7
CLEANUP file, 221
clearing command list with
    Alt+F7, 83
clobbering files, COPY and
    XCOPY, 161
closed loop, 130
closing tasks, 41

CLS command, 98
clusters, 276
    converting lost ones to files,
        279
    deleting lost, 279
    file storage, 169
    lost, 278-279
code,
    exit, 122-123, 251, 405-408
    key, 325
    pages, 4, 334
        alternate, 336-337
        changing for monitors,
            338-339
        default, 336-337
        displaying code page
            information, 351
        monitors, 342-343
        other than built-in
            codes, 341-342
        preparing, 345-346
        printers, 343-344
        reinstating, 350
        switching, 346-350
        typing characters, 335
        values, 334
CODEPAGE SELECT format,
    346
codes
    exit, 123, 251, 405-408
    key, 325
collapsing directories, 26
collating sequence, SORT, 72
color
    of screens, 318-319, 323
    schemes, setting in
        DOSSHELL.INI file, 56
colored message box, creating,
    322
.COM file, bypassing, 96
COM1- 4 devices
combining
    CALL with FOR, 134
    commands, 79
    FIND with FOR, 133
    IF with FOR, 134

COMMAND command, 5
command history list, viewing, 82
command interpreter
    locating, 182
    NDOS of Norton Utilities, 183
    primary, loading, 186
    secondary, 183-185
    SHELL, 181
    third-party, 183
command line
    editing, 79, 83
    editing keys, *see* DOSKEY command line editing keys, 84
    maximum characters, 133
command list, clearing with Alt + F7, 83
command macros., 79
command output, locating lines, 76-77
command prompt tasks, 41
command-line echoing, suppressing in batch files, 98-100
COMMAND.COM
    as secondary interpreter, 186
    file, 6
    file interpreter, 181
command1 | command2 redirection symbol, 60
commands, 80, 136
    APPEND, 150
    ASSIGN, 144-145, 377
    ATTRIB, 5
        manipulating archive attributes, 239
    automating, 65-68
    BACKUP, 5, 153-154, 238-240, 406
    BADFORM, 124
    BUFFERS, 8, 228
    CALL, 47-48, 117-118
    CD, 136
    CHCP, 351

CHKDSK, 5, 274, 277-278, 283-285
CLS, 98
combining, 79
    CALL with FOR, 134
    FIND with FOR, 133
    FOR with IF, 134
    on one line, 85
COMMAND, 5
COMP, 5, 264
CONFIG.SYS, 207
COPY, 152-154, 163, 168-170, 288
COUNTRY, 5, 334, 340-341
DATE, 5, 65
DEL, 5
DEL*.*, 97
DELOLDOS, 2, 7
DEVICE, 314
DEVICE, 200-201, 224
    CONFIG.SYS order using SMAARTDRV, 226
    of EMM386, 204
DEVICE=ANSI.SYS, 328
DEVICEHIGH, 314
DEVICEHIGH, 7, 210, 224, 342
    CONFIG.SYS order using SMARTDRV, 226
DIR, 6, 12, 74, 136, 178
    defaults, 17
    displaying branches, 13-14
    selecting files by attributes, 14-15
    sorting file list, 15-16
DISKCOMP, 269, 406
DISKCOPY, 6, 155, 288, 406
DISPLAY.SYS DEVICE, 343
DOS, 7
    commands restricted from network, 377-378
    replacing with macros, 91
DOS=HIGH, 202

DOS=UMB, 208
DOSKEY, 7
DOSSHELL, 22
DRIVPARM, 369-371
DT, 99
ECHO, 100-101, 322, 355
ECHO in batch files, 102
ECHO OFF, 100
ECHO ON, 100
ECOPY, 97
EDIT, 7, 71
EMM386, 7
Esc[m, 319
executing
    with batch files, 85
    with macros, 85
EXIT, 183
EXPAND, 7
FASTOPEN, 6, 229-230
FC, 264-267
FCBS, 8
FDISK, 6, 298
File Copy, 30, 52
File Delete, 30
File Menu, 27
File Properties, 52
File Run, 34
File Search, 32
FIND, 74-77
FOR, to create loops, 131-133
FORMAT, 6, 66-67, 97, 254-256, 300, 406
GOODFORM, 124
GOTO, 124-125
GRAFTABL, 6, 406
GRAPHICS, 6, 365-368
HELP, 7-10
IF, 121-124, 129
IF [NOT] EXIST, 127
IF ERRORLEVEL, 162-163
IF EXIST, 127
INSTALL, 7
JOIN, 377
KEYB, 6, 334-339, 346, 351, 406

LASTDRIVE, 147
LOADFIX, 7, 203
LOADHIGH, 7
MD, 136
MEM, 7, 198-200, 211
MIRROR, 8, 256-261, 300
MODE, 6, 329-330, 344-346, 357-360
MORE, 6, 142
Options Colors, 23
Options Display, 23
Options Enable Task Swapper, 37
Options File Display Options, 30
Options Refresh, 26
Options Select Across Directories, 30-31
PATH, 139-150
PAUSE, 103-105
PCL (page control language), 366
PCTRAACKR.DEL, 289
prefixing with @ symbol, 99-100
PRINT, 64, 361-364
PRINTER.SYS DEVICE, 344
PROMPT, 315, 320
PROMPT PG, 315
QBASIC, 8
RAMDRIVE.SYS DEVICE, 231
recalling
    former, 79
    last, 82
RECOVER, 96, 300-308
REM, 6, 102
RENAME, 97
REPLACE, 6, 97, 153-154, 172-173, 247, 407
RESTORE, 6, 153-154, 240, 247-249, 407
restricted, 144
SET, 38
    changing environment variable, 179

controlling environment variables, 176
creating DIRCMD variable, 178
creating TEMP variable, 177
deleting environment variable, 179
SETUP, 39
SETVER, 8, 17-19, 407
SHARE, 378-379
SHIFT, 110-113
SUBST, 144-148, 372, 377
SWITCHES, 8
SYS, 6
TIME, 6, 65
TREE, 6, 142-143
TRUENAME, 8, 149-150
two-line, editing, 83
TYPE, 317
TYPE COLTEST, 317
UNDELETE, 8, 247, 289-290, 294, 303
UNFORMAT, 8, 255-256, 295, 298-304
VERIFY OFF, 263
VERIFY ON, 263
View All Files, 30-32
View Dual File Lists, 29
View Single File List, 29
warnings about using BACKUP, 171
XCOPY, 6, 152-158, 238-240, 244, 288, 407-408
COMMON SHARED statement, 399
communication, international, 333
    code pages, 334-335
        displaying code page information, 351
        monitors, 342-343
        preparing, 345-346
        printers, 343-344
        reinstating, 350
        switching, 346-350

countries supported by DOS, 339-340
COUNTRY command, 334, 340-341
KEYB command, 334-337
keyboard layout, 336-337
other than built-in codes, 341-342
COMP command, 5, 264
comparing
    files, 264
    text strings, 128-129
compression of data on backup files, 239
computer viruses, 235, 259
COMSPEC variable, 178, 184
CON (console), 60
    device, 64, 312
    entering files from, 71
concatenating
    application data files, 166
    binary files, 167
    files, 154, 163-168, 240
conditions, IF ERRORLEVEL, 123
CONFIG.SYS command, 207
CONFIG.SYS file, 147-148, 181, 213, 314
    installing FASTOPEN, 6
    order of SMARTDRV's DEVICE[HIGH] command, 226
configuring
    disks, 370
    floppy disks, 372
    PRINT command, 362-364
    printers, 357-358
    serial ports, 358-360
conserving disk space on backup files, 239
constants (QBASIC), 386-387
CONTROL.nnn file, 240
controlling
    environment size with SHELL command, 182
    environment variables with SET command, 176

keyboard, 325
page frame address, 209
read-write arm movements, 218
sequences, 320
Shell, 24
conventional memory, 192, 203
converting
    EMS expanded memory to EMS extended memory, 198
    lost clusters to files, 279
    XMS extended memory to EMS expanded memory, 198
COPY command, 151-154, 163, 168-170, 288
    clobbering files, 161
copy commands
    advantages, 152-153
    disadvantages, 152-153
COPY program, 232
copying
    complete branches, 156
    files
        from different type floppy disks, 373-375
        insuring accuracy, 162-163
        non-ASCII, to devices, 171
        to and from devices, 168
        to same directory, 157
    floppy disks, 155
    to and from non-disk devices, 154
copying commands, 151
    BACKUP, 151
    COPY, 151
    REPLACE, 151
    XCOPY, 151
countries supported by DOS, 339-340
COUNTRY command, 5, 334, 340-341

country formats, 4
CPICOUNTRY.SYS file, 221
CRC
    errors, 305
    performed by drive control-ler, 263
    verification of files, 263
creating
    alternative drive names, 373-375
    batch files, 83, 99
        for pruning and grafting, 160
    colored message box, 322
    command macros., 79
    DIRCMD variable with SET command, 178
    directories, 157
    loops using FOR command, 131-133
    new directories, 157
    procedures (QBASIC pro-gram), 397-398
    programs with batch files, 93-94
    TEMP variable with SET command, 177
    top of screen banner, 320
cross-linked
    allocation units, 277, 280-281
    multiple files, 282-283
    single files, 281-282
Ctrl+/ control key, 28
Ctrl+\ control key, 28
Ctrl+Break key combination, 119, 130
Ctrl+C key combination, 119
Ctrl+d drive list control key, 25
Ctrl+End DOSKEY command line editing keys, 84
Ctrl+Esc task-swapping hotkey, 39
Ctrl+Home DOSKEY com-mand line editing keys, 84
Ctrl+P key combination, 356

Ctrl+PrintScreen key combina-tion, 356
Ctrl+T key combination, 85
current directory, 138
cursor control sequences, 320
cyclic redundancy check see CRC, 263

D

/D switch
    COMP command, 265
    MEM command, 200
    PRINT command, 362
    RESTORE command, 6, 249
    SETVER command, 19
data
    compression on backup files, 239
    lines, 69
    matching, locating follow-ing mismatch, 266
    protection facilities, 4
    protecting through third-party software, 270
    recovering using Norton Utilities' UnErase, 161
DATE command, 5, 65, 68
debugging QBASIC program, 403-404
DECLARE statement, 400
default
    code pages, 336-337
    DIR command, 17
    directories, 137
    overstrike or insert modes, changing, 84
    printer, 64
    program list view (View Program/File Lists), 44
defining
    functions, 402
    hot keys, 49
    macros, 86-90
        sample definitions, 87-88

new program group, 46
program items, 47
    help text, 49
    memory requirements,
        49-51
    optional fields, 48-49
    replaceable parameter
        dialog boxes, 51
    required fields, 47-48
    task switching limita-
        tions, 49-51
Defining Program Item dialog
    box, 52
defragmenting
    files, 222-223
        with DOS commands,
            288
    subdirectories, 222-223
Del
    command, 5
    control key, 28
    force-close task, 41
    hotkey in QBASIC Editor,
        383
    key, warning
DEL *.* command, 97
Delete DOSKEY command line
    editing keys, 84
deleted files
    recovering, 303
    tracking, 260
deleting
    environment variables, SET
        command, 179
    lost clusters, 279
    read-only and system files
        through Shell, 270
    unnecessary files, 220
    variables, environment, 184
DELOLDOS command, 2, 7
DELOLDOS.EXE file, 221
DEVICE command, 200-201,
    224, 314
    CONFIG.SYS order using
        SMARTDRV, 226
    of EMM386, 204

device drivers, 193, 200
    ANSI.SYS, 313-314
    CON, 312
    DRIVER.SYS, 369, 372
    loading, 198
DEVICE=ANSI.SYS command,
    328
DEVICEHIGH command, 7,
    210, 224, 314, 342
    CONFIG.SYS order using
        SMARTDRV, 226
dialog boxes
    Add Group, 46
    Add Program, 47-48
    associate file, 36
    Defining Program Item, 52
    File Display Options, 31
    replaceable parameters, 51
    Run, 34
    SUBs, 398
DIR command, 6, 12, 74, 136,
    178
    defaults, 17
    displaying branches, 13-14
    selecting files by attributes,
        14-15
    sorting file list, 15-16
DIRCMD environment vari-
    able, 17, 178
directories, 2
    collapsing, 26
    creating, 27
    current, 138
    default, 137
    deleting, 27
    displaying branches, 13-14
    DOS, 48
    expanding, 26
    finding true name of cur-
        rent, 149
    moving, 159-160
    multiple, handling files
        from, 30-31
    OLD_DOS.n., 2
    renaming, 27, 160
    root, 136, 232, 279

children, 136
    saving with MIRROR
        command, 260
Startup, 48
structure of, 141
testing for, 128
viewing DOS Shell's direc-
    tory tree, 142
directory
    listing, locating lines, 77-78
    structure, 219
    tree, 26-27
        restructuring, 144
disk full termination, 158-159
Disk Utilities group, 44-45
DISKCOMP command, 269,
    406
DISKCOPY command, 6, 155,
    288, 406
DISKCOPY program, 236
diskettes
    2.88M, 4
    Uninstall, 2
disks
    backup, storing, 238
    buffers, 227
    configuring, 370
    copying, 155
    drives, redefining, 369
    floppy
        adding external floppy
            disk drives, 375-376
        configuring, 372
        copying files from differ-
            ent type floppy disks,
            373-375
        for backup, 237, 246
        recovering CRC errors,
            305
        standard parameters,
            371
        write-protecting, 269
    hard
        for backup, 237
        partition table, 259
        recovering CRC errors,
            305

reformatting, 309
write-protecting by third-
   party software, 269
heads, parking programs,
   271
interleave factor, 218
space, conserving on
   backup files, 239
storage blocks
   allocation units, 169
   clusters, 169
structure, protecting, 257
display
   of partition, 297
   of text, shifting, 329
Display hidden/system files,
   270
DISPLAY.SYS DEVICE com-
   mand, 343
DISPLAY.SYS PRINTER.SYS
   file, 221
displayed messages, controlling
   in batch files, 98
displaying
   branches, 13-14
   code page information, 351
   file list options, 30
   files in one file list, 30
   paragraph symbol on moni-
      tor, 85
   value of specific variable,
      using batch files, 177
DO statement, 394-396
documentation of DOS 5,
   errors, 185-186
DOS
   accessing correct drive,
      370-371
   change line mechanism,
      372
   commands, 7, 91
   countries supported,
      339-340
   installing, 2
   loading into HMA, 202
   running on network,
      376-377

command restrictions,
   377-378
locking files, 378
logical drives, 378
sharing files, 378
special features/prob-
   lems, 378
verification of files
   general, 263
DOS 5
   documentation, 185-186
   keyboard layouts available,
      336-337
   new features, 4
DOS Shell see Shell
DOS utilities
   filters, 68-69
      FIND, 69
      MORE, 68-70
      SORT, 69-70
DOS=HIGH command, 202
DOS=UMB command, 208
DOSHELP.HLP file, 10
DOSKEY, 316
   buffer, 80-81
   combining two or more
      commands on one line, 85
   command line editing keys,
      84
   loading, 80
   macro special characters, 86
   macros, 328
   modes, 84
   starting, 80-81
   uninstalling, 81
DOSKEY command, 7
DOSKEY program, 3
DOSSHELL command, 21-22
DOSSHELL file, 221
DOSSHELL.INI, 53
DOSSHELL.INI file, 23, 52-56
   file associations section,
      56-57
   passwords in, 55
   programstarter section,
      55-56
   savestate section, 53

dot (.), single, path reference,
   137
dot (..), double, path reference, 137
dragging files, 29
drive controller, performing
   CRCs, 263
drive list, 25-26
DRIVER.SYS device driver,
   369, 372
DRIVER.SYS file, 221
drivers
   ANSI.SYS, 313-314
   CON, 312
   RAMDRIVE.SYS, 231
drivers, see device drivers, 193
drives, 137
   accessing correct drive,
      370-371
   adding external floppy disk
      drives, 375-376
   assigning fake names, 147
   choosing names, 147
   choosing names of, 147
   creating alternative drive
      names, 373-375
   diskette, switching with
      SUBST, 148
   hard, multiple, 4
   logical, on networks, 378
   RAM, 230
      creating, 231
      installation warning, 233
      using, 232
   reconstructing entire, 307
   substituting drive name for
      path, 145
DRIVPARM command,
   369-371
DT command, 99
dumb replacement parameters
   in batch fles, 113-114
duplicate tasks, 41
Dvorak keyboard, 327
dynamic allocation to environment, 185

E

/E switch
  COMMAND.COM command, 182
  KEYB command, 6
  XCOPY command, 157
ECHO batch command, 95
ECHO command, 100-102, 322, 355
ECHO OFF command, 100
ECHO ON command, 100
echo printing, 356
EDIT
  ASCII editors, 53
  command, 7, 71
  editor, 3, 10-11
EDIT program, 317
EDIT.HLP file, 11
editing
  two-line command, 83
  command line, 79, 83
Editor, QBASIC program, 382-384
/EDITOR switch, QBASIC command, 382
EDLIN editor, 10
EDLIN.EXE LINK.EXE file, 221
EGA.SYS file, 221
elements (QBASIC program), 389
ELSE statement, 391
EMM386, DEVICE command, 204
EMM386 command, 7
EMM386 program, 203-211
EMM386.EXE, 80
EMM386.EXE extended memory handler, 8
EMM386.EXE file, 198, 220
EMS (Expanded Memory Specification), 193-194
emulating expanded memory, 204
emulation mode, 354

emulators, 204
end-of-file indicator, 276
ENDSUB statement, 399-401
enhanced keyboard, 328
Enter drive list control key, 25
entering files from CON, 71
entries of caches, 230
environment, 175
  dynamic allocation of bytes to environment, 185
  size, controlling with SHELL command, 182
  variables, 176, 233
    accessing, 179
    adding, 184
    COMSPEC, 178
    controlling with SET command, 176
    deleting, 184
    DIRCMD, 17, 178
    modifying, 184
    PATH, 177
    preserving, 180
    PROMPT, 177
    restoring, 180
    TEMP, 38, 177-178
    versus replaceable parameters, 180
    warnings, 182
errors
  allocation, 284-285
  CRC, 305
  documentation of DOS 5, 185-186
  output, 61-62
  "Sector not found", 308-309
Esc[m command, 319
escape sequence, 314
  sending, using PROMPT command, 316
.EXE file, bypassing, 96
EXE2BIN.EXE DEBUG.EXE file, 221
executing batch files from floppy disks, 97-98
executing macros, 89

exit codes, 122-123, 251, 405-408
EXIT command, 183
EXPAND command, 7
expanded memory, 193-195
  caches versus extended memory caches, 225
  determining size, 209
  emulating, 204
  manager program, 194
  providing, 204
  turning on and off, 206
expanding directories, 26
extended
  character set, 322
  characters, 409
extended memory
  caches versus expanded memory caches, 225
  handlers
    EMM386.EXE, 8
    XMA2EMS.SYS, 8
    XMAEM.SYS, 8
  manager, 4-5
  manager programs
    HIMEM.SYS, 200
    HIMEM.SYS, problems, 201
    HIMEM.SYS XMS, 198
  specification see XMS, 197

F

F [NOT] EXIST command, 127
F EXIST command, 127
/F switch
  BACKUP command, 241
  CHKDSK command, 274, 278, 284
  TREE command, 143
F1 hotkey, 383
F2 hotkey, 383
F3 hotkey, 383
F4 hotkey, 383

F5 hotkey, 383
F6 hotkey, 383
F7 hotkey, 383
F8 (File Copy) key combination, 25
F8 hotkey, 383
F9 hotkey, 383
F10 hotkey, 383
facilities, data-protection, 4
fake drive name, assigning, 147
fallback sets, previous day's backups, 237, 246
FASTOPEN command, 6, 229-230
FASTOPEN program, 228-230
FASTOPEN.EXE file, 221
FATs, 217, 275, 284, 301
    bad sectors, 287
    displayed by third-party utility programs, 277
    saving with MIRROR command, 260
FC command, 264-267
FCBS command, 8
FDISK command, 6, 298
fields, 48-49
    Application Shortcut Key, 48
    memory
        XMS Memory KB Limit, 50
        XMS Memory KB Required, 50
    Pause after exit, 49
    required when defining program items, 47-48
file allocation table, see FAT, 217
file associations section, 56-57
File Copy
    (F8) key combination, 25
    command, 30
File Copy command, 52
File Delete command, 30
File Display Options dialog box, 31

file interpreter, COMMAND.COM, 181
file list
    displaying files in, 30
    displaying options, 30
    sorting, 15-16
    working with under Shell, 27-29
File menu, 24, 27
File Properties command, 52
File Run command, 34
File Search command, 32
FILEnnnn.CHK, 279
files
    appending, 165
    application data, concatenating, 166
    ASCII, 109
    asssociated, opening from Shell, 33
    AUTOEXEC.BAT, 39, 81, 179, 214, 232, 260
        starting Shell, 22
    backup
        assessing value, 236
        compression of data, 239
        conserving disk space, 239
        warning, 246
    BACKUP.nnn, 240
    BAS (from DOS directory), 221
    batch, preparing for other monitors, 319
    batch, see batch files, 93-94
    binary, concatenating, 167
    CLEANUP, 221
    clobbered, 161-162, 174
    .COM, bypassing, 96
    COMMAND.COM, 6
    comparing, 264
    concatenating, 154, 163-166, 240
    CONFIG.SYS, 147-148, 181, 213-314
        installing FASTOPEN, 6

CONTROL.nnn, 240
copying
    from different type floppy disks, 373-375
    insuring accuracy, 162-163
    to and from devices, 168
    to same directory, 157
CPI COUNTRY.SYS, 221
cross-linked, 280-281
    warning, 281
defragmenting, 222
defragmenting with DOS commands, 288
deleted
    recovering, 303
    tracking, 260
DELOLDOS.EXE, 221
DISPLAY.SYS
    PRINTER.SYS, 221
DOSHELP.HLP, 10
DOSSHELL, 221
DOSSHELL.INI, 23, 52-56
    file associations section, 56-57
    passwords in, 55
    programstarter section, 55-56
    savestate section, 53
dragging, 29
DRIVER.SYS, 221
EDIT.HLP, 11
EDLIN.EXE LINK.EXE, 221
EGA.SYS, 221
EMM386.EXE, 198, 220
.EXE, bypassing, 96
EXE2BIN.EXE
    DEBUG.EXE, 221
existing, replacing, 173
FASTOPEN.EXE, 221
FILEnnnn.CHK, 279
finding true location of, 149
fixing, 306
fragmentation, 287-288
fragmented, 277
general verification by DOS, 263

GRAFTABL.COM, 221
GRAPHICS.COM, 221
GRAPHICS.PRO, 221, 365
GW-BASIC, saving in ASCII
   form, 384
handling from mulltiple
   directories, 30-31
HIMEM.SYS, 220
IBMCACHE.SYS, 223
image, 301-304
including hidden and sys-
   tem files in directory, 270
individual, fixing, 306
KEYB.COM, 221
LAODFIX.EXE, 220
locking while networking,
   378
lost, locating, 32
missing, replacing, 172
moving, 162
MSHERC.COM, 221
multiple cross-linked,
   282-283
NLSFUNC.EXE, 221
preserving, 235
program, RECOVER com-
   mand, 308
program, opening from
   Shell, 33
protecting, 235
RAMDRIVE.SYS, 220
read-only, deleting through
   Shell, 270
README.TXT, 201
recovering with REPLACE
   command, 247
redirecting output to, 62-63
relocating, 222
restoring, made with
   XCOPY, 247
selected, restoring, 249
selecting by attributes, 14-15
selecting multiple, 28
setup, 53
SHARE.EXE, 221
sharing on network, 378

single, cross-linked, 281-282
size, 261
SMARTDRV.SYS, 220, 231
specific verification by DOS,
   263
strategy in accessing, 217
system, deleting through
   Shell, 270
temporary, pipe, 67-68
testing, 127
text, RECOVER command,
   308
TIMETRAK, 109
TXT PACKING.LST (from
   DOS directory), 221
undeleting, 288-293
verification
   CRCs, 263
   general, 263
with matching filenames,
   concatenating, 168
write-protecting by setting
   read-only or system attribute, 270
writing, 170
filespec, 138
filespecs
   absolute, 140
   global, 133
filters, 68-69
   FIND, 69
   MORE, 68-70
   SORT, 69-70
FIND command, 74-77
   combining with FOR command, 133
fixing files, 306
fixing individual files, 306
floppy disks
   adding external floppy disk
   drives, 375-376
   configuring, 372
   copying files from different
   type floppy disks, 373-375
   executing batch files from,
   97-98

for backup, 237
for backups, 246
recovering CRC errors, 305
standard parameters, 371
write-protecting, 269
FOR batch command, 95
FOR command
   combining
      with CALL command,
      134
      with FIND command,
      133
      with IF command, 134
   loops, 131-133
FORMAT command, 6, 66-67,
   97, 254-256, 300, 406
formats
   CODEPAGE SELECT, 346
   country, 4
   international, 339-340
   PREPARE, 345
   quick, /Q switch, 255
   recoverable, 257
   safe, 255
   unconditional, 255-256
formatting
   2.88M diskette, 6
   programs, low level, 309
fragmentation of files, 287-288
fragmented files, 277
frequency of backup, 237
function key "macros", 328
functions
   defining, 402
   LCASE$, 388
   LTRIM$, 388
   RTRIM$, 388
   UCASE$, 388
   user-defined, 396

G

global filespec, 133
global variables (QBASIC
   program), 399

GOODFORM command, 124
GOTO batch command, 95
GOTO command, 124-125
GOTO ERRORLINE statement, 385
GOTO statements, 391
GRAFTABL command, 6, 406
GRAFTABL.COM file, 221
grafting, 159
GRAPHICS command, 6, 365-366
    printer types, 366-367
    screen aspect ratio, 368
graphics mode, 44
GRAPHICS.COM file, 221
GRAPHICS.PRO file, 365
GW-BASIC program, 4

H

handlers
    A20, 201
    AT, 201
handlers of keystrokes, 212
hard disks
    architecture, 217
    description, 216
    for backup, 237
    interleave factor, 218-219
    layout, 217
    optimizing, 221-222
    partition table, 259
    recovering CRC errors, 305
    reformatting, 309
    write-protecting by third-party software, 269
hard drives, multiple, 4
HELP
    command, 7-10
    on-screen, 3, 9-10
hexadecimal numbers, 190-191
hidden files, including in directory, 270
high memory area, loading SMARTDRV.SYS into, 224

High Memory Area (HMA), 196-200
HIMEM program, 201
HIMEM.SYS extended memory manager, 197, 200-201, 204, 220
HMA, 200
    loading DOS into, 202
    loading SMARTDRV.SYS into, 224
hotkeys, 39
    active task list, 49
    defining, 49
    in QBASIC Editor, 383

I

IBM extended character set, 409
IBMCACHE.SYS file
    installing, 227
    memory caching system, 223
    versus SMARTDRV.SYS file, 226
    warning, 226
/ID switch, KEYB command, 6
IF batch command, 95
IF command, 121-124, 129
IF ERRORLEVEL command, 162-163
IF ERRORLEVEL condition, 123
IF statement, 391-392
IF with FOR commands, combining, 134
image files, 301-304
Immediate editor window, 403
incompatibilitie of printers, 64
indicators, end-of-file, 276
/Innnn switch, FC command, 268
input and output, redirecting, 60-66

Ins hotkey in QBASIC Editor, 383
insert mode, 84
INSTALL command, 7
installing
    DOS, 2
    FASTOPEN, 6
    FASTOPEN program, 229-230
    IBMCACHE.SYS, 227
    SMARTDRV.SYS, 224
    TSRs, 213
interleave
    factor, 218-219
    utility program, 219
international communication, 333
    code pages, 334-335
        displaying code page information, 351
        monitors, 342-343
        other than built-in codes, 341-342
        preparing, 345-346
        printers, 343-344
        reinstating, 350
        switching, 346-350
    countries supported by DOS, 339-340
    COUNTRY command, 334, 340-341
    KEYB command, 334-337
    keyboard layout, 336-337
international formats, 339-340
invalid
    allocation units, 277, 283
    subdirectories, 285-286
Invalid Directory message, 140

J

/J switch, UNFORMAT command, 303
JOIN command, 377

K

key codes, 325
key combinations
  Alt + F7, clearing command
    list, 83
  Ctrl+/, 28
  Ctrl+\, 28
  Ctrl+Break, 119, 130
  Ctrl+C, 119
  Ctrl+P, 356
  Ctrl+PrintScreen, 356
  F8 (File Copy), 25
  Shift+Cursor key, 28
  Shift+Enter, 28
  Shift+F8, 28
  Shift+Spacebar, 28
  task-swapping, 39
    Alt+Shift+Tab, 39
    Alt+Shift+Tab,Tab,…, 39
    Alt+Tab, 39
    Alt+Tab,Tab,…, 39
    Ctrl+Esc, 39
KEYB command, 6, 334-339,
  346, 351, 406
KEYB.COM file, 221
keyboards
  control, 325
  dispalying current keyboard
    information, 351
  Dvorak, 327
  layouts, changing, 338-339
  layouts available with DOS
    5, 336-337
  QWERTY, 327
  typematic feature, 330key-
    boards
keys
  assigning strings of text to,
    328
  Del, 28
  Enter, 28
  Print Screen, 64
  remapping, 327

Reserve Shortcut, 51
Spacebar, (in ADD mode
  only), 28
keystroke handlers, 212

L

/L switch
  BACKUP command, 241
  UNFORMAT command,
    295, 304
LASTDRIVE command, 147
/LB200 switch, FC command,
  268
/LBn switch, FC command,
  268
LCASE$ function, 388
Left arrow (drive list control
  key), 25
LIM 3.2 EMS expanded
  memory manager program,
  194
LIM 4.0 EMS expanded
  memory manager program,
  194
lines
  locating, 75-76
    in command output,
      76-77
    in directory listing, 77-78
  numbers in QBASIC,
    385-386
  of data, 69
  per inch (lpi), 357
LINES= parameter, 329
linking
  batch files, 116-119
    killing jobs, 119
    multiple, 119
/LIST switch, UNDELETE
  command, 294
LOADFIX command, 7, 203
LOADFIX.EXE file, 220
LOADHIGH, 80
LOADHIGH command, 7

loading device drivers, 198
  with DEVICEHIGH
    command, 210
  DOS into HMA, 202
  DOSKEY, 80
  HIMEM, precautions, 201
  primary command inter-
    preter, 186
  programs
    into conventional
      memory, 203
    into UMBs, 210
    into upper memory, 204
    into upper memory
      blocks, warning, 207
    TSRs, 198
  TSRs into UMBs using
    LOADHIGH command,
    210
locking
  files while networking, 378
  system, warning, 207
logical drives on networks, 378
logs, backup
  for fullback sets, 243
  of backup files, 241-242
look-ahead
  buffer, 227
  feature, SMARTDRV.SYS,
    223
LOOP statement, 394-396
loops, 130-131
  closed, 130
low-level formatting programs,
  309
LPT1 device, 64
LPT2 device, 64
LPT3 device, 64
LTRIM$ function, 388

M

/M switch, XCOPY command,
  158, 239, 246
/MACHINE switch, 201

macro special characters, *see*
   DOSKEY macro special
macros, 80-81, 85
   accessing all parameters, 89
   advantages, 85-86
   defining, 86-90
   disadvantages, 85-86
   DOSKEY, 328
   examples, 89
   executing, 89
   managing, 90
   replaceable parameters, 88
   turning off echoing, 90
   versus batch files, 85-86
Main program group, Disk
   Utilities, 44-45
managing
   extended memory
      High Memory Area
         (HMA), 196
   macros, 90
   memory
      by third-party programs,
         204
      UMBs, 208
maximum characters in command line, 133
MD command, 136
MEM
command, 7, 198-200, 211
   output, 203
   program, 197
memory
   address space, 190
   board, 193
   buffer, 175
   caching system,
      IBMCACHE.SYS, 223
   conventional, 192, 203
   EMS, 194
   emulating expanded, 204
   expanded, 193
      turning on and off, 206
   extended, 195
   extended versus expanded
      memory caches, 225

fields
   XMS Memory KB Limit,
      50
   XMS Memory KB Re-
      quired, 50
limitations of DOS, 189
managers
   by third-party programs,
      204
   HIMEM.SYS, 5
   EMM386, 4, 7
   HIMEM.SYS, 4
random access (RAM), 192
UMBs, 208
upper, 193
   loading programs into,
      204
XMS, 198
memory-mapped video, 312
message box, creating colored,
   322
messages
   controlling display in batch
      files, 98
      ECHO, 101
      ECHO in batch files, 102
      Invalid Directory, 140
   redirecting to standard
      output, 275
Microsoft Windows program,
   175-177
Microsoft Word program, 35,
   233, 317
minimizing read-write arm
   movements, 216
MIRROR command, 8,
   256-261, 300
MODE command, 6, 329-330,
   344-346, 357-360
modes
   ADD, 28
   emulation, 354
   graphics, 44
   insert, 84
   of operation, protected, 195
      switching in and out, 195

overstrike, 84
screen, 324
text, 44
video, 365
modifying
   program group definitions,
      52
   program items, 52
   program items definitions,
      52
   variables, environment, 184
modules (QBASIC program),
   396-397
monitors
   CGA, 51
   changing lines and col-
      umns, 329
   code pages, 334-343
      changing, 338-339
      values, 334
   color graphics adapter
      (CGA), 312
   DOS supported, 312
   extended graphics adapter
      (EGA), 312
   monochrome display
      adapter (MDA), 312
   video graphics array (VGA),
      312
MORE command, 6, 142
moving
   branches, 159
   directories, 159-160
   files, 162
/MSG switch, COMMAND
   command, 5
MSHERC.COM file, 221
multiple
   files
      cross-linked, 282-283
      restoring, 250
   hard drives, 4
   setups, 53

N

/N switch
  COMP command, 265
  RESTORE command, 248
naming
  batch files, 95
  drives with alternative drive
    names, 373-375
National Language Support
  feature, 348-350
NDOS command interpreter
  of Norton Utilities, 183
networks
  running DOS on, 376-377
    command restrictions,
      377-378
    locking files, 378
    logical drives, 378
    sharing files, 378
    special features/problems,
      378
NLSFUNC program, 348-350
NLSFUNC.EXE file, 221
NOEMS parameter on
  EMM386's DEVICE com-
  mand, 208
non-ASCII files
  copying to devices, 171
  updating time/date stamp,
    171
non-disk devices, copying to
  and from, 154
Norton Utilities programs, 183,
  287, 291, 306
  UnErase program,161, 262
  UnFormat program, 262
NUL device, 64
null parameters, 110-111
  testing for, 128-129
number system, binary, 191
numeric variables (QBASIC),
  387

O

/O switch, 15-17
OFF parameter, IN
  CONFIG.SYS command, 207
OLD_DOS.n. directory, 2
on-screen help, 3
open loops, 130
opening
  associated files from Shell,
    33
  program file from Shell, 33
optimizing
  directory structure in DOS
    Shell, 219
  hard disk, 221-222
Options Colors command, 23
Options Display command, 23
Options Enable Task Swapper
  command, 37
Options File Display Options,
  270
Options File Display Options
  command, 30
Options Refresh command, 26
Options Select Across Directories command, 30-31
  warning about enabling, 30
order of active task list, 40
order of SMARTDRV's
  DEVICE[HIGH] command
  in CONFIG.SYS file, 226
output
overstrike mode, 84
  default, 84
  versus insert mode, 84
overwriting versus appending,
  63

P

/P switch
  DEL command, 5
  MEM command, 200

possible system hang up,
  warning, 182
REPLACE command, 173
RESTORE command, 248
UNFORMAT command,
  295, 304
page frame
  address, controlling, 209
  in upper memory, 193
parameters
  accessing in macros, 89
  AUTO, IN CONFIG.SYS
    command, 207
  dumb replacement
    in batch fles, 113-114
  LINES =, 329
  NOEMS, on EMM386's
    DEVICE command, 208
  null, 110-111
    testing for, 128-129
  OFF, IN CONFIG.SYS com-
    mand, 207
  printer type, 366-367
  RAM, on EMM386's DE-
    VICE command, 208
  replaceable, 88-89, 128, 329
    in batch fles, 108-113
    in linking command,
      118-119
  standard for floppy disks,
    371
  status in Shell, 54
parking program for disk
  heads, 271
partition table
  computer virus targets, 259
  display, 297
  hard disk, 259
  information, 298
    saving with MIRROR
      command, 259
    viewing, 296
  restoring information, 296
/PARTN switch, UNFORMAT
  command, 295
passwords, in DOSSHELL.INI,
  55

protection, 46
PATH command, 139-140, 150
PATH variable, 177
paths, 136
    absolute, 136
    for searching, 177
    relative, 137
    resetting, 184
Pause after exit field, 49
PAUSE batch command, 95
PAUSE command, 103-105
PCL (page control language)
    commands, 366
PCTRACKR.DEL command,
    289
piping, 67-68
PostScript
    control information, 354
    printer driver, 354
PREPARE format, 345
PRINT command, 64, 361,
    362-364
Print Screen key, 64
printer type parameters,
    366-367
PRINTER.SYS DEVICE com-
    mand, 344
printers
    characters per inch (cpi),
        357
    code pages, 334, 343-344
        values, 334
    configuring, 357-358
    controlling with redirec-
        tion, 355
    drivers, 354
    incompatibility, 64
    lines per inch (lpi), 357
    serial
        configuring serial ports,
            358-360
        redirecting, 360-361
printing
    command prompt tree, 143
    echo printing, 356
    print queues, 364-365

redirecting standard out-
    put, 354
    text, 356
priorities of batch files, 96
PRN device, 64
procedures, creating (QBASIC
    program), 397-398
program file, opening from
    Shell, 33
program files, RECOVER
    command, 308
program groups
    defining, 46-52
    Main, 44-45
    password protection, 46
    versus program items, 44
program items
    defining, 47
        help text, 49
        memory requirements,
            49-51
        optional fields, 48-49
        replaceable parameter
            dialog boxes, 51
        required fields, 47-48
        task switching limita-
            tions, 49-51
    versus program groups, 44
program list
    Commands, 47
    Program Title, 47
program list views, 44
    View Program List, 44
    View Program/File Lists, 44
programs
    BASICA, 4
    batch, 242
    COPY, 232
    creating with batch files,
        93-94
    determining loaded, 199
    DISKCOPY, 236
    DOSKEY, 3
    EDIT, 317
    EMM386, 203-211
    expanded memory man-
        ager, 194

FASTOPEN, 228
    installing, 229-230
GW-BASIC, 4
HIMEM, 201
HIMEM.SYS, 204
HIMEM.SYS extended
    memory manager, 197
IBMCACHE, 223
LIM 3.2 EMS expanded
    memory manager, 194
LIM 4.0 EMS expanded
    memory manager, 194
loading into UMBs, 210
loading into upper memory
    blocks, warning, 207
low-level formatting, warn-
    ing, 309
MEM, 197
Microsoft Windows, 175-177
Microsoft Word, 233, 317
NLSFUNC, 348-350
Norton Utilities, 183, 287,
    291, 306
problems running in UMBs,
    210
QBASIC, 381-382
    case structure, 393-394
    constants, 386-387
    creating procedures,
        397-398
    debugging, 403-404
    DO statement, 394-396
    Editor, 382-384
    elements, 389
    functions, 402-403
    global variables, 399
    IF statements, 391-392
    line numbers, 385-386
    LOOP statement,
        394-396
    modules, 396-397
    passing values, 401-402
    record data types,
        389-390
    REMLINE.BAS program,
        397

running loaded pro-
  grams under, 384-385
subprograms, 399-401
typename, 389
user-defined functions,
  396
usertype, 389
variables, 386-389
QBasic, 4
REMLINE, 386
REMLINE.BAS, 397
running from Shell, 32-33
  associating file exten-
    sions with, 35-36
  by opening associated
    files, 33
  by opening program
    files, 33
  opeing program list
    item, 35
  secondary command
    prompt, 35
  with File Run command,
    34
running loaded programs
  under QBASIC program,
  384-385
SELECT, 8
SETUP, 2, 7-8, 149
sort, 74
SPACE.BAT, 108
START.BAT, 109
STOP.BAT, 109
terminate-and-stay-resident
  (TSRs) see TSRs
tracing, 403
UNDELETE, 8
UnErase by Norton Utili-
  ties, 161
UNFORMAT, 8, 294
using interleave utility, 219
utility for defragmenting
  and relocating files and
  subdire, 222-223
Windows 3.0, 224
  borrowing cache space,
    225

WordStar, 317
XCOPY, 232
programstarter section, 55
  color schemes, 56
prompt, resetting, 184
PROMPT PG command, 315
PROMPT command, 315, 320
PROMPT variable, 177
protected mode of operation,
  195
  switching in and out, 195
protecting
  data
    disk structure, 257
    third-party software, 270
  files, 235
providing expanded memory,
  204
pruning
  using batch files, 160
  with XCOPY command, 159

Q

/Q switch
  FORMAT command, 256
  PRINT command, 364
  quick format, 255
  SETVER command, 19
QBASIC command, 8
QBASIC program, 4, 381-382
  case structure, 393-394
  constants, 386-387
  creating procedures,
    397-398
  debugging, 403-404
  Editor, 382-384
    hotkeys, 383
  elements, 389
  functions, 402-403
  global variables, 399
  IF statements, 391-392
  line numbers, 385-386
  modules, 396-397
  passing values, 401-402

record data types, 389-390
REMLINE.BAS program,
  397
running loaded programs
  under, 384-385
statements
  DO, 394-396
  LOOP, 394-396
subprograms, 399-401
typename, 389
user-defined functions, 396
usertype, 389
variables, 386
  array, 388-389
  numeric, 387
  string, 387-388
quick format, 255
QWERTY keyboard, 327

R

/R switch, GRAPHICS com-
  mand, 367
RAM drive, 230-233
RAM parameter on EMM386's
  DEVICE command, 208
RAMDRIVE.SYS DEVICE com-
  mand, 231
RAMDRIVE.SYS driver, 231
RAMDRIVE.SYS file, 220
random-access memory
  (RAM), 192
RD command, 136
read-only files, deleting
  through Shell, 270
read-write arm movements
  controlling, 218
  factors determining, 217
README.TXT file, 201
real mode of operation, 195
reassigning address space, 194
recalling
  former commands, 79
  last command, 82
reconstructing entire drive,
  307

record data types (QBASIC), 389-390
RECOVER command, 96, 300-308
recoverable formats, 257
recovering
    clobbered files, 161
    data using Norton Utilities' UnErase, 161
    from RECOVER command, 308
    lost allocation units, 222
    missing files, 247
    subdirectories, 301-303
redirecting
    input to file or device, 65-66
    input and output, 60-62
        to devices, 63
    messages to standard output, 275
    output, 65
        to files, 62-63
output,using /C command-text switch, 187-188
    serial printers, 360-361
    SORT I/O, 72
    standard input, 67
    standard output controlling printers, 354-355
referencing batch file with using CALL
    warning, 134
reformatting hard disks, 309
relative path, 137
relocating files, 222
    using utility programs, 222-223
    subdirectories using utility programs, 222-223
REM, 81
REM batch command, 95
REM commands, 6, 102
remapping keys, 327
REMLINE program, 386
REMLINE.BAS program, 397
removing TSRs, 262

RENAME command, 97
renaming directories, 160
reorganizing directory structure in DOS Shell, 219
REPLACE command, 6, 97, 151-154, 172-173, 407
    recovering missing files, 247
replaceable parameters, 88-89, 128, 329
    dialog boxes, 51
    in batch fles, 108-113
    in linking command, 118-119
    versus environment variables, 180
replacing
    DOS commands with macros, 91
    existing files, 173
    missing files, 172
Reserve Shortcut Keys, 51
resetting
    path, 184
    prompt, 184
RESTORE command, 6, 153-154, 240, 247-248, 407
    warning, 249
restoring
    entire backup set, 250
    environment variables, 180
    files
        from supplemental backups, 250
        made with XCOPY, 247
    information on partition table, 296
    multiple files, 250
    selected files, 249
restricted commands, 144
restructuring directory tree, 144
Right arrow (drive list control key), 25
root directories, 136, 232
    children, 136
    parent of subdirectories, 136

saving with MIRROR command, 260
    size, 279
RTRIM$ function, 388
Run dialog box, 34
running loaded programs under QBASIC, 384-385
running programs from Shell, 32-33
    associating file extensions with programs, 35-36
    by opening associated files, 33
    by opening program files, 33
    opening program list item, 35
    secondary command prompt, 35
    with File Run command, 34

S

/S switch
    DIR command, 13-14
    XCOPY command, 157
safe format, 255
sample code page, 347-350
savestate section, 53
saving
    GW-BASIC files in ASCII form, 384
    partition table information with MIRROR command, 259
    Shell screen setup, 23
screens
    aspect ratio, 368
    color setting, 318-319, 323
    control sequences, 320
    modes, 324
    Shell, 23
    View All Files, 31, 32
search path, 177-179
searching files for text string, 76

secondary command inter-
  preter, 183-185
    COMMAND.COM, 186
  command prompt, 35
"Sector not found" errors,
  308-309
sector size, determining, 232
sectors, bad, 277, 287
SELECT CASE statement,
  393-394
SELECT program, 8
selected files, restoring, 249
selecting
  adjacent files, 28
  drives in Shell, 25
  files
    by attributes, 14-15
    from multiple directo-
      ries, 30
    multiple files, 28
    nonadjacent files, 28
sending escape sequence using
  PROMPT command, 316
sequences,
  cursor control, 320
  escape, 314
  screen control, 320
serial printers
  configuring serial ports,
    358-360
  redirecting, 360-361
SET command, 38
  changing environment
    variable, 179
  controlling environment
    variables, 176
  creating
    DIRCMD variable, 178
    TEMP variable, 177
  deleting environment vari-
    ables, 179
setting screen colors, 318-319,
  323
setup files in DOSSHELL.INI,
  53
  transferring to another
    computer, 52-53

SETUP command, 39
SETUP program, 2, 7-8, 149
setups, multiple, 53
SETVER command, 8, 17-19,
  407
SHARE command, 378-379
SHARE.EXE file, 221
sharing files on network, 378
SHELL command interpreter,
  181
Shell, 3
  controlling, 24
  controlling environment
    size, 182
  directory tree, 26-27
  drive list, 25-26
  file list, 27-29
  memory requirements, 50
  menus, File, 24
  opening program files, 33
  parameter status, 54
  running programs from,
    32-36
  screen, 23
  starting, 22
  task swapping capabilities,
    37-41
  using Del key to force-close
    task, warning, 41
SHIFT batch command, 95
SHIFT command, 110-113
Shift+Cursor key control key,
  28
Shift+Enter control key, 28
Shift+F8 control key, 28
Shift+Spacebar control key, 28
shifting text display, 329
single dot (.) path reference,
  137
single files, cross-linked,
  281-282
size
  of cache, 225
  of files, 261
  of root directory, 279
slack
  at end of cluster, 169

avoiding when accessing
  files
    ASCII method, 169
    binary method, 169
SMARTDRV.SYS, 5
SMARTDRV.SYS file, 220, 231
  assessing effectiveness, 226
  DOS 5, problems with Win-
    dows 386, version 2, 224
  installing, 224
  look-ahead feature, 223
  versus IBMCACHE.SYS, 226
  warning, 226
SORT
  collating sequence, 72
  limitations, 73
SORT I/O, redirecting, 72
sorting
  file list, 15-16
  programs, 74
SPACE.BAT program, 108-109
Spacebar control key, 28
Spacebar drive list control key,
  25
specific verification of files by
  DOS, 263
standard
  error output, 61-62
  input, redirecting, 67
  parallel printer, 64
starting
  DOSKEY, 80-81
  Shell, 22
Startup Directory, 48
statements
  CALL, 401-402
  COMMON SHARED, 399
  DECLARE, 400
  DO, 394-396
  ELSE, 391
  ENDSUB, 399-401
  GOTO, 391
  GOTO ERRORLINE, 385
  IF, 391-392
  LOOP, 394-396
  SELECT CASE, 393-394

430 Peter Norton's Advanced DOS 5 Guide

SUB, 399-401
WHILE...WEND, 391
STOP.BAT program, 109
storing backup disks, 238
strategies
accessing files, 217
for backup, 237
string variables (QBASIC),
387-388
strings of text, assigning to
keys, 328
structure of directories, 141
SUB statement, 399-401
subdirectories, 26, 232
children of root directories,
136
defragmenting, 222
invalid, 285-286
locating, 27
parent of, 136
recovering, 301-303
relocating, 222
subprograms (QBASIC pro-
gram), 399-401
SUBs dialog box, 398
SUBST command, 144, 372,
377
SUBST, 145-148
substituting drive name for
path, 145
supplemental backup, daily
using BACKUP command,
243
using XCOPY command,
245
supplemental backups. restoring files from, 250
supplemental backups, daily,
238
supplementary batch files,
105-108
suppressing command-line
echoing in batch files, 98-100
swapping tasks, 37-41
switches
/A
BACKUP command, 243

COMP command, 265
COPY command, 170
DIR command, 14-17
FC command, 267
REPLACE command,
247
RESTORE command,
250
SEE CH. 14, 270
TREE command, 143
using XCOPY command,
246
/ALL
UNDELETE command,
294
/AS, 270
/Ax, 270
/B
COPY command, 170
GRAPHICS command,
368
PRINT command, 363
using to copy non-ASCII
files to devices, 171
/C
COMP command, 265
MEM command, 199,
210-211
PRINT command, 364
/C command-text, using to
redirect output, 187-188
/D
COMP command, 265
MEM command, 200
PRINT command, 362
RESTORE command, 6,
249
SETVER command, 19
/E
COMMAND.COM com-
mand, 182
KEYB command, 6
XCOPY command, 157
/EDITOR, QBASIC com-
mand, 382

/F
BACKUP command, 241
CHKDSK command,
274, 278, 284
TREE command, 143
/ID, KEYB command, 6
Innnn, FC command, 268
/J, UNFORMAT command,
303
/L
BACKUP command, 241
UNFORMAT command,
295, 304
/LB200, FC command, 268
/LBn, FC command, 268
/LIST, UNDELETE com-
mand, 294
/M, XCOPY command, 158,
239, 246
/MSG, COMMAND com-
mand, 5
/N
COMP command, 265
RESTORE command,
248
/O, DIR command, 15-17
/P
DEL command, 5
MEM command, 200
REPLACE command,
173
RESTORE command,
248
UNFORMAT command,
295, 304
warning, possible system
hang up, 182
/PARTN, UNFORMAT
command, 295
/Q
FORMAT command, 256
PRINT command, 364
quick format, 255
SETVER command, 19
/R, GRAPHICS command,
367

/S
DIR command, 13-14
XCOPY command, 157
/T, PRINT command, 364
/Td, MIRROR command, 261
/TEST, UNFORMAT command, 301-304
/U
FORMAT command, 256
REPLACE command, 6, 174
UNFORMAT command, 295, 300
/V
DISKCOPY command, 6, 269
XCOPY command, 161
/W (Wait), 97
/X
DEVICE=ANSI.SYS command, 328
FASTOPEN command, 6
SWITCHES command, 8
switching
code pages, 346-350
diskette drives with SUBST, 148
in and out of protected mode of operatio, 195
symbols, using > redirection, warning, 63
SYS command, 6
system files
deleting through Shell, 270
including in directory, 270

T

/T switch, PRINT command, 364
tape cartridges for backup, 237
task swapping, 37-41, 44
DOSSHELL command, 21
hotkeys, 39-40

in Shell, 38-40
/Td switch, MIRROR command, 261
TEMP enviromental variable, 38, 178
temporary files, pipe, 67-68
terminate-and-stay-resident programs see TSRs
termination of batch files, 118
/TEST switch, UNFORMAT command, 301-304
testing files, 127-129
text
display, shifting, 329
files, RECOVER command, 308
mode, 44
printing, 356
strings
searching files for, 76
comparing, 128-129
third-party
cache systems, 227
command interpreter, using, 183
TIME
command, 65
automating with ECHO, 68
TIME command, 6
time/date stamps for changing files, 154
updating by concatenating files, 167
on non-ASCII files, 171
TIMEOUT.BAT batch file, 47
TIMETRAK file, 109
tracing programs, 403
tracking deleted files, 260
transferring setup to another computer, 52-53
tree, 136
command prompt, printing, 143
viewing DOS Shell's directory tree, 142

TREE command, 6, 142-143
Tree menu, 26
TRUENAME command, 8, 149-150
TSRs, 193, 200, 212
installing, 213
loading, 198
into UMBs using LOADHIGH command, 210
removing, 262
turning expanded memory on and off, 206
two-key sort, 73-74
two-line command editing, 83
TXT PACKING.LST (from DOS directory) file, 221
TYPE COLTEST command, 317
TYPE command, 317
typematic feature of keyboards, 330
typename (QBASIC program), 389

U

/U switch
FORMAT command, 256
REPLACE command, 6, 174
UNFORMAT command, 295, 300
UCASE$ function, 388
UMBs
loading programs into, 210
problems in running programs, 210
unconditional format, 255-256
warning, 256
UNDELETE command, 8, 247, 289-290, 303
warning, 294
undeleting files, 288, 290-293
warning, 290

UnErase, Norton Utilities'
program, 161, 262
UNFORMAT command, 8,
255-256, 294-295, 298-303
warning, 300, 304
UnFormat program of Norton
Utilities, 262
Uninstall diskette, 2
uninstalling DOSKEY, 81
unnecessary files, deleting, 220
updating files, dangers, 150
updating time/date stamp on
non-ASCII files, 171
updating time/date stamps by
concatenating files, 167
upper memory, 193
blocks *see* UMBs, 208
loading programs into, 204
user-defined functions, 396
usertype (QBASIC program),
389
using > redirection symbol,
warning, 63
using Del key to force-close
task, warning, 41
using third-party command
interpreter, 183
utilities
filters, 68-69
FIND, 69
MORE, 68-70
SORT, 69-70
programs for
defragmenting and relo-
cating files and
subdirectories, 222-223

V

/V switch
COPY command, 263
DISKCOPY command, 6,
263, 269
XCOPY command, 161, 263

values
of code pages, 334
passing (QBASIC program),
401-402
variables
accessing environment, 179
COMSPEC, 178
specifying, 184
DIRCMD, 178
displaying value of specific
variable, using batch files,
177
environment, 179-184, 233
PATH, 177
PROMPT, 177
(QBASIC), global, 399
(QBASIC), 386-389
TEMP, 177-178
VDISK.SYS see
RAMDRIVE.SYS, 231
VERIFY OFF command, 263
VERIFY ON command, 263
video
buffer, 312
modes, 365
monitors see monitors, 312
View All Files command, 30-32
View Dual File Lists command,
29
View Single File List command,
29
viewing
command history list with
DOSKEY /H, 82
DOS Shell's directory tree,
142
partition table information,
296
virtual drive *see* RAM drive, 230
viruses, computer,235, 259,
270-271

W

/W switch (Wait), 97
warnings
> redirection symbol, 63
allocation errors on pro-
gram file, 285
ASSIGN command, 145
BACKUP command, 171
backup files, 246
cache system
IBMCACHE.SYS, 226
SMARTDRV.SYS, 226
CHKDSK command, 274
CHKDSK with /F switch
running under DOS
Shell, 278
running under Microsoft
Windows, 278
cross-linked files, 281
Del key to force-close task,
41
DELOLDOS command, 2
DOSSHELL.INI, 53
enabling Options Select
Across Directories com-
mand, 30
environment variables, 182
interweave utility programs,
219
loading programs into
upper memory blocks, 207
locking up system, 207
low-level formatting pro-
grams, 309
RAM drive installation, 233
RECOVER command, 306,
307
referencing batch file with
using CALL, 134
RESTORE command, 249
turning off echoing of
macro, 90
unconditional format, 256
UNDELETE command, 294

undeleting files, 290
UNFORMAT command,
   300, 304
   WHILE...WEND statement,
   391
Windows 3.0 program, 224
      borrowing cache space,
      225
Windows 386, version 2
   problems with DOS.5
   SMARTDRV.SYS, 224
WordStar program, 317
write-protecting, 269
   files by setting read-only or
      system attribute, 270
   floppy disks, 269
writing files
   ASCII method, 170
   binary method, 170

X

/X switch
   DEVICE=ANSI.SYS com-
      mand, 328
   FASTOPEN command, 6
XCOPY command, 6, 97,
   151-158, 232, 238-240, 244,
   288, 407-408
   advantages with files, 239
   clobbering, 161
   disadvantages with files, 239
   using to avoid disk full
      termination, 158-159
   versus DISKCOPY com-
      mand, 155
 232
XMA2EMS.SYS extended
   memory handlers, 8
XMAEM.SYS extended
   memory handlers, 8
XMS extended memory specification
   manager, 197
XMS memory, 198